# ENABLING REFLECTIVE THINKING

**Reflective Practice in Learning and Teaching**

*Edited by*
*Kathryn Coleman and Adele Flood*

# ENABLING REFLECTIVE THINKING

**Reflective Practice in Learning and Teaching**

*Edited by*
*Kathryn Coleman and Adele Flood*

COMMON GROUND PUBLISHING 2016

First published in 2016
as part of The Learner Book Imprint
and the Creativity in Learning and Teaching book series

Common Ground Publishing
2001 S. 1st St., Suite 202
University of Illinois Research Park
Champaign, IL
61821

Copyright © Kathryn Coleman and Adele Flood 2016

All rights reserved. Apart from fair dealing for the purposes of study, research, criticism or review as permitted under the applicable copyright legislation, no part of this book may be reproduced by any process without written permission from the publisher.

Library of Congress Cataloging-in-Publication Data

Names: Coleman, Kathryn, editor. | Flood, Adele, editor.
Title: Enabling reflective thinking : reflective practice in learning and
  teaching / edited by Kathryn Coleman and Adele Flood.
Description: Champaign, IL : Common Ground Publishing, [2016] | Includes
  bibliographical references and index.
Identifiers: LCCN 2016012296 (print) | LCCN 2016023838 (ebook) | ISBN
  9781612298672 (hbk : alk. paper) | ISBN 9781612298689 (pbk : alk. paper) |
  ISBN 9781612298696 (pdf)
Subjects: LCSH: Reflective learning. | Reflective teaching.
Classification: LCC LB1027.23 .E538 2016 (print) | LCC LB1027.23 (ebook) |
  DDC 371.102--dc23
LC record available at https://lccn.loc.gov/2016012296

Cover Photo Credit: Belinda Allen, Mangrove mandala

# Table of Contents

Acknowledgments — xi
Editor Biographies — xii
Contributing Author Biographies — xiii

Introduction
    Adele Flood and Kathryn Coleman — xxii

*Chapter 1*
Novice Reflections: Developing Metacognitive Habits of Mind — 1
    Ruth Benander and Brenda Refaei

*Chapter 2*
Doctoral Research: An Unacknowledged Source of Creativity and Innovation — 18
    Francia Kinchington

*Chapter 3*
Reflections on Cultural Differences between Individualistic and Collective Societies: Adaptation to Individualism Orientated Learning and Teaching — 36
    Xiaoli Jiang

*Chapter 4*
Mutual Mentoring for Faculty Professional Development: A Radical Model — 58
    Laurie Fox

## Chapter 5
Does 'One Child Policy' Produce Little 'Emperors and Princesses'?: Fostering Critical Thinking and Reflective Learning in a Chinese Language Course  79
    Yanyin Zhang

## Chapter 6
Teacher Education for Reflective Thinking in Teaching: Field Experiences of Teacher Trainees in South Africa  100
    Simeon Maile

## Chapter 7
Breaking Online Tradition: Journaling as Authentic Interaction, Reflective Practice, and Crystallization of Self  132
    Marianne Vander Dussen & Michelann Parr

## Chapter 8
Digital Natives as Critically Reflexive Practitioners  147
    Susan Beierling and James Paul

## Chapter 9
Closing the Loop: Using Reflection in Teaching Management and Leadership Subjects in Higher Education  164
    Zelma Bone

## Chapter 10
Reflective Practice through Reflecting Writing  179
    Abraham Motlhabane

## Chapter 11
Creating Intergenerational Portraits through "Life Stories" in Communication Studies  193
    Marilyn J. Matelski

*Table of Contents*

*Chapter 12*
Interactive Reflection in a Photomedia Participatory e-Feed Learning Culture    211
    Kathryn Meyer Grushka and Aaron Bellette

*Chapter 13*
Reflective Practice: A Way of Life    234
    Gabriel Julien

*Chapter 14*
The Effects of an Intervention Program Based on Metacognitive Strategies on Young Students' Writing    248
    Konstantinos Mastrothanasis and Athina Geladari

*Chapter 15*
Facilitating Collaborative Reflection: Researching with College Students with Intellectual Disabilities    270
    John Kubiak

*Chapter 16*
Students as Bricoleurs: Eliciting Creativity in a Cluttered World    297
    Gail Matthews-DeNatale and Amy Cozart-Lundin

*Chapter 17*
Developing Mindfulness, Reflection and Transformative Learning with Diverse College Students    318
    Hedva Lewittes

*Chapter 18*
Design Thinking, Universal Design, & Distance/Mobile Education: Impact on Learning    340
    Barbara Schwartz-Bechet, Roelien Bos-Wierda and Ron Barendsen

## Chapter 19
Developing Self-management Capacity in Student Learning: A Pilot Implementation of Blended Learning Strategies in the Study of Business Law    354
   Jacquelyn Cranney, Leela Cejnar and Vik Nithy

## Afterword
   Kathryn Coleman    370

## The Creative Graduate: Cultivating and Assessing Creativity with ePortfolios
   Belinda Allen and Kathryn Coleman    371

# ACKNOWLEDGMENTS

This curated collection of 19 chapters, flows and invites discourse into reflective practice and reflective thinking in teaching and learning. It is indebted to our authors who have shared their practice, research and personal inquiry here.

We would like to say a continued thank you to Common Ground Publishing for the community that they inspire and the support they provide for edited books like these. This is our fourth book for Common Ground Publishing and the second in our invited series on Creativity. This book is a great example of what the scholarship of learning and teaching in education looks like. We are privileged to have worked with all of these authors via their research and practice and thank them for their generosity.

The following chapters are the reason we do this, to share what it is that reflective practitioners in education do so well, share and collaborate.

# Editor Biographies

**Kathryn Coleman** is an a/r/tographer from Melbourne, Australia. She has twenty years of experience teaching both secondary and higher art and design education and is current a Phd Candidate at Melbourne Graduate School of Education. Kate's research specifically focuses on increasing the integration of digital technologies into the artworld and educational setting through digital badges, portfolios and digital identity formation. Kate is an active member of the Board of Director's for the Association for Authentic, Experiential and Evidence Based Learning (AAEEBL).

**Dr Adele Flood** has taught and worked across all levels of Education with an ongoing particular interest in Visual Arts Education. In the Tertiary Sector she has worked in Teacher Education for a number of years and more recently in Academic Development. Adele has expertise in curriculum development, assessment strategies and the alignment of Graduate Attributes with assessment and practice. She is a past president of Australian Institute of Art Education (AIAE) and was on the research board of The International Society of Education through Art (InSEA), and the executive of Art Education Australia. She has written extensively on creativity and her most recent research is concerned with ideas of identity. She has a strong belief in the need of an individual to be heard and that notions of self should be explored by engaging in creative practice. In her current research Adele is exploring further, the ways recording narratives in visual diaries or journals can add to a person's understanding of self thereby enabling a change in their practice. Adele presents her research regularly at both national and international conferences and she has many published papers in the fields of Art Education, Narrative Inquiry and the Scholarship of Learning and Teaching. She has attended several UNESCO international learning summits and represented Australia at the UNESCO Regional forum in Nadi.

# Contributing Author Biographies

**Belinda Allen** is a digital photomedia artist based in Sydney, Australia. Belinda also works in higher education as an educational designer and researcher at the University of New South Wales. Since graduating with the prize in Printmaking at the South Australian School of Art, she has worked for many years in a variety of photographic and digital media, sometimes incorporating painting, drawing and sculptural assemblage. Belinda is a long-time resident of Bundeena in the Royal National Park south of Sydney, and regularly exhibits in solo and group exhibitions. (https://belindaallen.wordpress.com/exhibitions). Belinda's cover for this edited collection is called Mangrove Mandala.

**Ron Barendsen** graduated in Social Sciences and in Educational Sciences. He taught Geography in a number of lower secondary schools and has been the owner of a software company, developing educational games and simulations for public and educational institutions. For the past 15 years Ron has lectured Educational Sciences and e-pedagogy at NHL University of Applied Sciences in the Netherlands. As a specialist in Curriculum Design, e-pedagogy and Blended Learning Ron was and has been involved in a number of national and international projects with a focus on ICT's, competency based learning, UDL and Design Thinking, Ron currently coordinates the NHL InnovationLab – together with his colleague Roelien Wierda - which is a unit focusing on Innovative practices and research in education. Besides, he is co-founder of MySchoolsNetwork, an international social network for schools, moderated by student teachers.

**Susan Beierling** is a PhD Candidate with the Werklund School of Education at the University of Calgary, specializing in Curriculum and Learning. Turning a life-long struggle with body image into an academic journey Susan's research utilizes phenomenological hermeneutics in an effort to gain and provide deeper understanding of what it means to be a human being, in specific reference to overweight women. Ms. Beierling is interested such research areas as: hermeneutics, interpretive inquiry, guided conversations, critical and interpretive theories, body image, construction of the self and sense of belonging. Susan is also a Sessional Instructor, in the Bachelor of Education program, Werklund School of Education, instructing Professional Development and Life-Long Learning (2014 – Ongoing).

**Aaron Bellette** is lecturer in photomedia at Avondale College of Higher Education. Bellette is currently undertaking a PhD in tertiary education, specifically dealing with the development of photographic visual learning in blended and online learning. Aaron is also a recognized artist photographer.

**Dr. Ruth Benander** is from Cincinnati, Ohio, USA. She is a faculty member in the English department where she teaches developmental, first-year, and second year writing courses. She has also served as the Co-director of the college Learning and Teaching Center. Ruth is concerned with studying acculturation and identity development in academic culture. She has published articles on the role of reflection in acculturation and pedagogy. Currently, Ruth is examining differing perceptions of identity representation in digital environments and the development of basic writers as they move into college writing.

**Zelma Bone** has been an academic on Orange and Bathurst campuses of University of New England, University of Sydney and Charles Sturt University, Australia for 25 years and has played an active role in curriculum design and course development. In recent years Zelma has been Courses Manager for Undergraduate programs in the Faculty of Business as well as teaching in the areas of leadership and management. Zelma has led or co-lead study tours to Indonesia, Japan, England, Europe, China and Argentina. During post-graduate studies she has concentrated on training and development within organizations and has developed a keen interest in action research and action learning. Recent research includes study in the areas of community development (natural resource management, aged-care services) as well as workplace learning, practice-based education and gender and leadership. Reflection has always been a key component of her own practice and an integral part of subject and course design.

**Dr Leela Cejnar** is a Senior Lecturer in the Business School at the University of New South Wales (UNSW). Leela's primary area of research is competition law. However, as convener of a large, undergraduate (first year) business law cohort, Leela has developed a research interest in student motivation in "large class learning" and, more recently, in developing self-management capacity in student learning. Leela is also interested in exploring further whether *learning* takes place more effectively *online or face-to-face in large cohorts*. Leela is presently studying for a Master of Education at UNSW.

*Contributing Author Biographies* xv

**Amy Cozart-Lundin** is a recent graduate of the eLearning and Instructional Design M.Ed. program at Northeastern University. Amy spent 13+ years in the retail visual merchandising industry, and now has shifted her creative eye for design to the creation of eLearning experiences. Passionate about enhancing community learning, she has volunteered with an adult literacy center in Detroit, and serves as an ePals mentor with In2Books. Amy most recently completed an internship with the Northeastern University Online Experiential Learning design team, working remotely with the team in Boston, MA from her home in Detroit, MI.

**Associate Professor Jacquelyn Cranney**, Psychology, UNSW, has successfully delivered useful outcomes to the tertiary education sector, particularly through her work on psychological literacy (the intentional application of psychological science to meet personal, professional and societal needs), educational models and accreditation standards, SoTL, and evidence-based self-management for all university students. She is an OLT and UNSW Fellow, is a member of several national and international education committees, and has received recognition at many levels for her dedication to improving the current and future value of higher education.

**Laurie Fox** is a Professor in the Program for Advancement of Learning (PAL) at Curry College in Milton, MA where she coordinates Curry's Faculty Peer Support Program grounded in reflective practice. She has worked with students of all ages as a reading, speech, and learning specialist, classroom teacher, diagnostician, counselor, and professional-level educational therapist (ET/P) and is a recipient of the Lorenz Excellence in Teaching award. Research and publication areas have included daily stress, learning disabilities, executive function, academic success factors, and mutual mentoring. She is the senior editor of *Changing Lives Through Metacognitive Relationships: LD/ADHD and College Success* and co-author of the *Learning Disabilities Reference* (*LDR*). A former Association of Educational Therapists' Study Group Leader for Greater Boston, MA, she is a contributing book reviewer for and editorial board member of the journal, *The Educational Therapist*.

**Athina Geladari** is primary school teacher. She holds a bachelor in Primary School Education and a master degree in Arts and New Technologies in Teaching (University of Western Macedonia, Greece). Currently she is a PhD Candidate at the Aristotle University of Thessaloniki in the field of Pedagogy. She holds a scholarship in differentiating instruction by the School of Education of Harvard University. Her research and publication interests focus on teaching of the second/foreign language, teachers' development and the evaluation of the language skills. She has participated in many conferences regarding language acquisition and has published many papers in international journals.

**Kathryn Grushka** is a Senior Lecturer at the University of Newcastle's School of Education. Kathryn is a nationally recognized artist and visual / design teacher educator, curriculum writer, and practicing artist. Her research interests span learning, cognition, embodied visual knowing and subjectivity insights, visual pedagogies, multi modal learning, e-learning, narrative, and arts health.

**Dr. Xiaoli Jiang** was born in Tianjin, China. She currently is the Program Leader of the Bachelor of Arts (International Studies) at the Faculty of Education and Arts, Federation University Australia. In 2009 and 2012 she received the Australian Award for University Teaching: Citation for outstanding contributions to student learning. She is one of very few people in Australia who has attained this prestigious award twice. Her research interests are in the areas of cross-cultural self-esteem, cross cultural studies in education and children's self-esteem development as well as Chinese culture, history, education and self-esteem.

**Dr. Gabriel Julien** is a part time lecturer in Psychology at the University of the West Indies, Open Campus. He is also an external evaluator with the Accreditation Council of Trinidad and Tobago and an associate editor for the International Journal of English and Literature. He has referred several papers for: The International Journal of Learning, The International Journal of English and Literature, The British Journal of Counselling, Preventing Chronic Disease, and African Journal of Political Science and International Relations. He has published five articles and has presented three of them at an International Learning Conference at the University in Barcelona, the University of Hong Kong and the University of London. Dr. Julien has done extensive action research among street children in Trinidad and Tobago and in Latin America, including Argentina, Colombia, Costa Rica, Chile and Venezuela. Today, he continues to work assiduously among street children and youths in both rural and urban areas of the country.

**Francia Kinchington** is a Principal Lecturer and University Teaching Fellow within the Faculty of Education and Health at the University of Greenwich

(London, UK). She is an experienced doctoral supervisor and examiner (Education and Health) has extensive European and International experience and involvement in European projects with a research interest in creativity, leadership, doctoral education and health.

**John Kubiak D.Ed.** lectures at the School of Education, Trinity College Dublin (TCD) where he co-ordinates the Certificate in Contemporary Living (CCL), a two-year post-secondary educational program for people with intellectual disabilities. John's doctoral research was conducted with the input of CCL students and has led to the development of a model of how people with intellectual disabilities learn while in tertiary education. In 2012 John was a recipient of TCD's prestigious Provost Teaching Award. In May 2013 he was awarded a Post-doctorate research position and bursary with TCD's School of Education and is a member of the research group 'Inclusion in Education and Society'. His research interests include: social inclusion; inclusive research; learning and people with intellectual disabilities.

**Hedva Lewittes Ph. D.** is a Professor of Education and Psychology and Director of Academic Assessment at the State University of New York, Old Westbury. She has authored articles about women's identity development in adulthood and aging and her research on women's participation in discussions and friendships. Focusing on teaching and learning, she trained her college's faculty to assess critical thinking in introductory to advanced level courses. She has written about a critical thinking rubric as the basis of curriculum and assessment and about using collaborative groups to engage students in analyzing knowledge. In an article about her Adulthood and Aging course she discusses teaching critical and reflective thinking and the relationship between them. Developing a meditation practice has encouraged her creativity as a teacher. At recent conferences she has presented on mindfulness and intentional learning and social Justice. She is energized and inspired by her students' determination and wisdom.

**Professor Simeon Maile** obtained his PhD with specialization in Educational Management in 2000 from the University of Pretoria. To date, five doctoral candidates and 28 master's students have successfully completed their studies under his supervision. He has presented 33 papers at national and international conferences. He has published twenty-six articles in refereed accredited national and international journals, six chapter books and two books. Three of his book manuscripts are being prepared for publication. Currently he chairs the research section in the Department of Educational Studies. Prof Maile has received institutional awards and national and international grants for his research. His research interests cut across Educational Management, Education and Development, Education and Politics, Research Methods for the Social and Human Sciences, Economics of Education, Education Policy Analysis, and Education Labor Relations.

**Konstantinos Mastrothanasis** is a teacher. He graduated from the Department of Primary Education of the University of Western Macedonia. His post-graduate studies concern the organization and administration of education (Università degli Studi Guglielmo Marconi), management and emerging technologies (Harokopio University). He has specialized in adult education from the Democritus University of Thrace and the teaching of Greek as mother, second/foreign language from the University of Patras and the University of Harvard. He has written articles in several journals and chapters in books. He has participated as a speaker at several international conferences in Greece and abroad.

**Dr. Marilyn J. Matelski** is a tenured full professor at Boston College, having received her B.A. from Michigan State University, as well as M.A. and Ph.D. degrees from the University of Colorado at Boulder. She has taught in the Communication Department at BC since 1978, where she served as Chairperson from 1995 to 1998. Her scholarly interests include areas of intercultural communication, cultural diversity and media studies. She has authored and/or co-authored fourteen books, more than a dozen journal articles and numerous convention papers on topics ranging from soap operas to Vatican Radio. Most recently, she has concentrated her research efforts on indigenous people and social change in Ecuador and the U.S., emphasizing the relationship between corporate social responsibility and cultural survival.

**Dr Gail Matthews-DeNatale** is an Assistant Teaching Professor at Northeastern University's Graduate School of Education, where she also leads the M.Ed. program in eLearning and Instructional Design. Prior to Northeastern, Gail held positions at Simmons College, George Mason University, and The University of South Carolina Gail is recognized nationally for her innovative work with authentic assessment and experiential learning, specifically in the areas of ePortfolios, Digital Storytelling, and Blended/Hybrid Learning. She is the recipient of numerous awards, including Northeastern University's Award for Teaching Excellence, the Online Learning Consortium's Learning Effectiveness

Award, and Nova Southeastern University's International Exemplary Course Award. Gail's grants and leadership roles include Northeastern University's FIPSE-funded involvement in the Connect to Learning consortium and the Simmons College Blended Learning Initiative that was funded by the Alfred P. Sloan Foundation.

**Dr Abraham Motlhabane** is an associate professor at the University of South Africa in the College of Education within Department of Science and Technology Education. Abraham specializes in Science and Technology Education.

**Vik Nithy** is the director of One Can Grow, an organization that guides young people toward careers of passion and purpose. A psychology graduate, Vik completed his undergraduate honours thesis on cognitive neuroscience, moving on to study student well-being at the University of New South Wales, Australia. With One Can Grow, Vik delivers workshops to high school and University students on topics ranging from procrastination and mindfulness to collaborative social innovation.

**Michelann Parr** began her teaching career in the elementary classroom, covering grades from Kindergarten to Grade 6 for over ten years. Her teaching experience includes training in early literacy intervention and work with students who struggle to read and write the traditional way. She now teaches language, literacy, and special education, at both graduate and undergraduate levels, in the Schulich School of Education at Nipissing University in North Bay. She is a frequent conference presenter and workshop leaders on successful approaches to teaching literacy, poetry, writing, drama, and infusing technology into real world literacy. She will be presenting hands-on workshops on word solving and phonemic awareness as well as the essentials of planning for balanced literacy with a focus on reading, writing, and talk.

**Dr James Paul** retired July 2014, after 23 years at the Werklund School of Education, the University of Calgary, and he is now Werklund Associate Professor Emeritus. Dr. Jim Paul had two significant career paths – (i) he was a University academic, scholar, researcher, lecturer, graduate studies supervisor, and an administrator specializing in teacher education pre-service and in-service curriculum, instruction, assessment-evaluation design, development, and implementation theories and practices; (ii) Dr. Paul has extensive international education, leadership, design, monitoring and evaluation capacity development and enhancement project experience in nations such as South Africa (1999 – 2005) and China (2001 – 2007) and in a community health-education project in Nigeria (2007- 2011) and a teacher certification design project in Afghanistan (2012-2013).

**Brenda Refaei** is from Cincinnati, Ohio, USA. She is the composition coordinator at the University of Cincinnati Blue Ash College where she teaches developmental, first-year, and second-year writing courses. Brenda is especially interested in exploring effective pedagogical approaches to writing instruction and has published articles on service-learning, problem-based learning, and information literacy approaches in first-year writing courses. Currently, Brenda is examining how different audiences approach reading ePortfolios and how an emporium model can propel basic writers into first-year writing courses.

**Dr. Barbara Schwartz-Bechet,** Chair and Professor, in the Department of Special and Early Education has been in the field of education for over 25 years. Dr. Schwartz-Bechet received her doctorate in Applied Behavior Analysis from Columbia University/Teachers College in New York City. She began her career as a regular education teacher, with a BS in elementary education and later became a special education teacher, with a MS in Ed., working with students' ages several months through the age of 21. She continued on with her career as an educational evaluator, and later as principal of several schools in New York City. Upon relocation to Maryland, Dr. Schwartz-Bechet supervised and taught graduate special education students at Johns Hopkins University and was an associate professor of education at Bowie State University for 13 years. Dr. Schwartz-Bechet also evaluated children under the Maryland Child Find program with physician Dr. Renee Wachtel in Howard County Maryland. Dr. Schwartz-Bechet was instrumental in the creation, facilitation & vitality of three special education Professional Development Schools in Prince George's County MD. She is widely published and has presented nationally and internationally. Her current research interests include personalized instruction in online formats, mentoring, professional development schools for children with special needs, virtual schooling and virtual professional development schools, technology integration for low performing schools, and athletic opportunities for children with special needs.

**Marianne Vander Dussen** is an award-winning teacher, researcher and visual artist based out of North Bay, Ontario, Canada. She is in the final stages of her

Master of Education at Nipissing University, focusing on critical literacy, social justice and storytelling. Marianne is a dedicated advocate for equity, arts-based pedagogy, and community initiatives, and hopes to channel these life-long passions into PhD research. Marianne is excited to be on the cusp of her future in academia and educational research, and grateful for the opportunity to be a part of this publication.

**Roelien Wierda** graduated in English language and literature and in Educational Sciences. She taught English in higher secondary school for 15 years after which she started lecturing linguistics and educational sciences at NHL University of Applied Sciences in the Netherlands.

As a specialist in Curriculum Design, blended and hybrid learning she was and has been involved in a number of national and international projects with a focus on ICT's, competency based learning, UDL and Design Thinking. Roelien currently coordinates the NHL InnovationLab – together with her colleague Ron Barendsen - which is a unit focusing on Innovative practices and research in education. Besides, she is co-founder of MySchoolsNetwork, an international social network for schools, moderated by student teachers.

**Yanyin Zhang** holds a PhD in linguistics and is Senior Lecturer in the College of Asia and the Pacific, the Australian National University. She has many years of teaching experience in Applied Linguistics, TESOL and Chinese, and has taught in Australia, China, Vietnam, and the US. Her research interests cover second language acquisition, second language pedagogy, and international education, and she has published widely in these areas.

# Introduction

*Adele Flood and Kathryn Coleman*

This book contains a wide variety of subject areas written by a diverse number of people coming to it from varying levels of experience and cultural backgrounds from across the world of education. If we were to choose any recurring themes, our thoughts turn to two important aspects of reflective learning: motivation and self efficacy. In these writings which are concerned with enabling reflective thinking and practice in learning and teaching, the primary desire of the writers is to make explicit how they have employed various teaching and learning practices to elicit self efficacy within their students.

Generally, motivation is a reason or set of reasons for engaging in a particular behavior. The reasons include basic needs, goals, state of being, an ideal that is desirable. Motivation also refers to initiation, direction, intensity and persistence of human behavior. Motivation in education can have several effects on how students learn and their behavior towards subject matter. It can direct behavior toward particular goals - lead to increase effort and energy; increase initiation of, and persistence in activities; enhance cognitive processing; determine what consequences are reinforcing; lead to improved performance. There are two kinds of motivation: Intrinsic motivation that brings pleasure, or makes people feel what they are learning is morally significant and Extrinsic motivation which comes when a student compelled to do something because of external factors.

Self-efficacy is an impression that one is capable of performing in a certain manner or attaining certain goals. It is a belief that one has the capabilities to execute the courses of actions required to manage prospective situations. It is also a belief (whether or not accurate) that one has the power to produce that effect. Self efficacy relates to person's perception of their ability to reach a goal.

In the following chapters we find the use of both intrinsic and extrinsic motivating factors employed. Each writer clearly displays through their teaching methodologies a clear desire to engage learners with both enjoyable and content focused learning. The chapters provide a comprehensive look at all levels of teaching and learning, from PhD supervision to investigating an intervention

*Introduction* xxiii

program in writing practices, to developing mindfulness in diverse student cohorts, online practices and so on.

A particular pleasure for the editors is the recurrence of the creative processes employed by such a diverse range of teachers in various learning communities. It is gratifying to see that values we hold dear regarding creativity in learning and teaching are displayed by educators in all these programs. This is manifested in the creative responses from students and can only happen when students are fortunate enough to experience teachers who understand how to motivate learners and then allow them to become self motivated learners.

In *Novice Reflections: Developing Metacognitive Habits of Mind* Ruth Benander & Brenda Refaei provide a comprehensive account of how they enhance students ability to use the power of reflection for development of personal growth. In Chapter 1, the authors "recommend ways to support… progression and how to cultivate the habit of reflection for students who are new to academic culture and the expectations that they have control of their choices" (p.1). They found in their study that "Instructors of developmental writing courses need to be willing to accept shorter reflections initially and gradually coax longer and deeper reflections, in both formal and informal contexts, as students become more comfortable with this way of thinking"(p.13). Francia Kinchington investigates the importance of reflection in Doctoral research suggesting it is an unacknowledged source of creativity and innovation in Chapter 2. She shares, doctoral candidate feedback suggesting that the "creative research process is onerous, not only for the individual but their family and close friends. It is lengthy and life changing, but a price they report worth paying because it enables intellectual challenge and fulfilment and the opportunity to make an original contribution to knowledge within one's field of study" (p.32).

Xiaoli Jiang in Chapter 3, identifies the core issues of difficulties of individual adaptations, from a collective oriented environment to an individualistic society. The chapter "reveals several fundamental differences between individualistic and collective cultures that result in dissimilarities in pedagogy, teaching and learning practices. It identifies that in individualistic and collective societies teacher's different roles have a close association with their respective power structure and social hierarchy" (p.35). The chapter highlights "how individuals could adapt to a very different work environment via observation, comparison, reflection, making sense of differences, challenging the 'old' self and at the same time actively learning and adjusting to the new" (p.53) through reflections on a very personal journey. In Chapter 4, Laurie Fox reveals a personalized faculty peer support programme. The author suggests, that minimal institutional management can be highly effective for self-motivated practitioners and scholars in a learning/work community. This highly inspiring reflection on the professional learning program describes how "Faculty are invited to connect with each other to support self-determined professional development work" and how "participants self-select partner(s), meeting times, places, and topics (teaching, writing, research, curriculum development, etc.), and self-direct activity, sharing equal mentor status and session time" (p.58).

Yanyin Zhang in Chapter 5, argues that reflective practices do not seem to occupy the mainstream second language pedagogy, research interests and teacher training courses. The author tells us that "the mission of education, including language education, is in part to develop the capacity to recognize, understand, and appreciate the contrast and to overcome single perspectives and culture-conditioned assumptions so as to embrace and tolerate differences through cultural interpretation and deep intellectual exchange and understanding. This does not happen automatically. It needs active fostering and nurturing" (p.95). In Chapter 6, Simeon Maile provides a thought provoking account of a country in a state of change. His research tells us "the findings reveal a complex problem of disjuncture between theory and practice. What students learn from teacher education programs seems to have dissonance with realities prevailing in schools" (p.124) while he writes of South Africa, these problems are universal for teacher trainers.

Marianne Vander Dussen & Michelann Parr, reflect on their current research and practice in Chapter 7. The authors "argue that there is room for a more private space between student and instructor, where each has room to negotiate previously-held assumptions in an effort to further develop practice, understand theory, and perhaps shift paradigms. In this way, journaling serves as private inquiry, reflective thought, and crystallization, where thoughts and ideas can be tested, explored, and rehearsed prior to putting them out there into the public sphere" (p.131). Susan Beierling & James Paul in Chapter 8 argue that our "slowly-evolving education system is ill equipped to meet the learning and development and self-awareness needs of today's and tomorrow's technologically mediated, and even perhaps brain-altered, Digital Natives". They "suggest that through a reimagined, for the $21^{st}$ century, critically reflective know thyself inquiry practice, such as Currere 2.0, educators, especially those at post-secondary teacher preparation institutions, may be able to establish solid self-aware groundings so Digital Natives are not "blown about by the winds of cultural and pedagogic" and technological, "preference" (Brookfield, 1995, p. 265)" (p.159)

*Introduction* xxv

In Closing the Loop, author Zelma Bone describes using reflection in teaching management and leadership subjects in higher education. Chapter 9 presents Dr Bone's "personal journey as an educator incorporating reflection into teaching and assessment design and illustrating how reflection can be used in a variety of ways to enhance the learning process" (p.163). Chapters 10, 11 12 and 13 continue with investigations of reflective practice through storming an imagery.

Abraham Motlhabane presents how *"reflective practice* is interpreted and understood in a number of different ways, in this context it is viewed as a means by which teachers are able to develop a greater level of self-awareness about the nature and impact of their classroom practice" (p.178). The chapter presents how "Teachers can learn enormously by reflecting on their personal views in terms of their current classroom practice. And by comparing their current views with documented literature and the reality in the classroom, fresh ideas about improving classroom practice can emerge" (p.188). Marilyn J. Matelski in Chapter 11 focuses on creating intergenerational portraits through "Life Stories" in Communication Studies. Here students are invited to personalize the literature and to create common links between multi- generational populations. By sharing family information through a prism of systems and cultural dimensions in "a capstone project representing the assimilation and culmination of smaller assignments throughout the semester—is intended to *personalize* the literature and to create common links between multi-generational populations"(p.192).

Authors Kathryn Grushka and Aaron Bellette in Chapter 12 focus "on the affordances of social media to address online learner identities and support the development of critical self-reflective and creative dispositions in student-directed on-line learning. It reports on an aspect of an ethics approved study titled Photographic Participatory Inquiry, researching the participatory pedagogies of photomedia students in the blended e-learning environment" (p.211). The following chapter by author Gabriel Julien argues that reflective practice if it is to be effective, must be an ongoing part of all aspects of life. Julien suggests "reflective practice ought to be a way of life." Some guidelines on the reflective learning process are offered and the difference between reflection-in-action and reflection-on-action is discussed. The author addresses some difficulties that may arise during the process and he offers some suggestions in decision making; additionally, the use of the reflective diary is presented. The chapter concludes with the hope that practitioners will value and appreciate the importance of reflective practice (p.234).

Mastrothanasis Konstantinos & Athina Geladari provide us with insights into the effects of an intervention program based on metacognitive strategies on young students' writing. The researchers investigate "the effect of metacognitive strategies in writing. More specifically, the main hypothesis was focused on whether the implementation of an intervention program of development and use of metacognitive strategies, in the last two grades of primary school ($5^{th}$ and $6^{th}$), will have a positive effect on student performance on writing" (p.251). In the following chapter, John Kubiak describes, facilitating collaborative reflection through researching with college students with intellectual disabilities. Kubiak states that "the main purpose of the study was to explore how co-operative reflection could be used as a methodological lens to enable students with ID to have some agency in the process of research" (p.288).

In Chapter 16, Students as Bricoleurs: Eliciting Creativity in a Cluttered World, Gail Matthews-DeNatale and Amy Cozart-Lundin bring us back explicitly to creativity. They ask: What is creativity? and how is it related to learning? The authors suggest that this "question is central to educators who value creativity, because it helps us consider the pedagogical purpose of eliciting it in our students (p.295). This is furthered by the authors definitive statement, "Creativity is a capability that needs to be cultivated, and each form of creativity involves fundamental skills and techniques" (p.304). In Developing Mindfulness, Reflection and Transformative Learning with Diverse College Students Hedva Lewittes presents a Psychology course that she teaches at the State University of New York, Old Westbury. Chapter 17 takes us through how Lewittes, a reflective practitioner "guides students in contemplative inquiry using brief meditations, journals and reflective essays to guide students in contemplative inquiry" (p.319). Authors of these chapters express their beliefs in student empowered learning and position themselves as part of the learning process alongside the students' learning development.

Chapters 18 and 19 provide specific examples of how learning can be empowered through the construction of carefully implemented programs. Barbara Schwartz-Bechet, Roelien Bos-Wierda and Ron Barendsen describe how through design thinking, universal design, & distance/mobile education impact learning. They present "a case study approach ...to present the integration of the principles associated with Universal Design for Learning and Design Thinking with mobile technologies" (p.340). The authors tell us that "Creative aspects of teaching and learning need to be identified, modeled, and understood to affect the behaviors of educators. Instructional practices are presented, analyzed, and reflected upon as exemplars of learning are identified through expressions of knowledge presented through a variety of approaches and in various formats and contexts" (p.340).

Jacquelyn Cranney, Leela Cejnar and Vik Nithy in Chapter 19 share a pilot implementation of blended learning strategies in the study of business law at an Australian University. The chapter looks at developing self-management capacity in student learning and "represents an initial attempt to gauge the receptivity of students and staff to the integration of evidence-based self-management strategies into the curriculum of a large first-year (non-psychology) course" (p.364).

While this has barely touched the surface of the extensive knowledge and practice found in this volume of works. Suffice to say that when re-reading these chapters the editors are proud to be associated with such energized and enthusiastic educators. The value we see in this collection is not only the specific content of each study but also the willingness of all contributors to share their outstanding practice in ways that others may replicate within their own future teaching experiences. We hope it provides the reader with the motivation to bring about the development of self efficacy not only within their students but also within themselves and their learning communities.

CHAPTER 1

# Novice Reflections: Developing Metacognitive Habits of Mind

*Ruth Benander and Brenda Refaei*

Students need to practice the skill of reflection in order to learn the habits of mind that make reflection useful for personal growth. In Basic Writing courses, students need to not only learn the skills of reading and writing, but also the skill of thinking about these skills. Starting the habit of reflecting early in Basic Writing courses is important so that students might be able to have as much practice in this habit as possible. Students at this level often find it effortful to think about why they make choices. They are doing reflection in their writing so that they can understand what moves they need to make as writers. Basic Writing students need to build personal agency in their academic lives as well as in their writing. Instructors need to help students understand that they *do* have choices, and there are specific reasons to make these choices. In this case study, we outline the progression of novice writers and reflectors as they are introduced to reflection and begin to practice this habit. We analyzed three types of student reflection, written and spoken, and formal and informal. We suggest that the depth of reflection may be related to the format and context in which the students produce their reflections. We recommend ways to support this progression and how to cultivate the habit of reflection for students who are new to academic culture and the expectations that they have control of their choices.

## INTRODUCTION

At two-year open access colleges, more than half of the student population places into developmental education (Bailey, 2009; U.S. Department of Education, 2004). It is essential for our college to productively address supporting students who are not prepared for college level writing while empowering them to be successful in their college careers. With calls from state legislatures to reduce funding and support to developmental education, we must find more effective ways to support students as they prepare for college-level work. One such effective way is to make developmental students active participants in their own learning. Students need to practice the skill of reflection in order to learn the metacognitive habits of mind that make reflection useful for personal growth. In developmental English courses, students need to not only learn the skills of reading and writing, but also the skill of thinking about these skills. Given the writing skill levels of students in developmental writing courses, we find that the depth of reflection a student can engage in may depend on the form in which the reflection is expressed.

To address the problem of spending a year in developmental coursework, we created a blended learning accelerated option for the lowest level of developmental reading and writing that would allow a student to complete the requirements for college level English and thus enter that course after one semester of developmental reading and writing rather than two. Central to this work were reflective assignments that asked students to identify their own goals for each module and to reflect upon whether they met their goals or not at the end of the module. Students also reflected upon their reading skills through reading logs. At the end of the term, students were asked to talk through a final course reflection about their learning throughout the course. This chapter discusses how we built scaffolded reflective activities to help students understand that they *do* have choices in how they approach their reading and writing, and there are specific reasons to make those choices. In this case study, we outline the progression of novice writers and reflectors as they are introduced to reflection and begin to practice this habit. We outline the varieties of reflection they engaged in, both spoken and written. Finally, we recommend ways to support this progression and how to cultivate the habit of reflection for students who are new to academic culture and the expectations that they have control of their choices.

## LITERATURE REVIEW

Students placed in the lowest level English course at our institution must take a full-year of developmental work before being eligible for college-level work in composition. Students placed in the lowest levels of developmental course work are most likely to leave college without obtaining their desired degree. Edgecomb et al. (2014) found that accelerated developmental English courses that are well aligned with first-year composition courses indicated long term benefits for those who were able to complete them, which included better completion of college level English and more college credits accrued over time. Edgecomb et al.'s (2014) work suggests that developmental courses need to be intentionally designed to prepare students for their work in first-year writing courses.

Once placed in the developmental program, students offered an accelerated path to college English are more likely to remain in college. Edgecomb et al. (2014, p. 14) write, in their study of the Chabot College accelerated developmental English experiment, "Reducing the number of developmental courses and limiting the exit points increases retention and persistence." Our accelerated path involves online self-paced modules in a blended learning environment. Alber-Morgan et al. (2007) observe that guided feedback is essential for good writing, and Priemer and Ploog (2007) similarly observe that students with basic writing skills benefit most from guided writing about topics of personal interest. Thus, these modules allow students to practice skills that will help them achieve college level writing in self-paced online modules accompanied by instructor and peer-feedback as they progress at their own pace. Stine (2010) supports the use of multi-modal writing to create a mix of learning activities that allow students to explore their own interests and yet benefit from the instructor's guidance and the peer writing group's feedback. The blended learning environment facilitates this group interaction and personalization. Rutschow and Schneider (2011, p. 33) write of modularized fast-track courses, "These approaches show trends of relatively strong increases in students' achievement…" Students complete the online basic writing skills modules and complete the required writing assignments in class, receiving instructor assistance and feedback when they need it, and receiving peer reviews when they have a piece of writing ready. MacArthur and Philippakos (2013) note that teaching self-regulated learning techniques such as goal setting and reflection can result in substantial gains in writing skills and motivation to persist.

Reflection is essential in helping students transfer what they learn in the writing classroom to other writing situations (Yancey et. al, 2014). Denton (2011, p. 840) examined various definitions of reflection. He argued that two key characteristics of reflection are "time and thorough exploration." Quinton and Smallbone (2010) suggested that not enough time is spent on reflection at the college-level. They developed questions to guide second and third-year students' reflections on feedback. Students could describe their emotional reaction and judge the accurateness of the assessment, but not all students were able to say how they would use the feedback to prepare for future assignments. They suggest that students need to understand the feedback and how it can be used to change what they do in the next assignment. Denton (2011) in his examination of reflections further explains that students need distance from their work. Parisi (2014) and Sommers (2011) describe ways writing instructors can use to help students in developmental writing classes develop distance from their work.

Parisi has students write reflections to "others" who influence how they view themselves as writers, while Sommers has students examine belief statements about writing. Both Sommers and Parisi follow Bower's (2003) advice to develop reflective writing throughout the term. She concludes her analysis of reflective cover letters by saying "[t]o be effective, reflective thinking should be bound up in the philosophy of writing as a whole, recognizing the development of reflective ability is highly individualized and creatively cognitive" (Bowers, 2003, p. 64).

## OUR STUDENTS

At our college, approximately 40% place into our lowest level developmental English course, and approximately 65% place into our second level developmental English course. Of these students who place into developmental English, approximately 70% persist into college level English. For this vulnerable population to be ready for college level courses, they not only need to learn the structure and mechanics of an essay in edited written standard English, they also need to be fully aware of how they learned this information.

We completely redesigned the first level of developmental English at our college by creating online modules developed to support students as they attempt to engage in an accelerated developmental reading and writing course to place into first-year composition at the end of the semester. We hoped to help students at the lowest level complete the developmental sequence more quickly. Currently, students who place into the college's first developmental reading and writing course must pass portfolio review and take another preparatory composition course before they are admitted to first-year composition. Instructors in the course used these modules to allow students to progress through the course at their own pace. Students had the opportunity to create portfolios that would allow them to place into first-year composition instead of taking another level of developmental writing coursework. To address the needs of students who needed more support, they were able to take the next level of developmental reading and writing before college level English.

A typical class session involved all the students in the course meeting in the classroom and using tablets or computers to work through the modules resulting in multi-page written assignments. There were periodic breaks for short instruction sessions, peer review, and personal consultations. Students progressed through the modules at their own paces. Students who were motivated to move faster could complete the requirements for a college level English entrance portfolio in one semester, and students who needed more time to work through the assignments could complete a portfolio for entrance into the next level of preparatory composition. The modules emphasized goal setting and reflection on the goals to support self-regulated learning as a way to help basic writers gain the organizational skills they will need in addition to the writing skills required in college level English. Students in this revised modularized course could choose the fast-track or not, according to their preferences. Nevertheless, we recognize that this strategy is not appropriate for all of our students, and we designed an environment that accommodates those who are ready for the fast-track and those who are not. To understand the role of reflection in supporting preparatory students' writing, we collected the following data: written module reflections, reading logs, written informal reflective free writing, and spoken final course reflections.

## THE EFFECT OF CHOICE

In personalizing the course, students were allowed to choose their own readings and topics to write about. Students explored a great range of subjects and interactions with the texts. In an end of class survey, all students agreed that they liked being able to choose their own topics, no topic was repeated by any student. Topics varied from the Charlie Hebdo attacks to multicultural approaches to body scarification to women in sports to gay rights. These basic writing students interacted with the texts they chose with varied strategies such as the following:

- Recommended action/proposing solutions
- Analysis of implications
- Agreeing and disagreeing with authors
- Agreeing with a difference
- Discussing reasoning (this is happening because...)
- International comparisons
- Expressing personal points of view,
- Offering multiple examples
- Using evidence to support a position
- Description of events

The flexible nature of the course seemed to allow students to be more creative with the topics that interested them as well as how they chose to approach the topics.

In having such a personalized nature to the essays, the instructors did need to cultivate an eclectic approach to instruction where students had to explain their readings to each other in detail so that their discussion partners could understand their topics. Often students would resist completing a paper because they wanted to find more articles to read on the topic. Nevertheless, the students who were less engaged felt the strain of this freedom of choice and often needed more support at the start of each essay. Ultimately, the students created more complex responses to the essay topics than if the instructors had been choosing the topics for them due to their personal interest and being free from any external expectations from the instructor.

To facilitate guiding the students through such varied readings, we designed reading logs for the students to complete as they worked through an article (see Appendix A for the reading log assignment). The reading log was intended to help them develop the habit of mind of preparing to read, reading, and reflecting on the reading and the reading process. The reading log included a "Before you read", "During reading," and "After you read" sections that asked student to predict, summarize, discuss insights, and reflect on their reading process. They completed reading logs for each reading they read for the essays.

## STUDENT REFLECTIONS: FORMAL, WRITTEN

We used module reflections as a way for students to set their own goals for working through the modules. At first, students had difficulty with this goal setting activity. When asked what they wanted to complete in class that day, some students would say they wanted to become better spellers. We had to work through how to narrow down their goals to levels that could be achieved in one class session. As Quinton and Smallbone (2010) recommend we set aside reflection time during the class to help students establish their learning goals. In the end of course survey, the majority of students indicated that the learning goals reflections were helpful in monitoring their learning.

At the beginning of the course, most of the students had poor perceptions of themselves as writers. As a warm up activity, we asked students to describe their experiences as a writer. One student said she was a bad writer because she had bad handwriting. Several students mentioned they were not good spellers. They associated writing chiefly with correctness and neatness. As the course progressed, students were nominating more process oriented goals such as, "I want the reader to be on my side," and "I want to learn to paraphrase better." Focusing explicitly on the goals of each new essay helped students go beyond surface concerns to rhetorical concerns.

In her work with first-year English students, Jensen (2011, p. 49) described how reflective activities helped students "develop self-regulation and critical reflection skills." She developed six criteria to evaluate her students' final reflective statements in their ePortfolios:

1. Reflections that only named the final project (e.g., "Final research paper" or "This is the final paper I wrote for my freshman writing class.")
2. Reflections that not only named the paper but also added a description of the paper itself or the process used to write it
3. Reflections that identified learning outcomes of the assigned paper
4. Reflections that included statements related to self-regulation strategies
5. Reflections that included statements relating learning in this course to other college courses
6. Reflections that included statements relating learning in this course to life beyond college. (Jensen 2011, p. 54)

We applied these same criteria to our students' module reflections (see Appendix B for the personal goal prompts). We also counted the number of words in each of their entries as a way to measure the depth of the reflection. More words don't necessarily mean a deeper reflection, but a shortage of words generally indicated a surface level reflection where students were writing something to complete the assignment instead of thinking about their learning.

As students began each module, they were asked to identify the learning outcomes listed in the module and to comment on what they personally wanted to learn from completing the module. The first module on reading led students to identify some of the strategies they would apply to their reading assignments such as using context clues to understand new vocabulary *or as one student said,* "to appreciate the words on the pages," finding important details, and annotating the text. This module focused on reading strategies students could use in a variety of contexts so it was good most students' reflections included statements related to self-regulation strategies. Responses ranged from a low of 17 words to a high of 176 words. In brief responses, one student wrote, "I want to learn how to write an argument and how the steps go in writing one." In contrast, another student began a lengthier discussion, beginning with surface concerns and then moving on to rhetorical concerns,

> In the next essay I need to work on my grammar. I need to work on putting commas in my sentences and make sure that I put them correctly in my sentences. I need to avoid run on sentences. Describing the information better to keep the reader interested of what I have to say to

have successful support and show this issue is important and how my experience should change the reader's understanding on the issue.

By the time the students are more comfortable with what this kind of writing is asking for, some are able to give more elaborated answers, but many need to practice at the single sentence level for a longer time, one idea at a time.

In the rest of the modules, students' reflections were less focused on self-regulation strategies. The scores were mostly 4s and 2s indicating that some students understood how to apply the course concepts to their own work as writers while others were able to describe the writing project they were working on. The number of words used in the reflections also fell off after the module one reflection with an average of **88** words although the reflections did expand to rhetorical concerns from surface editing concerns.

## STUDENT REFLECTION: FORMAL, SPOKEN

By the end of the course, we had noted how difficult the written reflections remained, and wanted to find out if students were able to generate deeper reflections if the stress of writing was removed. For the final reflections, we interviewed students about their portfolio of writing. We asked them to take us on a tour of their portfolio and describe what they learned as they wrote each essay. In the spoken interviews, students were able to go into more depth concerning their insights about their learning and the strategies they used to create the essays responding to the instructor's spoken prompts.

As pointed out in Jensen 2011 and reflected in our own data, reflecting in writing is an effortful task, as reflected in the prevalence of description and brevity. For students who already have difficulty with writing, asking for complicated cognitive tasks in writing may compound the difficulty. Since academic written English is a new way for these students to express their experiences, it may not be effective to ask them to engage in complex analysis of these experiences in a form that is already difficult for them. Because we are asking them to engage in difficult reflection, we must be very careful to scaffold the assignments. In this course, we asked for short reflections throughout the term, which could be short and descriptive. However, we intended these short descriptive reflections to help build the habit of mind that is reflection, allowing them to engage in deeper reflections as they become more comfortable with academic written English.

In a similar research study concerning study abroad reflective writing, Page and Benander (2011) found that even students writing at the college level did not naturally reflect on their experiences beyond brief descriptions. Indeed, in unstructured reflections, the syntax and verb use was also limited to simple forms. When students were explicitly asked to describe, analyze, and evaluate in prompts that guided how to engage in reflective thinking, the reflections became longer, more connective of a broad range of experiences, and more grammatically complex. Page and Benander also found that students who were asked to reflect in the language they were studying provided brief descriptions as their reflections since their language facility limited their expression.

We see similar patterns in the developmental writing course of this study. For these writers, written English is at the very least a second dialect if not a second language. With students with low writing facility, it is not surprising that reflections would be brief and descriptive. However, this pattern was not duplicated in spoken guided reflections where facility with writing did not affect the quality of the reflection. At the end of the course, for the final reflective piece, the instructors reviewed each student's portfolio in a recorded interview with the student. In these guided, spoken reflections, we see more elaborated reflections that went beyond description to reflect on learning outcomes, self-regulation strategies, and learning in other courses.

Table 1: Numbers of References to Reflective Topics in Spoken Interviews

|  | Name of Project | Name and Description | Learning outcomes | Self-regulation strategies | Learning in other courses | Learning in life beyond college |
| --- | --- | --- | --- | --- | --- | --- |
| Student A | 3 | 3 | 7 | 8 | 2 | 0 |
| Student B | 0 | 0 | 3 | 12 | 2 | 0 |
| Student C | 2 | 2 | 3 | 5 | 0 | 0 |
| Student D | 1 | 2 | 0 | 16 | 2 | 3 |
| Student E | 0 | 2 | 7 | 14 | 4 | 1 |

*Note. Student interviews were coded for references to each of the categories. The references were totaled for each student interview.*

Students were able to articulate their successes in addressing the learning outcomes in their essays and discuss their self-regulation strategies in the spoken reflections in ways that were more complex than in their written reflections.

## STUDENT REFLECTION: INFORMAL, WRITTEN

Often the audience of the reflection is the instructor (Bower, 2003), particularly in pieces where the student is reflecting on how a project has changed through different revisions. Final reflective pieces may conceivably have a wider audience where a student discusses his or her experience of a class, yet, for many students, the instructor or immediate evaluator is perceived to be the principal audience. When the student is reflecting with the self as the audience, reflection becomes more focused on the experience of the author. Nevertheless, as many researchers have shown, the prompt still conditions the response.

In an activity to highlight finding a personal voice in writing, we invited the Program Coordinator for Multicultural Affairs to multiple sections of a basic writing class. She did an interactive presentation on code-switching and finding a place for personal cultural expression in academic writing. The original prompt that the Program Coordinator had been using to assess presentations was, "*What did you learn?*" In the past, she reported anecdotally that this resulted in descriptions of what she had presented, with an average length of a sentence or two. In an effort personalize the reflection and invite students to reflect more deeply on what they had heard, we changed the prompt to be, "Summarize what the Program Coordinator said, and explain what new insights you came to related to those main points." In this case, the reflection did go into their portfolios, but the reflections were purely personal and not formally related to any assignment.

In an analysis of these reflections, students did describe the ideas of the presentation, which makes sense given the prompt to "summarize." In the insights paragraph that followed, students most often discussed self-regulation strategies, but several students made reference to learning beyond college, and a few described connections to learning in other courses.

Table 2: Number of references to reflective topics in informal, written reflection

|  | Named project | Name and description | Learning outcomes | Self-regulated learning strategies | Learning in other courses | Learning in life beyond college |
|---|---|---|---|---|---|---|
| Number of references | 0 | 43 | 8 | 36 | 4 | 17 |

*Note. 31 students completed reflections. The reflections were coded for references to each category. The total number of references per category for all student responses is represented in this table.*

In these reflections, responses ranged from 11 words to 238, with a mean of 98 words. "Naming and description" and "self-regulated learning strategies" were the primary forms of reflection in the "insights" section.

In this form of reflection, the students easily applied the described activities to their own experiences and strategies for success in reading and writing. We believe that, given the reality of "you get what you ask for" in reflective writing, these students would have been able to generate references to learning in other courses and learning in life beyond college had we asked them to think about it. Nevertheless, at this level of writing, addressing the description and insights, with an average word generation of 151 words, took twenty minutes. We were asking the students to reflect on their personal experiences, which made the task easier, but we asked for it in writing, which made the task harder.

## IMPLICATIONS FOR TEACHING

### Form Influences Depth of Reflection

For students who are struggling to express themselves in writing, and who are new to the college environment, the form of reflection appears to affect the depth of reflection. When we asked our basic writers to reflect in writing, they needed to engage in two difficult tasks, reflection and writing, at the same time. Formal writing about course content with the instructor as the perceived audience resulted in limited reflections that were mostly observations of what they did. Bower (2003) noted similar limited reflections when the instructor was the audience.

Nevertheless, this does not imply that they were not able to reflect on their writing. In the context of reflecting on their writing in a spoken interview with their instructor, the reflections were more extended and varied than in the written format. In the spoken reflections, the instructor was able to give more individualized scaffolding, and the students did not need to negotiate formal writing to express themselves. When students were asked to write informally, with no concern for formal constraints, they were able to reflect on their writing beyond just describing what they did in an assignment. In this informal, personal writing, where the audience was more themselves than the instructor, the students were able to articulate their writing strategies and self-regulated learning strategies more frequently than in their formal written reflections. For example, students nominated such strategies as, "I learn [to] get connections together [to] create a new things to make it happen", "When you talk to somebody and you disagree instead of calling them "wrong" or "a bad person" try to hear them out and gain knowledge of what they have to say.", and "I think the guy Mike how he shifted his voices in the video were really neat. I feel that would be a great technique to use in an essay or just like a freestyle writing. I don't think that using this type of technique in different classes would be a bad thing."

The implication of this variation in reflective depth depending on format informs how we ask for reflective work from basic writers. While we wish to help them develop the necessary skills for formal reflection, we need to acknowledge the writing skills required to be successful in formal written reflection. To help our students learn how to reflect, perhaps it might be most supportive of learning this skill by asking them to reflect in spoken interviews, making recordings of spoken reflections, or by recording peer review exercises. We might also ask for informal reflections as part of class meetings to encourage this kind of written expression without the concerns of formal written situations. This effect of format on depth of reflection emphasizes the importance of scaffolding for basic writers learning to reflect.

**Scaffolding is Important**

Scaffolding of reflective assignments is essential in helping students to develop their own awareness of themselves as writers. In order to be successful in their other college courses, they need to build a framework for metacognitive reflection that will support them in their college writing. This habit of mind is necessary for adapting to the different types of writing required in different disciplines. Most students in our pre-college course do not have experience in setting their own writing goals in educational settings. We work with them to set realistic goals in terms they understand so they can measure their own progress in meeting the goals they have set for themselves. d'Erizans and Bibbo (2015) applied Dweck's "growth mindset" in K-12 students' ePortfolios by asking students to reflect on their own "growth mindsets". They quote Karen Hinnett, educational developer at the UK Center for Legal Education, "Reflection is a way of thinking about learning and helping individual learners to understand what, how and why they learn. It is about developing the capacity to make judgments and evaluating where learning might take you" (d'Erizans & Bibbo, 2015, p. 80). The reflective assignments students completed in our course asked them to consider "what, how, and why" they were making the choices they did as readers and writers. Arcario, Enyon, and Clark (2005, p.16) describe how students at LaGuardia Community College use reflective essays in their ePortfolios "to explore their changing sense of themselves." They suggest that this reflective assignment is, in part, responsible for their increase in student retention. With this recommendation, we attempt to include assignments that ask students to reflect on their changing identities as writers and as members of an academic discourse community.

Good reflection depends upon opportunities to discuss learning with others. We built in opportunities to discuss their work with others in the class through peer reviews, meetings with the tutors and the instructor, and through the class discussions. Denton (2011) argues that such interaction is necessary for learning and for reflection. Citing Vygotsky and Bruner, Denton (2011, p. 844) says, "learning involves interaction and this interaction has the potential to assist learners in taking a metacognitive-step, as it were, away from the objective at hand to evaluate their progress." Students were able to learn from their peers about the choices they were making as writers and readers. In their reflections on the suggestions their peers gave them about improving their papers, students were able to describe how they would use the feedback to make changes to their writing to improve how others would read it. Their peers served as an audience to help them assess how effectively they were able to communicate their ideas in their writing.

We wanted students to take ownership of their own learning in the course. They needed to be active participants in their writing through choosing their own topics to read and write about. They had to set their own reading and writing goals and monitor their progress in meeting them. These actions are often new to students in developmental writing courses. *Masui and De Corte* (2005, p. 366) suggest that active learning is necessary to develop "cognitive and motivational self-regulation." They argue that instructors need to change their role from experts who transmit knowledge to coaches who guide students' learning by setting up stimulating learning environments.

Students in our course did not come in knowing how to reflect on their learning. In fact, they often did not understand what the benefit of such activity might be for them. They began with brief descriptions of their work, but as they engaged in these activities throughout the semester, they saw their value and began to write more and deeper reflections on their learning as writers. Instructors of developmental writing courses need to be willing to accept shorter reflections initially and gradually coax longer and deeper reflections, in both formal and informal contexts, as students become more comfortable with this way of thinking. This is an important move for them because as they enter the first-year writing course, they will be expected to engage in reflective writing. Having this experience in the developmental writing course helps set the stage for them to be successful in the first-year writing course.

## REFERENCES

Alber-Morgan, S. R. Hessler, T. & Konrad, M. (2007). Teaching writing for keeps. *Education and Treatment of Children, 30* (3): 107-128. Retrieved from http://go.galegroup.com/ps/i.do?id=GALE%7CA167691057&v=2.1&u=ucinc_main&it=r&p=EAIM&sw=w&asid=b7a80e15da298363e3f8a16bf79d6246.

Arcario, P. Eynon, B. & Clark, J. E. (2005). Making connections: Integrated learning, integrated lives. *Peer Review 7*(4): 15-17. Retrieved from http://go.galegroup.com/ps/i.do?id=GALE%7CA137915259&v=2.1&u=ucinc_main&it=r&p=EAIM&sw=w&asid=2fd12f716e6cb411b0b5f5d596d81a3c.

Bailey, T. (2009). Challenge and opportunity: Rethinking the role and function of developmental education in community college. *New Directions for Community Colleges 145,* 11–30. DOI: 10.1002/cc.352.

Bower, L. L. (2003). Student reflection and critical thinking: A rhetorical analysis of 88 portfolio cover letters. *Journal of Basic Writing 22* (2): 47-65.

Denton, D. (2011) Reflection and Learning: Characteristic, obstacles, and implications. *Educational Philosophy and Theory 43,* (8):383-352. DOI: 10.1111/j.1469-5812.2009.00600.x.

d'Erizans, R. & Bibbo, T. (2015). Time to reflect ePortfolios and the development of growth mindsets. *Independent Schools Journal.* 78-85.

Edgecomb, N. Smith Jaggars, S. Xu, D. & Barragan, M. Accelerating the Integrated Instruction of Developmental Reading and Writing at Chabot College. *Community College Research Center Working Papers, 71.* http://ccrc.tc.columbia.edu/publications/accelerating-integrated-instruction-at-chabot.html

Jenson, J. (2011). Promoting self-regulation and critical reflection through writing students' use of electronic portfolios. *International Journal of ePortfolio 1*(1): 49-60. Retrieved from http://www.theijep.com/pdf/ijep19.pdf.

MacArthur, C. A., & Philippakos, Z. A. (2013). Self-regulated strategy instruction in developmental writing: A design research project. Community College Review, 0091552113484580.

Masui, C. & De Corte, E. (2005). Learning to reflect and to attribute constructively as basic components of self-regulated learning. *British Journal of Educational Psychology 75*: 351-372. DOI: 10.1348/000709905x25030.

Page, D. & Benander, R. (2011). Promoting cultural proficiency through reflective assignments in study abroad. *International Journal of Arts and Sciences 4*(25): 205-216.

Parisi, H. (2014). Third-party address: A dialogic option in portfolio reflection for basic writers. *Teaching English in the Two-Year College 42* (2): 7-26.

Priemer, B. & Ploog, M. (2007). The Influence of Text Production on Learning with the Internet. *British Journal of Educational Technology 38* (4): 613-622. DOI: 10.1111/j.1467-8535.2006.00646.x.

Quinton, S. & Smallbone, T. (2010). Feeding forward: Using feedback to promote student reflection and learning--a teaching model. *Innovations* in *Education and Teaching International* 47 (1): 125-135. DOI: 10.1080/147032909035911.

Rutschow, E. Z. & Schneider, E. (2011). Unlocking the Gate: What we know about improving developmental education. MDRC. Retrieved from http://www.mdrc.org/sites/default/files/full_595.pdf.

Sommers, J. (2011). Reflection revisited: The class collage. *Journal of Basic Writing* 30 (3): 99-129. Retrieved from http://search.proquest.com/docview/910328875?accountid=2909.

Stine, Linda. (2010). Basically Unheard: Developmental Writers and the Conversation on Online Learning. *Teaching English in the Two-Year College* 38(2): 132-148. Print.

U.S. Department of Education. (2004). The condition of education. *National Center for Educational Statistics*: p. ix. Retrieved from https://nces.ed.gov/pubs2004/2004077.pdf.

Yancey, K. B., Robertson, L. & Taczak, K. (2014). *Writing across Contexts: Transfer, Composition, and Sites of Writing*. Boulder, CO: University Press of Colorado.

## Appendix A

Reading Log
Your Name:                Date You Read the Article:
MLA Citation of the article:
URL of the article:
Answer these questions before you read the article:
1. How long do you think it will take you to read this article?
2. What are your objectives for reading?
3. What do you need to know from this text?

After you read the article, answer the following questions:
1. Purpose (Why did the author write this article?)
2. Audience (Who did the author have in mind when writing this article?)
3. Type of Text (What kind of article is it?)
4. What reading strategies did you try?
5. How did the reading strategies help?
6. Key Vocabulary: (list three words readers need to know in order to understand the article. Write both the words and their definitions.)
7. Use each of the three key vocabulary words in three sentences you create.
8. Write two questions you have about the article you read.

9. Summary of the article in three sentences:
10. The most important insights about this reading that I would like to share with others are:
11. Estimated time to read vs. actual time to read:
12. The following are two things affected how good or bad my reading was:

## APPENDIX B

Personal Goals Prompts

Planning your learning. Before you begin working on the module, read through it and answer the following 2 questions.
1. Name the student learning outcomes for this module. What are you supposed to learn?
2. What do you personally want to learn from completing this module?

Peer Review. Now that you have had your writing evaluated by a peer, answer the following 3 questions.
1. What did your peer like about your paper?
2. What did your peer suggestion you change in your paper?
3. Describe what you will change in your paper based upon your peer's suggestions.

Assessing your learning. Now that you have completed working on this module, answer the following 4 questions.
1. Describe what you were supposed to learn in this module.
2. What did you actually learn in this module?
3. How can you use the information in this module in other reading or writing activities you need to do?
4. What is the most important information in this module that other college students should know?

CHAPTER 2

# Doctoral Research: An Unacknowledged Source of Creativity and Innovation

*Francia Kinchington*

This chapter conceptualises doctoral research as a creative endeavor, where both creative and analytical thinking are brought together in a research process that is underpinned by a fundamental tenant - that of originality. My observations and reflections are based on my experience over the past 15 years as a doctoral supervisor with over 16 completions; as an examiner, Chair of PhD examinations and as a doctoral programme leader (PhD and Professional Doctorate in Education (EdD) during the period 2010-2015 with an average annual cohort of 60 students. During this period I have worked closely with doctoral students across a range of education and health disciplines, evaluated their progress and interviewed them on completion. Many have reported that they were not the same people on completion of their thesis that they were at the beginning of their doctoral journey. They report that the process has been transformational; it has changed them in terms of their intellectual understanding, their ability to problem solve and the way they see 'the world' but it has also changed them as individuals in terms of their researcher identity, reflexivity and intellectual and personal confidence in engaging in research. In the eyes of one researcher,

> It sounds like a cliché to say that doctoral study has changed my life, but since I joined the programme I have presented at 9 conferences (three abroad), co-authored a book chapter and an article on topics I would not have dreamed of two years ago, and been awarded a contract to author a book for a major educational publisher. I'm not saying the doctorate is responsible for this – I am! – but the doctoral programme has undoubtedly given me the confidence to push beyond the boundaries of my normal comfort zone.

Doctoral researchers' development is one of creative evolution and is framed by the criteria set out by *The framework for higher education qualifications in England, Wales and Northern Ireland* (FHEQ) (QAA, 2008) level 8 and *The framework for higher education qualifications in Scotland* (SCQF) (QAA, 2001), level 12, both of which fall within the remit of the UK Quality Assurance Agency (QAA). The level descriptors state that doctoral degrees be awarded for research that demonstrates the following criteria:

- the creation and interpretation of new knowledge, through original research or other advanced scholarship, of a quality to satisfy peer review, extend the forefront of the discipline, and merit publication;
- a systematic acquisition and understanding of a substantial body of knowledge which is at the forefront of an academic discipline or area of professional practice;
- the general ability to conceptualize, design and implement a project for the generation of new knowledge, applications or understanding at the forefront of the discipline, and to adjust the project design in the light of unforeseen problems;
- a detailed understanding of applicable techniques for research and advanced academic enquiry.

Implicit within the first two criteria are notions of originality, innovation and creativity. A thesis must demonstrate and articulate a statement of originality, for example in tackling an under-researched area or population; using a novel approach or methodology; or in examining a well researched area through a novel approach or theoretical lens. The original contribution of a thesis can be in terms of a major contribution to a given field, but it could equally provide a missing part of a jigsaw puzzle within an extensively researched area, contributing a small incremental step that can be picked up by future research. The contribution can be to a field; a body of knowledge and in the case of professional doctorates, where candidates' research is directly aligned to their working context, individual creativity can lead to organizational innovation. A doctoral thesis which is unable to demonstrate an original contribution is unlikely to pass, however well written.

From the outset doctoral research follows a process of creativity. However, unlike artists or musicians who see themselves as creative and have a self-acknowledged creative identity evolved through their discipline, practice and personality, candidates engaging in doctoral research would not claim creativity as one of their prime characteristics. Once registered on a research programme, however, they are required to engage in creativity. This is a capacity which the candidate develops over time; an attribute that is hidden and often goes unacknowledged as it is integrated and embedded within the research process. Failure to articulate this attribute will result in an inability to complete their thesis because the candidate will be unable to engage in problem finding or problem solving or be unable to resolve complex issues to appropriate solutions that are central to demonstrating originality. What is particularly interesting is that doctoral candidates do not lay claim to engaging in a creative process, rather, they will describe and conceptualize a research process framed by theoretical paradigm and a process which will underpin their research from start to completion. They will counter that that their engagement in a scientific or theoretically framed process is not contaminated by assumptions of serendipity, imagination, inspiration, chance and insight; yet these elements are common to both research and creative processes and should be embraced as part of the wider process. Of interest is whether the constituent problem solving and creativity enhancing skills be taught but Mayer (1997:386) suggests that there is a lack of convincing evidence that 'global skills can be learned in context-free environments' suggesting that the learning, experimentation and experience of creative engagement is context bound.

Louis Pasteur claimed that in the field of observation 'chance only favors the prepared mind' and that is certainly the case for doctoral research where the research candidates enter the process with intellectual and subject expertise and with a positive attitude to engaging in research; they are primed and receptive to exploration, changes in understanding and paradigm shifts. These individuals often take a heuristic approach to their problem finding, problem solving and research design, adjusting their ideas and understanding over a period of time to get 'best fit' in terms of addressing their research question, so that the process is meandering rather than linear. Sternberg (2006:88) proposes an investment theory of creativity which

> requires a confluence of six distinct but interrelated resources: intellectual abilities, knowledge, styles of thinking, personality, motivation, and environment.

His notion of confluence brings together these six components, proposing that

> First, there may be thresholds for some components (e.g., knowledge) below which creativity is not possible regardless of the levels on other components. Second, partial compensation may occur in which a

strength on one component (e.g., motivation) counteracts a weakness on another component (e.g. environment). Third, interactions may occur between components, such as intelligence and motivation, in which high levels on both components could multiplicatively enhance creativity (Sternberg 2006:90).

The Vitae Researcher Development Framework (RDF) (2010:2) within Domain A: Knowledge and Intellectual Abilities, cites creativity as one of the three sub-domains, comprising: inquiring mind; intellectual insight; innovation; argument construction and intellectual risk. These elements give rise to specific behaviors (D1), namely, developing new ways of working, has novel ideas and realizes their potential (D2); identifying new trends; creates new opportunities (D3); developing convincing and persuasive arguments to defend research (D7); Takes intellectual risks; challenges the status quo (E3). These behaviors are underpinned by specific attitudes of taking 'a creative, imaginative and inquiring approach to research and being open to new sources of ideas'.

As an expression of this 'creative, imaginative and enquiring approach', it is useful to refer to Sternberg (2006:96) and his articulation of eight types of creativity which typify the range of creative approaches which contribute to moving ideas and knowledge forward. Of the eight the following seven can be directly applied to doctoral research, in the fundamental criteria of demonstrating originality:

i. Redefinition: The contribution is an attempt to redefine where the field is. The current status of the field thus is seen from different points of view. The propulsion leads to circular motion, such that the creative work leads back to where the field is but as viewed in a different way;
ii. Forward incrimination: The contribution is an attempt to move the field forward in the direction it already is going. The propulsion leads to forward motion;
iii. Advance forward incrimination. The contribution is an attempt to move the field forward in the direction it is already going but by moving beyond where others are ready for it to go. The propulsion leads to forward motion that is accelerated beyond the expected rate of forward progression;
iv. Rejection of current paradigms and attempt to replace them through Redirection: The contribution is an attempt to redirect the field from

where it is toward a different direction. The propulsion thus leads to motion in a direction that diverges from the way the field is currently moving;
v. Reconstruction/Redirection: The contribution is an attempt to move the field back to where it once was (a reconstruction of the past) so that it may move onward from that point, but in a direction different from the one it took from that point onward. The propulsion thus leads to motion that is backward and then redirective;
vi. Reinitiation: The contribution is an attempt to move the field to a different, as-yet-unreached, starting point and then to move from that point. The propulsion is thus from a new starting point in a direction that is different from that the field previously has pursued;
vii. Synthesis of Current Paradigms.(Sternberg 2006:96).

Neither creativity nor research is engaged in by individuals who prefer entropy; their preference is for challenge and discovery, they share characteristics such as the ability to deal with ambiguity whilst being able to maintain their focus, and derive satisfaction from this experience. Research is framed by observation and curiosity and asks questions of 'how', 'why', 'what is the relationship between x and y?' It seeks an answer to a question, where neither the framing of the question nor the solution exists. This requires the candidate to identify the problem and frame it within a question or hypothesis. Getzels acknowledges this critical starting point, observing

> The world is of course teeming with dilemmas. But the dilemmas do not present themselves automatically as problems capable of resolution or even sensible contemplation. They must be posed and formulated in fruitful and often radical ways if they are to be moved toward solution. The way the problem is posed is the way the dilemma will be resolved (Getzels 1979:167).

Sternberg offers another perspective to 'problem finding', applying an economic and investment theory to creativity, underpinned by the idea of buying low and selling high. He writes

> Buying low means pursuing ideas that are unknown or out of favor but that have growth potential. Often, when these ideas are first presented, they encounter resistance. The creative individual persists in the face of

this resistance and eventually sells high, moving on to the next new or unpopular idea (Sternberg 2006:86-7).

Implicit within this is a notion of a willingness to engage in a high risk strategy, a single- mindedness and the ability to spot an opportunity, in a sense to 'problem find' and see it through.

Having identified a problem, the doctoral candidate is required to gather and interrogate existing knowledge and theory, demonstrating their scholarship and the wider theoretical framework within which their study is located, but importantly verifying the original potential of their research. They are required to create their own process of investigation that is robust and ethical and that is underpinned by their own philosophy and understanding of knowledge and the world (ontology and epistemology). Data is gathered, analyzed and interpreted and placed within a theoretical framework drawing insights, relationships whether positive or negative, developing models, but essentially resulting in deeper understanding. As for any artist or scientist, the creative process towards an original contribution is not linear. It is fraught with blind alleys, a lack of clarity and misinterpretation, but it requires and ultimately demonstrates the third point in the FHEQ level 8 descriptors which is a flexibility of mind, single mindedness and persistence 'to adjust the project design in the light of unforeseen problems'. Unlike many other creative endeavors which are framed by repetition (albeit with different outcomes), a doctoral study is a singular event which may take up to six years of part time study or up to four years of full time study, from inception to completion. Once started and the candidate registered, the research cannot be put to one side and picked up a year later. The journey towards completion is governed by a ticking clock, insecurity, and cycles of elation followed by self-doubt. Unlike an artist or a musician, the journey towards completion is not solitary since the candidate will normally have two supervisors who will have made the journey before. The best supervisors have methodological and subject expertise and importantly, they have the experience and aptitude to mentor and create an independent, reflective researcher with their passion for their research intact even after five or so years. They will know when to challenge and when to reassure, supporting the candidate to the stage where their knowledge surpasses that of their supervisors so that they are able to (within the English system) present their work to a closed panel of expert examiners who will decide the outcome, in the viva voce. At this point the candidate

> defends his or her research in the viva, and demonstrates deep knowledge and understanding of the field of study, and originality of

thought, either in the creation of new knowledge or in the novel application of existing knowledge (QAA, 2011:23).

The criteria of originality and the creation of new knowledge guide the examiners in their questioning and decision making and ultimately decide the viva outcome.

- Candidates engaged in doctoral research demonstrate common characteristics:
- Entry level of qualification (in terms of subject and methodological knowledge, often post Master's level)
- A willingness to engage in research that does not have an obvious outcome
- Flexibility of mind; intrinsic motivation; curiosity; problem solving aptitude
- Ability to engage in a high risk strategy, comprising both intellectual risk taking and emotional risk taking, where they risk the censure of their peers;
- Tolerance of ambiguity: ability to cope with a significant amount of environmental ambiguity;
- Use meta-cognition to enhance their engagement and adapt to their learning environment;
- Ability to manage bias (bracket preconceptions emerging from their professional background and experience as an 'insider researcher' in order to carry out research in an objective way);
- Willingness to engage in an iterative process;
- Ability to deconstruct; reconstruct and synthesize ideas;
- Engage in the testing of ideas and concepts as part of the journey to completion;
- Ability to make decisions related to the direction and development of their research;
- Demonstrate single-minded concentration with intrinsic motivation;
- Demonstrate tenacity and hard work, acknowledging a research journey that will take up to six years prior to completion.

Two key elements are present in terms of doctoral research: that the individual is self motivated with a capacity and interest in carrying out self-generated research, and secondly, that the research takes place in a psychologically safe context where the individual is free to make and learn from mistakes. Although this creative research process is individually focused, there is an important wider context that must be acknowledged, namely that the individual is part of a wider researcher cohort. This provides momentum; models practice; enables transparency of the creative research journey and provides a forum for discussion, critique, psychological safety in the exploration of ideas and research design, intellectual challenge and emotional support. This cohort approach provided by most doctoral or graduate schools parallels the team approach in research and organizations proposed by Amabile (1996) and developed by DeRue and Rosso, (2009:223) in their theory of rapid creativity in teams and the conditions and speed which teams generate creative ideas. It is proposed that belonging to such a research-orientated creative community of practice in a shared world with common relationships, identity, shared interests, practice and repertoire of resources and experiences (Wenger 1998:72), is fundamental to providing the support necessary for ensuring timely completion of doctoral research particular where they are enabled to come together as cohorts of early researchers sharing experiences, broadening their understanding of research methodology and discussing their research with one another. Doctoral research students inhabit a discrete professional world or community of practice in a similar way to that of musicians or artists, developing and reinforcing practitioner identity which according to Wenger (2010:180) includes:

- Understanding what matters, what the enterprise of the community is, and how it gives rise to a perspective on the world;
- Being able (and allowed) to engage productively with others in the community;
- Using appropriately the repertoire of resources that the community has accumulated through its history of learning.

Research has proposed a number of characteristics as fundamental to creative individuals, namely, general intelligence, experience in the field, self motivation and the ability to think creatively (Amabile 1988:128); imagination, problem solving, ego (self satisfaction) labor (hard work) and value (to society) (Glück, Ernst and Unger 2002:64); specific aspects of individuals' learning styles with reference to salutogenesis (experiencing one's own achievements as meaningful), meta-cognition, self-efficacy and the ability to adapt to learning environments (Boström and Lassen 2006:185); judgment enabling adaptation to difficulties that arise (Nadal-Burgues, 2014:817).

Separate from characteristics are ideas and research which aims to explore and explain the processes which take place during creative engagement. These include creative problem solving and 'flow'. Wilson and Thompson (2014:369) report that (Sio and Ormerod, 2009) carried out a meta-analysis which has suggested that

> the benefits of incubation for creative problem-solving are maximized when people engage in an undemanding task, such as reading, during a period of interruption than when they complete a cognitively demanding task or just rest.

The research of doctoral students is characterized by series of problems, some major and some minor, some of which present as unique problems, others as potentially interrelated clusters all representing stumbling blocks requiring incubation and problem resolution, exacerbated by the pressure of time. Feelings of stress brought about by pressure that time is running out are counterproductive to problem solving. However as Sio and Ormerod point out, engagement in undemanding tasks help, and for doctoral student's mundane tasks such as 'tidying up' one's list of references is a perfect task since although focused, is repetitive and tedious and allows the mind to wander whilst at the same time contributes to the completion of the thesis.

Csikszentmihalyi (1996:111-113) through his description of 'flow' has sought to articulate the characteristics of the process that creative individuals experience when they are focused on creative engagement. He writes:

> This optimal experience is what I have called flow because many of the respondents described the feeling when things were going well as an almost automatic, effortless, yet highly focused state of consciousness.... The flow experience was described in almost identical terms regardless of the activity that produced it.

This makes a valuable contribution because it seeks to penetrate the creative process to explain the experience from 'within' an individual. These nine elements were identified as:

1. There are clear goals every step of the way;
2. There is immediate feedback to one's actions;
3. There is a balance between challenges and skills;
4. Actions and emotions are merged;

5. Distractions are excluded from consciousness (intense concentration thrives when distractions are blocked from one's consciousness);
6. There is no worry of failure;
7. Self consciousness disappears;
8. The sense of time becomes distorted (focus in the activity dissipates the sense of time);
9. The activity becomes autotelic (joy of discovery, of solving a problem ....what is rewarding is the pursuit of the problem and its solution).

These elements, particularly 3, 5, 7 and 8 have been reported repeatedly by doctoral candidates in their writing-up stage where the focus is on synthesis, bringing together the key ideas within each of the chapters into a coherent whole. These elements are experienced in terms of satisfaction, a sense of achievement and a pleasure and associated with the few points within the process where the candidate experiences a sense of control.

Aside from the intensely personal experiences of the creative process, a range of elements are proposed by researchers as central to creativity:

- Product/ideas focus: (Amabile 1988:126) creativity is the process of novel and useful ideas by an individual or a small group of individuals working together;
- Emphasis on novelty (Stein 1974);
- Personality and intellectual characteristics (Findlay and Lumsden) which when expressed result in acts of creativity;
- Combination of personality and context (materials, events, people, circumstances of one's life) (Rogers 1954).

The research process engaged in by a doctoral candidate incorporates key phases of creative engagement such as those proposed by Wallas (1926); Rossman (1931); Osborn (1953) and Barron (1988). These have been explored in Tables 1a- 1d that follow, detailing the relationship between the respective models and the process of doctoral research.

Table 1a: Relationship between Wallas (1926) and the process of doctoral research

| Wallas (1926) | Relationship of model to the process of doctoral research |
|---|---|
| Preparation (definition of issue, observation, and study) | This takes place in the justification of the study, the creation of the research questions, the review of literature and the initial claim for originality. |
| Incubation (laying the issue aside for a time) | This is present in the initial stages of working out the research question; the development of the methodology and research design and in the interpretation of the data. |
| Illumination (the moment when a new idea finally emerges) | This often occurs in the final stages involving the interpretation of the data and articulation of models and the framing of the original contribution. |
| Verification | This takes place in the demonstration of how the data relates to the analysis and final conclusions of the thesis. |

Table 1b: Relationship between Rossman (1931) and the process of doctoral research

| Rossman (1931) (extended Wallas' original four steps to seven) | Relationship of model to the process of doctoral research |
|---|---|
| Observation of a need or difficulty | This takes place in the justification of the study, the creation of the research questions, claim for originality |
| Analysis of the need | Claim for originality verified through an examination of the literature and through the research design used |
| A survey of all available information | Review of literature |
| A formulation of all objective solutions | Within the methodology, research design, pilot study, analysis of data |
| A critical analysis of these solutions for their advantages and disadvantages | Research design, analysis of data and presentation of findings |

*Doctoral Research*

| | |
|---|---|
| The birth of the new idea - - the invention | This is focused within the Findings and Conclusions chapters; the claim for originality and articulation of models |
| Experimentation to test out the most promising solution, and the selection and perfection of the final embodiment | Research design, pilot study, analysis of data, and summarized within the Conclusions chapter |

Table 1c: Relationship between Osborn (1953) and the process of doctoral research

| Osborn (1953) (brainstorming; combination of analysis and imagination) | Relationship of model to the process of doctoral research |
|---|---|
| Orientation: pointing up the problem | This takes place in the justification of the study, the creation of the research questions |
| Preparation: gathering pertinent data | Evidenced within the review of literature and the initial claim for originality. |
| Analysis: breaking down the relevant material | Demonstrated in the research design |
| Ideation: piling up alternatives by way of ideas | Piloting elements as part of the research design |
| Incubation: letting up, to invite illumination | This often occurs in the final stages involving the interpretation of the data and articulation of models and the framing of the original contribution. |
| Synthesis: putting the pieces together | Demonstrated in the way in which the data is used to answer the research questions |
| Evaluation: judging the resulting ideas | Demonstrated in the critical analysis of the analysis of findings; the Conclusions and the claim for originality |

Table 1d: Relationship between Barron (1988) and the process of doctoral research

| Barron (1988) | Relationship of model to the process of doctoral research |
|---|---|
| The tone of Barron's model supports the popular view of creativity as a mysterious process involving subconscious thoughts beyond the control of the creator. | |
| Conception (in a prepared mind) | Justification of research area, research questions based on observation, experience and professional background |
| Gestation (time, intricately coordinated) | Acceptance of a lengthy period of gestation (between 3-6 years dependent on whether engaged in full time of part time study) |
| Parturation (suffering to be born, emergence to light) | All doctoral candidates would attest to this especially in maintaining motivation and momentum during the lengthy research period of up to six years |
| Bringing up the baby (further period of development) | Recommendations following conclusions and identification of areas for further research; writing papers for publication and presenting findings at conferences to ensure that the research is disseminated to the widest audience |

Berg, Taatila and Volkmann (2012: 6) propose a four step model of teaching for creativity which encompasses five key dimensions, namely: problem recognition, goal generation, searching (for information), idea generation and evaluation/implementation which are then cross referenced to person, product, process and environment. Of particular interest are the following which relate directly to the process engaged by doctoral students in carrying out their research.

    i.    Person: Students are enabled to judge emergent solutions and acquire the skills to implement them. The acquisition of convergent thinking skills is thus paramount. The ability to make decisions and accept responsibility plays a role here and tolerance for ambiguity is important; Students learn to allow time for incubation, reflection and selection;

ii. A product has to have value, and thus correspond to certain rules or standards the students have to learn. A reflective and critical element which sets limits and rules has thus to be introduced;

iii. Process: Enable [students] to evaluate solutions with regard to usability, and the risks involved. Introduce convergent thinking skills. Employ realistic exercises to promote such abilities;

iv. An environment that stimulates originality and divergent thinking is required. Different environments for different stages of the project may be useful. An atmosphere of safety to experiment openly and of open interaction is required.

Having explored how the stages of creativity presented by key researchers such as Wallas and Barron relate to elements within the process of research, it is useful to view both how creativity relates to the research process and the personal responses of individuals engaged in doctoral research. Table 2 sets out the research process and the relationship to the creative process.

Table 2: An exploration of the relationship between research process and creativity processes

| Research Process: Phases | Relationship of creative process to research | Personal responses to Creative process |
| --- | --- | --- |
| Intention to engage in the research process | Preparation; Intention to engage in the creative process | Anticipation, preparing oneself, accepting element of risk taking |
| Developing focus and research question/s | Problem finding | Search within oneself as to the appropriateness of the aspect to explore/ focus of research |
| Identification of area of originality | Analysis of Need | Engaging with the element of psychological risk |
| Placing the research in context | A survey of all available information | Analytical; reflective; incubation |
| Interrogating the literature | A survey of all available information | Analytical; reflective; Incubation; evaluation |

| | | |
|---|---|---|
| a critical analysis of paradigm, methodology; Interrogating and justifying the paradigm, methodological lens | A critical analysis of solutions for their advantages and disadvantages; Preparation; Ideation | Incubation; ideation |
| Articulating and justifying the research design | Ideation; Synthesis | Ideation; incubation; evaluation |
| Carrying out a pilot study | Trialing ideas, techniques, materials | Making sense of what has emerged from trials and using the outcomes to decide the direction of the next step; Incubation |
| Deciding and justifying the sample and methodology | Ideation; Incubation | Incubation |
| Carrying out the research | Experimentation; | Ideation; incubation; evaluation |
| Gathering and preparing the data (whether textual or statistical) for analysis | Incubation; | Incubation |
| Analyzing the data | A critical analysis of solutions for their advantages and disadvantages; Synthesis | Incubation; synthesis; Evaluation |
| Interrogating the data to gain insight and deeper understanding (for example thematic analysis; examining the nature of the statistical relationships etc.) | Verification; Incubation | Incubation; synthesis; evaluation |
| Drawing conclusions which are used to resolve the initial questions posed | Synthesis; The birth of a new idea- the invention | Incubation; Synthesis |

| Drawing the research process together as a whole, drawing conclusions, identifying limitations and the claim for originality emerging from the research | Synthesis; Evaluation; Verification | Incubation; Synthesis |
|---|---|---|
| Presenting research for public scrutiny (viva voce within the UK system); publication of papers following viva voce | Parturation; 'Bringing up the baby' | Accepting element of risk; potential for personal and public humiliation or vindication of the years' worth of sacrifice and work |

What emerges from Table 2 is the notion of iterative practice as far as the individual is concerned. The creative process is not experienced as linear, but moves slowly forward in an iterative manner, at times hesitantly and at other times in spurts where layers are built upon layers towards completion of the study.

Creativity is often held to be the domain of particular groups with gate keepers who guard it either physically or metaphorically, allowing only initiates to engage in the process and the understanding or interpretation of the product and its value to society. It is acknowledged that the process of research reflects these characteristics and that although the subject domain terms and language differ, the principles are similar. Once admission is granted, the creative process is, in the case of doctoral researchers, used as with any artist or musician to explore, re-envision and create new ways of understanding and the creation of new knowledge. However, there is a cost. Feedback from doctoral candidates is that engaging in this creative research process is onerous, not only for the individual but their family and close friends. It is lengthy and life changing, but a price they report worth paying because it enables intellectual challenge and fulfilment and the opportunity to make an original contribution to knowledge within one's field of study. That, is something special.

## REFERENCES

Amabile, M. (1988) A Model of Creativity and Innovation in Organisations, *Research in Organisational Behaviour*, Vol. 10, 123-167

Barron, F. (1988) "Putting creativity to work" in Sternberg, RJ (ed.) *The Nature of Creativity*. Cambridge: Cambridge Univ. Press

Berg, H., Taatila, V. and Volkmann, C. (2012), Fostering creativity – a holistic framework for teaching creativity, *Development and Learning in Organizations: An International Journal*, Vol. 26:6, 5 – 8

Bostrom, L. and Lassen, L.M. (2006) Unravelling learning, learning styles, learning strategies and meta-cognition, *Education and Training*, Vol. 48:23, 178-189

Csikszentmihalyi, M. (1996). *Creativity: Flow and the psychology of discovery and invention*. New York: Harper/Collins

DeRue, D.S and Rosso, B. (2009) Toward a theory of rapid creativity in teams, In Creativity in Groups, *Research on Managing Groups and Teams*, Vol.12, 195–228

Getzels, J.W. (1979) *Cognitive Science* 3, (2) 167-172

Glück, J., Ernst, R. and Unger, F. (2002) How Creatives Define Creativity: Definitions Reflect Different Types of Creativity, Creativity Research Journal, Vol. 14, 55-67

Mayer, R.E. (1997) *Thinking, Problem Solving, Cognition*, (2$^{nd}$. Ed.) New York: W.H. Freeman and Co.

Nadal-Burgues, N. (2014),"Project specification: creativity and rhetoric in scientific research", *Journal of Organizational Change Management,* Vol. 27:5, 807 – 818

Osborn, A (1953) *Applied Imagination*. New York: Charles Scribner.

Rossman, J (1931) *The Psychology of the Inventor*. Washington DC: Inventor's Publishing.

Sternberg, R.J. (2006) The Nature of Creativity, *Creativity Research Journal* Vol. 18, No. 1, 87–98

Vitae (2010) Researcher Development Framework, Careers Research and Advisory Centre (CRAC) Ltd [www.vitae.ac.uk]

Wenger, E. (1998) *Communities of Practice: Learning, Meaning and Identity*, Cambridge: Cambridge University Press

Wenger, E. (2010) Social Learning Systems: the Career of a Concept, In Blackmore, C. (ed.), *Social Learning Systems and Communities of Practice*, The Open University in association with Springer-Verlag London Ltd.

Wilson, E.R. and Thompson, L.L. (2014), Creativity and negotiation research: the integrative potential, *International Journal of Conflict Management*, Vol. 25:4, 359 – 386

CHAPTER 3

# Reflections on Cultural Differences between Individualistic and Collective Societies: Adaptation to Individualism Orientated Learning and Teaching

*Xiaoli Jiang*

This chapter reveals several fundamental differences between individualistic and collective cultures that result in dissimilarities in pedagogy, teaching and learning practices. It identifies that in individualistic and collective societies teacher's different roles have a close association with their respective power structure and social hierarchy. Different ways of establishing and maintaining individual self-esteem and perceiving self in relation to others have played an important part in the differences. Further, the chapter utilized a case study of a university academic with a collective cultural background and investigated her personal reflective journey on the quest of understanding herself, her home and host cultures from childhood development, self-esteem development and self-evaluation perspectives. It identifies the core issues of difficulties of individual adaptations from a collective orientated environment to an individualistic society and teaching learning context. The chapter could assist migrants, especially migrant teachers to better understand the self and others in individualistic and collective societies, help with personal reflection and improve teaching and learning practices.

## DIFFERENCES IN LEARNING, TEACHING AND PEDAGOGY BETWEEN INDIVIDUALISTIC AND COLLECTIVE SOCIETIES.

There are marked differences between East and West in learning and teaching practices. From a pedagogy perspective, Eastern education often emphasizes conformity, discipline, behavior control and academic achievement (Rao, Ng & Pearson, 2010). A teacher directed approach and direct instruction on subject teaching are the predominate teaching philosophy and strategy. Content based learning and learning through practicing are the main ways of learning. Whole class teaching and teacher directed activities are the main forms of classroom organization and activities, normally with all students involved in the same activity (Pearson & Rao, 2003). In contrast, Western education emphasizes a student's individuality and initiative via student centered learning and integrated teaching. Learning approaches are inquiry based and learning through doing. Student initiated and process oriented activities play a vital role in teaching and learning activities (Rao, Ng & Pearson, 2010).

The fundamental difference between the two approaches lies in the different cultural and societal values. According to Hofstede's famous IBM research (2001, p. 215) non-Western societies such Confucianism oriented Eastern societies, Arab and South America countries mostly have collective cultures. These cultures stress group consensus, conformity and self-sacrifice.

> Individuals view themselves as parts of one or more collective such as family, co-workers, tribe, or nation; are primarily motivated by the norms of, and duties imposed by, those collectives; are willing to give priority to the goals of these collectives over their own personal goals; and emphasize their connectedness to members of these collectives. (Triandies, 1995, p. 2).

Education is one of the conforming approaches and part of a process to develop individuals' adaptation to collective society. In a collective society as such, an important feature is legitimate inequality between those who are more powerful and those who are less powerful. It is a common belief in collective society that there should be an order of inequality in this world in which everyone has his/her rightful place; high and low are protected by this order (Hofstede, 2001, p. 98). Educational institutions play a big part in maintaining this social order and hierarchy. For example, school teachers are viewed as gurus who transfer personal wisdom and initiate all communication in class. Students are dependent on teachers and treat teachers with high respect, even outside class (Hofstede, 2001, p. 107). There is a mandated inequality in the relationship between students and teachers. A teacher centered learning environment reinforces a teacher's authority and power. In return, power provides individual (teacher) with a feeling of control, psychological security and individual worth due to respect and obedient behaviors of the students.

However, in Western individualistic societies such the USA and Australia, human relationships are operated in a very different manner. According to Traindies (1995) individuals are loosely linked and view themselves as independent of collectives.

> They "are primarily motivated by their own preferences, needs, rights, and the contracts they have established with others; give priority to their personal goals over the goals of others; and emphasize rational analysis of the advantages and disadvantages to associating with others." (p. 2).

Along with the development of liberalism in Western societies, student centered learning is also flourishing, reflecting a change of culture and advance of individualism. Again, education pedagogy plays an important part in the cultural change via reinforcing the cultural values of the West. An important part of the development of individualism is advocating equality and fairness in society and education, so that each individual's full potential can be fully explored, value and uniqueness can be recognized. Power distance in Western societies is low (Hofstede, 2001, p. 87). This is also reflected in the relationship between teachers and students. Teachers treat students as equals and vice versa (Hofstede, 2001, p. 107). Consequently, teachers do not have, neither want to, the same power over their students as their collective counterparts. There is little resistance to let students initiate some communication in class and individual interests are accommodated.

## CHALLENGES WHEN TRANSFERRING FROM TEACHING IN A COLLECTIVE SOCIETY TO AN INDIVIDUALISM ORIENTATED SOCIETY

The first, probably the most challenging part to a teacher from a collective culture is the relationships between teacher and students. As identified above, in collective societies, teachers are perceived as gurus and treated with respect. Teachers have ultimate power in the classroom and student obedience is the norm. Students are not allowed to question teachers and any interruptive behaviors in classrooms are discouraged and often punished.

However, in Western university classrooms, students and teachers are largely equals. Teachers do not automatically receive respect, but need to earn it. Students often question or even argue their points against that of teachers. Contrary to Eastern classroom culture, students are the people who need to be treated with respect.

I observed an incident in a class at a metropolitan university in Australia when I was a post graduate student studying with undergraduate students:

> A senior lecturer with a collective cultural background, who had lived in Australia for 12 years, was teaching a class of both undergraduate and post-graduate students. Suddenly he stopped his lecture and pointed at

four students: "Michael, Amy, Lyn and Tom[1], don't talk. Some students have told me that they did not understand some of my lectures. If you talk in the class, how can you understand?" Tom was sitting in front of the other three students named by the lecturer. He responded "I did not talk". The lecturer raised his voice "You were talking." "I was not" responded Tom. "You were talking" the lecturer shouted. Tom stood up and walked out of the lecture theatre. The lecturer yelled at Tom: "You withdraw, don't come back!" Then he turned to the class: "I don't want bad eggs in the class". At this time Michael stood up and walked out as well. The lecturer again yelled: "You withdraw, don't come back!"

The action of the lecturer pointing a finger at students who are talking in the class can happen quite often in collective cultural classrooms. Rarely do students talk back to their lecturer. Students from collective cultures generally remain mute and it would be the end of the story. However, Australian students do not have the same idea of hierarchy and power structure as the students from collective societies. Teachers theoretically are equal to them and they believe that they could not be accused of something that they had not done. The unusual disobedient behavior was not something the lecturer was prepared for given his native cultural values. He felt a sense of loss of control. Students' challenge to his authority angered him. Consequently, he raised his voice and students walked out of the classroom. This case highlights significant different views as how a teacher should relate to his/her students and the equality/inequality of the relationship, especially the power structure in classroom.

Most of the times a conflict like this in classrooms in Western societies are not handled so openly and confrontationally by lecturers from collective cultural backgrounds. Many choose not to react so strongly. They tolerate the "talking", questioning and disagreement from students in university classrooms. However, it doesn't mean all are happy to be at the receiver's end of such a situation. Deep down they have doubts, dilemmas and their professional satisfaction may be affected, because the respect embedded in the teaching position they used to receive in their home country is no longer a given entitlement. Some of the sanctioned bad behaviors are no long considered as bad. The rules have changed in terms of good and bad, right and wrong. This causes confusion, frustration and self-doubt. Individual adaptation is clearly required to handle "challenging"

---

[1] All people's names in the cases of this paper have been changed from their real names for reasons of confidentiality

behavioral patterns of students that associate with individualistic cultural values and beliefs such as equality and low power distance.

Further, the nature of a collective culture is also reflected by a tendency of teachers to treat students as a group (Hofstede, 2001, p. 236). Because of the larger numbers that the teachers have to handle in collective society classes, individual student needs are often not considered as important compared to those in individualistic societies. Teaching and learning are normally conducted for the group. Whole class teaching and teacher directed activities are the main forms of classroom organization and activities. Normally all students are involved in the same activity (Pearson & Rao, 2003). At the university level, lecture style of delivery of information/knowledge is prevalent and rote learning is the dominate form of learning. However, in the individualistic society, students are the center of learning. They are recognized as diverse individuals and have different needs requiring consideration and accommodation in teaching practice and learning design. For a teacher from a collective teaching environment, often it will take considerable time to comprehend this difference and adjust to individual orientated teaching and learning approaches that initially appear to be in a similar teaching context – lecturing the class.

## COMPARATIVE RESEARCH ON SELF, EVALUATION OF SELF, EDUCATION AND PARENTING STYLES AND MAKING SENSE OF FUNDAMENTAL CULTURAL DIFFERENCES BEHIND THE CHALLENGES

Most of the challenges previously mentioned originated from how an individual view's him/herself, relates to people in his/her associate groups (including family, friends and community etc.) and accepts his/her rightful place/power in the group in different societies. Research has long recognized fundamental differences in the way we see our self in collective and individualistic cultures. It has been revealed that people from collective societies are bound by their relationships with family and the community. (Triandis, 1995). The nature of the self is fluid, embedded, interdependent, situated, particularistic and self is evaluated in the form of a lower self versus a higher self which is set up according to the social role, group and family expectations (Heine, 2001; Kim, Triandis, Kagitcibasi, Choi, & Yoon, 1994). For example, my initial Chinese thinking was more collective, sensitive and considering other people's opinions, especially from in-group, towards me and my conduct. In Chinese culture people believe their conduct should not be self-driven, but driven by family, community and even national interests. The feeling about self is often dependent on other people's views toward ourselves and the way they treat us. Research supports this common observation via identifying that students from collective cultures are more likely to evaluate themselves based on social or external dimensions and their self-esteem is more likely to be interdependent (Sinha, Willson & Warson, 2000; Tafarodi, Swann, and William, 1996; Tafarodi & Lang, 1999, Wang & Ollendick, 2001). This contrasts with the individualism orientated Western societies where the individual is socialized to be more self-sufficient and independent. The self is developed towards uniqueness, autonomy, freedom and intrinsic worth of the individual (Heine, 2001; Triandis, 1995). People are more likely to evaluate themselves based on the autonomous or internal dimension, and their self-esteem is more independent (Sinha, Willson & Warson, 2000; Tafarodi, Swann, and William, 1996; Tafarodi & Lang, 1999, Wang & Ollendick, 2001).

Comparative studies in education and parenting styles have provided a picture of pathways for developing children as collective individuals in some of those societies. These studies reveal children from collective Asian cultures such as Chinese, Japanese and Indian societies are given highly controlling feedback and are discouraged from independent, active or exploratory activities. (Bond, 1991; Sinha, 1999, Woronoff, 1997). Shame and isolation of the child from the group are dominant punishment techniques. Highly disciplinary and controlling feedback make a child dependent so that he/she is more likely to adopt group values and comply with the example of authorities, resulting in minimizing the child's need for self-expression, independence, self-mastery, creativity and overall personal development. (Wang & Ollendick, 2001). It has been consistently reported that Chinese parents are highly restrictive and controlling, or "authoritarian" where unquestioned obedience to authority is stressed rather than two-way open communication between children and parents (Chao, 2001, Zhou, Eisenberg, Wang, & Reiser, 2004). Education practices in many collective Asian cultures are designed to make children conform via strong compliance training and group influence (Sinha, 1999; Shangguan, 1999). In this context, children learn to live up to externally imposed criteria to feel worthy. Their degree of self-esteem is in proportion to the extent to which one measures up relative to others. Thus their feeling about themselves are more likely to depend on other people's evaluation, not their own. Those people's evaluations are a powerful motivator (Deci & Ryan, 1995).

One of the major implications of these practices is that people from a collective society normally have developed this so called "face" or "honor" from a very young age. "Face" or "honor" is highly dependent on other people's opinions and subject to external evaluations. It is considered a part of self-esteem that is highly contingent to external factors and potentially volatile depending on an individual's achievements and perceptions of others (Jiang, Guan, and Prosser, 2005). In collective societies everyone has his/her own rightful place, together with a certain level of power according to his/her role in the family, workplace, community and society. A high power distance and clear hierarchy is explicit. Hierarchy means existential inequality (Hofstede, 2001, p. 98). An individual's power allocation plays an important role in maintaining and boosting the high power individual's positive feelings about their "face"/" honor" – consequently their self-esteem. Teachers in many collective societies are highly respected. For example, in Confucian cultures, teachers are treated as parents. There is a Teacher's Day (10$^{th}$ September) in China to show respect to those who are educating the younger generations. In Hindu cultures, teachers/academics belong to the highest caste, above kings and warriors. The high respect ensures teachers' prestige and power in society and over the young people in classrooms. It acts as an important foundation to support individual teacher's self-esteem by providing them with "face" and "honor" in daily work. A teacher has great power to tell students what to do and students must follow the orders. Any misbehaviors would be condemned by the teacher, principal, fellow students and even parents of the misbehaving students. A punishment often follows. Teachers become accustomed to their conforming behavior pattern and exercise great power or control over students. This explains the fundamental differences in cultural values that guide different learning and teaching between East and West and underline the challenges that teachers with a collective background may face in individualistic culture oriented classrooms.

## SELF-REFLECTION ON PAST LEARNING AND TEACHING EXPERIENCES, UNDERSTANDING OF SELF IN DIFFERENT CULTURES, AND MAKING CHANGES TO SELF, STUDENT LEARNING DESIGN AND TEACHING PRACTICES.

### Deep Self-reflection and Making Changes to Myself - A Critical Part of My Adaptation Journey.

I grew up in a collective society and completed the majority of my education, including a bachelor and a master's degree in teaching, in a collective environment. The education I experienced was largely teacher-centered, classes were large and rote learning the main teaching methodology together with intense competition. However, after arriving in Australia in the early 90's I have been very fortunate to have opportunities to study and teach in Australian schools, plus research and teach in cross culture areas in a university. During the years of my interactions with different education institutions and communities in Australia, and to some extent in the UK and USA, I observed many people in Western societies perceive themselves as unique individuals and prioritize their own needs above others in family, school, university and community. Social hierarchy is much lower and each individual is supposed to be equal to others. To understand why and how this kind of culture was developed, research on individualism and collectivism and the self in these cultures became my major focus for seeking theoretical explanations of differences in cultural behaviors. I was most interested in how individuals view self as a unique entity and guiding their way of relating to others and react to others' feedback and control temptations.

In addition to my understanding and reflections on the differences between individualistic and collective cultures, relevant power distance, inequality and the self in those cultures, I extended my research into cross-cultural self-esteem and stability of self-esteem studies to further understand the self. Cross-cultural research has investigated differences between collective self-esteem and personal self-esteem (De Cremer & Oosterwegel, 2000; Kao & Nagata, 1997; Sato & Cameron, 1999). Tafarodi and his colleagues tested their so called 'cultural trade-off' hypothesis: people from collectivist cultures were higher in self-liking and lower in self-competence than their western counterparts. The research compared Chinese with Americans, (Tafarodi, et al, 1996) and Malaysians with British people (Tafarodi & Lang, 1999). The scores for self-liking (more social or outer dimension of self-esteem) and self-competence (more autonomous or inner dimension of self-esteem) were compared. Results supported the hypothesis that type of culture was associated with differences in self-liking and self-esteem. In general, it has been widely accepted that the self in collectivist cultures is enmeshed and contextualized, so that self-esteem is interdependent and based on external evaluation. The self in individualist cultures is self-contained, isolated and clearly bounded. Self-esteem is independent and more internally evaluated (Tafarodi & Lang, 1999). These studies have contributed greatly to my understanding of the self in relation to others (particularly significant others) in different cultures.

When reflecting on the impact of external evaluation tendency on a collective background person in this individualistic society, I started to understand that the cause of an often aggravated self-doubt and identity crises is the lack of collective protection on a contextualized, interdependent and external evaluation oriented self-esteem. In collective societies individuals endeavor to maintain and give "face" or "honor" or contingent part of self-esteem (Jiang & Prosser, 2002) to their in-groups. Respect and compliance from students is a part of it. This acts as a protection to sustain teachers' positive self feelings. However, in individualistic oriented classrooms a teacher's feeling of worth or self-esteem could be severely challenged from time to time because of his/her original collective culture values. The power that a teacher had over students is partially removed. What teachers say is not always right, and students can challenge teachers in terms of their knowledge, opinions, teaching approaches, results, organization of the courses etc. Even communication styles between teachers and students have changed. For example, e-mails are often sent to me without mentioning my name, a basic "Hi" or "Hello": some students ask whatever they want bluntly. According to my home culture, this is very disrespectful. Initially I thought this was all because of me who did not deserve their respect. Clearly these could all negatively impact on the feeling of authority and control of an individual with a collective background due mainly to their original implanted social status. Teachers could have a feeling of loss of control and being devalued.

After years of observation and reflection, it came to my realization that for someone like me working in a Western culture orientated university with a collective background, the ultimate challenge is to the self. However, this has rarely been admitted or mentioned, let alone addressed. Different student values and behaviors challenge our previously established identity - who we are, consequently our self-esteem – our feeling about ourselves and self-worth. It is further complicated by language issues. Very often people with a collective culture background have English as their second language. It is always a handicap regardless of how much hard work we have completed in English studies. The daily academic tasks are not always easy when completing them with our second language. Culturally, societal rules have changed dramatically. Many behaviors that were good in our collective society are no longer desirable. All of these inevitably create some self-doubt and potentially damage self-esteem, impacting on our happiness and wellbeing.

Personally, understanding the reasons for the differences and challenging my interpretation of adverse events and consequent feelings about myself is the most empowering step towards self-reflection and adaptation to an individualistic culture. My research and teaching at primary schools have complemented my reflection via providing firsthand knowledge and experiences on how children were brought up in Australia, their daily activities, their relationships with teachers and parents. In the context of my cross-cultural self-esteem research and teaching I started to make sense of university students' behaviors. It is individualism's equality, individual freedom and self-autonomy, implanted into children at a very young age, reinforced in school years via teaching and learning practices, teacher response to student needs and individual attention they have received, made these children/students vastly different from those in my home country. A much lower power distance and social hierarchy than that of a collective society are very obvious in children's daily school life and their association with their teachers. It establishes a significant contrast from what I knew before.

I gradually learnt to interpret external events differently and challenge my original cultural values in terms what is right and wrong, good and bad, polite and rude, respect and disrespect etc. These gradually overhauled my home-grown ideas and native power structure, in particular, after I learned and later taught Charles Taylor's theory *"Politics of recognition"*. In his theory, Canadian philosopher Charles Taylor (1992) believes every individual human being is unique and this uniqueness and individual identity should be respected, recognized and accepted. Taylor further states when rejecting or misrecognizing individuals' uniqueness, their identity and potential, we risk destroying those individuals by damaging their self-esteem and causing them discontent. Ill feelings and conflicts could arise as a result. Taylor's positive freedom advocates equality and to be fully one's self. It allows an individual's potential to be maximized and their wellbeing achieved. Taylor's theory had a profound impact on my understanding of the importance of equality, recognition of each individual's uniqueness and consequently positive aspects of Western individualism. I began to fully appreciate why lower power distance and more equality are needed in the development of student self-esteem and positive views towards life and academic studies. I have also recognized that my own self-esteem developed in a collective culture is vulnerable to external negative views. I gradually trained myself to evaluate myself according to my own deeds and be less sensitive to external elements not under my control. Slowly I have developed a unique sense of self identity. This has been the critical element in removing my self-doubt and solving an identity crisis.

## Making Changes to Student Learning Designs and Teaching Practices Based on 'Flow' Theory in an Individualism Orientated Environment

After serious reflective 'soul searching', my understanding of the self in a different cultural context has acted as a catalyst to spark fundamental changes in my teaching practice and communication with students. I put myself on an equal footing with all my students and communicate with them as equals and treat them as unique individuals. I explore suitable teaching approaches and learning designs to address diverse student needs and attempt to make their learning an enjoyable experience.

The guiding philosophy for accommodating diverse student needs in my teaching is 'flow' theory, a psychological theory that promotes optimal experiences (Csikszentmihalyi, & Csikszentmihalyi, 1988). It was a part of my Ph. D. studies.

In the mid-seventies, the phenomena of people enjoying rock climbing, painting, playing chess and music, and dancing for long hours without expecting to be rich or famous aroused the attention of some researchers. Extrinsic rewards could not explain these behaviors. Based on research into intrinsic motivation and the play of children, Csikszentmihalyi (1975) investigated a range of these types of experiences and termed them as "flow" experience. "Flow Theory" was developed. "Flow" is "a state of experience that is autotelic or intrinsically rewarding, hence, it provides its own motivation" (Csikszentmihalyi, 1975, p.191). In flow, most of the dimensions of experience reach their positive peaks. People feel a sense of control, cheerfulness, freedom, clarity, satisfaction, motivation, happiness as well as deep enjoyment (Csikszentmihalyi, & Csikszentmihalyi, 1988; Csikszentmihalyi, 2008).

According to 'flow' theory, optimal ('flow') experience in any activity is desirable and motivational (Csikszentmihalyi, & Csikszentmihalyi, 1988). The 'flow' experience has the following major characteristics: a challenging activity that requires skills; clear goals and immediate feedback (one knows instantly how well one is doing), and the paradox of control (Csikszentmihalyi, 1992).

Every human activity has the potential to become a 'flow' experience providing the activity achieves a good balance between the challenges and an individual's skills. If the challenges are far greater than the person's skills, this generally produces anxiety. If the person's skills are far higher than the challenges, this can result in boredom. When challenges are approximately equal to skill levels, a person experiences a feeling of enjoyment and involvement – 'flow' (Csikszentmihalyi, 1993). Human beings and their self-esteem can grow as a result of their 'flow' experiences. Student learning experiences are no exception. I hypothesized that creating 'flow'-like learning experiences for students could be a way to create an enjoyable learning environment, to enhance independent learning outcomes and to avoid student boredom and/or anxiety. I have also recognized that creating 'flow'-like learning experiences is about understanding student skills, being sensitive to their diverse needs and designing teaching and learning activities accordingly. It is a radical departure from my original collective pedagogy that treat students as a group via lecturing them with

one-way communication and assessing them in a traditional manner. My reflection on cultural differences have generated reflective teaching and learning practices, guided by 'flow' theory, in two areas to accommodate an individualistic student learning style.
This is achieved via:

### Creating Visually Enhanced and Narratively Enriched Learning Activities and Resources Together with Challenging Questions and Positive Strategies

I teach nine courses in International Studies and my students are from different undergraduate programs in Arts, Education, Physical Education, Psychology and Social Welfare. They are also drawn from quite diverse backgrounds. The cohort typically includes high school graduates, mature age students, disadvantaged rural and low socio-economic students, Asian international full fee paying and European and American exchange students as well as African refugee students. I facilitate student centered learning focusing on serving student needs and their interests, not just give student traditional lectures. I want to make sure the content matches the different base knowledge and skill levels of my students and create 'flow' like learning experiences for all.

Research has shown that people remember visual images more easily, and better than they remember words. Using imagery can make learning more fun and interesting (Small, 2013). As a result, I spend many hours producing visually enhanced lecture PowerPoints by incorporating relevant photographs, video clips, YouTube clips and internet sites. I also carefully seek examples, cases and stories to provide enriched narratives in the delivery of lectures. For example, in a course named Asia in Focus, 'Confucianism and related culture' is one of the topics. In Confucianism, filial piety is an important concept, and a concept that most Australian students, who have lived in an individualist culture, may have difficulty in understanding. Initially students are asked about their prior knowledge on filial piety, then two pictures demonstrating the concept 'fly in' the PowerPoint slide with my brief explanations. I then use a five-minute video clip from a BBC documentary which recorded the daily life of a son practicing filial piety towards his parents. After the video clip, I further describe other practices of filial piety in China utilizing a story-telling approach. This tangible approach inspires students to enthusiastically engage in their learning. As a result, they have a much better understanding of filial piety and feel good about their new knowledge. All of the above approaches are based on 'flow' theory and are designed to enable students to connect their existing knowledge and experience with the new, making the challenges suitable for their skills. Students then obtain immediate feedback from the learning activities, that is, they have gained something new and meaningful. According to 'flow' theory this type of feedback provides students with an intrinsic reward and a feeling of being in control, nurturing personal growth and providing motivation to learn (Csikszentmihalyi & Csikszentmihalyi, 1988).

With the aim to fully engage students in their learning, in all my lecture preparation I design manageable questions as suitable challenges and integrate the questions at appropriate times during the lecture. This approach seeks to challenge all students to think and invites them to work with me in class. It also acts as a break from my talking and heightens student attention to the class. Students' correct or innovative answers provide an opportunity for them to receive immediate feedback on what they are doing well. The students report that they feel connected to their learning. In the language of Csikszentmihalyi, they are experiencing mini 'flow'-like time and are engaged in the moment. At the same time students have opportunities to express their opinions toward many issues on globalization, multiculturalism and world politics. Shernoff (2013), when researching optimal learning environment, identified that lectures can be made engaging by frequent questioning the class, transforming the activity into an interactive presentation. A teacher's higher level of enthusiasm and creativity during a lecture actually creates some of the highest levels of student engagement in his study sample – indicating they are experiencing flow.

In tutorials I use the same principle to provide students with challenging but manageable questions for group discussions. Everyone has a chance in a non-threatening environment within a small group to discuss the issues. Laptops and iPads are encouraged to be used for searching relevant information, students from each group then share their ideas. Importantly, everyone's ideas are appreciated based on my commitment to the development of their self-esteem and freedom of speech. This approach makes students feel in control, with improved self-confidence.

Due to the nature of international studies, my courses attract a large percentage of students with different cultural and linguistic backgrounds, including international and African refugee students. Their level of English language is often relatively low. In this multicultural and multi lingual environment, my approach of combining appropriate visually enhanced PowerPoint slides and video clips/YouTube in teaching is critically important to ensure the learning challenges for everyone are manageable. When some students cannot read the notes of the PowerPoint slides quickly enough or cannot understand some of the vocabulary, the visual images help to provide them with basic information that connects their original knowledge with the new concept. It reduces difficulties in their learning tasks, making their learning better balanced between challenges and their existing language and culture skills. International students in their evaluations comment that, *"the teacher gives lessons weaving in pictures and video, benefiting our study and making the course rich and colorful at the same time"*; *"Although it is very difficult for me to be in the class, I still feel comfortable because I like the challenge"*.

Based on the international nature of my course, I often invite international students and past refugees to make their unique contributions to the classes based on their own experiences and knowledge. Encouragement and appreciation always follow. For example, I encouraged several past refugee students to make their presentations on African refugee issues based on their own migration experiences. Their presentations and contributions in class discussions impacted profoundly on the local students –particularly in understanding their living conditions, schooling, the dangers and the length of time they endured at refugee camps. Students were surprised to learn that some refugees walked many months to reach the camps and were there for 15 years. The students with a refugee background have made their unique and powerful contribution to the learning experiences of the local students. It helps the refugee students to feel good about themselves and benefits their personal development.

## APPROACHES TO ASSESSMENT AND FEEDBACK THAT FOSTER INDEPENDENT LEARNING

In one of my program reviews, students expressed a strong desire to have more practical oriented elements in the program to assist in their future employment preparation. I immediately amended my assessment methods to address this feedback. I focused on building students' practical skills using independent discovery methods. Student feedback has been sought throughout the modification of assessments and helped me to refine my practice.

Firstly, I provide students with independent learning opportunities through assessment tasks that challenge them in far more creative ways than simply doing library research. For example, a course named Global Community and Mobile Citizens addresses migrant and multiculturalism issues. I provide students with opportunities to attend general meetings at the Ballarat Regional Multicultural Council and to write a report on this as their major assignment. This approach to assessment and feedback allows students to establish contact with migrants in local Australian communities and observe such things as: how migrant communities are structured; how they function; what support they receive; and the issues they face. It is designed to broaden student thinking and to expose them to real community work. Alternatively, students in this course could also write a report on their visit to the Immigration Museum in Melbourne (IMM). They are required to analyze and interpret the exhibition artefacts in relation to migration and multicultural history in Australia utilizing theories discussed in the course. Similarly, for a Chinese history course I teach, I provide two authentic assessment choices. Students can either visit the Chinese artefacts and history exhibition in the Asian Galleries of the National Gallery of Victoria in Melbourne or write a traditional essay. In a course called Going Global: Making Sense of Globalization, I provide students with an option to research and report on an Australian based international non-government organization and make recommendations for the organization based on their research analysis. In a course titled Intercultural Competence and Communication, I focus on improving student independent cross-cultural problem solving skills through writing an e-mail response to solve an intercultural conflict, job application for a position in an Asian country, and analyzing intercultural conflict cases.

Secondly, I emphasize peer learning in the commonly used assessment approach - oral presentation. The oral presentation for assessment purpose is only a by-product or a stimuli for the learning. Because of my understanding of Australian individualistic culture and student ability and preferences, I truly believe students are very capable of doing part of the teaching and has the benefit of developing their independent learning skills. Teaching peers can empower and motivate student learning. The key is to provide students with suitable challenges that match their current skills. In all the courses I teach, the purpose of tutorial presentations is to allow students to share their independent research outcomes with the aim of stimulating fellow students to participate and learn from each other.

In some of my courses, as an assessment task, each presenter is required to independently study one chapter of the textbook and share their understanding and questions with the rest of the group in an oral presentation. To ensure the quality of their 'presentation/teaching', I provide detailed assessment criteria and specify that students need to demonstrate "appropriate use of audio and visual materials (e.g. PowerPoint, thoughtfully selected videos/You Tubes, handouts etc.)", demonstrate "ability to generate class involvement and discussion"; and generate "good learning outcomes."

Similarly, in other courses I have provided students with assessment choices. They have been free to investigate and present one of the areas required in the course guide. Each week's presenters have a clear goal to reinforce a specific topic of interest that complements that week's lecture content and tutorial discussions areas. Sometimes oral presentations are assessed by a panel of four to five peers. Every student is assigned to a panel twice a semester to assess five to eight student presentations. They are required to provide presenters with constructive feedback which acknowledges the achievements and provides advice for future improvements. Student assessors' feedback is provided anonymously to the presenters via e-mail within one day of the presentation. I verify the quality of the assessors' comments and accuracy of the marks to ensure the peer assessments are fair and accurate.

To maximize student peer learning outcomes, in the first tutorial of the semester students are given time to discuss the benefits and potential issues in implementing peer assessment. Students brainstorm approaches that may be useful to involve and increase student participation during presentations. In this process the learning benefit of peer assessment and clear assessment criteria are reinforced and students develop very favorable responses to the process. "Enables students to develop their knowledge in different ways."

Thirdly, I conduct tests/exams based on incremental learning. In each course I teach, normally there is a test that accounts for 30% of the total mark. The test is designed to enhance independent student learning via the comprehensive nature of the questions. For example, one of the test questions in the course of Intercultural Competence and Communication is:

> "Utilize cross-cultural theories regarding power distance, face and self-esteem in different cultures, to explain likely conflicts when people communicate across individualistic and collective cultures. Describe how you might minimize these conflicts. (15 marks)"

To answer a question like this, students need to independently review and analyze their studies over the semester. They need to demonstrate a holistic understanding of course content and apply the knowledge to the real world to solve problems. To promote student learning I provide the questions in the first week of the semester and they are available on the course shell - Moodle. On the day of the test students are only allowed to bring in pens to write their answers on the blank test books provided.

The test provides students with a suitable challenge that matches their newly learned knowledge and skills. Students are largely free from the anxiety that a normal test would bring. Students are in full control of their own destiny. The feedback and reward are inherited in the student's own preparation and ability to successfully answer the questions.

## OUTCOMES OF THE REFLECTIVE ADAPTATION AND CHANGES

I have gained overwhelming student support for my changes in learning and teaching approaches based on my reflection of cultural and pedagogy differences and understanding of students in individualistic societies. Student evaluation of my teaching has been consistently high ranging between 4.2 and 5 with an average of 4.55 out of maximum score of 5. Typical student comments on my visually enhanced and narratively enriched learning activities and resources include: *"Lectures have been really visual and help my understanding"; "The use of video and PowerPoint make learning this unit interesting and comprehensive"; "The use of videos helps me to understand the different countries and cultures, instead of just reading about them";* Some of the comments on my questioning and interactive style of approach: *"I like the way Dr Jiang conducts lectures and tutorials. They promote learning and the retention of that knowledge". "The discussion generated in classes, and the informal lecture style have meant that I have been able to gain a better understanding of the material"; "Xiaoli was extremely genuine, friendly, enthusiastic, well informed, open to opinion and provided excellent learning opportunities".*

In 2009, I was awarded an Australian University Teaching Award: Citation for Outstanding Contributions to Student Learning in this area because of utilizing these approaches.

On my changes to assessments, I have conducted several anonymous student surveys to gain their feedback for continued improvement. Results demonstrated that on the reports that are an alternative from traditional essay and require student independent discovery, between 65% and 83% of student respondents believed this approach was either 'much better' or 'better' to assist their learning than a traditional essay. Typical of the comments I receive are the following student observations: *"A welcome change from the traditional essay." "I can choose the option that I feel my learning skills and knowledge will be best suited to." "Choice on what and how we present our content is a much better way of learning as we can look at the topics in varying ways compared to having a direct question we have to answer in a traditional essay." "Aids interest and understanding of the topic."* The assessments open student eyes to a different world and spark students' interests in their involvement in voluntary work to assist newly arrived migrants and some undertake honors studies in these areas.

I have observed over a number of semesters the effectiveness of presentations that emphasize the peer learning approach. In a recent series of presentations 89% of the students used colorful and visual pictures in their PowerPoint presentations to assist their communication, and 81% of the students used other visual aids such as videos, and You Tube clips, 91% of the students designed suitable questions to engage fellow students during their presentations. Some organized role play and other class activities. Many conducted quiz competitions and rewarded their classmates with sweets. These sessions are fun with high levels of student participation. The positive feedback is immediate. It is evident that students have engaged robust discussions, numerous interactions and often drawn abundant applause at the end. Presentations have become an activity where students feel in control, gain great satisfaction and build their skills and confidence. The preparation and delivery of oral presentations are at the core of becoming an independent learner. Students reported they: *"Develop skills in how to present in front of tutorial class." "Learn better through doing, keeps students focused & involved throughout presentation."* Typical of the views are the following student observations: *"An effective way for people to do better in oral presentations." "Important as it helps engage the audience."*

In terms of peer assessment, student feedback overwhelmingly recognizes the benefits to the assessors. In the class evaluation/survey of my assessment approaches students commented *"It does make you concentrate on the presentation and gives you more of an idea of how to present well." "We concentrate more on the skills of presentation."* Students also believed that by writing constructive feedback including suggestions for improvement, they learn how to communicate their point of view with greater sensitivity. *"It helps us to learn how to mark others as well as pay attention on the presentations"*

For the test approach, student feedback indicated that 92.3% of the students support this assessment approach for its learning value. They commented: *"Very surprised at first. But now realize it allows you to learn something well and not just cram everything into memory only to be forgotten after exam.";* *"Ensures students engage with the course content for the duration of the semester as they know what they will be assessed on." "Less test anxiety."* and *"It puts the responsibility of learning back on the individual".*

"In 2012" I was awarded my second Australian University Teaching Citation for Outstanding Contribution to Student Learning as a result of my utilization of these assessment approaches.

However, the most rewarding outcome is probably the feeling of personal enlightenment after all the confusion and self-doubt. The enlightenment is a result of the constant self-reflection and search for answers to perceived differences, internalizing and making sense of my adopted culture and society, changing the role of self in classrooms and society, and accepting a new social status that is equal to students and others. The soul search journey has achieved a new sense of control after losing the old grip. The new control is established on having control on my internal self, my identity, my evaluation of self and my own destiny. The control is also rested on my understanding of others, the unwritten cultural rules of the society and community that I call home. It has resulted in a much needed personal growth and happiness derived from the deep self-reflection.

## CONCLUSION

Every societal culture is developed from its own unique historical, environmental and societal context and its values, beliefs and customs. Education plays an important role in this development and reinforces the culture and societal values. However, globalization and international migration provide challenges to all cultures to reflect and learn from others, adapting and renewing itself for the better.

The significant differences in pedagogy in learning and teaching between collective and individualistic societies originated from their culture values, beliefs and different education standpoints. Reflecting and understanding the underlying reasons is the most important element to an adaptation.

Migration and taking up an academic position using a second language in an unfamiliar cultural environment was never meant to be easy. Different culture values, behaviors, societal norms and academic practices could challenge a migrant scholar immensely in terms of his/her value, worth, even existence. People reflect and adapt initially for survival needs. However, my personal journey illustrated in this chapter has revealed how individuals could adapt to a very different work environment via observation, comparison, reflection (to a large extent self-education), making sense of differences, challenging the 'old' self and at the same time actively learning and adjusting to the new. The adaptation may not be a smooth pathway. However, the rewards are in the twists and turns, especially the reflection and consequent enlightenment.

Further, different cultural backgrounds could also contribute to teaching and learning practices and enrich student experiences. In my case, my childhood upbringing that focused on caring for others has positively impacted on my adaptation through a high level of empathy, being sensitive to student needs and perceptive to changes. A deep reflection and adaptation to individualism orientated learning and teaching could be started without much ethnocentricity baggage. At the same time, the different personal backgrounds can be an invaluable asset to establish a unique teaching and learning context that provide students with fresh interpretations of the world and ways of life that they have never heard and experienced before. Enriched teaching and enhanced learning outcomes could be achieved by culturally and linguistically diverse teaching staff in a multicultural environment.

## REFERENCES

Bond, M. H. (1991). *Beyond the Chinese face*. Hong King: Oxford University Press.

Chao, R. K. (2001). Extending research on the consequences of parenting style for the Chinese Americans and European Americans. *Child Development.* 72(6). 1832-1843.

Csikszentmihalyi, M. & Csikszentmihalyi, I. S. (Eds.) (1988). *Optimal experience: Psychological studies of flow in consciousness.* New Your: Cambridge University Press.

Csikszentmihalyi, M. (1975). *Beyond Boredom and anxiety: The experience of play in work and games.* San Francisco: Jossey-Bass Publishers.

Csikszentmihalyi, M. (1992). *Flow: The psychology of happiness.* London: Rider.

Csikszentmihalyi, M. (1993). The evolving self: A psychology for the third millennium. New York: HarperCollins.

Csikszentmihalyi, M. (2008). *Flow: The psychology of optimal experience.* New York: Harper Perennial.

De Cremer, D., & Oosterwegel, A. (2000). Collective self-esteem, personal self-esteem, and collective efficacy in in-group and out group relations. *Current Psychology. 18*, (4). 326-340.

Deci, E. L. and Ryan, R. M. (1995). Human autonomy: The basis for true self-esteem. In M. H. Kernis (Ed.). *Efficacy, agency and self-esteem.* (pp. 31-50). New York: Plenum Press.

Heine, S. J. (2001) Self as cultural product: An examination of East Asian and North American Selves. *Journal of Personality, 69*, 881-906.

Hofstede, G. (2001). *Cultures and organizations: Software of the mind.* London: McGraw-Hill book.

Jiang, X. & Prosser, L. E. K. (2002). A case study of Chinese contingent self-esteem. In *Self-Concept Research: Driving International Research*

Agendas, *Proceedings of the Second International SELF Research Conference.* Sydney: University of Western Sydney.

Jiang, X., Guan, X. & L. Prosser, (2005). Contingent self-esteem: A cross-cultural comparative study between Chinese and Australian university students, In *Proceedings* of *Asian Association of Social Psychology, 6th Biennial Conference.* Wellington: University of Wellington.

Kao, E. M., & Nagata, D. K. (1997). Explanatory style, family expressiveness, and self-esteem among Asian American and European American college students. *Journal of Social Psychology. 137,* (4). 435-445.

Kim U., Triandis, H. C., Kagitcibasi, C., Choi, S., & Yoon, G. (1994). Introduction. In U. Kim, H. C. Triandis, C. Kagitcibasi, S. Choi, & G. Yoon, *Individualism and collectivism.* Thousand Oaks: Sage.

Pearson, E., & Rao, N. (2003). Socialisation goals, parenting practices, and social competence in Chinese and English preschoolers. *Early Child Development and Care,* 173(1), 131–146.

Rao, N., Ng, S. S. N., & Pearson, E. (2010). Preschool pedagogy: A fusion of traditional Chinese beliefs and contemporary notions of appropriate practice. In C. K. K. Chan, & N. Rao (Eds.), *Revisiting the Chinese learner: Changing contexts, changing education* (pp. 255–280). Hong Kong: The University of Hong Kong, Comparative Education Research Centre=Springer Academic.

Sato, T., & Cameron, J. E. (1999) The relationship between collective self-esteem and self-construal in Japan and Canada. *Journal of Social Psychology. 139,* (4). 426-436.

Shangguan, Z. (1999). *Talking about Chinese: 100 ways of describing Chinese.* Beijing: Chinese Youth Publishing House.

Shernoff, D. J. (2013). Optimal Learning Environments to Promote Student Engagement. New York: Spring Sciences & Business

Sinha, B. K.; Wilson, L. R. & Warson, D. C. (2000). Stress and coping among students in India and Canada. *Journal of Behavioural Sciences.* 32(4), 218-225

Sinha, D. (1999). Cross-cultural psychology: The Asian scenario. In J. Pandey, D. Sinha, & D. P.S. Bhawuk (Eds.), *Asian contributions to cross-cultural psychology.* (pp. 20-41).

Small, T. (2013). Brain Boosting Secrets. Surrey: Terry Small Learning Institute. New Delhi: Sage.

Tafarodi, R. W. & Lang, J. M. (1999). Self-esteem and the culture trade-off. *Journal of Cross-Cultural Psychology, 30,* 620-639.

Tafarodi, R. W.; Swann, Jr. & William, B. (1996). Individualism-collectivism and global self-esteem: Evidence for a culture trade-off. *Journal of Cross-Cultural Psychology, 27,* 651-673.

Taylor, C. (1992). The politics of recognition. In A. Gutmann, (Ed.). *Multiculturalism and "the politics of recognition": An essay by Charles Taylor.* Princeton: Princeton UP. pp. 25-73

Triandis, H. C. (1995). *Individualism & Collectivism.* San Francisco: Westview Press.

Wang, Y. & Ollendick, T. H. (2001). A cross-cultural and developmental analysis of self-esteem in Chinese and Western children. *Clinical Child and Family Psychology Review.* 4(3), 253-273

Woronoff, J. (1997). *The Japanese Social Crisis.* London: Macmillan Press.

Zhou, Q., Eisenberg, N., Wang, Y. & Reiser, M. (2004). Chinese children's effortful control and dispositional anger/frustration: Relations to parenting styles and children's social functioning. *Developmental Psychology.* 40(3), 352-366.

CHAPTER 4

# Mutual Mentoring for Faculty Professional Development: A Radical Model

*Laurie Fox*

This program description presents a unique, radically open and simple mutual mentoring model for post-secondary institutions. The Faculty Peer Support Program invites any and all faculty members to connect for personalized professional development support. Participants self-select partner(s), meeting times, places, and topics. They self-direct activity, sharing equal mentor status and session time. Individual interests and learning styles are respected. Its uncomplicated design encourages involvement and renders it easy to run and replicate at no cost. Fifteen years of data yield consistently high degrees of satisfaction; 99% say they would participate again. The theoretical foundation is reflective practice, supported by mutual mentoring and adult learning theory.

"Teacher Training Effort Called Expensive Waste: Billions Spent, but Classroom Gains are Elusive" (Layton, 2015, p. A9). This is not the headline we want to read. Research is yielding little or no correlation between traditional faculty professional development activities and teaching improvement. How many faculty skip joyfully off to long workshops where presenters point to slides on a common-denominator topic? Not I.

There is tension between what is normally offered for faculty professional development and what is naturally desired. That strain can be a goldmine for creative solutions. Reflective practice is grounded in such energy – the awareness that something is off the mark, unsatisfied, or warrants attention. It serves a problem solving function (Dewey, 1933), to analyze critical incidents and dilemmas (Brookfield, 1995), or to go beyond superficial understanding with undivided attention as Parker Palmer gleaned from the Quakers (1998). We can grumble, bringing iPads, work, and caffeine or we can reflect on what we need and self-direct authentic, experiential, and problem-based learning for ourselves.

Most of us subscribe to the rugged individualism ethic we've been taught and reflect alone, often with our pillows at night. This can help but there are drawbacks. In addition to losing sleep, we are naturally biased in our perceptions and revert to counterfactual thinking where critical analysis drifts toward congruency with one's original beliefs (McGarr & McCormack, 2015). Humans learn with and from each other (Vygotsky, 1995). In helping others, we help ourselves cope (Vaillant, 1977). Additionally, research suggests that reflection with others has greater influence on awareness and on behavior change (Wlodarsky & Walters, 2006). Palmer (1998) reminds us that, "If surgery and the law were practiced as privately as teaching, we would still treat most patients with leeches and dunk defendants in millponds" (p. 144). Reflecting together, however, doesn't have to draw from sabre-tooth-tiger models of what has always been done (Peddiwell, n.d.).

Despite increasingly varied offerings for higher education faculty development, few invite personalized collegial support attuned to unique interests and learning styles of each faculty member. Few are open to all regardless of rank. Few share equal mentoring. Few are private and provide extensive free choice and self-direction. This Faculty Peer Support Program was created to comprehensively address these legitimate needs, augmenting more traditional institutionally structured offerings. Literature reviews yielded no identical, radically simple program to serve as progenitor. It thus serves as an exemplar of creative program development.

Faculty are invited to connect with each other to support self-determined professional development work. Participants self-select partner(s), meeting times, places, and topics (teaching, writing, research, curriculum development, etc.), and self-direct activity, sharing equal mentor status and session time. Some meet as partners; some in groups of varying sizes. Meetings range from three to more than 11 during the academic year. Participation is voluntary and private; a handshake on confidentiality fosters trust.

The program's elegant design renders it inviting, uncomplicated to run and to participate, and easy to replicate at no cost beyond one person's minimal coordination and data analysis time. A fall semester email and introduction page is sent to every faculty member at this traditional New England liberal arts institution serving about 2000 students (see Table 1). Interested participants speak with each other, notify the volunteer coordinator of who is working with whom, and then commit to meet for at least five hours or five times on their own. Basic reflection guidelines are sent (see Table 2) along with an evaluation questionnaire that frontloads suggestions for *Organization, Goals,* and *Relationship Roles* (see Appendix). Those who invest the connection time and complete the questionnaire receive a hardcopy Certificate of Participation sanctioned by the institution as evidence of professional development worthy of inclusion in faculty portfolios. Evaluation data is added to longitudinal program research which currently spans 15 years.

Table 1: Introduction to the Faculty Peer Support Program for Professional Development

**Faculty Peer Support Program**
**For**
**Professional Development**

**This is a voluntary professional development program**
based on the philosophy that we are lifelong learners. We have internal wisdom worth hearing & sharing with colleagues.

**You meet with someone of choice**
to talk about something of personal professional interest. There are no boundaries on what that can mean. Discussions are confidential. You can collaborate, coach, mentor, research, reflect, support, plan, ask – whatever you choose.

**Groups**
are possible, too (professional reading, writing support, etc.). Feel free to start one.

**You meet**
5 hours or 5 times (more if you wish) ....at your convenience.

**It's simple on purpose**
Just email me to say who is meeting with whom.

**I respond**
with a few reflective practice guidelines and an evaluation form.

**A Certificate of Participation**
for your file will be sent (once questionnaire is returned).

**This is a gift**
of time and attention for yourself as an ever-evolving professional.

---

## HISTORICAL CONTEXT

When the program began in 2000, the norm for higher education faculty development was institutional leadership of group activities such as workshops, speakers, and retreats. While serving a valid need, the offerings tended to lack flexibility, choice, and personalization for addressing idiosyncratic interests. While there has been a shift in the last decade toward offering more peer options, they usually have one foot in the new mutual mentoring paradigm and the other grounded in tradition. Most activities still rely on a mentor/mentee model that is defined as experience-superior individuals paired with mentees or protégés of lesser experience. This can be beneficial to both but the hierarchical dynamic is not equal. Most continue to operate from external management that diminishes self-direction, individualization, and free choice. Most focus on new and underrepresented faculty who lack collegial connection when, in fact, all need some form of inspiration and support for a profession replete with rapid changes, dilemmas, and pressures. This Faculty Peer Support Program model is part of that new mutual mentoring movement but, by setting fewer boundaries with less external management, it offers more.

It was begun by this faculty member, frustrated by lack of question time following a presentation. Her need to be more proficient at analyzing students' Wechsler Adult Intelligence Scale results prompted outreach to a colleague with that expertise who, in turn, needed teaching support related to students' reading problems. Each offered the other reflective support for teaching and learning issues of individual concern. Departmental colleagues were asked if mutual peer support might help them, too. Their feedback gave rise to the concept of a minimally structured program with no pressure to participate. With chairperson permission, the Faculty Peer Support Program, including its evaluation questionnaire, was offered as a pilot to all 33 faculty teaching in one department during academic years 2000 to 2006. 97% expressed interest in participating again. The degree of satisfaction was so high that institutional sanctioning by the chief academic officer was sought and received. The program continues to operate with strong indicators of success. The overall peer support experience, as reported by the 343 participations to date, yielded a modal rating of *very satisfied*. 99% say they would participate again.

Table 2: Ten Guidelines for Reflective Faculty Peer Support

1. A handshake on confidentiality and no carry-over to evaluation
2. Regular meeting dates / times
3. Meet at least 5 times or hours
4. Express what you need / want from the other(s); i.e., your goals and how to be helpful to you
5. Clarify how you'd like to share the time
6. Please fill out the program evaluation in spring
7. Listen patiently, ask, encourage
8. Look for patterns in thinking or actions
9. Listen for underlying assumptions
10. Let the coordinator know if you need help in any form

> *If we want to grow in our practice, we have two primary places to go:*
> *the inner ground from which good teaching comes and*
> *to the community of fellow teachers*
> *from whom we can learn more about our craft....*
> *in that space we receive ourselves as well as the other.*
> *As we reach for the questions that will help the focus person*
> *go deeper into his or her truth,*
> *we find ourselves drawn*
> *more deeply*
> *into*
> *our*
> *own*
> *truth.* (Palmer, 1998, pp. 141, 154).
>
> Palmer, P.J. (1998). *The courage to teach.* San Francisco: Jossey-Bass

## THEORETICAL CONTEXT

### Reflective Practice and Faculty Adult Learners

Americans, in general, and faculty, in particular, spend more time doing than reflecting (York-Barr, Sommers, Ghere & Montie, 2001). Dewey (1933) speaks of the resulting loss of open-mindedness and, in its place, becoming indifferent or dogmatic, both deleterious to teaching. He grounds reflective practice in problem solving. Struggles as academics, especially with today's pressures to meet diverse student needs and to adapt to profound and rapid industry-specific changes, are perfect fodder for reflective peer support. Educators need synthesis time to fill gaps in knowledge and to learn from their 'puzzlement' (Daly, Pachler & Lambert, 2004; Dewey, 1933; Reagan, Charles & Brubacher, 2000).

Faculty, like all students, learn at different rates via different styles, are ready at different times, have different interests and talents, and can thrive in caring, collaborative relationships. A program that fosters personalized initiative aligns faculty development with the research domain of adult learning and self-direction (Brookfield, 1985; TEAL, 2011) now appearing in mentoring literature (Pololi & Knight, 2005).

> However, with the increasing inclusion of diverse participants in the conversation about adult education, it has become clear that there is no such thing as one kind of learner, one learning goal, one way to learn, nor one setting in which learning takes place. Many theorists have convincingly demonstrated that commonly held assumptions about generic learners and learning are irrelevant and even willfully oppressive

when recklessly applied to all kinds of people without regard for their unique life experiences and attributes... (Kilgore, 2001, p. 53)

Austin and Sorcellini's work in 2013 (as cited in Mitchell, 2015) notes that faculty development can address issues of institutional change and quality. Educators, however, especially in group workshops, tend to focus on teaching strategies. Deeper reflection, the path to master teacher, goes beyond and requires both time and commitment to hear our stories, learning about the self and deep-seated beliefs as well as the information (Miflin, 2004; Palmer, 1998, Schon, 1987; Shadiow, 2012). Self-reflection can have the greatest impact on professional development (Lopez-Real & Kwan, 2005). Research suggests that reflection can indeed contribute to teaching effectiveness (Behling, Weir, & Jorgensen, 2006; LaPrade, Gilpatrick, & Perkins, 2014; Wlodarsky & Walters, 2006).

Seminal studies in adult development have addressed the need for supportive work relationships (Gilligan, 1982; Levinson, 1978), a variety of which has long been recommended for academia (Hill, Bahniuk, & Dobos, 1989). Isaacs (1999) reminded us, however, that people tend to resist ideas that seem imposed. Freedom of choice and self-empowerment are more likely to inspire participation and follow-through (Reagan, et al., 2000). Chandler & Eby (2010) note that "...people who volunteer for mentoring are more likely to fulfill one another's expectations..." (p. 5, as cited in Jones & Corner, 2012) motivated, in part, by internal rather than external factors – a foundation of adult learning. The more personalized the experience, the greater the likelihood of engagement, internalization, and, ultimately, actualization of potential (Gibbs, Angelides & Michaelides, 2004). "Critical and postmodern theorists alike believe that knowledge is socially constructed and takes form in the eyes of the knower, rather than being acquired from an existing reality that resides 'out there'" (Kilgore, 2001, p. 53).

## REFLECTIVE PRACTICE AND MUTUAL MENTORING

Research suggested more than 20 years ago that untenured faculty in higher education and those inhibited by authority figures are more inclined to seek peer support for improvement (Harnish &Wild, 1993). Mutual mentoring has roots in these natural inclinations and is evolving to include more institutional options. Sorcinelli and Yun (2007b), for example, encouraged networks of reciprocal partnerships based on reports that multiple mentors can be more beneficial than one (deJanasz & Sullivan, 2004; Girves, Lepeda & Gwathmey, 2005; VanEmmerick, 2004; Wasburn, 2007).

Although mentoring literature uses the phrase *mutual mentoring* and, recently, *horizontal mentorship*, the reference is often to networks where connections may or may not be mutual or reciprocal (Bessett, 2015; Emerson, 2015; DeCastro, Sambuco, Ubel, Stewart, & Jagsi, 2013) or to structured groups with a trained master teacher/coach whose role is primarily to organize and facilitate (Behling, Weir, & Jorgensen, 2006). *Reciprocal mentoring, lateral mentoring*, or *informal mentoring* are more likely to connote mutuality, egalitarianism, choice, and friendship (Bessett, 2015; Inzer & Crawford, 2005). At least 50 definitions of mentoring appear in the literature, reflecting varying disciplines and contextual meaning (Jones & Corner, 2012). Assumptions, therefore, must be made with care.

Differences in ascribed power and participants' hierarchical position remain common - differences that can negatively impact relationship authenticity, mutuality, and connection (Morrison, 2011). Benefits to the mentor, such as professional rejuvenation, are valuable, but are often generated secondarily (Lopez-Real & Kwan, 2005). Unequal role stereotypes continue to be perpetuated by the terms *mentor* and either *mentee* or *protégé* – the longstanding currency of the field.

Additionally, while new models are opening to mid-career and senior faculty, most are still geared toward new, tenure-track, junior faculty or those considered vulnerable due to underrepresented status, usually according to race or gender (Angelique, Kyle & Taylor, 2002; Driscoll, Parkes, Tilley-Lubbs, Brill & Bannister, 2009; Girves, et al., 2005; Sorcinelli & Yun, 2007a). A recent study of women faculty in engineering found that traditional mentoring did not align with their own stories (Buzzanel, Long, Anderson, Kokini, & Batra, 2015). Expansion of mentoring opportunities is recommended for women in male-prevalent departments to counterbalance social exclusion. "The interactional dimension is central to making academic departments more inviting to diverse faculty, and hence a fundamental step in transforming the image of the disembodied ideal scholar" (Morimoto & Azjicek, 2014, p. 144). New Latino faculty were more intrinsically motivated when feeling connected to others (Lechuga, 2012). Notably, few programs are open to all.

Historic work by Kram and Isabella (1985) found that adult peer relationships serve critical functions of mutual exchange, hierarchical equality, and empathic support. Peer mentoring communities are emerging from faculty awareness of their specific needs and beliefs that they can achieve more in partnerships (Bottoms, Pegg, Adams, Vu, Risser, & Kern, 2013; Butcher, Bezzina, & Moran, 2011; Gillespie & Robertson, 2010) especially when there is an existing collaborative colleague relationship (Tahtinen, Mainela, Natti, & Saraniemi, 2012). The concept of mentoring is shifting toward that of a journey with equal relationships built on trust (Awaya, McEwan, Heyler, Linsky, Lum, & Wakukawa, 2003; Wlodarsky & Walters, 2006), toward intentional yet informal discourse (Harvard, 2014), and within relevant contexts that appreciate social factors (Hansman, 2006; Nolan, Morrissey, & Dumenden, 2013).

Dialogue can loosen rigidity and is more likely in committed relationships that feel safe. Schon (1987) refers to the reciprocally reflective dialogue that informs artistry of all forms. Parker Palmer (1998) is famous for saying that we don't ask to be fixed but rather simply to be heard. Reflecting, dialogue, and active listening are recommended by the National Education Association and POD, the Professional and Organizational Development Network in Higher Education (Bell & Thomas, 2007; Lee, 2009).

> Through reflection and communication focused on common professional concerns, each others' ideas become less strange, and the search for new and better ways of achieving professional goals becomes a common and collaborative process rather than an isolated and individual effort....In short, reflective practice recognized the importance of dialogues for learning, stresses the importance of collaborative effort    toward common goals and calls for teachers to be active learners...(A. Cimer, S. Cimer, & Vekli, 2013, p. 142).

## EVALUATION OF THE FACULTY PEER SUPPORT PROGRAM MODEL

Fifteen years of data have been generated from 343 participations drawn from each of the 14 ongoing departments since the program began in 2000. Participations during the six pilot years averaged 11 per year within one department of 33; since going campus wide, where full-time faculty average 119 and part-time 318, participations averaged 23 per year, ranging from 17 to 49. Self-reported results indicate effectiveness of the model in meeting individuals' goals - the primary purpose of the program. In the process, the program has built active reflective learning communities among peers across ranks and departments.

The program questionnaire (see Appendix) collected both quantitative and qualitative data. Seven quantitative items assessed *degree of satisfaction* via a five-point scale ranging from (1) *not satisfied* to (5) *very satisfied*. Seven items, spread among the sections, provided information on *meeting days, times,* duration, and *frequency,* and on participants' *goals, relationship roles,* and interest in *participating again.* Qualitative feedback came from eight optional open-ended questions (*Please briefly explain any of the above*) and an *Overall* section asking for *General Strengths/Benefits of the Program, General Weaknesses/Drawbacks of the Program, Suggestions,* and *What Was Accomplished/Worked On.* Questionnaires were submitted anonymously by hardcopy or as an email attachment per participants' preference.

## OUTCOMES

**Overall.** Based on a 59% return rate, the composite *Degree of Satisfaction with the Overall Peer Support Experience* evidenced a consistent yearly mode of 5 (*very satisfied*) with a mean of 4.6("mostly satisfied"). Every other *degree of satisfaction* item (*Introductory Information, Scheduling of Sessions, Goals Met, Roles You Assumed, Roles Your Partner/Others Assumed*) yielded the same composite mode. 99% of the participants responded "*Yes*" to the question, *Would You Consider Participating Again*? Table 3 provides other summary data for questionnaire sections *Organization, Goals, Relationship Roles,* and *Demographics.*

Table 3: Modal Responses for Items on the Faculty Peer Support Program Questionnaire
2000 – 2015

Survey items

| | |
|---|---|
| 4. Times met | 3 – 5; 6 - 8 |
| 5. Duration | 46 – 60 minutes |
| 6. Time of Day | 12 – 2 pm |
| 7. Day of Week | Wednesday |
| 9. Goals | Teaching, Project Support, Friendship |
| 10. Relationship Roles Assumed | Collaborator, Listener, Speaker, Mentor |

Demographics

| | |
|---|---|
| 22. Sex | Female |
| 23. Age | 50s |
| 24. Racial/Ethnic Group | Caucasian/White/European |
| 25. Years at this College | 1 – 5 |
| 26. Rank | Associate Professor |

Note. based on average of 59% returned questionnaires from 343 participations representing 14 out of 14 departments; open to one department averaging 16 full-time, 17 part-time, 33 total for six pilot years (2000 – 2006) (67 participations) and open to all college faculty averaging 119 full-time, 318 part-time, 437 total for nine years (2006 – 2015) (343 participations).

---

**Organization.** Most met three to eight times for an hour each time between noon and 2 p.m. on Wednesdays, the institution's faculty meeting day when most are on campus. Meeting nine or more times was the mode for 2012 – 2015, likely due to weekly scheduled meetings. The *degree of satisfaction* of session scheduling was the only questionnaire item with a mean rating below 4.5 at 4.2 (the low range of *mostly satisfied*). While the mode was 5 (*very satisfied*), many struggled to find meeting time. The most frequent qualitative theme for *Organization* was how participants scheduled their meeting times. Most established a routine and structure. Curiously, some connected on weekends and over winter and summer break; some communicated part of the time by email or by phone. Time and scheduling challenges constituted the second most common theme. The third most common was that days varied and/or the meetings were informal.

**Goals.** Most discussion goals (question nine) were in the categories of *Teaching, Project Support,* and *Friendship*. Narrative data themes focused, in order, on *Support & Feedback, Reflection,* and *Course-Specific Projects*. Projects commonly involved writing - professional and creative - and course development.

The *degree of satisfaction* with meeting individualized goals had a composite mean of 4.5 (*mostly satisfied*) and a mode of 5 (*very satisfied*). One group had multiple problems with organization which impacted satisfaction with goals. Comments suggested that reflection on those problems yielded ideas for improvement which were realized in subsequent years.

**Relationship Roles.** *Collaborator* was the most common *Relationship Role* followed by *Listener, Speaker,* and *Mentor* as checked in question 12. By far the most common narrative spoke of roles varying, changing, and taking turns. The terms *collaborator, mentor,* and *mentee* appeared often. Group support was a secondary theme followed by one combining the concepts of shared and equal. The average was *mostly satisfied* (4.5) for *satisfaction* with the *Roles They Assumed* and that their *Partner/Others Assumed* (4.6); the modal response was *very satisfied* (5) with both.

**Demographics.** The majority of respondents were senior full-time faculty (Assistant, Associate, and Full Professor) (57% of respondents) women (82%) at the institution for five or fewer years (36%) who were Caucasian/White/European (64%) and in their 50s (33%). Faculty there six to 15 years represented an additional 32% of participations. Most were full-time professors at the Associate Professor rank (31%). About equal numbers of Assistant and Full Professors represented a total of 26%. Part time faculty constituted 24%. A noteworthy number were in their 40s (25%). Interestingly, some respondents chose to skip all or certain demographic answers. Most (87% to 90%) responded to rank, years at the college, and sex. Fewer responded to age (78%) and least responded to racial/ethnic group (68%) where they could describe it in their own words. All of the 14 ongoing departments since 2000 were represented.

Table 4: Most Frequent Qualitative Themes from the Faculty Peer Support Program Questionnaire 2000–2015 by Section

Organization
    How scheduled meeting times
    Time & scheduling challenges
    Days varied/meetings informal
Goals
    Support & feedback
    Reflection
    Course-specific projects
Relationship Roles
    Varied
    Group support
    Shared & equal

Strengths/Benefits of the Program
    Reflection
    Support & Collaboration
    Opportunity
Weaknesses/Drawbacks of the Program
    Time and scheduling
    None
What Did You Accomplish/Work On?
    Teaching-related work
    Writing (Scholarly & Creative)
    Connection with others

*Note.* based on average of 59% returned questionnaires from 343 participations representing 14 out of 14 departments; open to one department averaging 16 full-time, 17 part-time, 33 total for six pilot years (2000 – 2006) (67 participations) and open to all college faculty averaging 119 full-time, 318 part-time, 437 total for nine years (2006 – 2015) (343 participations).

---

**Composite qualitative themes.** Table 4 summarizes most frequent qualitative themes by questionnaire section, also noted in the outcomes section above for *Organization, Goals,* and *Relationship Roles.* Among those three areas, the most common narratives, in order, spoke of:

- Idiosynchratic scheduling and structuring (including challenges)
    - "Setting a schedule for the semester worked well"; "Our offices were side by side so access was a great help"; "Scheduling was a challenge."

- Varying roles
    - "We took turns"; "Each had a chance to assume a different role"; "Our roles fluctuated but there was always equality and mutual respect."
- Goals of support and reflection
    - "Talking with writers about writing inspired me every time"; "Feedback & support"; "Sharing insight with a caring, non-judgmental listener."

**General Strengths/Benefits of the Program most often cited related to Reflective Practice:**

"This program provides me a safe place to hash out areas of wonder and concern"; "Participation in this constructivist mutual mentoring process required an internal drive for self-reflection – invaluable"; "Shared reflection."

**The second most common narrative theme for *Strengths/Benefits* was *Support*, especially via Collaboration:**

"Such a supportive and engaging experience"; "Benefit is collaboration and sharing ideas – will continue"; "Felt supported. Very helpful feedback."

**The third narrative theme in *Strengths/Benefits* was *Opportunity*:**

"Good opportunity to interact with others"; "A wonderful opportunity to find the support that sustains us and to grow as a professional"; "Valuable opportunity."

## GENERAL WEAKNESSES OR DRAWBACKS COMMENTS FOCUSED OVERWHELMINGLY ON TIME AND SCHEDULING

**Challenges:**

"Busy schedules"; "Time constraints"; "Time to meet, especially with part-time people."

The second most common *Weakness/Drawback* narrative theme was *None*. Most *Suggestions for Improvement*, related to the *Weakness/Drawbacks* question, said *None* or related to *Scheduling* themselves more effectively, followed by some who wanted partnering instead of groups and some who wished for more groups and longer time for groups. Multiple comments expressed desire for lighter teaching loads to increase participation, "So there's time to take advantage of this program."

In response to the question *"What did you accomplish/work on during your peer support time?"* participants mentioned, in order of frequency:

- Teaching-related work (48% of comments)
- Writing (Scholarly and Creative) (34%)
- Connection with others, including relationships, friendships, and mentoring (14%)

*Overall Experience* comments supported the quantitative data and the themes. There were frequent references to continuing, to having participated for a long time, or to it being fun and enjoyable, appreciating the confidentiality and commitment and the value placed on stimulating, supportive, professional exchange. *"Frankly, these meetings are the one sure place where I feel heard. I plan to continue."*

## Discussion and Implications

The Faculty Peer Support Program has generated a 15-year, high degree of satisfaction with 99% expressing interest in participating again. It serves as an effective faculty development model for those who are self-directed, can self-select partners, and have goals for professional development that can be articulated and translated into action. This research suggests that those post-secondary faculty are mostly senior ranking Caucasian women in their 50s at the institution for five or fewer years, followed closely by faculty there six to 15 years. Responses also reflect satisfaction with – and desire for - meaningful human connection and support as faculty work productively together.

Those who might desire more external structure, who lack available peers or assertiveness to self-select partners, or whose goals or action plans are less clear, may thrive, at least at first, in a more traditional model where those are provided. Some faculty may need assistance setting up connections with peers. Others, perhaps males whose participation was minimal, may not be comfortable participating in an equalized, nurturing activity that is different from the historic individualism of higher education and American life. Results help to strengthen the notion that women may experience mentoring differently than men, seeking egalitarianism, inclusivity, and friendship in the process.

Arranging mutually convenient meeting time will likely be a challenge for any faculty professional development program. It may, however, be less so for this model given the high degree of commitment to one or a few self-selected partners. With participants accountable for achieving their own goals there may be deeper, more personalized motivation.

It is to the industry's benefit to promote programs that acknowledge individual differences and preferences and that provide authentic, experiential, and problem-based learning, for therein lay the creative energies of faculty that inspire personally meaningful work. A program like this, neither top-down nor bottom-up, taps the theoretical foundations of reflective practice, adult learning, and mutual mentoring and deserves its rightful place on the faculty development menu of options. It may appear to be a grassroots concept for now, but its research-based merits nourish the academy and its evolution into a creative 21$^{st}$ century paradigm shift.

Its elegant design renders the Faculty Peer Support Program innovative and easily transferable to other educational settings. Results provide compelling evidence to replicate similar reflection-based programs where minimal institutional management can be highly effective for self-motivated practitioners and scholars in a learning/work community. Indeed, less can be more.

## REFERENCES

Angelique, H., Kyle, K., & Taylor, E. (2002). Mentors and muses: New strategies for academic success. *Innovative Higher Education, 26*(3), 195-209.

Awaya, A., McEwan, H., Heyler, D., Linsky, S., Lum, D., & Wakukawa, P. (2003). Mentoring as a journey. *Teaching and Teacher Education, 19*(1), 45-56.

Behling, K., Weir, C., & Jorgensen, C. (2006). Equity and excellence in higher education- reflective practice implementation guide: A tool for college faculty. Durham, NH: Institute on Disabilities.

Bell, D. & Thomas, E. (2007). A mentoring process to support teachers' growth and retention. *Academic Leadership, 5*(4), 1.

Harvard Graduate School of Education (2014). *Benchmark Best Practices: Mentoring*. Retrieved from http://sites.gse.harvard.edu/sites/default/files/coache/files/coache_bench markbestpractice s_mentoring_0.pdf

Bessette, L.S. (2015). Reciprocal mentoring: Rethinking the traditional model. *Women in Higher Education, 24*(1), 18-19.

Bottoms, S., Pegg, J., Adams, A., Wu, K., Risser, H.S., & Kern, A.L. (2013). Mentoring from the outside: The role of a peer mentoring community in the development of early career education faculty. *Mentoring & Tutoring: Partnership in Learning, 21*(2), 195-218.

Brookfield, S. D. (Ed.) (1985). *Self-directed learning: From theory to practice.* San Francisco, CA: Jossey-Bass.

Butcher, J., Bezzina, M., & Moran, W. (2011). Transformational partnerships: A new agenda for higher education. *Innovative Higher Education, 36*(1), 29-40.

Buzzanell, P.M., Long, Z., Anderson, L.B., Kokini, K., & Batra, J.C. (2015). Mentoring in academe: A feminist poststructural lens on stories of women engineering faculty of color. *Management Communication Quarterly, 29*(3), 440-457.

Cimer, A., Cimer, S.O., Vekli, G.S. (2013). How does reflection help teachers to become effective teachers? *International Journal of Educational Research, 1*(4), 133-149.

Daly, C., Pachler, N., & Lambert, D. (2004). Teacher learning: towards a professional academy. *Teaching in Higher Education, 9*(1), 99-111.

DeCastro, R., Sambuco, S., Ubel, P., Stewart, A., & Jagsi, R. (2013). Mentor networks in academic medicine: Moving beyond a dyadic conception of mentoring for junior faculty researchers. *Academic Medicine, 88*(4), 488-496.

deJanasz, S.C., & Sullivan, S.E. (2004). Multiple mentoring in academe: Developing the professional network. *Journal of Vocational Behavior, 64*(2), 263-283.

Dewey, J. (1933). *How we think.* Boston, MA: D.C. Heath.

Driscoll, L.G., Parkes, K.A., Tilley-Lubbs, G.A., Brill, J.G., & Pitts Bannister, V.R. (2009). Navigating the lonely sea: Peer mentoring and collaboration among aspiring women scholars. *Mentoring & Tutoring: Partnership in Learning, 17*(1), 5-21.

Emerson College. (n.d.). *Faculty mentoring at Emerson College.* Retrieved from http://www.emerson.edu/academics/academic-services/academic-affairs/faculty- mentoring

Gibbs, P., Angelides, P., & Michaelides, P. (2004). Preliminary thoughts on a praxis of higher education teaching. *Teaching in Higher Education, 9*(2), 183-194.

Gillespie, K.J., & Robertson, D.L. (Eds.) (2010). *A guide to faculty development (2nd ed.).* San Francisco, CA: Jossey-Bass.

Gilligan, C. (1982). *In a different voice.* Cambridge, MA: Harvard University Press.

Girves, J.S., Zepeda, Y., & Gwathmey, J.K. (2005). Mentoring in a post-affirmative action world. *Journal of Social Issues, 61*(3), 449-479.

Hansman, C.A. (2001). Context-based adult learning. In S.B. Merriam (Ed.), *New directions for adult and continuing education* (pp. 43-51). San Francisco, CA: Jossey-Bass.

Harnish, D., & Wild, L.A. (1993, August/September). Faculty peer mentoring: A strategy for improving instruction. *AACC Journal,* 22-27.

Hill, S. E. K., Bahniuk, M. H., & Dobos, J. (1989, January). The impact of mentoring and collegial support on faculty success: An analysis of support behavior, information adequacy, and communication apprehension. *Communication Education, 38,* 15-31.

Inzer, L.D., & Crawford, C.B. (2005). A review of formal and informal mentoring: Processes, problems, and design. *Journal of Leadership Education, 4*(1), 31-50.

Isaacs, W. (1999). *Dialogue and the art of thinking together.* New York, NY: Currency.

Jones, R. & Corner, J. (2012). Seeing the forest and the trees: A complex adaptive systems lens for mentoring. *Human Relations, 65*(3), 391-411.

Kilgore, D.W. (2001). Critical and postmodern perspectives on adult learning. In S.B. Merriam (Ed.), *New directions for adult and continuing education* (pp. 53-61). San Francisco, CA: Jossey-Bass.

Kram, K.E., & Isabella, L.A. (1985). Mentoring alternatives: The role of peer relationships in career development. *Academy of Management Journal, 24*(1), 110-132.

LaPrade, K., Gilpatrick, M., & Perkins, D. (2014). Impact of reflective practice on online teaching performance in higher education. *Merlot Journal of Online Learning and Teaching, 10*(4), 625-638.

Layton, L. (August 5, 2015). Teacher training effort called expensive waste. Boston Globe, p. A9.

Lechuga, V.M. (2012). Latino faculty in STEM disciplines: Motivation to engage in research activities. *Journal of Latinos and Education, 11*(2), 107-123.

Lee, V. (2009, Winter). President's message. *POD Network News*, 1-2.

Levinson, D.J. (1978). *The seasons of a man's life.* New York, NY: Ballantine.

Lopez-Real, F., & Kwan, T. (2005). Mentors' perceptions of their own professional development during mentoring. *Journal of Education for Teaching, 31*(1), 15-24.

McGarr, O., & McCormack, O. (2015). Counterfactual mutation of critical classroom incidents: Implications for reflective practice in initial teacher education. *European Journal of Teacher Education.* Retrieved from http://www.tandfonline.com/doi/abs/10.1080/02619768.2015.1066329

Mifflin, B. (2004). Adult learning, self-directed learning and problem-based learning: Deconstructing the connections. *Teaching in Higher Education, 9*(1), 43-53.

Mitchell, N. N. (2015). *Faculty perceptions of the Teaching and Learning Center on faculty development: A descriptive study* (Doctoral dissertation). Retrieved from http://nsuworks.nova.edu/fse_etd/12.

Morimoto, S.A., & Zajicek, A. (2014). Dismantling the 'Master's House': Feminist reflections on institutional transformation. *Critical Sociology, 40*(1), 135-150.

Morrison, K.E. (2011, May). *Growth fostering relationships: The relational-cultural theory in the mentor/mentee relationship.* A presentation at the New England Faculty Development Consortium Conference, Worcester, MA.

Nolan, A., Morrissey, A., & Dumenden, I. (2013). Expectations of mentoring in a time of change: Views of new and professionally isolated early childhood teachers in Victoria, Australia. *Early Years: An International Research Journal, 33*(2), 161-171

Palmer, P.J. (1998). *The courage to teach.* San Francisco, CA: Jossey-Bass.

Peddiwell, J.A. (n.d.). The saber-tooth curriculum. Retrieved from http://www.nassauboces.org/cms/lib5/ny18000988/centricity/domain/57/thesabertoothcur riculumshort.pdf

Pololi, L., & Knight, S. (2005). Mentoring faculty in academic medicine: A new paradigm? *Journal of General Internal Medicine, 20*, 866-870.

Reagan, T.G., Charles, W.C., & Brubacher, J.W. (2000). *Becoming a reflective educator: How to build a culture of inquiry in the schools* (2nd ed.). Thousand Oaks, CA: Corwin Press.

Schon, D. A. (1987). *Educating the reflective practitioner*. San Francisco, CA: Jossey-Bass.

Sorcinelli, M.D., & Yun, J. (2007a). Building a network of mentors: A guide for engineering educators. Retrieved from http://www.works.bepress.com/marydean_sorcinelli/28

Sorcinelli, M.D., & Yun, J. (2007b). From mentor to mentoring networks: Mentoring in the new academy. *Change, 39*(6), 58-61.

Tahtinen, J., Mainela, T., Natti, S., & Saraniemi, S. (2012). Intradepartmental faculty mentoring in teaching marketing. *Journal of Marketing Education, 34*(1), 5-18.

TEAL teaching excellence in adult literacy (2011). *TEAL Center fact sheet no. 11: Adult learning theories*. Retrieved from https://teal.ed.gov/tealguide/adultlearning

van Emmerick, I.J.H. (2004). The more you can get the better: Mentoring constellations and intrinsic career success. *Career Development International, 9*(6/7), 578.

Wasburn, M.H. (2007). Mentoring women faculty: An instrumental case study of strategic collaboration. *Mentoring & Tutoring: Partnership in Learning, 15*(1), 57-72.

Shadiow, L.K. (2012). *What our stories teach us: A guide to critical reflection for college faculty*. San Francisco: Jossey-Bass.

Vaillant, G.E. (1977). *Adaptation to life: How the best and the brightest came of age*. Boston, MA: Little, Brown and Company.

Vygotsky, L. (1995). The social construction of knowledge. In K.C. Barrett, K.D. Kallio, R.M. McBride, C.M. Moore, & M.A. Wilson, *Child development* (p. 295). New York, NY: Glencoe.

Wlodarsky, R.L. & Walters, H.D. (2006). The reflective practitioner in higher education: The nature and characteristics of reflective practice among teacher education faculty. *National Forum of Teacher Education Journal, 16*(3), 1-16.

York-Barr, J., Sommers, W.A., Ghere, G.S., & Montie, J. (2001). *Reflective practice to improve schools: An action guide to educators*. Thousand Oaks, CA: Corwin Press.

*Note. From "A Personalized Faculty Peer Support Program: Less Can Be More," by L. Fox, May 2012. The Journal of Faculty Development, 26(2), pp. 55-61. Copyright 2012 by New Forums Press, Inc. Adapted with permission.*

APPENDIX

Faculty Peer Support Program Questionnaire

## Organization
<u>To what degree of satisfaction</u> were the following:
1. the introductory information
       1    2    3    4    5
       not    slightly  moderately  mostly    very
       satisfied satisfied satisfied satisfied satisfied
2. the process of matching partners in order of receipt-not applicable
3. your scheduling of sessions
       1    2    3    4    5
       not    slightly  moderately  mostly    very
       satisfied satisfied satisfied satisfied satisfied
4. How many times did you meet (as best you can recall) ?
   ___ 0-2 ___ 3-5 ___ 6-8 ___ 9-11 ___ more than 11
5. What was the duration of most sessions?
   ___ 5-15 min. ___ 16-30 min. ___ 31-45 min. ___ 46-60 min. ___ more than 60 min.
6. What time of day did you usually meet?
   ___ 8-10 am ___ 10-12 am ___ 12-2 pm ___ 2-4 pm ___ 4-6 pm ___ after 6 pm
7. What day of the week did you usually meet?
   ___ Monday ___ Tuesday ___ Wednesday ___ Thursday ___ Friday ___ other
8. Please briefly explain any of the above (optional):

### Goals
9. Your discussion goals were in which category(ies0:
   ___ teaching ___ research ___ diagnosis ___ professional reading ___ project support ___ friendship ___ personal metacognition ___ gain specific information
   ___ gain general information ___ reflection at the moment ___ other
10. To what degree of satisfaction were your goals met?
        1    2    3    4    5
        not    slightly  moderately  mostly    very
        satisfied satisfied satisfied satisfied satisfied
11. Please briefly explain any of the above (optional):

### Relationship Roles
12. The relationship roles assumed by you and your partner(s) were in which category(ies)?
    ___ listener ___ speaker ___ mentor / teacher ___ mentored / protégé ___ coach ___ collaborator ___ other (please name it if you can):

13. To what degree of satisfaction were the roles <u>you</u> assumed?
    1         2          3            4           5
    not     slightly  moderately   mostly      very
    satisfied satisfied satisfied satisfied satisfied
14. To what degree of satisfaction were the roles <u>your partner / others</u> assumed?
    1         2          3            4           5
    not     slightly  moderately   mostly      very
    satisfied satisfied satisfied satisfied satisfied
15. Please briefly explain any of the above (optional):

**Overall**

16. To what degree of satisfaction was your overall peer support experience?
    1         2          3            4           5
    not     slightly  moderately   mostly      very
    satisfied satisfied satisfied satisfied satisfied
17. Would you consider participating again sometime? ___yes ___no
18. Please briefly explain the above (optional):
19. General strengths / benefits of the program (not previously mentioned) (optional):
20. General weaknesses / drawbacks of the program (not previously mentioned) (optional):
21. Suggestions (not previously mentioned) (optional):

**Demographic Data**
22. Sex ___Female ___Male
23. Age ___20s ___30s ___40s ___50s ___60s ___70s
24. Racial/Ethnic Group (please use your own words): _____
25. Years at this college ___1 ___2 ___3 ___4 ___5 ___6-10 ___11-15 ___16-20 ___more than 20
26. Rank (please write in): _____
Also:
27. What did you accomplish / work on during your peer support time?

Copyright 2000

CHAPTER 5

# Does 'One Child Policy' Produce Little 'Emperors and Princesses'?: Fostering Critical Thinking and Reflective Learning in a Chinese Language Course

*Yanyin Zhang*

Is it possible to foster critical thinking and reflective learning in a foreign language course? If yes, how is it done so that learners will develop an intellectual capacity to truly comprehend and understand the target country, its language, its people, its culture, and its past, present and future? In their paper on the goal of foreign language teaching at the tertiary level, Kinoshita and Zhang (2014) call for a reconceptualization of foreign language teaching. Not downgrading the role of linguistic and functional aspects of language learning, they advocate an approach that views foreign language teaching as 'a form of liberal arts' education that 'contributes to the intellectual development beyond language facility' (p.90). Although this aspect of foreign language teaching is neither denied nor discounted by any of the current teaching approaches, it does not seem to occupy the mainstream second language pedagogy, research interests and teacher training courses. In this chapter, I will offer a critical reflection of a pedagogical practice that gives explicit expression and equal weight to language 'teaching' (functional skill training) and 'education' (intellectual development). I will focus on the latter, discussing the rationale, the procedure and the learning outcome of a suite of activities that push students beyond the classroom walls and engage them through zero-distance contact and interaction with ideas and objects of their learning: the Chinese language and its speakers.

## INTRODUCTION

In her book on language teaching theory and practice and, Ur (2006) makes a distinction between 'training' and 'education' in regard to professional preparations for language teachers. According to Ur, 'training' emphasizes skills and techniques in a profession, while 'education' is a process that 'develops moral, cultural, social and intellectual aspects of the whole person as an individual and member of society' (p.3). A quick perusal of a few pre- and in-service language teacher training textbooks (e.g., Harmer 2007, Ur 2006) and second language research and pedagogy journals (e.g., *Foreign Language Annals, ELT Journal, Language, Culture and Curriculum, Language and Curriculum, Applied Linguistics, Language Education*) shows 'training' to be the predominant approach in the current language teaching field.

In their call for a reconceptualization of foreign language teaching at the tertiary level, Kinoshita and Zhang (2014) advocate an 'education' position. They state that language teaching should be viewed as a form of 'liberal arts education' that 'contributes to the intellectual development beyond language facility' (p.90). This echoes the call to 'develop a cultured person' in language studies by Rivers as early as 1968, who regarded a successful language learner to be a person who not only has second language linguistic skills, but who also has intellectual faculties, comprehension and the imagination, and is capable of examining his/her long-held and culturally-determined attitudes, reactions and unspoken assumptions. This 'critical thinking' aspect of language studies, although never downgraded or discounted, does not seem to occupy a central position in the mainstream second language teaching, research interests and professional development.

Is it possible to foster 'critical thinking' and along with it, reflective learning in a foreign language classroom? And how is it done so that such endeavors give language learners substantive opportunities to develop their intellectual capacity that would ultimately assist their understanding of the target country, its language, its people, its culture, and its past, present and future?

In this chapter, I will discuss a pedagogical practice in a high-intermediate L2 Chinese language course that gives explicit expression and equal weight to 'training' (functional skills) and 'education' (intellectual development). I will focus on the 'education' aspect, discussing the conceptualization, the design, and the implementation of a syllabus that aims to nurture the intellectual capacity of language learners through reflective learning in order to achieve a balanced, nuanced and emic understanding of one unique aspect of the target language country – the 'One Child Policy' of China.

## FOREIGN LANGUAGE EDUCATION: GOALS AND VALUES

What is the goal and value of foreign language teaching and learning? The answer to this question changes over time along with the changing world. At the beginning of the 20$^{th}$ century, Jesperson (1904), in his book 'How to Teach a

Foreign Language,' stated, '[T]he highest purpose in the teaching of languages may be said to be the access to the best thoughts and institutions of a foreign nation, its literature, culture – in short, the spirit of the nation in the widest sense of the word.' (cited in Rivers, 1968, p.261). Similarly, in 1933, the Secondary Education Board of Milton Massachusetts claimed that the main value of foreign language study was 'the breaking down of the barriers of provincialism and the building up of the spirit of international understanding and friendship, leading toward world peace' (cited in Rivers, 1968, p.261). These goals, noble as they were, can hardly be said to match the dominant teaching methods of those days: grammar translation, rote learning, and laborious memorization of texts.

With the rapid advancement of science and technology after WWII, the world has become increasingly mobile. The concept of 'globalization' and 'global village' permeates every corner of life. Direct intercultural communication and experience of a foreign culture becomes a reality enjoyed by millions of people. As a result, foreign languages take on a more instrumental role. 'Knowing what' about a language (the linguistic elements) is increasingly giving way in favor of 'knowing how' to use the target language in actual communication. The ability to do things in a foreign language becomes the ultimate goal in many language teaching methodologies (e.g., Communicative Language Teaching, Task-Based Language Teaching), whose relevance and efficacy are measured through their 'communicative' values. Learning outcomes are frequently expressed through 'can-do' descriptors in tests and policies (e.g., IELTS, Common European Framework of Reference for Languages). Foreign language studies appear increasingly similar to vocational training characterized by a strong utilitarian purpose and orientation.

There are, however, voices that call for re-setting the priority of language teaching from that of linguistic and communicative focus to one that emphasizes intercultural experience and understanding. According to Liddicoat and Scarino (2013), for example, the goal of language education is to develop 'an intercultural perspective by learners as their own experience of linguistic and cultural diversity' (p.7). They state that 'interactions and experiences' should be the center piece of language teaching and learning process. Kinoshita and Zhang (2014) go a step further, advocating a position that views foreign language studies at the tertiary level as a form of liberal arts education that promotes 'an attitude of intellectual openness, especially to inquiry, discovery, new ideas and perspectives' (Blaich, Bost, Chan and Lynch 2004, p.13). Kinoshita and Zhang argue that language education is in a good position to cultivate such an attitude as well as general intellectual development such as critical mind and analytical skills, all of which are the goals of liberal arts education at the tertiary level (see also Winter, McClelland and Stewart 1981).

Learning a foreign language as adults presents unique characteristics, challenges, and opportunities. For one thing, it is the only type of learning that adults are not as good as young children (Bley-Vroman 1990, Hyltenstam and Abrahamson 2003). Secondly, high-level cognitive functions such as analytical skills and problems-solving strategies are utilized by learners from day one to access an abstract system of sign-meaning association -- language. Hypothesis-testing, trial-and-error, instant and constant feedback are exercised in the learning process all the time. As culture-specific values and practices are often built in linguistic structures and expressions (e.g. grammaticalized respect system in Japanese, lexicalized gender value in Chinese), language learning offers a window for learners to see and experience a different life and culture from their own, and along with it, a different value system rooted in tradition, history, and political systems of the country in which the language is spoken. Cultural clashes occur implicitly and explicitly, and learners' value systems are challenged from time to time. All this provides opportunities for developing high-level intellectual capacity and personal attributes. According to a group of graduates who learned L2 Japanese previously in a university, two of the most benefits they had gained in the Japanese language courses were general personal character development and language skills (Kinoshita and Zhang 2014). The former refers to 'emphasizing, recognizing one's own assumptions and seeing all sides of an issue', and the latter refers to skills associated with traditional language learning. Nearly half of the graduates mentioned the benefits corresponding to the liberal arts education goals: critical thinking, analytical skills, learning how to learn, empathizing, recognizing one's own assumptions, and participating in and enjoying cultural experience.

The reflections by the graduates in Kinoshita and Zhang (2014) demonstrate the long-term value of a short-term language course that emphasizes on both 'training' and 'education.' The question is, 'how do we incorporate intellectual arts education in a language classroom in such a way that it is an integral part of the curriculum?' In the following, a pedagogical practice in a language course that embraces the concept of critical thinking and understanding through reflective learning is presented and discussed.

## From 'Knowing It' （知其然） to 'Knowing Why It'（知其所以然）

**The Course**

The course is a 3rd year Chinese language course at an Australian university', designed for students at a high intermediate proficiency level. Being the last course in Chinese major, it aims to further develop students' language skills and cultural understanding through reading and discussing major topics in contemporary China. The students and the teacher meet four hours per week in lectures and tutorials. The medium of instruction and assessment is Chinese.

The majority of the students are undergraduates of non-Chinese background. They study in a range of disciplines such as arts, law, economics, finance, and science. Many of them have been to China and Taiwan for short-term studies or tourism.

The course book *Reading into a New China* 《变化中的中国》(Li and Liu 2010) contains 10 units, each covering a 'hot' topic in contemporary China. For example, before the single child policy, a woman's position, environment problem, divorce, love in old age, consumer behavior, technology, economic development, business, Chinese modern families. Adopting a topic-based approach, the book is aimed to 'provide maximum opportunities for thinking and discussion, promoting the development of both linguistic and communication skills.' (p.x). The reading texts are characterized by the written style (书面语) typically used in Chinese writings and formal speeches, including works of literature, official documents, essays, newspapers and TV news broadcast. Sentences are long and complex, and the texts contain many fixed and idiomatic expressions (成语，惯用语), and are written with formal and semi-formal vocabularies.

These two features -- hot topics in China today and literary styles – determine the pedagogical foci of the course. In order to be able to process the texts linguistically, students need to learn a new set of vocabularies and expressions typically used in writing. They need to be able to parse long and complex sentences for meaning, and develop a sensitivity to the distinction between spoken and written styles. The linguistic training therefore centers on enhancing the students' ability to comprehend the written texts, and their skill to write Chinese essays in a less colloquial manner.

In tandem to linguistic training is attention to nurturing students' critical understanding of the current issues in rapidly changing China. As mentioned before, students in this course are mostly 3rd year undergraduates. Many of them have studied Chinese culture, history, and society in other courses. Some have been to China, and have had direct experience with its people and its everyday culture. Through media and formal studies, they know many things about China, including some of the topics covered in the course book. However, what does their 'know' look like? How much and how deeply do they 'know' and from what perspectives? 'Knowing' is a mental state that has many cognitive levels, from superficial recognition ('knowing it' 知其然) to substantial understanding ('knowing why it' 知其所以然). The latter requires not only extensive readings and in-depth study, but also an emic perspective based on 'an insider's view of the context and a deep understanding of what is relevant in it for participants' (Otega, 2009, pp.228-229, also Markee and Kasper 2004). It is the latter that the course is aiming for: to foster a critical understanding and perspective of China that is informed, balanced, and nuanced.

## What Do Students Already 'Know'?

Learners come to learning situations with certain amount of knowledge acquired in life and in previous studies. Adult learners have also developed a belief system based on their culture, tradition and life experience. Education, especially tertiary education in humanities and social sciences, is aimed at engaging learners in an intellectual exercise that examines one's own knowledge and belief systematically, deeply, and critically to attain a renewed understanding of others'. In this Chinese course, the first step toward this goal is to find out what the students already 'know' about China's One Child Policy, a topic that interests the majority of the students in the course.

The answer: they know a lot, and they don't know a lot. They know China has a huge population. They know the purpose of the policy is population control. They also know that female babies are not often welcome, and in some areas of China, there appears gender imbalance due to practices rooted in old tradition and exasperated by the policy. On the other hand, the vast majority of the students do not know the population figure of China (or Australia for that matter). They do not know when the policy was introduced, nor the historical events that led to its introduction. They also do not know the outcome of the policy, the significance and contribution of the policy to China as a country, to Chinese families and people as individuals, and to the world. They believe that Chinese people do not like it, and that it has produced a generation of spoilt children who behave like 'little emperors and princesses.'

This description can apply to almost every topic in the course book, i.e., students know 'it', but not 'why it' or 'how it.' This type of knowledge and understanding can hardly be productive because the knowledge structure is incomplete. It involves little substantive understanding and comprehension of the issue, let alone from an emic perspective. Applications of this type of knowledge will result in unbalanced critique, reinforcing bias and misunderstanding.

## Course Design and Implementation: A Liberal Arts Orientation

If the course is to be treated as a predominantly 'language' course, the 'why' and the 'how' of the 'One Child Policy' will occupy a periphery position as background information. But if intellectual development serves as the pedagogical basis of the course and critical understanding is the mission, the 'why' and the 'how' must be an integral part of the course from teaching to assessments.

Central to the implementation of a liberal arts education model in a foreign language course such as the one discussed here is the emic approach. It underpins all pedagogical activities. Direct contact with Chinese people is essential because their lived experience serves as the input from which exploration of new perspectives as well as critical self-reflections are triggered. However, direct interactions (直接互动) and personal experience 亲身体验) are two of the most salient deficiencies in a foreign language setting (李 2014, also Liddicoat and Scarino, 2013). Despite this, there are successful practices that engage learners with target language speakers through e-Chat and through inviting target language speakers into classrooms (Zhang, 2005, Kinoshita, 2007). The present Chinese course adopts an 'open door' policy: it invites native speakers of Chinese IN and pushes students OUT. Through direct engagements between the students and the Chinese people inside and outside the classroom, it provides opportunities for cultural and intellectual exchange that inevitably motivates students to question, to explore, and to critically examine and reflect on their own views and knowledge about China.

## ACTIVITY A. Inviting IN: Guest Speaker -- Chinese 'Single Child'

'One Child Policy' is the topic of Unit 13 '贝贝进行曲' (*The March of Beibei*). This policy was adopted by Chinese government in the late 1970s in response to the population explosion over the past decades. One of the criticisms of the policy is that single child are all spoilt like 'little emperors and princesses.' The reading text in Unit 13 expresses this view. It describes a small boy called Beibei behaving badly. He is selfish, self-centered, and obsessed with material comfort.

Is that an accurate and fair characterization of the generation of 'single child' in China? What is the life like for this group of children when they grow up? Are they pampered and spoilt beyond reason like Beibei?

The best way to answer these questions is to meet a product of the policy, a single child from China. There are many Chinese students in the university, and the vast majority of them are single child in their family. Although there are direct contacts between them and the Australian students during their studies, questions such as 'what is it like to grow up as a single child?' 'how does it feel like to be a single child?' or 'what is your opinion about the "One Child Policy" are hardly the topics of interest in their social and academic conversations.

A Chinese international student in her early 20s was invited to class. In about 10 minutes at the start of the lecture, she spoke (in Chinese) about her life in China. She talked about her childhood and teenage years, her daily life in those years, her (extended) family, her parents, their expectations and requirements of her, major events in her life, etc. In a nutshell, her life as a single child was very busy; she had no weekends because all weekends were spent on extracurricular activities; all her wishes and requests were satisfied by her parents but in return, she was expected in no uncertain terms to maintain excellent academic performance. She was not lonely as a small child because she was living in an extended family. Her life became somewhat lonely after she started school and moved back to live with her parents. Parental pressure and pampering, she said, was pretty much the characteristics of the life of her schoolmates and friends in China who were all single child.

In the Q&A that followed, students asked her many questions, for example, her feelings of her life as a single child, and her views of the 'one child policy'. They also wondered about how she dealt with the pressure from parents. They were shocked by the tragic reaction (suicide) of her friend to similar parental pressures. In response, the Chinese student said overall, she found her childhood to be rather fulfilling and satisfying. She tried her best to meet her parents' expectations and was successful in her academic achievements. She thought the policy was necessary, and had no qualms about it.

*Comments*: The purpose of inviting a Chinese 'single child' into the classroom is to present students a live experience so that they hear the first-hand account from a culture insider who is the product of the 'One Child Policy.' The Chinese student's story contains factual information unknown to students, as well as culture-specific ways of child-rearing, Chinese-style parent-child relationship, and traditional Chinese values and emphases on offspring and education. Her brief oral 'autobiography' reveals stark differences between the life and upbringing of the Australian students, including Chinese background students, and that of the single child in China. Much of the story, common as it is in China and to the Chinese people, is new and rather shocking to the Australian students.

Personal experiences are a powerful means to trigger memories and comparison. A person standing in front of the class, telling her story and the story of her fellow single child, and offering her own thoughts on the policy, is more believable than the (stereotype) depiction often seen and heard in the media and in publications. The ensuing reflections on one's current knowledge and assumptions are inevitable. The direct input from and interaction with a native-speaking single child is the first step in a journey toward developing an intellectual capacity to think critically and learn reflectively.

**ACTIVITY B. Lecture: China's One Child Policy**

The personal story of the Chinese student was followed by a short lecture (15 minutes, in Chinese) on the history of Chinese population issues. The lecture began with the debate in the 1950s between Peking University Professor MA Yingchu and Chairman Mao, and it went through subsequent policy changes in each of the decades up to 2013. The lecture also gave a brief sketch of the issues and pressures confronting the single child as they grew up and had their own families. The sketch was couched in a wider context in which culture-specific practices rooted in Chinese traditional and societal expectations of filial piety and duty were discussed. Together, the oral autobiography and the lecture presented a multi-dimensional picture of the policy, its germination, outcome and implication. The lecture concluded with the advice that one needed to view an issue, any issue, from multiple perspectives, and that a single-lens approach was to be avoided.

*Comments*: The lecture is aimed to complement the experiential knowledge (感性认识) obtained from the guest speaker with rational knowledge (理性认识) based on facts. This is similar to university courses in humanity and social sciences in which students learn about political, historical and social issues. A significant population control policy such as China's 'One Child Policy' needs to be understood in the context in which it was born because a comprehensive and informed knowledge is more likely to lead to a deeper and better understanding. The lecture, short as it was, outlined the background of the policy, showing that the Chinese population problem was a complex issue and that the policy was not a 'knee-jerking' reaction of the government of the day, but a response to an urgent situation that the country had been confronting over many decades. It was a 'necessary evil' that China had to have at that time. The lecture encouraged students to take a relative and emic perspective, and called for a critical analysis of the policy based on historical, cultural, and political factors.

## ACTIVITY C. Debate: 'One Child is Good'

Tutorials follow the lectures, and are intended to reinforce learning through practice. Of the two tutorials in the course, one is designated to essay writing, and the other to speaking. Following the lecture in which students learned about the life of a Chinese single child, the background of the policy, and the key language points, the practice phase in the oral tutorial requires students to exercise their newly learned linguistic and background knowledge to produce a coherent argument.

The task was debate. The topic: One child is good: Agree/Disagree (一个孩子好：同意／不同意). Every student was asked to take a position although the position did not have to represent one's true belief. To prepare for the debate, students studied the textbook material, the guest speaker's speech, and the background information provided in the lecture and in other courses. A few students carried out research on the internet.

In the first 15-20 minutes of the tutorial, students discussed their arguments and supporting evidence in their respective teams. The teacher was on hand to provide vocabularies on request and to guide students on possible arguments.

During the debate, students from each team took turns to speak, each for about 1-2 minutes. Free debate followed afterwards. The teacher served as 'umpire,' tallying each valid (not 'correct') point made in the debate. In the last 5 minutes, the teacher gave a summary feedback, mentioning all the valid points, announcing the winning team, and inviting further contribution.

The debate was heated. Students in the 'agree' team cited famous and successful people who are single child (e.g., Condoleezza Rice) to support their argument. Students in the 'disagree' team used Beibei as a counter example. Students expressed their opinions from family, social, and environment perspectives. There were a few Australian students who were single child, and they argued passionately in favor of single child.

*Comments*: The experiential and rational input given by the guest speaker and the teacher provides food for thought. Further understanding and learning require active digestion of the food, through some form of 'output.' According to Swaine (1985), it is language output that ultimately drives acquisition because it calls for learners to process L2 material via active engagement in grammatical encoding and monitoring processes. Although Swain's thesis is concerned with language acquisition, it applies equally to intellectual development. To be able to articulate one's opinion clearly and convincingly, whether in L1 or L2, requires clear thinking, genuine understanding, logical reasoning, as well as linguistic facility. Debate in L2 offers a platform to integrate these skills because it is as much a linguistic exercise as an intellectual one.

In the debate, students engaged closely with the issue, drawing on their own experience to argue for and against the topic statement. As every student is someone's child, with or without siblings, they never ran out of things to say. The debate was a continuous cycle of critical reflection in which students not only articulated their thoughts and views, but also listened to (counter-)arguments and evidence and formulated fresh arguments from various perspectives. Following the input, this activity sees the emergence of evidence-based reflective understanding and sophisticated reasoning.

## ACTIVITY D. Pushing OUT: An Inquiry-based Project

'Pushing out' means 'learning beyond classroom walls.' After the input (the guest speaker, the lecture) and the output (the debate), a series of tasks are designed that integrate the linguistic and intellectual skills through an inquiry-based project that pushes students out of the classroom to further investigate an issue that interests them.

The teaching and learning activities prior to this point are organized and managed by the teacher. The teacher invited the guest speaker, sourced the lecture material, and delivered the lecture. The teacher set the debate topic, lay down the rules, and facilitated the debate. Scaffoldded and carefully choreographed, these classroom activities offered essential linguistic, intellectual, and factual input and training necessary for critical thinking and reflective learning to take place. But that is not enough. Students need to go out there, taking initiatives to engage in linguistic and intellectual exchanges with target language speakers in order to learn more.

The project, called 'language use project' (语言应用作业) is designed for that purpose. It is comprised of three tasks: interviewing a native speaker of Chinese, writing an essay based on the interview, and presenting the interview and the essay. These three tasks have an inherent connection that further stretches students' linguistic and intellectual skills. Like all activities in the course, the project is to be completed in Chinese. A guideline (in Chinese) is provided that sets out the tasks, the requirements, the assessment criteria, and some suggestions.

**Task 1.** Interview: Students are to interview a Chinese person on an issue of interest (10-20min). The interviewee must be a native-speaker of standard modern

Chinese as a first language. Students are given a choice to work in pairs or individually. The interviews are recorded and uploaded on the course website. Although the interview itself is not assessed, it is used as a reference for the assessment.

In the guideline, suggestions about possible talking points are offered. For example, if the interviewee is a single child, the interview can focus on her/his life as a child, how she/he was brought up, her/his family, current life, thoughts and plans for the future, and views on 'single child' and the 'One Child Policy.'

In this student-initiated cross-cultural encounter, students interviewed their neighbors, workmates, dorm-mates, and friends, including family friends. A few interviewed their parents. The majority of students interviewed Chinese students who are single child. The interview topics ranged from the 'One Child Policy' and marriage and divorce in China, to environmental problems, the employment situation in a Chinese city, the economic development and significance, and the Chinese consumer behavior.

*Comments:* For students to attain a deep understanding of the 'One Child Policy,' or any issue for that matter, nothing is better than activities that remove the physical distance and mental detachment of an outsider. Unlike the meeting with the Chinese guest speaker in class, the interview task gives students autonomy to discuss with a Chinese single child, alone and away from the prying eyes of the teacher. It invites students to explore their questions and curiosities through direct interactions with target language speakers who were of a similar age as them. The task is open-ended, intimate, and personalized. Students are 'pushed OUT' of the classroom, not only physically, but intellectually and pedagogically, to see and hear for themselves the views and perspectives of someone who 'personifies' the policy. 'It also invites the interviewees to share their life stories and opinions freely and analytically, perhaps for the first time, in a cross-cultural face-to-face encounter in which a genuine and meaningful intellectual exchange takes place.

The interview was also a real communication occasion to test students' L2 Chinese linguistic skills. Unlike language practice and test inside the classroom where the teacher tailors her speech to the level of the learner, a native target language speaker does not do so readily or successfully. Students need to use considerable L2 linguistic and communicative skills to carry out a natural conversation with someone they do not know. They must be able to successfully approach someone and obtain their agreement, to explain the purpose, to negotiate for meaning where clarifications and confirmations are needed, and to sustain the conversation until mission accomplished.

**Task 2**. Essay: The interview serves as the basis for an essay (800-1000 words in Chinese). In the essay, students are required to introduce the interviewee and summarize their conversation. They could write in a genre of their choosing: argumentative, descriptive, comparative or biographic.

*Comment*: Like all pedagogical activities in the course, the interview-based essay serves dual pedagogical functions: linguistic and intellectual. Linguistically, students exercise their listening and writing skills through reproducing the interview in a structured, coherent and literary style in Chinese. Intellectually, the essay task presents an opportunity for students to express their thoughts, not any thoughts, but informed thoughts on the issue. By now, students should have become aware that 1) one cannot judge the practice of another culture exclusively from the point of view of one's own culture, 2) a productive critique can only be exercised on the basis of comprehensive knowledge and informed understanding of facts and local situations, 3) nothing is black or white.

**Task 3**. Presentation: Students present their interviews (and essays) in class (10-15 minutes per student). This serves as the final speaking test for the course. PowerPoint slides, if used, can only show pictures, titles and a few key words. Each presentation is followed by Q&A in which the presenter answers questions and explains his/her analysis, and and sometimes defends them and argues against opinions that disagree to his/her own. The presentation takes many forms: PowerPoint slides, and free speech with or without notes.

*Comments:* The presentation task is built on the interview and the essay tasks. It is the culmination of the inquiry-based project, offering an opportunity for students to showcase their linguistic skills as well as their new knowledge and fresh understanding of 'why it' of an issue. It is also an occasion for students to learn from each other and grow together. The benefits of the interaction with Chinese native speakers in the interview task are most evident in the quality of the presentation. The range of topics and questions are diverse, demonstrating the level of interests, enthusiasm and engagement.

Indeed, the inquiry-based project shows amply that with sufficient preparation and nurturing, student-led learning activities beyond the classroom walls promote intellectual development in a meaningful and productive way.

## Learning Outcome

The section above presents and discusses a liberal arts oriented pedagogical practice and how it is implemented in a high-intermediate Chinese language course. In this section, the learning outcome is examined. Out of 35 essays, 21 students wrote on the 'One Child Policy', reporting on their interviews with

Chinese students who were single child. The rest discussed environmental problems (3), consumer behavior (3), economic development (3), divorce (3), employment (1), and changes after the economic reform (1). Of the 21 essays on the population policy, 5 gave a recount of the interviewees' stories, and 16 contained reflective analysis and thoughts that displayed discovery and renewed understanding.

Many students discussed the benefits and drawbacks of the policy, and analyzed the pros and the cons of the policy critically. The policy was no longer viewed in black and white, but against the outcome it has achieved and possible improvements in the future. The analytical perspective, critical as it is, indicates a level of intellectual maturity in terms of balanced reflections (benefits and problems), tempered and tentative conclusions (可能 'maybe', 有可能 'possibly'), and the use of facts from authoritative sources (根据… 'according to…'). The following are two examples (1) (2). (See original Chinese versions in the Appendix).

1. The one child policy introduced in the 80s indeed lowered the birth rate, but it also invoked a debate on whether 'single child is good or not good.' The good aspects include first, the child will get all the love from his/her family. Secondly, the child will have a fairly worry-free and happy life. On the other hand, because single child does not have siblings, they may not know how to share, and they may be rather selfish. They may possibly be weak in social interactions, and their life may be lonely. If their parents spoil them, then they will not be independent when growing up. (S17)

2. According to BBC, the policy has succeeded in reducing 0.4 billion people in China in 30 years. At the same time, the one child policy has brought about many problems.

People's rights…

Old people who have lost their child…

Along with the relax of the policy in recent years, the number of old people with no child will decrease. In terms of people's rights, the government now allows couples who are single child on both sides to have two children. After many years, the government will relax the policy even more, and these problems will be reduced as a result. (S16)

In this liberal arts-oriented course, students embarked on a journey of discovery. They learned 'it' as well as 'why it' of every topic in the course book and their political and historical background. They also had face-to-face encounter and interaction with Chinese single child and learned about the lives and views of those who are the direct products of the population policy. The zero-distance communication was a unique opportunity for students to hold an intellectual dialogue with a so-called 'little emperor' or 'princess.' Through these, students' existing knowledge was restructured and renewed understanding emerged. This is illustrated in Examples (3), (4) and (5):

3. When I was a child, my sisters and I played together. We got along very well, and we had very happy life. During that time, I felt that it was ideal to have siblings. As I grew older, I heard about China's One Child Policy. I thought that being an only child would be very lonely so my opinion towards the policy was not positive. However, after learning more about the policy, I gradually understood why the Chinese government introduced this policy. (S1)

4. After I interviewed a female single child, I found many of the views held by Westerners are fallacies. Therefore, I am writing this article to denounce the rubbish. ... Westerners think Chinese one child policy has produced many social problems, for instance, 'little emperors'... In my dormitory, there are about 500 students. We must share one big kitchen. If xxx is a little emperor, she might hate to share. Yet everyday, I see her cooking while chatting with other students. She also often happily lets other people taste the food she has cooked.... The way her parents raised her allows her to become independent gradually. We can see from her example that Chinese single child are not necessarily little emperors... After interviewing xxx, I now know that this policy is not all bad. (S18)

5. Through this conversation, we have discovered some problems which very probably reflect the same population aging problems facing our country... (S6)

In these excerpts, students looked inward by examining their assumptions and beliefs. This led to discoveries and change of attitudes and views. After 'studying many things about the policy,' Student #1's previous 'not positive' opinion about the 'One Child Policy' was replaced by a 'gradual understanding of why Chinese government introduced this policy.' Similarly, after interviewing a single child, student #18 'discovered that many Western views about the policy are fallacies and that the policy is not all bad after all.' The example of his interviewee shows 'clearly that Chinese single child is not necessarily little emperors'. From the conversation with a Chinese single child, student #6 'discovered some problems' and related them to similar issues in his own country Australia.

It is evident that the discovery and renewed understanding are the result of the conversations with target language speakers as well as the study of the facts and issues surrounding the policy. The subsequent change of attitudes and views are testimony to an emerging intellectual openness to new ideas and adoption of emic perspectives. These are exactly what the liberal arts education aims to achieve.

The inquiry-based project, especially the conversation with a Chinese student who is of the same age as the students in the class, invites critical comparison and thoughtful comments. Some students related what they heard to their own life, offering their thoughts on the 'One Child Policy' and its implications. The following examples (6) and (7) are two examples illustrate this:

6. Western single child also faces the same pressure…and experiences the same loneliness. Although the one child policy has problems, it does not have major issues. Parents are very important. If they are able to care for their children, quantity is not important. (S19)

7. Xxx said his experience in the 3-year senior high school was very hard because in China, the national college entrance examination determines one's future. Starting from Year 1 in the senior high, he prepares for tests everyday. Because there is only one child for parents, the child bears a lot of pressure. Xxx is also lonely. Not only didn't he have siblings, he had no chance to play with friends. As someone of the same age, my experience in the Australian students was very different. First, although there is also final examination in Australia, the Australian university entrance examination is rather light. College students don't need to prepare the exam from Year 1. Secondly, until Year 3, I played with my friends. Finally, I am not single child…and don't feel 'lonely.' (S10)

According to student #19, single child family is not unique to China. Single child in western families experienced 'the same pressure and the same loneliness.' Being a single child, she apparently could identify with the Chinese student's life experience. Her conclusion was that the policy, though having 'shortcomings,' was not problematic because it was not the number of children in a family, but the role of the parents, that was the issue. In contrast, #10 was very happy about his life in school and at home because he was not a single child and he went to school in Australia. This student expressed a feeling of 'being lucky' and this lucky feeling was the result of the interview and comparison.

Comparison is a means for students to recognize cross-cultural gaps and personal issues, which serves as the basis for critical reflection. Students actively engaged in comparison on different levels: personal, analytical, intellectual, and policy. This resulted in an enhanced capacity for empathy and for seeing an issue from all sides – a liberal arts education value.

The inquiry-based cross-cultural interaction between Australian and Chinese students had a rather unexpected and pleasant side result. It presented Chinese student interviewees a chance as well to reflect on their life and articulate their thoughts on the population problem confronting China today, including the 'One Child Policy.' Most of the students expressed a positive acceptance of the policy despite its problems, stating that it was absolutely necessary for China at that time. They recognized the population impact on the environment in China. Even though 'loneliness' and 'pressure' were constant themes in their stories, they all felt overwhelmingly that they had had a happy and fairly normal childhood. They owed the opportunity to study in Australia to being a single child because they understood that their parents would not have been able to have the financial strength to send them to Australia to study if there was more than one child in the family. Despite this, when asked about their future family plan, they all said they would like to have more than one child – a 'contradiction' that did not escape the interviewers.

## Conclusion

A foreign language course, especially an intermediate or high proficiency one in universities, can and should orient itself toward intellectual arts education akin to humanity and social science courses. The pedagogical practice presented in this chapter made a conscious and purposeful effort to engage students in an intellectual (and linguistic) journey toward capacity building in critical thinking and reflective learning. Intercultural interactions and experience (Liddicoat and Scarino, 2013) are part of the journey. The entire course curriculum is designed to open up the classroom to allow students to experience, to make connection, and to see with their mind active. Rather than teaching uninterpreted and often unrelated culture-specific facts such as traditional holidays and ceremonies, gift-giving customs, taboos, food and so on, the education-oriented Chinese course endeavors to explore basic beliefs, values and attitudes of both one's own and the target language speaker's. The opinions students eventually form are not as important as their enhanced ability to think, explore and comprehend issues in a balanced, nuanced, and informed manner. As Kramsch (1993) pointed out, the world contained multi-elements with huge differences, but different cultures also have a lot in common beneath surface variations (Rivers 1968). The mission of education, including language education, is in part to develop the capacity to recognize, understand, and appreciate the contrast and to overcome single perspectives and culture-conditioned assumptions so as to embrace and tolerate differences through cultural interpretation and deep intellectual exchange and understanding. This does not happen automatically. It needs active fostering and nurturing. Second language courses at the tertiary level should embrace this approach, aiming for 'education' by promoting intellectual development as well as L2 linguistic competency so that foreign language learners do not clothe their 'cultural offensiveness in the best local diction' (Bishop 1960, cited in Rivers 1968).

Back to the question 'Does One Child Policy produce little emperors and princesses'? Taught with a linguistic focus, students' answer is likely to be 'yes,' because there is no evidence in the textbook to support a 'no' answer. With an intellectual arts orientation, however, students may not have a definitive answer because the 'why it' involves a complex web of factors each of which is connected to various types of reality past and present. What is clear is that students progressed from 'knowing it' to 'knowing why it' through activities that invite them to interact with target language speakers meaningfully and experience their life through direct communication. This zero-distance intercultural contact is supplemented by lectures, debate, essay writing and presentation. This suite of activities support each other, aiming to nurture critical thinking through reflective learning and deep understanding of contemporary issues in China. The coherent feature of these pedagogical activities is captured in part by a student, '*More interestingly, the content we have learned in class is very similar to XXXX's actual experience.*' (10)

## REFERENCES

Blaich, C., Bost, A., Chan, E. and Lynch, R. (2004). Defining liberal arts education. Unpublished manuscript.

Bley-Vroman, R. (1990). The logical problem of foreign language learning. *Linguistic Analysis,* 20 (1-2), 3-47.

Harmer, J. (2007). *The Practice of English Language Teaching*. Essex: Pearson Education Limited.

Hyltenstam, K., and Abrahamsson, N. (2003). Maturational constraints in SLA. In J.Doughty and M.Long (Eds.), *The Handbook of Second Language Acquisition*, (pp.538-588). Oxford: Blackwell.

Jespersen, O. (1904). *How to Teach a Foreign Language*. London: Allen and Unwin Ltd.

Kinoshita, Y. (2008). Using an audio-video chat program in language learning. In F., Zhang and B. Barber (Eds.), *The Handbook of Research on Computer-Enhanced Language Acquisition and Learning* (pp.507-520). London: IGI Global.

Kinoshita, Y. and Zhang, Y. (2014). Why do we teach languages at universities? Re-conceptualization of foreign language education. *Selected Proceedings of the Second National LCNAU Colloquium*, pp. 87-100.

Kramsch, C. (1993). Language study as a border study: Experiencing difference. *European Journal of Education*. 28/3, pp.349-358.

Li, D., and Liu, I. (2010). *Reading into a New China: Integrated Skills for Advanced Chinese.*《变化中的中国》(Vol 2). Boston: Cheng & Tsui Company, Inc.

李朝晖 (2014). 目的语与非目的语的语言环境文化学习方式探讨。《汉语国际传播研究》6 (1), pp. 145-151. [Li, Z. Discussion on the methods of cultural studies in target and non-target language settings. *Chinese Language International Communication Research*]

Liddicoat, A., and Scarino, A. (2013). *Intercultural Language Teaching and Learning*. Hoboken, N.J.: Wiley-Blackwell.

Markee, N., and Kasper, G. (2004). Classroom talks: An introduction. *Modern Language Journal,* 88, pp.491-500.

Otega, L. (2009). *Understanding Second Language Acquisition*. London: Hodder Education.

Rivers, W. (1968). *Teaching Foreign Language Skills*. Chicago: The University of Chicago Press.

Swain, M. (1985). Communicative competence: Some roles of comprehensible input and comprehensible output in its development. In S.M.Gass and C.G.Madden (Eds.), *Input in Second Language Acquisition* (pp.235-253). Rowley, MA: Newbury House.

Ur, P. (2006). *A Course in Language Teaching*. Cambridge: Cambridge University Press.

Winter, D., McClelland, D., and Stewart, A. (1981). A new case for the liberal arts: Assessing institutional goals and student development. San Francisco: Jossey-Bass.

Zhang, Y. (2005). Introducing native speakers to the foreign language classroom. *Journal of American Chinese Teachers Association*, 40 (3), pp.71-90.

## APPENDIX

1 八十年代出的独生子女确实使生育率下降了，但也产生了一个'独生子女是好或不好'的辩论。好处包括第一，孩子会得到家庭全部的爱，第二是孩子会有已过很轻松和比较高兴的生活。但另一方面，由于独生子女是没有兄弟姐［么子女］可能就不会分享，反而会比较自私，也有可能社会交流能力比较差，生活比较孤独。如果受到父母的溺爱，孩子长大就不会独立。(#17)

2 根据 BBC 的统计，政策成功的在三十年里中国人口下降，减少了四亿的人。与此同时，独生子女政策［也］带来［了］种种问题：
一、人民的权利问题。。。
二、失独老人现象。。。
随着近年来政府慢慢放松独生子女政策，这种失独老人现象未来会减少。人民的权利问题方面，政府现在让双独家庭有两个孩子。在许多年里政府应该又会再放松，这些问题也慢慢减少。　　(#16)

3 小的时候，我跟我的两个妹妹一起玩，我们感情很好，过的很快乐。那时候我觉得有兄弟姐妹是非常理想的。我长大后，听说了中国独生子女的政策。因为以前我对独生子女政策的看法不太好，所以我觉得独生子会很孤单。但是，在我学了很多关于独生子女政策以后，我渐渐明白了为什么中国政府有这个政策。（1）

4 我采访了一位独生女以后，发现了很多西方人对独生子女政策的观点都是谬论，于是我写了这篇文章来揭穿这些谬论。。。。西方人觉得中国独生子女政策造成［了］很多社会问题，比如说'小皇帝'。。。。在我宿舍里大概有五百个学生，我们必须合用一个大厨房。如果 xxx 是小皇帝的话，她可能会讨厌跟别人一起用一个厨房。可是我天天看她一边做饭，一边和其他人聊天，她经常很高兴地让别人尝他自己做的菜。。。她父母的教养方式让她慢慢的独立了。从她的例子中可以看得很清楚：中国独生子女不一定是小皇帝。。。采访 xxx 以后，我现在知道了这［个］政策不完全是坏的。（18）

5 此番谈话，我们发现了一些问题而这些也有可能反应我国的同样面临的老年化的问题。。。（6）

6 西方独生子女也有面临着同样的压力，。。。并且经历同样的孤独。。。独生子女政策虽然存在缺点，但没有非常大的问题。父母是很重要的，如果他们能很好的照顾小孩，数量并不重要。（19）

7 Xxx 说他三年高中经历很'辛苦'，因为在中国，高考决定人生。从高一开始，他每天都准备高考。因为父母只有一个孩子，所以给孩子很多压力。Xxx 也很孤独。不但没有兄弟姐妹，而且没有机会跟朋友们玩。而作为同龄人，我的澳洲高中经历完全不一样。首先，虽然澳洲也有期末考试，但澳洲'高考'比较轻松。澳洲高中学生不用从高一开始准备考试。其次，直到

高三，我仍然跟朋友们玩。最后，我不是已过独生子。。。所以我没有感觉'孤独'。（10）

8 ...跟 xxx 真正的经历很像。（10）

CHAPTER 6

# Teacher Education for Reflective Thinking in Teaching: Field Experiences of Teacher Trainees in South Africa

*Simeon Maile*

Since 1994 South African teachers experienced a barrage of changes in the curriculum, which introduced new ways of educating teachers and embedded new approaches to teaching. Burgeoning research shows that teachers are struggling to implement new approaches as required by the new policy regime. The central thesis of this article is that reflective thinking is a skill that must be learnt in teacher education programmes. Informing this thesis is the assumption that without proper training in reflective practice, teachers are likely to fail to apply reflective thinking in the classroom. At the center of the investigation is the question: how well prepared South African teachers are to apply reflective thinking in teaching? Therefore, the purpose of this study is investigates whether or not South African teachers are adequately prepared to be critical reflective thinkers in their teaching. Answers to this question are drawn, through qualitative research approaches, from extensive literature review, and five teachers located in Gauteng province. The findings reveal that teachers have sound theoretical grounding in critical reflection, but are hamstrung by resource deficiency, lack pedagogical innovation and creativity to apply critical reflective thinking in the various stages of their teaching.

## INTRODUCTION

Since 1994 South African education system experienced a barrage of changes ranging from structural to curriculum changes. The changes were introduced to transform the education system from apartheid to the new democratic dispensation. Apartheid education system entrenched structural allocations characterized by inequality and discrimination on the basis of race. Different racial groups were treated unequally with preference given to the white communities. Under apartheid there were 19 racially and ethnically divided education departments (McLennan, 1995). These included 11 separate education departments (also known as Bantustans) for the Black population (Sayed and Kanjee, 2013). These separate departments were made up of 6 departments in self-governing states, 4 in independent states and the central government department administering education for Africans living in designated areas for Whites. Furthermore, Sayed and Kanjee, (2013) point out that in addition to these, there were three separate services in the tricameral parliament for Whites, Coloreds and Indians, which were organized into four semi-independent provincial departments. Further, there was a Department of Education responsible for setting national norms and standards, controlling policy and making budgetary allocations. What is remarkable with the system of education during apartheid was that there were substantial disparities in the provision of education which was characterized by disproportionate share of resources. Departments for white education received higher allocations resulting in unequal distribution of educational facilities and learning resources. The resource imbalances were heavily skewed against the Bantustan departments.

Similarly, discriminatory and inequalities were applied to teacher education in the higher education system. Bunting (1994) describes the inequalities permeating higher education as constituted by exclusion and deprivation of resources. In terms of the Bantu Education Act of 1953, African teachers were trained in separate colleges and universities allocated to their racial group. Other racial groups such as Whites, Coloureds and Indians have their separate colleges and universities. In addition to racial segregation, teacher education was ethnically divided (Sayed, 2004). Each homeland (a province like region allocated for a specific ethnic group) had a university and colleges to train teachers. The education of teachers in the colleges and homeland universities was aligned to Christian National Education policy which utilized religion to buttress in the outcome of the training. Teachers were trained to function as state functionaries whose primary task teach curriculum content, using officially selected textbooks. The graduates of apartheid college system were not trained to question authority. Consequently, teaching followed the ideology of apartheid. Teachers and learners were submissive, non-critical, non-reflective and non-progressive. Easton (2008) refer to this kind of training as the factory model which domesticated teachers to meekish and subservient approach to teaching characterized by conformity.

The problem of apartheid teacher education system is that it trained teachers to be submissive, non-critical, non-reflective and non-progressive. This had far reaching consequences in the new dispensation. Being domesticated and subservient, teachers were confined to conveyor belt role. They had no role in the development of teaching and no focus on the context in which teaching was taking place. Teaching remained a mechanistic practice (Schon, 1983). The notion of reflection was not there in the practice of teaching. As such, the new dispensation inherited teachers whose values are diametrically opposed to democratic values of non-racism, non-sexism, democracy, and equality. To aggravate matters, the new schooling curriculum took the direction of progressive teaching and learning inspired by human rights discourse and Freirean Peoples' Education Movement predominant in the 1980s (Kraak, 1999). Progressive teaching and human rights discourse requires specific skills such as adaptation, critical thinking, problem solving, active learning and engaged learning – the skills which teachers do not have. The changed philosophy and principles of education permeating the schooling system became a challenge to many teachers. To achieve the aims of the new curriculum new knowledge, skills and attitudes are required from teachers.

The radical changes in the schooling curriculum obliged changes in teacher education offered in public higher education institutions. It would seem that changes in teacher education were wrought in response to sweeping changes the curriculum of the schooling system. The discourse on curriculum change in the schooling system in South Africa is characterized by chopping and changing resulting into uncertainty, and volatility arising from constant changes in the curriculum. Arguments in this article will exclude schooling curriculum changes, but I will only refer to some elements of to enhance my thesis. In this article I argue that teachers are struggling to make a transition to progressive teaching as required by the new curriculum. The focus is on teacher education simply because the teachers are trained and equipped, mainly in public higher education institutions offering teacher education programmes. The assumption is that in training the new teachers, public higher education institutions, will infuse critical reflective skills which will enable them to be, for example, adaptive experts, problem solvers, or facilitators of active learning. The investigation is driven by the question: how well prepared South African teachers are to apply critical reflective thinking in their classroom teaching. The unit of analysis is new teachers because the role of critical reflective thinking was only made a requirement for teacher education recently. In the subsequent discussion of this article, the lexicon of my argument is landscaped to include conceptualization – which covers the main variables such as teacher education, critical reflective thinking and classroom teaching; current debates; policy trajectory which tracks some of the claims made in this section; scientific theories on critical reflective thinking; research strategy; findings; conclusions and recommendations.

## CONCEPTUAL ARCHITECTURE AND ANALYTICAL FRAMEWORK

This study utilizes multiple theories to explain the problem under investigation. The theory of multiples embodies the idea that any phenomenon renders itself to multiple discoveries and explanations. Forrester (2002) argues that no discovery can be made to meet the needs of human beings as a new thing on its own. Forrester (2002) is of the view that discoveries constitute knowledge accumulated over time. She argues that changes in human knowledge resulted from basic nature of human beings. She attributes the human ability to learn, to understand, to remember and human curiosity as drivers of human urge to learn more about their environment. This increases human knowledge. Human beings make scientific advances from the already existing knowledge by refining the existing knowledge which has been around for a long time and by logically reasoning from scientific laws. In human knowledge the properties and structure of nature are acquired in a particular order. Certain things are discovered before other things. Because the structure and properties of the universe become known to us in a particular order- which could be either from simple to more complex. Forrester concluded that we learn the world in a particular order and that order is due to the relationship between ourselves and the world.

Like Forrester, I believe that all scientific discoveries are potential multiples. There are many scientists continuing the on the works of their predecessors. Normally a particular scientific fact may remain undiscovered for thousand of year and then be discovered separately by two or more individuals. As such discoveries could have not been discovered until certain scientific facts had been discovered. For me this suggests that those other facts have been uncovered then the discovery of further scientific facts will be inevitable. Radical new ideas without clear precedent emerge more or less *ab ninito*. The architecture of the concept embraces an analysis of teacher education and policy trajectory; critical reflective thinking and classroom teaching.

**Teacher Education and Policy Trajectory**

Theorizing teacher education plunges us into a galaxy of proposals characterized by conceptual inexactitudes, anecdotal evidence, huge methodological questions, insufficiently grounded proposals, copouts, and problems of measurement tools (Maile, 2015). The discourse of this study is framed on what teachers know and practice in the evolving system. Debates on critical reflective thinking are underpinned by need to provide quality education. In this way teachers' critical reflective thinking knowledge invokes what Maile (2015) regards as characteristics of excellent teachers. In his research, Maile (2015) discovered that current research advances many proposals on what constitute an excellent teacher, but without consensus. What remains unanswered is the question: what makes a good teacher? In his quest for answers to this question, Maile (2015) suggests, from empirical evidence, that good teachers are made. In other words, knowing what makes a good teacher should start at the point when teachers are first prepared to become teachers. For this reason, an in-depth analysis of literature on teacher preparation is undertaken to establish how current programmes on teacher education prepare teachers for critical reflective thinking. Maile's (2015) thesis is continued in this article. However, the focus now is on how well prepared teachers are for critical reflective thinking. This question delves deeper into teachers' knowledge and skill – an aspect which has, in recent years, come under scrutiny for varying reasons. Among other reasons, there is discourse linking teachers' knowledge and skill with student learning (de Clerq & Shalem, 2014). De Clerq and Shalem (2014) argue that the knowledge that teachers acquire in various teacher education programmes should have a positive influence on student outcomes.

De Clerq and Shalem 's argument emerges from a bigger intellectual debate which argues that South Africa's education is in crisis. Cutting edge research (Bloch, 2009; Fleisch, 2008; Taylor and Vinjevold, 1999; Taylor, Muller, & Vinjevold, 2003; Christie, Butler, & Potterton, 2007; Sayed, Kanjee, & Nkomo, 2013, Spaull, 2013 & 2014) demonstrate that the crisis is aggravated by the poor quality of teaching. For instance, Bloch (2009:58) laments that:

"Schooling in South Africa is a national disaster. The vast majority of our schools are not simply producing the outcomes that are their chief objective. What is more, international tests suggest that South African schools are among the world's worst performers in maths and literacy."

Bloch's argument ties well with De Clerq and Shalem 's thesis which highlighted sources of weakness in teachers' practice and how teachers learn. They identified the sources of weakness as lack of link between curriculum learning outcomes and teachers' content knowledge. What they argue is that teachers must have more practice in their learning than being fed with theoretical knowledge that they never practice on. Put simply, De Clerq and Shalem argue that teachers should in their training get more chance to practice. Without more practice of teaching the knowledge that teachers gain from teacher education programmes will not be enough to enable them to deal with complexities of teaching. De Clerq and Shalem 's argument goes deeper into the quality teacher education programmes.

To respond to the crisis in teacher education the Department of Education introduced a series of interventions. The precursor to changes in teacher education was the *Norms and Standards for Teacher Education* introduced by Minister Sibusiso Bengu's Committee for Teacher Education Policy (COTEP) in 1995. The COTEP document set in motion the discourse of required competences for teacher qualifications. *The Norms and Standards for Teacher Education* (NSTE) uses an outcomes approach to teacher education and provides a detailed descriptions of what a competent educator can demonstrate (Parker, 2001). This policy emphasized teacher performance or practice as domain that help bring to bear the ability of teachers. It enjoins training providers to produce teachers who have the knowledge, skills and values necessary to make learning in schools more relevant to socio-economic needs of South Africa. Once again, context is embedded in the description of teacher competence. *The Norms and Standards for Teacher Education* defines and identifies a competent teacher through the seven roles: Learning mediator; interpreter and designer of learning programmes; leader, administrator and manager; scholar, researchers and lifelong learner; assessor; a community, citizenship and pastoral role and a learning area/subject/discipline/phase specialist role. Together these seven roles are seen as constituting a description of teacher excellence in the context of the *Norms and Standards for Teacher Education.*

The seven roles did not address the problem of teacher critical reflection adequately. The *Norms and Standards for Teacher Education* emphasized the notion of integrated and applied competence as the primary definition of teacher excellence without guiding higher education institutions through a new academic policy on how they infuse the Norms and Standards in their teacher education programmes. At the time of introducing the *Norms and Standards for Teacher Education* there was no policy for higher education regulating academic programme offering. Subsequent policies on teacher education (Department of Education, 2005; Department of Education 2006) still grapple with teachers not being sufficiently equipped to meet the needs of the education system. The Department of Education (2006) streamlined teacher education by prescribing frameworks for Initial Professional Education of teachers (IPET) and Continuing Professional Teacher Development (CPTD). Similarly, the Department of Education (2005) proposed an overarching framework that aims to develop a coherent teacher education system and promised to focus sharply on a decisive role of teacher education. While the Department of Education (2005) purports to develop clarity and coherence across the various authorities and policies that play a part on teacher education, the chronic problem of teachers lacking in conceptual and content knowledge hat underpins critical reflective thinking has not been addressed by policy endeavors.

To address this, the Department of Education adopted a two pronged strategy. The first strategy included *The Higher Education Qualifications Framework* (HEQF) (Department of Education, 2007) 's *Norms and Standards for Teacher Education* which were reviewed to align teacher education with the new policy. In essence it means replacing the Norms and Standards for Teacher Education to provide teacher education providers with guidelines with regard to the development of HEQF aligned qualifications and teacher education programmes.

The second strategy involves the Higher Education Qualifications Council (HEQC) which was saddled with the responsibility of reviewing of teacher qualifications and re- accreditation process. These processes involved Bachelor of Education (B.Ed) degree, Postgraduate Certificate in Education (PGCE) and the Advanced Certificate in Education (ACE). The review provided valuable information on the quality and design of the programmes. The department of Higher Education and Training's (2011) policy entitled, *Minimum Requirements for Teacher Education Qualifications*, responded to the HEQC review by introducing guidelines that describes clear requirements for the development of learning programmes; allows for institutional flexibility in the design and implementation of learning programmes; requires all teacher education programmes to address the poor content and conceptual knowledge among teachers; enjoins programmes to apply reflexive integrated and applied knowledge to enable teachers to acquire different types of knowledge and practices in the learning programmes; and retains the seven roles of teachers which must be interpreted as functions. This policy acknowledges that teaching is a complex activity similar to Shulman's (1983) invective. The *Minimum Requirements for Teacher Education Qualifications* refutes a purely skills based approach which relies on evidence of demonstrable outcomes as measures of teacher excellence. This policy pays attention to various types learning such as disciplinary, pedagogical, practical, fundamental and situational learning, it seems that the *Minimum Requirements for Teacher Education Qualifications* gravitates to a mix of knowledge, values and attitudes that define a newly qualified teacher. It can be inferred from Appendix C: basic competencies of a Beginner Teacher of *Minimum Requirements for Teacher Education Qualifications* (MIRTEQ), that an excellent teacher must have sound subject knowledge; must know how to teach their subjects; must know their learners and how they learn; must know how to communicate effectively; must be knowledgeable about the school curriculum; must understand diversity in the South African context; must be able to manage classrooms effectively; must be able to assess learners; must positive work ethic; and must be able to reflect critically.

The debates around the schooling crisis raise another important question as to placement of teacher trainees. Currently many institutions allow teacher trainees the freedom to choose schools where they want to do teaching practice. This is a problem given the fact that many schools are dysfunctional (O'Connell, 2013). Dysfunctional schools are mainly characterized by leadership crisis, culture of late coming, absenteeism, disregard for law, unsafe environment, bunking lessons, etc. The central argument is that teacher trainees are likely to learn wrong habits by being placed in such schools. That will defeat the purpose of teaching practice-which is to learn best skills, attitudes and knowledge practices exhibited by practicing teachers (Azeem, 2011; Zepeda &Aviles, 2008). Hence, most universities in South Africa are beginning to control student placement. In some cases, universities develop a list of functional schools in consultation with districts. The schools that make it to this list are normally selected on the basis of having high percentage of learner performance in exit grades (7 and 12). In addition to academic performance, O'Connell (2013) point out that functional schools are schools that: are in session for the stipulated number of hours per day and learners and teachers arrive on time; re operating for the stipulated number of school days in the school year according to an approved timetable; have rules and regulations that are known and adhered to by educators and learners alike; have efficient administrative system in place; have functioning school governing bodies (SGBs) and constituted school management teams (SMTs); have clear system of monitoring performance and achievement; have teachers demonstrating commitment and adherence to ethics; assess learner performance at regular intervals and feedback is provided to learners and parents; have learner support mechanism; have sound financial management system; and have an active and regular extracurricular programme.

Under these conditions, teacher trainees are likely to have an opportunity not only to teach but also internalize the correct habits and characteristics of effective teachers and learn how to create a conducive learning environment. This is not to say that these are perfect conditions. In a country with a history of structural inefficiencies it is impossible to have perfect teaching conditions. However, a correct balance is needed, and this list gravitates towards equilibrium.

Equilibrium has eluded us when taking into consideration the imperatives of the digital age. Bates (2015) argues that teachers face unprecedented change. Technology has pervaded different layers of management and operations of the teaching profession. Teaching can no longer be the same. Technology challenges the current conceptions of teaching, yet traditional forms of teaching remain indelible in the construction of teaching. Teaching needs to transcend traditional boundaries of time and space by using technology to teach in and outside the classroom (De Jager, 2014). Conceptions of teaching needs to adopt paradigmatic shift, which Kuhn (1970) describes as scientific revolution characterized by successive transition from traditional paradigm to digital paradigm through revolution in a developmental pattern. To make such transition in our conceptions of teaching practice we will need to reconsider traditional epistemologies (Doll, 1993) which coerce us to stick to foundations to which we may want to hang on to escape the tide of the digital age. Teaching has to develop an organic character: must develop and mature (Beck, Giddens & Lash, 1994). For teaching to develop and mature, it needs to make successive revolutions to digital age. New teachers have to be trained in digital technology to acquire skills that are incompatible with knowledge based economy. New teachers have to be trained to take lead in the use of technology in and outside the classrooms. In a developing context teacher trainees are only exposed to traditional aspects of teaching. The new technologies have not yet reached many lecture rooms. Universities have to develop the workforce that is ready to take up technological innovations

**Critical Reflective Thinking**

Current literature on teacher education indicates that traditional views on and attitudes to teaching and teacher education are changing. Researcher on teacher education agree with the argument drawn from De Clerq and Shalem (2014) which shows that teacher learning must be linked with student performance. This argument concurs that the most important factor influencing learner performance is the quality of classroom teaching. This sentiment is reflected in the Department of Education's (2005a) *National Framework for Teacher Education* which elevated the quality of classroom teaching to national discourse. The Department of Education's focus on the quality of classroom teaching is used as a strategy to address the crisis in education (Sayed, Kanjee, & Nkomo, 2013). The Department of Education's strategy is that in order to effectively change the schooling system teacher education also needs to change. Thus teachers are made change agents who facilitate quality learning.

The argument on how well prepared teachers are for critical reflective thinking resides within the discourse on teacher as gents of change in the education system. Critical reflective thinking integrates competence and performance. Teachers are saddled with a bigger role of assisting learners to achieve the desired results. This ability, according to Medley and Crook (1978), cannot be developed through theoretical learning of teaching as assumes the existence of a particular relationship between teachers and learners. Such a relationship can only be realized in practice. Similarly, the integration of competence and performance requires microscopic assessment of what teachers do in the classroom. To be competent in teaching requires a combination of learning from relevant teaching theories and learning to practice during teacher preparation.

Being a critical reflective teacher, which is set out as a new requirement in the policy discussed above, can be established through intuitive logic and situated interpretive judgments. This argument places social anthropology at the center of teaching. Social anthropology places the context of teaching at the center (Tosh, 2010). The use of context springs from the science of teaching that a sense of the whole must always inform understanding of the parts. Teaching and learning must address the entire social structure. It is insufficient to exclude the social structure in teaching. A critical reflective thinking teacher will always pitch his/her teaching on the social structure. Structuralism approach to teaching is embedded in the sociological perspective of education which base theoretical presuppositions on the concept of social structure as a precondition for teaching and learning. Structuralism views the society as fundamental to human knowledge existing to offer appropriated explanations of knowledge (McKay & Romm, 1992).

Reference to social structure is invoked to demonstrate that teaching should be linked to social institutions by querying the mode of production and class structure prevailing in the society. Critical reflective teaching embraces structural analysis to liberate learners by intervening in the learner's social reality to conscientize them of hidden elements of the erstwhile apartheid practices (Freire, 2000). It embraces critical consciousness. Paulo Freire (2000; 2001 & 2003) articulates this in his trilogy: *Pedagogy for the Oppressed* (2003); *Pedagogy of Freedom. Ethics, democracy and civic courage* (2001) and *Education for critical consciousness* (2000).

The notion of social consciousness embodied in critical reflective is very important for the South African context. To date critical research is demonstrating that the project of transformation is failing simply because of the technicist approach to teaching which is encapsulated in Mr Thomas Gradgrind ( a school principal in Dickens (1994))'s words when welcoming a new teacher:

> Now, what I want is Facts. Teach these boys and girls nothing but facts. Facts alone are wanted in life. Plant nothing else, and root out everything else. You can only form the minds of reasoning from animals upon facts: nothing else will be of service to them……..Stick to facts, Sir.

Mr Thomas Gradgrind's methods of teaching are cold and do not embrace social consciousness. His methodology excludes two basic essential elements of teaching such as consideration of the learning environment and the use of personal qualities (Maile, 2015). Maile 's (2015) research shows that, scholars around the world agree that quality teaching takes into account the learning environment and personal qualities. Any teaching excluding these essential elements is likely to fail.

In general, reflection is considered to be a form thinking that involves thoughtful and deep consideration of professional and practical knowledge. This requires constant referencing to an organized network of facts and experiences obtained over time (Stewart, Keegan & Stevens, 2008). Stewart, Keegan and Stevens (2008) tap into the idea of teachers as intellectuals. Applying thoughtful and deep consideration for knowledge requires an attitude towards ideas which is concerned with the link between the idea and material container. Fuller (2005) refers to the process of relationship forming as similar to Plato's believe that ideas are always trying to escape their material containers to return to pristine state of unity. This normally occurs when teachers do not reflect on their teaching their ideas return to the source and become dormant. Instead, by applying reflection teachers engage in some struggle to mediate material containers of ideas with some form and purpose, which in turn will bring more perfection to the practice of teaching.

The idea of mediating the material containers ties well with the notion of social consciousness. It entails that teachers, as intellectuals, need to champion particular ideas to uncover hidden meanings in the material containers (Fuller, 2005). Teachers need to go against conventional boundaries of teaching. Fuller's (2005) caveat invokes Rousseau's (1998) idea of *The Social Contract*, which enjoins teachers to subjugate their desires to the interest of the learners. As organic intellectuals (Gramsci, 1971), teachers are obliged to reflect on socio-economic conditions that have a bearing on the lesson offered. Ideas that form part of the lesson should be linked to the context.

This is similar to Schon's (1987) argument in which he stated that reflective practice is a critical process of refining one's artistry in a specific discipline. Schon recommends reflective practice for beginner teachers to compare their own practices to those of successful practitioners. The question is how do beginner teachers begin to apply reflective practice? Schon (1987) proposes the use of frames to explain how teachers perceive the situations in which they work. Basically the beginner teacher will use the frame to interpret and organize their environment to guide their behavior. The beginner teacher's frame is constituted by his/her past experiences. This is in line with Kennedy's (1991) study in which she examined pre-service and in-service teacher education programmes and discovered that novice teachers strongly believed in their role models, the teachers who they liked while still students at high school. Kennedy find out that no matter what enrichment programme the students are exposed to; they will stick to their role models. Novice teachers will have fewer frames because of their limited experiences. The novice teacher can change their practices for the betterment of their practice through deliberate and mindful acts of self-evaluation. In the case of teacher trainees in my university, teacher trainees have, in their lesson plan, a section that they use daily or weekly to reflect on their lessons. The lesson plans oblige the teacher trainees to use past events to influence future lessons.

They are also trained to reflect during the lesson. This type of reflection happens while the lesson is taking place. In this type of reflection, the teacher trainee analyzes what they are doing while they are doing it. The teacher trainee needs to have a mental picture of the whole lesson. Like an artist the teacher have a complete picture of the drawing before putting it on paper. The teacher looks into his/her class while teaching and tries to understand what is happening while it is happening. The teacher constantly requires to replay the events of the lesson in his/her mind while teaching (Steffy, Wolfe, Pash & Enz, 2000). To achieve this, the teacher must frame problems subconsciously, generate a hypothesis and immediately test it. Many of our teacher trainees struggle to practice this kind of reflection. Our research demonstrates that this type of reflection requires many years of practice and extensive experience in teaching (Banoobhai, 2011).

Conceptually, critical reflective thinking is skill-driven characterized by teachers seeing themselves as agents of social change (Katz, 2008). Such skills driven individuals will be innovative by infusing their teaching within the social environment. It does not matter where they find themselves (Taggart & Wilson, 2005), such professionals are adaptive.

## Classroom Teaching

Classroom teaching forms part of the broader conceptual framework because an analysis of a complex phenomenon like critical reflective thinking in teaching requires us to reflect on the practice of teaching. Thus, classroom teaching is essential in the assessment of how teachers apply what they have learnt in the theory of teaching. It is in the classroom where we determine how well prepared teachers are for critical reflective thinking. This section reflects on the essential elements of teaching such as instruction, learning environment and personal qualities. Although, I am mindful of the fact that the one-size-fits-all approach will not assist us in establishing how well prepared teachers are for critical reflective thinking, these elements are selected to focus the narrative and discourse on teacher preparedness, and to apply critical reflective thinking. I have taken Korthagen 's (2004) caution regarding the fact that the context is posing a serious challenge to one-size-fits-all approach.

Furthermore, the Department of Education (2005b) identified teaching and learning conditions as being not conducive for ideal teaching. Similarly, the Department of Education (2007) acknowledges in the *National Policy Framework for Teacher Education and Development in South Africa*, that teaching is complex. The Department is of the view that the complexity of teaching is exacerbated by the context in which teaching takes place. Hence it must be considered that teachers work under extremely complex conditions largely debilitated by remnants of apartheid. The Department also recognizes that the constantly changing policies needed to bring about change in education increases the complexity of teaching. Morrow (2007: 28) also is of the view that

> Our schooling system is far from healthy conditions…in some regions and sectors, the system is close to total collapse.

I am not under the illusion that classroom teaching happens under ideal teaching situation with small teacher-learner ratio, with all learners having textbooks, desks, etc. My conception of classroom teaching is that it is an activity guided by the intention to promote learning. To some the use of the word intention will represent a copout, and a *laizes faire* approach allowing chaos to prevail in the classroom (Morrow, 2007). This is a problem of learning to teach in developing context. Many theories of what constitute excellent teaching will have no application in context with limited resources. Both teaching materials and infrastructure of schools are important conditions of determine success in teaching (Kruijer, 2010). Kruijer (2010) argues that when this conditions are deficient; teachers are likely not able to apply critical reflective teaching. To navigate a middle path, we can use Halmos, Moise and Piranian 's (1975) assertion that teaching is an art. If we regard teaching as an art, we will allow for teachers' creativity and improvisation which will require an open-ended instrument used for assessment of classroom teaching. Such an approach does allow replication. Consequently, the purpose of this research will be defeated. This will risk the disposition of the discourse.

In a report classified as a benchmark study entitled *Schools that work. Report to the Minister of Education*, Christie, Buttler and Potterson (2007) demonstrate that despite precarious deprivations, disadvantaged schools can still hold quality classroom teaching based on teachers' competence in traditional methods, determination to defeat the disadvantage, regard for school as vital modern institution, subject knowledge of teachers, promoting hard work, leadership motivation and having positive ethos. This argument takes us back to the claim I made earlier that teaching should be linked to the context. If openness is applied in disadvantaged schools, similarly, teachers in well resourced schools should be encouraged to innovate and improvise in their teaching. Therefore, the model for critical reflective teaching should be based on Darling-Hammond and Bransford 's (2005) adaptive experts- which entails teacher preparedness to learn from teaching.

The question remains, what should teachers do to demonstrate preparedness of critical reflective thinking? In other words, what aspects of classroom teaching will demonstrate preparedness of critical reflective thinking? This question is important because answers to it will assist in identifying indicators of preparedness of teachers in critically reflecting on their teaching.

Current practice of critical reflection is not structured to allow for 'dialogical spaces' where teacher trainees share contextualized experiences (van Wyk, 2013) in a nonthreatening environment. Structure constrains as students are forced to provide answers to items provided in the template. A free-style approach allows for individualized reflection. Van Wyk (2013) discovered in his study that even the less confident student prefers an open reflection. This is tantamount to improvisational and context dependent practice which resists the notion stability characterized by techniques, judgment, and robust curriculum. Ball and Forzani (2009) investigated the work of teaching and its challenges, and found out that teaching practice is complicated by improvisation and context bound judgments. In fact, Ball and Forzani (2009) build on Lambert and Graziani 's (2009) argument that improvisation and context bound judgments compels supervisors of teacher trainees to invent from the scratch and tailor their responses to fit a particular student. In this way stable and learnable practices are shoved aside. Rich and scientifically proven ideas about teaching practice which can provide dependable skills and substantial structure are suspended. This deprives teacher trainees valuable knowledge of what experienced teachers know and do. A large body of research on teacher education confirms that learning from experienced teachers provide excellent learning moments (Darling-Hammond, 1998). The work of Ball and Forzani (2009) comes in handy to defend learning from experienced teachers. Ball and Forzani (2009) argues that teaching is not about being oneself. In defending their claim, Ball and Forzani (2009) point out that the locus of the role of the teacher is other people. Acting in the interests of the learner is the core imperative of the role of teaching. This would entail deliberate suspension of the aspects of one's self. Therefore, during teaching practice teacher trainees need to be exposed to unnatural orientation towards learners. Teacher educators need to plough in the minds of teacher trainees that the teacher 's primary responsibility is to see teaching from the perspective of others.

So far arguments raised above reject improvisation and context bound judgments for lowering the quality of teaching practice (Mashava & Chigombe, 2013). Research (Mashava & Chigombe (2013: s139) investigating the effectiveness of teaching practice in its current form concur with this claim in this way:

> Students are deployed to schools whilst they are still raw, not much time is available to fully prepare them for the task ahead of them, the assumption is that they will ultimately learn

This implies that students are send to schools while they have not mastered the theory of teaching. Taking Mashava and Chigombe's (2013) findings seriously we will need to look into the question of when is the right time to deploy students to schools. I am asking this question because preparing teachers to be thoughtful, critical, conscientious and reflective practitioners is complex (Mthiyane & Grant, 2013). Cutting edge research has already informed us that our teachers do not have the right skills and content knowledge to teach. To ask for thinking from teachers, is almost like asking the impossible. To critique and assess oneself is not easy. I deal with the issue of self correction in the discussion below. For now, I want deal with the issue of the right time to deploy students to schools. The emphasis of the right time will help increase the quality of teaching practice (Mashava & Chigombe, 2013; and Oliver & Koeberg, 2013). Current research shows that universities differ with regards to the timing of deployment of student teachers to teach in schools. Our model of teaching practice (Scott, 2013; Kagoda & Katabaro, 2013) is of the allows, in a four teaching programme, for first year students to complete three weeks observation of experienced teachers at work. We are aware that at this stage students are not yet exposed to content knowledge, they lack teaching skills, do not know how to plan, prepare and deliver a lesson. Many are shy to stand in front of a formal classroom.

Returning to the debate on the structure reflection, Chen (2013) utilizes the concept meta-teaching. Chen (2013) argues that provides a framework underpinned by teacher support to reflect on the entire teaching process. Chen departs from the notion that the student is observed as an object by himself in pursuit of self-improvement. In this way the teacher, concludes Chen, teaches him/herself to teach. In Chen 's view reflection is a means for self-correction. The problem with this approach is that one can only self-correct if one knows what is right and what went wrong. For the teacher to self-correct he/she needs knowledge of teaching (Sosibo, 2013). A residual, but very important question is, what must teachers know to self correct themselves? A loud, but very scientific voice (Bloch, 2009; Fleisch, 2008; Taylor and Vinjevold, 1999; Taylor, Muller, & Vinjevold, 2003; Christie, Butler, & Potterton, 2007; Sayed, Kanjee, & Nkomo, 2013, Spaull, 2013 & 2014) reverberates throughout South Africa that teachers cannot teach. Therefore, the idea that they can self-correct does not hold.

To answer the question, what must teachers know to self correct themselves, Ishumi (2013) prescribes medication normally used for chronic illnesses, such as improvement in academic qualifications of teachers and teacher professional development. The problem with chronic illness medication is that it does not cure the disease, but only make the patient to live with the it. Surely, we cannot allow teachers to live with the disease. It is going to cost us immensely. The system may even collapse causing domino effects in other sectors. For teachers to self-correct they need to have sufficient content and conceptual knowledge; must know how to teach their subjects; must know their learners and how they learn; must know how to communicate effectively; must be knowledgeable about the school curriculum; must understand diversity in the South African context; must be able to manage classrooms effectively; must be able to assess learners; and must demonstrate positive work ethic (Maile, 2015).

## Research Strategy

The study seeks to investigate how well prepared teachers are to apply critical reflective thinking in their classroom teaching. Answers on the question of *how* requires the investigator to see the phenomenon unfolding in practice. For this reason, I selected qualitative approaches to investigate the phenomenon. I used observations and interviews to draw data from teacher trainees currently at fourth year level of Tshwane University of Technology Bachelor of Education (B.Ed) undergraduate degree. The choice of fourth-year level students was informed by the fact that at fourth-year level, these students are regarded as fully prepared to take teaching role. Such students have complete subject content knowledge and other subjects for teaching theory such as General Subject Didactics (GSD). The teaching practice forms the main activity with regards to their academic work. All have passed History at Third Year Level and have also passed GSD at Third Year level and were currently registered for GSD 4. All were teaching History at Grade 10 in the different schools they were doing teaching practice. They spend six months in the field practicing under the guidance of mentors based at the school where they are placed. A total of five fourth-year level students were selected from the current registered B.Ed students. At the time of conducting this research the students were out in the field doing teaching practice.

Firstly, I observed the lessons the students prepared according to our lesson plans (see Appendix A for a sample). The lesson plans wee structured in a similar way because the students used the template they received from GSD lecturers. This enhanced the consistency of the evaluation process. The observation utilized a structure drafted according to guidelines provided by specialist such Stuhlman, Hamre, Downer and Pianta's (2015); Estacion, McMahon, Quint, Melamud, and Stephens' (2004); Hora and Ferrare's (2013); and also referred to scholarly works of Randhawa and Fu (1973); Rosenshine (1970); and Cohen (1988).

Secondly, I interviewed the same students I have observed application critical reflective thinking would require talking to them asking them about the lessons I have observed. This strategy enabled me to gain insights into their thinking processes. Before I engaged the students on their reflections on the lessons they offered I gave them feedback on (a) aspects of their lessons in which they performed well, (b) aspects of their lessons in which they have not performed well, and (c) suggestions on how they can improve their performance. Following the feedback, I interviewed them through semi structured interviews using the following questions:

- What has worked and why?
- What has not worked and why?
- How could you have done better?

Data drawn included lesson observations.

The second set of data was the feedback which was structured according to (a) successes, (b) gaps, and (c) improvement suggestions. Similarly, data gathered from interviews was also arranged according to (a) what has worked, (b) what has not worked, and (c) what can be done to improve. I utilized the same structure in presentation of the findings.

## FINDINGS

### Observation

Data gathered through observations was structured according to successes, gaps and suggestions for improvement. I used the same information to give them feedback on the lessons they have prepared.

### Successes

*Lesson plan*

The results from observations show that students use the template given to them during GSD lectures. All the different aspects of the lesson plan are attended to. All the general information section of the lesson plan was competed satisfactorily. Aspects included in this section include date, subject name, name of the school, theme and topic of the lesson.

The students also lesson aims and objectives identified relevant sources and teaching and learning media for the lesson. All the students utilized the introduction and actualization of prior knowledge- which is useful to determine the learners' prior knowledge on the topic they have selected to teach them.

The exposition of the content was carried out very well. In this section the students broke down the topic into sub-headings consistent with the objectives of the lesson. Following this the students were able to develop teaching and learning activities which were delivered according to correct methods. The activities ranged from self-assessment to group assessment and included setting homework for the learners.

## Gaps

My observations during the presentations of lessons I picked up some areas which needs attention. During the presentation students depended a lot on the textbook. It appears that they have not internalized the content. They keep reading from the book without giving explanations demonstrating their own understanding of the content. The lessons were nearly read out to students.

Over dependence on textbook can be an indicator of poor subject content knowledge. It appears the students have not mastered the subject content they were teaching. This is a problem because the students were currently at fourth year level of their studies. This is a final year. As such they are expected to have sound knowledge of their subjects, especially their majors.

With poor content knowledge they also applied insufficient pedagogy. What they taught was not made practical through relevant examples. They presented the lesson as if it had not practical link with the world of the learner. In their lesson plans they had written learners' prior knowledge but that was not functionalized.

Many of our students come from deep rural areas where their ethnic language is used predominantly. In the schooling system English is used a language of learning and teaching. our students encounter difficulties with their lesson presentation, especially if it is entirely presented in English. Some students who find the learners speaking the same language end up presenting their lessons in vernacular.

Another problem experienced by the respondents relates to composure. The students still lacked composure during the presentation of their lessons. Some hide their faces by taking a lot of time writing on the chalk. However, I noticed that some of them have not mastered the skill of writing short notes. Instead they use longer sentences. And they write everything that is contained in their lesson plans. This leads to another problem of lesson plans appearing to be copied pages of the textbooks (Objective overload). They are very long. As such, the students could not finish their lessons on time. Some topics were left hanging because they dealt with many topics in one lesson. With frustrations of poor time management, their confidence declines and end up losing the energy to teach.

In all the lessons I have observed student struggled to make transition from one objective to another. They jumped from one objective sequentially without showing causal link of the objective. Some claim to have used scaffolding strategy, but the evidence gathered during their presentations showed that students moved from one objective to another in staccatos. In most cases they were inflexible. It appears to the scaffolding is only an upward movement. They could not move back and forth especially when students ask questions relating previous objective.

*Suggestions for Improvement*

After the observations of each lesson I immediately held some discussions to give feedback to students. I showed each of the students their weaknesses, and gave some suggestions as to how they can improve their teaching. On the problem of dependence on the textbook I suggested that in their preparation they should master the content by studying it like a student preparing for a test, not just skim reading. I also suggested to them that they should teach in the subject they have majored in, not their minors. They agreed that this would increase their level of confidence. They have said that they lacked composure and confidence in teaching in the subject they have not majored in. This will help solve the problem of poor subject content knowledge. It may increase the depth of presentation and thereby avert the problem of insufficient pedagogy.

The problem of language of teaching is a general problem experienced by many teachers in South Africa. South Africa has eleven official languages spread across the former homelands characterized by ethnic regional preponderance. In the region where this study was undertaken, there is no clear ethnic dominance in terms of language. Consequently, the use of one mother tongue is difficult. As such teachers need to be multi-lingual. However, English is used as a language of teaching in schools and in universities. I suggest that multi-lingualism should be set as a requirement for teacher qualification. With problems of inadequate linguistic development for many ethnic languages, it means that teachers have to master English as many scientific theories contained in the subjects exist in English in South Africa. English remains the major tool teachers must know if they are to be successful teachers.

The problem of making transition from one objective to another can be averted by first, mastering the content of the subject. In other words, teachers need to know the subject they are teaching. They must have sound conceptual knowledge which will enable them to move ideas between concepts.

**Interviews**

During interviews I focused specifically on the reflection part of the lesson plan. Teacher reflection forms the last part of the lesson plan. Students complete this section immediately after completing their lesson presentation. Normally, they will have the discussion of their lessons with their mentors. But this time I came in to interview them, and the results are presented as follows:

## What has Worked

*Learning the Theory of Teaching*

From the interviews the students tend to appreciate the opportunity of being trained in the theory of teaching before they go on teaching practice. Hence Student A stated that:

> when I came to this university I first enrolled for engineering, but I failed my first year and lost interest in the course. The following year changed to teaching. I started from first year and was introduced to different theories of teaching. Coupled with this, was observations we did at first year and micro teaching we did from second year till fourth year. This training gave me a sound background as to what a teacher needs to do.

It seems initial training in the theory of teaching works better for the student. It gives the students opportunity to familiarize themselves with the nitty-gritty's of teaching. it appears that students are comfortable with doing observations at first year level because they are not yet introduced to strategies of teaching. It appears they will not what to do in the classroom. In support of this view Student C argued that:

> imagine if one was required to teach at first year level. That was going to be a disaster. I would not know which methods to use in teaching.

Similarly, Student E said:

> at first year level I will not know the content. I do not think the knowledge I gained from high school is enough. The problem is that at school we used rote learning. We studied to pass not to teach others. A teacher needs to have in-depth knowledge about the subject he is teaching. I support the idea of doing teaching in practice from second year level.

In the same vein, Student B said:

> the strength of the idea of doing teaching in practice from second year level is that with micro-teaching one will have gained thorough knowledge of teaching. Because in micro-teaching our peers assess us

and our mentors give us constructive criticism. At this level the classroom is simulated and one faces people one is familiar with. This assisted in building my confidence.

From these statements a lesson that can be drawn is that previous experience has an impact in teaching practice. Students apply what they experienced before. The experience ranges from learning at university and the role model one had while still at school. Student D said:

> I have always loved teaching. Teaching was my first choice. I was inspired by my History teacher. That man knew the subject. He presented it in such a way that every student understood it. He used everyday student experiences to make examples.

Student D continued to confirm the importance of previous experience by saying that:

> I was lucky when I enrolled for history at this university I found a lecturer who uses the same style as the teacher who taught me history at high school. I modeled my teaching according to my role models. Every time I am in the classroom I imagine myself as my heroes.

### The Lesson Plan

Some students find the idea of being provided with a lesson plan working. Their reflections asserted the need for lesson plan. Student D said:

> the idea of being provided with the lesson plan works very well for. It helps narrow the focus of the lesson. In the absence of a lesson plan it is possible to present disjointed ideas and students will not know what is important and what is not. The whole teaching time will be lost.

Student A supported Student D by saying that:

> the lesson plan is like a compass. It gives direction during the lesson. It is important in history which is full of contradictions and contestations. Imagine a situation where learners are allowed to ay what ever comes into their mind. Classrooms will be turned into chaos.

## Placement in a School of One's Choice

Recently our university changed policy with regards to placement of students for teaching practice. Previously students chose schools that they wanted to do teaching practice. The new policy requires that the students choose from the list developed from functioning schools. During the interviews this theme emerged out of the frustrations students experienced with the change. Student C argued that:

> the problem with choosing a school from the university list is that one 's choice is limited. Schools from my area are not classified functional. I have to choose schools from very far with cultural and language difference. I struggle to make examples in the learner's language. Sometimes I feel teaching is difficult. Just image, I have to learn a new language to serve my learners with distinction. And that is a problem.

Similarly, Student B lamented that:

> language is a problem. In may life I have not used English for the entire forty-five minutes. I struggle to make examples. Some of my translations are very bad. I hear that you say my lesson had many gaps. You mist understand I come from a different context. As such contextualizing the lesson was problem. I cannot use the learner's prior knowledge.

## Having the Right Mentor

Some students agree that having a mentor is useful. They feel that they learn a lot from the mentors. These mentors are experienced teachers based on the school of the student's choice. The mentors are given a workshop on different aspects of teaching practice by the Teaching Practice Office. Student B said that:

> my struggles with the context were solved by the mentor. He knows the school and the villages around the school. He has a good sense of what learners do in their culture and how they express some concepts linguistically. He is very useful.

## What has not Worked

On the idea of utilizing learners' prior knowledge students struggled to find the right to find appropriate examples to support topics selected from the textbooks. It appears this problem happen because students do not share the same cultural environment as their students. The issue of cultural difference has serious impact on conceptual formation for students. Student E reveals that:

> when I entered the classroom I knew immediately that it was not going to be easy for me. I speak a different language and the learners speak a different language. Even though my language group Bantu languages, my language belongs to the Nguni group. Culturally Nguni people will not find difficulty with AmaZulu, AmaXhosa, AmaSwati, and AmaNdebele. The school where I chose to be placed is dominated by Sotho group comprising of Bapedi, Batswana and Basotho with a mix of BaTsonga and VhaVenda. As such my context and theirs differed enormously. So I stuck to the textbook.

Similarly, Student C agreed that:

> I also experienced a problem with cultural difference. I know that my job requires me as a teacher to reach out to learners. I know I am not supposed to pummel learners with my cultural beliefs and values. I think a successful teacher will have to make an effort to, ethnologically, understand the lesson according to the life-world of the child.

Furthermore, Student B pointed out that:

> when I teach I look at the facial expression of the learners. I can see when they are frustrated. This time it was clear that I was alone. The learners appear to have no clue of what I was talking about. I could feel that if I was using their language they will be enthusiastic about the lesson.

Student E added that:

> in my preparations I struggled to find correct translation in the language of the learners. As such my examples remained in English, and this was a problem to many children.

Some students do not like the idea of a lesson plan. They regard as limiting to their creativity. They feel bottled up by the lesson plan lacking flexibility. When I ask them as to what other things would they consider necessary for a lesson but not catered for by the lesson plan, Student A said:

> I have a problem with the lesson plan. It puts one's ideas in boxes which one has to fill as if that is the only knowledge. We need to acknowledge that there are many sides to a story. The plan has no room for contradictions and contestations forming the core of history.

In the same vein, Student E argues that:

> learners should be introduced to other ideas. As history teacher I am forced to teach the things that I do not believe in. For example, why would I teach about Ghandi, he is hero in India but in South Africa his statements reflect discriminatory tendencies against black. And this is hidden in history. We have our own heroes. They should form part of history.

Students showed over dependence on textbook. When I asked why they read from textbooks frequently, Student A argued that:

> "I think the whole idea of reading textbooks is not bad. Learners need to know where to find the information and hear the teacher reading some of the difficult terms aloud. History has many difficult words. I assist them by reading. I think what is not working is when I read all the time. In think one needs a proper mix.

Furthermore, Student B concurs that:

> when learners lack textbooks I know that they will not have any chance of seeing the words I have used in the lesson. I read aloud to give them a sense of the sound of the word and I also write the word in the chalkboard. However, the problem is that one keeps doing that all that time. That is why it not working.

Those who did not like the idea of mentors, seem to have discouraged by poor professionalism demonstrated by the mentors. The students argue that they have nothing to learn from their mentors. Student D said:

> at the school where I ma doing teaching practice I have no mentor. On paper I have, but in practice I have none. This teacher who is supposed to be my mentor is absent on many occasions. When he is present he bunks classes. Learners are complaining. I tried to attend to my learners

and he is now accusing me of turning his learners against him. We do not like each other.

And Student A concur that:

my mentor does do her job well. She does not accompany me to class. Since I started teaching I have taken over everything about the subject. I teach and assess. She does nothing.

Furthermore, Student E said:

my mentor is very old. When I request him to assist me with forms for Integrated Quality Management System (IQMS) he refuses and gives an excuse that he is old, so IQMS is for young people. He is just waiting for his pension. He poses not threat to my marks. He just gives me higher marks.

*What can be Done*

Generally, the findings reveal a complex problem of disjuncture between theory and practice. What students learn from teacher education programs seems to have dissonance with realities prevailing in schools. Problems of theory not linked with practice, and practice weakly grounded on theory have always been there. To bridge the sterile relationship universities, need to make knowledge useful (Du Pre', 2009) by opening program knowledge to accommodate excluded episteme (Morrow, 2007). Drawing expert knowledge from role models may be one of the initial steps in the accommodation of excluded knowledge.

## Discussion

Existing theory (Darling-Hammond & Bransford, 2005; Kennedy, 1991; Morrow, 2007; Schon, 1987) on teaching teaches us that learning to teach is difficult. These researchers argue that teaching is complex phenomenon. For our South African context, Morrow s' (2007) provide an excellent guideline. Morrow argues that judging teaching in South Africa is a difficult process. The difficulty is compounded by inequalities in resource endowments permeating the schooling system. No matter how best the preparation can be, teachers are paralyzed by resource deficiencies. Some teachers have to teach without proper sanitation, with no roof over their heads, with no books, etc. such conditions are insurmountable for novice teachers. The novice teachers are grounded in the theory of teaching, which has no room for deviations. The contextual deficiencies seem to affect many teachers, including the experienced ones.

The dynamic elements of teaching also affect teaching practice. Since 1994 there has been a barrage of changes affecting teachers in the area of the curriculum. Teaching is longer the same. The new curriculum introduced new skills which old teachers have limited knowledge of. The new curriculum requires learner-centered approaches and a new content that promotes progressive ideas. For old teachers to be familiar with the new curriculum they will need to be trained intensively. New teachers have the advantage of probably being trained in the new curriculum changes. The negative relationship between teacher trainees and their mentors is probably affected by the knowledge gap that exists between them. The mentors may probably loose confidence to advice the trainees on aspects of teaching- an area they have limited knowledge of.

Kennedy (1991) writes on the effects of role models on teacher trainees. Kennedy's (1991)research reveals that teacher trainees emulate their role models despite the scientific knowledge passed on to them during theory of teaching classes. Depending on whether the role model was good or not, the trainee will still teach in the same way they have been taught. Research needs to tap into this to improve the theory, because as I have indicated no theory can best provide all knowledge about any phenomenon.

Challenges emerging from the context of teaching, should be taken seriously. Korthagen (2004) has studied the characteristics of excellent teachers and found that teachers who comply to the context are successful. Context can make or break teaching. Teaching should capture the reality of everyday life (Berger & Luckmann, 1991). In this way teachers will show social consciousness alluded to earlier. Accommodating contextual imperatives in the lesson plan requires in-depth preparation strategies that are not only based on textbook knowledge, but also researched and mediated knowledge arrived at through interaction with parents, peers and the environment (Du Plessis, Conley & Du Plessis, 2012 and De Jager, 2014)

## REFERENCES

Azeem, M. (2011). The problems of prospective teachers during teaching practice. In *Academic Research International, Vol. 1, Issue 2, September 2011*, 308-316.

Ball, D.L., and Forzani, F.M. (2009). The work of teaching and the challenge of teacher education. In *Journal of Teacher Education, Vol.60, No.5,* 497-511.

Banoobhai, M. (2011). *Teacher education for critical reflective classroom practice: A qualitative case study.* Unpublished Doctorate in Education Thesis. Tshwane University of Technology.

Bates, A.W. (2015). *Teaching in a digital age.* Toronto: Ryerson University Press.

Beck, U., Giddens, A., and Lash, S. (1994). *Reflexive modernization. Politics, tradition and aesthetics in the modern social order.* Oxford: Blackwell.

Berger, P., and Luckmann, T. (1991). *The social construction of realiy. A treatise in the sociology of knowledge.* London: Penguin.

Bloch, G. (2009). *The toxic mix. What's wrong with South Africa's schools and how to fix it.* Cape Town: Tafelberg.

Bunting, I. (1994). *A legacy of inequalities. Higher Education in South Africa.* Cape Town: UCT Press.

Chen, X. (2013). Meta-teaching: Meaning and strategy. In *Africa Education Review, Vol.10 Supplement 1,* s63-s74.

Christie, P., Butler, D., and Potterton, M. (2007). *Schools that work. Report to the Minister of Education.* Pretoria: Department of Education.

Cohen, D.K. (1988). *Teaching practice: Plus Ca change. Issue paper 88-3.* Washington, D.C.: Office of Educational Research and Improvement.

Council on Higher Education. (2013). *A proposal for undergraduate curriculum reform in South Africa: The case for a flexible curriculum structure. Report of the task team on Undergraduate Curriculum Structure.* Pretoria: CHE.

Easton, L.B. (2008). From professional development to professional learning. Teaching a developing profession. In *Phi Delta Kappan.* June Edition. 755-761.

Darling-Hammond, L., and Bransford, J. (eds). (2005). *Preparing teachers for a changing world: What teachers should learn to be able to do.* San Frascisco: Jossey-Bass.

Darling-Hammond, L. (1998). Teachers and teaching: Testing policy hypotheses from a national commission report. In *Educational Researcher, Vol.27, No.1, (January-February, 1998),* 5-15.

De Clerq, F.,and Shalem, Y. (2014). Teacher knowledge and professional development. In F., Maringe and M., Prew (eds). *Twenty years of education transformation in Gauteng . 1994 to 2014. An independent review.* Johannesburg: Gauteng Department of Education.

De Jager, T. (2014). *General Subject Didactics.* Pretoria: Van Schaik.

Department of Education. (2007). *The National Policy Framework for Teacher Education and Development in South Africa.* Pretoria: Department of Education.

Department of Education. (2005a). *Report of the Ministerial Committee on Teacher Education. A national framework for teacher education.* Pretoria: Government Printers.

Department of Education. (2005b).*Teachers for the Future. Meeting teacher shortages to achieve education for all.* Pretoria: Government Printers.

Dickens, C. (1994). *Hard times.* London: Penguin.

Doll, W.E. (1993). *A post-modern perspective on curriculum.* New York: Teachers College Press.

Du Plessis, P., Conley, L., and Du Plessis, E. (2012). *Teaching and learning in South African schools.* Pretoria: van Schaik.

Du Pre', R. 2009. The place and role of Universities of Technology in South Africa. Bloemfontein: South African Technology Network.

Estacion, A., McMahon, T., Quint, J., Melamud, B., and Stephens, L. (2004*).  Conducting classroom observation in First Things First Schools. MDRC Working paper on Research Methodology.* June 2004.

Fleisch, B. (2008). *Primary education in crisis. Why South African school children underachieve in reading and mathematics.* Kenwyn: Juta.

Forrester, R. (2002). *A theory of History.* Available URL: http//:www.paradise.net.nz/Rochelle/ Date visited: 20 June 2015.

Freire, P. (2003). *Pedagogy for the Oppressed.* New York: Continuum.

Freire, P. (2001) *Pedagogy of Freedom. Ethics, democracy and civic courage.* New York: Rowan and Littlefield

Freire, P. (2000). *Education for critical consciousness.* New York: Continuum.

Fuller, S. (2005). *The intellectual.* Toronto: Penguin.

Gramsci, A. (1971). *Selections from prison notebooks.* London: Lawrence and Wishart.

Halmos, P.R., Moise, E.E., and Piranian, G. (1975). The problem of learning to teach. In the *American Mathematical Monthly, Vol. 82. No.5 (May, 1975),* 466-476.

Hora, M.T., and Ferrare, J.J. (2013). *A review of classroom observation techniques in postsecondary settings. WCER Working Paper No. 2013-1,* February 2013.

Kagoda, A.M., and Katabaro, J. (2013). Funding teaching practice in two east Arican universities: its influence on the behavior and practices of a supervisor. In *Africa Education Review, Vol.10 Supplement 1,* s117-s133.

Katza, S.J. (2008). Towards a new history of teacher education: a view from critical pedagogy. In *American Educational History Journal, Vol.35 (1),* 41-49.

Kennedy, M.M. (1991). Some surprising findings on how teachers learn to teach. In *Educational Leadership, November 1991,* 14-17.

Korthagen, F.A.J. (2004). In search of the essence of a good teacher: towards a more holistic approach in teacher education. In *Teaching and Teacher Education, Vol.20*.pp.77-97.

Kraak, A. (1999). Competing education and training policy discourses: A 'systemic' versus 'unit standard' framework. In J Jansen, and P. Christie. (eds). *Changing curriculum. Studies on outcomes-based Education in South Africa.* Kenwyn: Juta.

Kruijer, H. (2010). *Learning how to teach. The upgrading of unqualified primary teachers in Sub-Saharan Africa. Lessons from Tanzania, Malawi, and Nigeria.* Switzerland: Education International.

Kuhn, T.S. (1970). *The structure of scientific revolutions. 2nd edition.* Chicago: University of Chicago Press.

Lambert, M., and Graziani, F. (2009). Instructional activities as a tool for teachers' and teacher educators' learning. In *Elementary School Journal, Vol. 109, No.5,* 491-509.

Maile, S. (2015*). Essential characteristics of excellent teachers as determinants of quality education.* Forthcoming.

Mashava, R., and Chigombe, A. (2013). Teaching practice and the quality dilemma: Lessons from experiences of student teachers in Masvingo Province. In Africa *Education Review, Vol.10 Supplement 1,* s134-s148.

Mckay, V., and Romm, N. (1992). *People's education in theoretical perspectives. Towards the development of critical humanist approach.* Johannesburg: Maskew Miller Longman.

McLennan, A. (1995). Into the future: restructuring the public service. In P., Fitzgerald, A., McLennan, & B. Munslow. (eds). *Managing sustainable development in South Africa.* Cape Town: Oxford University Press.

Medley, D.M., and Crook, P.R. (1978). Research in teacher competency and teaching tasks. *Theory into practice, Vol. xix* (4), 294-301.

Morrow, W. (2007). *Learning to teach in South Africa.* Cape Town: HSRC.

Mthiyane, S.E., and Grant, C. (2013). Re-imagining novice teachers as leaders in building a community of educational leaders and researchers. In *Africa Education Review, Vol.10 Supplement 1,* s207-s225.

O'Connell, J. (2013). The education quality improvement partnership programme: A whole school development framework. In Sayed, Y., Kanjee, A., & Nkomo, M., (eds). *The search for quality education in post-apartheid South Africa. Interventions to improve learning and teaching.* Cape Town: HSRC.

Oliver, H., and Koeberg, J. (2013). Quality assurance: Adapting SERVQUAL to measure the perceived quality of pre-service teachers' teaching practice. In *Africa Education Review, Vol.10 Supplement 1,* s183-s206.

Randhawa, B.S., and Fu, L.L.W. (1973). Assessment and effect of some classroom environment variables. In *Review of Educational Research, Vol.43, No.3 (Summer, 1973,* 303-321.

Rosenshine, B. (1970). Evaluation of classroom instruction. In *Review of Educational Research, Vol.40. No. 2 (April, 1970),* 279-300.

Rousseau, J. (1998). *The social contract.* London: Wordsworth.

Sayed, Y and Kanjee, A. (2013). Overview of education policy change in post-apartheid South Africa. In Y., Sayed, A., Kanjee, & M. Nkomo (eds). *The search for quality education in post-apartheid South Africa. Interventions to improve learning and teaching.* Cape Town: HSRC.

Sayed, Y., Kanjee, A., & Nkomo, M., (eds). (2013). *The search for quality education in post-apartheid South Africa. Interventions to improve learning and teaching.* Cape Town: HSRC.

Sayed, Y. (2004). The case of teacher education in post-apartheid Soth Africa: politics and priorities. In L. Chisholm. (ed). *Changing class: Education and social change in post-apartheid South Africa.* Cape Town: HSRC.

Schon, D. (1987). The reflective practitioner: how professional think in action. New York: Basic Books.

Schon, D. (1983). *The reflective practitioner: how professional think in action.* New York: Basic Books.

Scott, A. (2013). Teaching practice at the University of Namibia: Quo Vadis? In *Africa Education Review, Vol.10 Supplement 1,* s149-s158.

Sosibo, L. (2013). Accountability in teacher education: Positioning pre-service teachers as evaluators of their performance. In *Africa Education Review, Vol.10 Supplement 1,* s159-s182.

Spaull, N. (2013). Assessment results don't make sense. In *Mail and Guardian,* December 13 to 19 2013, p.9.

Steffy, B.E., Wolfe, M.P., Pash, S.H. and Enz, B.J. (2000). *Life cycle of the career teacher.* Thousand Oaks: Corwin Press.

Stuhlman, M.W., Hamre, B.K., Downer, J.T., and Pianta, R.C. (2015). *A practitioner's guide to conducting classroom observation: What the research tells us about choosing and using observational systems.* Virginia: University of Virginia.

Taggart, G.L., and Wilson, A.P. (2005). *Promoting reflective thinking in teachers: 50 action strategies.* New Delhi: Sage.

Taylor, N., Muller, J. and Vinjevold, P. (2003). *Getting schools working. Research and systematic school reform in South Africa.* Johannesburg: Pearson Education.

Taylor, N., and Vinjevold, P. (1999). *Getting learning right. Report of the President's Education Initiative Project.* Johannesburg: JET.

Tosh, J. (2010). *The pursuit of History. Aims methods and new directions in the study of modern History. $5^{th}$ Edition.* London: Pearson.

Van Wyk, M.M. (2013). Using blogs as a means of enhancing reflective teaching practice in open distance learning ecologies. In Africa *Education Review, Vol.10 Supplement 1,* s47-s62.

Zepeda, B.P., and Aviles, H.H. (2008). A reflective teaching practice experience: case study. In *Memorias del iv foro nacional ce studios en lengaus (Fonael 2008),* 338-352.

CHAPTER 7

## Breaking Online Tradition: Journaling as Authentic Interaction, Reflective Practice, and Crystallization of Self

*Marianne Vander Dussen & Michelann Parr*

Graduate-level work, particularly in an online setting, is lonely work. Even with a strong social support system, the fiercely intellectual and cerebral nature of graduate studies entails many solitary ventures into the *border country* (McCormack, 2014), where the comfort of the familiar and the discomfort of the unknown intersect. Coupled with a lack of face-to-face contact, student-instructor interactions are most often filtered through digital media, whether by email, online discussion boards, or Skype, requiring additional effort and outreach by the instructor in order to establish a teacher presence (Holzweiss, Joyner, Fuller, Henderson, & Young, 2014). Notwithstanding the benefits of collaboration in online learning, we argue that there is room for a more private space between student and instructor, where each has room to negotiate previously-held assumptions in an effort to further develop practice, understand theory, and perhaps shift paradigms. In this way, journaling serves as private inquiry, reflective thought, and crystallization, where thoughts and ideas can be tested, explored, and rehearsed prior to putting them out there into the public sphere. In the graduate course, *Meanings of Literacy: Theory into Practice*, the context within which this inquiry took place, journals served as ongoing, one-on-one interactions between student and instructor; they allowed us to chart our progress through the course, crystallize our personal conceptualizations of literacy, and develop a metacognitive awareness of ourselves as writers, interpreters, collaborators, and members of an academic community.

To provide a sincere snapshot of the experience of journaling as an inquiry-based, reflective practice, we offer two perspectives: that of student (Marianne), and that of instructor (Michelann), who together built a relationship of trust and support that expanded the conduit of learning, empowering Marianne to build her reflective practice in preparation for a lifetime of academic research, while providing Michelann with insight and awareness into her students' lives to provide them with the support they needed to transcend their isolation and truly feel a part of their online learning community. Keeping our key learnings in front of us at all times, we have attempted to capture our questions, intents, purposes, impressions, and reflections. At the conclusion of the chapter, we offer a set of conditions that can enhance relationship-building and interaction through journaling in a predominantly online course.

## The Student Perspective

I began the Meanings of Literacy course in my first term of graduate studies, and so my journal captured and chronicled the intensity of my transition period from the collegiality and comfort of teacher's college into the unsettling isolation of the Master's program. As a student who thrives in conversation-based learning, I knew that I needed to forge some kind of connection with my instructors to ensure my constant and consistent engagement with the material. Meanings of Literacy provided that opportunity, and since it was one of the first graduate level courses I took, I threw myself into every element of the course wholeheartedly by engaging with both my colleagues and instructor in consistent and ongoing dialogue, reading and re-reading our assigned articles, and diving headfirst into the journaling component, wanting to prove my dedication not only to my instructor, but also to myself. As the journals spiraled recursively and allowed me to reflect upon course-specific learning, starting the program with journaling ensured that reflective practice became habitual and interconnected to not just the course, but the entirety of the program and representative of my supervisee relationship with Michelann.

### The Romantic Expectations of Graduate Work

Prior to beginning my studies at the graduate level in the Schulich School of Education at Nipissing University, I had somewhat antiquated projections of what my learning experience would look like. Even though I was fully aware that our graduate program was entirely online, I pictured my future learning through a nostalgia-infused filter; I pictured myself surrounded by stacks of books, wearing cozy wool knits as I worked late into the night with a steaming mug of tea, blissfully content as I lived out my dream of being an academic. Completely unaware that I had romanticized the rigors of graduate work due to popular representations in film and books; I was shocked and devastated by the intense loneliness I felt after only one week of online learning. As a full-time student on scholarship, I had little outside interaction, and had unwittingly placed myself under house arrest.

## The Realities of an Online Course

Having attended teacher's college, the year prior, I sorely missed the daily interactions and social aspect of learning from my peers. Online conversations felt stilted and overly formal by comparison. My graduate level colleagues were scattered across the globe, and all of us were doing our best to tailor our language to become fluent in academic-ese. Even worse, I had completely underestimated the value that I intrinsically placed on having my instructor there in person, and had not yet come to understand the technological *teacher presence*, meaning the design and facilitation of my courses (Holzweiss et al., 2014), and the strong yet not immediately visible impact it would have on each of my courses.

## The Good, the Bad, and the Ugly

Meanings of Literacy had been strongly recommended to me by Michelann, who served not only as my faculty advisor for the program, but also as chair of graduate studies and the supervisor for my graduate assistant work. Through a few in-person meetings, I'd been able to establish a rapport, but her position as professor, advisor, and supervisor made me want to be on my best behavior. In person, I tried to be tactful, professional, and confident, even though beneath my carefully polished veneer, I was wrestling with Imposter Phenomenon (Clance & Imes, 1978) and strong feelings of isolation. Alone, with my soulless computer as my constant and only companion, I latched onto my journal as a way to build an authentic connection with not only my instructor, but myself. I promised myself that I would document the good, the bad, and the ugly. I'd write small observations of my work habits, discuss my own shortcomings, and be held accountable to keeping my reflection momentum going by knowing that Michelann would be privy to it all.

## The Anger. The Loneliness. The Disconnect

Early in the course, I wrote several frustrated, dark, angry passages. I cited my own inability to read highly academic language, my loneliness, my sense of disconnect between myself and my peers. But as time went on, I could trace the journey by reflecting upon my journals. In September 2014, approximately four weeks into my studies, I wrote:

> I don't regret journaling during those dark times to remember just how awful and yucky it is, while acknowledging that I am also in control and can definitely shift towards a more positive mindset.

As always, Michelann was there, and had been there from the very beginning, who offered this in reply:

> Sometimes, we need to confront these doubts and certainties head on. There are many researchers who discuss writing our way out of the darkness (Max Van Manen (2002) being one); it is important that we have an outlet, somewhere to go with our thoughts, somewhere to look up, look out, look in, look around.

### The Key Patterns

The concept of *looking out, looking in* kept re-emerging, partially as a result of the research Michelann and I were conducting in the field of family engagement. As outlined by Pushor (2011), the practice of checking one's assumptions at the door could lead to more beneficial and authentic engagement with families. Applied to the Meanings of Literacy course, I used my journal as a way to check my own assumptions, challenge my own preconceptions, and look at the roots of how they formed. I used family stories, personal anecdotes, and steeped them heavily in both emotion and criticality to gain access to both the rawness and realness of the place in which they originated, while retaining a level of detachment to analyze the emerging patterns of learning which had begun to unfold.

*A meaningful connection.* The first was that through my journal, I had started to build a meaningful connection to my instructor. Since there were no other students present, I was able to write informally, share my deepest anxieties and boldest ideas, and display personal artifacts and memories without fear of condemnation or judgment. In my mind, Michelann had merged with my journal, and her gentle nudging and questioning helped me to cement and feel confident with my unique theory of literacy. In a state of both vulnerability and safety, the journals allowed for a transcendence of not only life experience into personal literacy theory, but for a repositioning of professor and student into more equal partners in learning. Although there was an inherent power dynamic in play (she did, after all, have to give me a grade for my efforts), I felt more connected, both to the course and to who she is as a person. Just as the journals had broken open my shell and allowed my repressed insecurities to breathe, they had allowed me to glimpse a more human, approachable guide and mentor, who has remained a source of academic strength and professional inspiration ever since.

*Crystallization.* The second pattern I found was the notion of *crystallization* (Janesick, 2000; Richardson, 1994). Unlike the word *transformation*, its more academically fashionable counterpart, crystallization does not mean a metamorphosis of ignorance to knowledge, but rather acknowledging that the struggle has, is, and will always be there, and is a part of the process as the learning spreads outwards. Through reflective practice, I gained insights into each and every one of these micro-conflicts between self and other (theory, reading, personal challenge, etc.) while being able to observe the crystallization of epistemological awareness and the formation of an identity as a student, teacher, and researcher, each composed of thousands of smaller moments of coalescence and understanding. I could look back into my journals and see glimpses of what eventually became my personal philosophy of literacy, the trend itself visible in the rearview mirror yet invisible at the time.

## The Enlightenment

At the end of the term, I drew from the periods of despair to realize how it had transformed into a personal statement of literacy, as well as a manifesto of citizenry that reflected so many of my personal beliefs that I had fleshed out in the context of literacy:

> Earlier in the term, I found myself overwhelmed by the sheer magnitude of oppression and injustice that exists in the world. Today, I understand the responsibility I have to resist. It's what my mentors do, it's what many citizens of the City of North Bay are doing, and it's what many brave people around the world are doing. But Eva Olsson, a Holocaust survivor and public speaker, summed it up the best: beware of the bystander. I don't have the right to bemoan the intensity of the challenge ahead of me, brave women fought for my right to have a voice and it's my duty to exercise it and use it to push for equity. Racism, sexism, religious intolerance, greed, are all alive and well and thriving, and I must do everything in my power to help my students see the lines of power, control, domination and assimilation, and help them find ways to challenge this if they so choose.

I realized that there is a difference between pure testimony and authentic reflection, particularly within a contemporary context of ubiquitous life documentation occurring through social media. If a journal entry, photograph, or clever one-liner is the raw data, then it is the reflection itself that allows for a greater pattern to be viewed, critiqued, and understood (Boud, 2001). Recursive spiraling back through the darkness, through the documented confusion, allows for the learning to be propelled further in a controlled, directed manner.

As I learned to use my reflections to become more intentional and mindful with my habits, contemplations, and decisions, my ability to work in an academic setting became stronger. Loneliness became the necessary gateway through which I could explore and learn to navigate the deepest recesses of my mind and all its preconceptions, and grow holistically as a student, a researcher, an academic, and a person. Looking inwards and outwards helped me re-conceptualize the chaos of the unknown as fractals in a greater pattern; the more I was aware of it, the better prepared I could be to face new challenges as they barreled towards me.

## THE LETDOWN. THE WAY FORWARD.

When the course ended, I felt somewhat adrift without the anchor of my journal (which had reached 37 pages, single-spaced), so when the time came to begin my thesis work, I began a new one. But something (more specifically, someone) was missing; Michelann. So I invited her again to be a part of the process, using this same strategy to help me experiment with writing strategies, mitigate known factors of distraction, and confront feelings of fear and insecurity head-on. It's a new, updated version of the *border country*, but the reassurance of the journal helps to pre-empt and dismantle obstacles before they have an opportunity to manifest.

## THE INSTRUCTOR PERSPECTIVE: BREAKING ONLINE TRADITION

### The Context and the Purpose

The course was *Meanings of Literacy: Theory into Practice*. The context was online, a course that brings together students from all over the world, drawing on unique contexts to explore literacy, diverse experiences of students and instructor, and multiple conceptualizations of literacy. Inquiry and collaboration extended over twelve weeks, each with a different theme including literacy's past, present, and future; measurement and assessment of literacy; situated and localized literacies; child, adult, and youth literacies; family and community literacies; Aboriginal literacies; new and old literacies. Each theme challenges students to work through assumptions, conceptualizations, perceptions, and often misperceptions; this is not always a comfortable journey.

## The Purpose

I had strong memories of engaging in conversation with my self and my colleagues and supervisors throughout my own graduate journey – just like it was yesterday, I could remember the impact of a very well placed comment, question, even a raised eyebrow (Richardson, Parr, & Campbell, 2008). I also had Dewey (1933, 1973), Schön (1983, 1987), and van Manen (2002) reminding me that if I wanted to impact change, I needed to invoke the more personal inquiry and reflective practice, as well as interrogating and discussing with colleagues. My goal was to figure out how to facilitate, with students all over the world, a personal yet dialogic and collaborative experience, much like I had experienced early in my graduate work in a face-to-face setting, where

> Narrative, poetry, snippets of songs, lived experiences, and formal research writing became part of my repertoire, both personally and professionally. Using writing and dialoguing with others as processes of understanding enabled me to explore, experiment, create, and imagine a personal and professional world different than the one in which I was engaged. These realizations freed me to play with words and ideas, talk about them, saving draft after draft so that I could continually revisit my process work, seeing the development of ideas and the nature of my thought processes. (Richardson, Parr, & Campbell, 2008, p. 284)

## The Question

As I sat down to review my syllabus for this session of *Meanings of Literacy*, I wondered whether interactive journals would provide a forum to support students in their exploration of the intensely personal and situated nature of literacy within their localized contexts; essentially, I wanted them to be more comfortable, without vulnerability, agreeing, disagreeing, holding fast to deeply held assumptions, or setting them aside. I had worked with this textual material before as a graduate student, an instructor, and a writer, and I knew that it required a healthy blend of personal inquiry, interrogation, and often, a subtle pressure. This was not always easily accomplished in a public forum grounded in writing, with large numbers of students. Reviewing my course tasks (e.g., discussion boards, team assignments, debates, final paper), I wondered about the benefits of online interactive journaling:

> How might online journaling, as a private space between student and instructor, be beneficial within the context of a predominantly online course? How does journaling add value to collaborative discussions? How will students use their journals if given the freedom to personalize, explore course content in a way less-structured and lower risk than the discussion board? What are the conditions for effective journaling between students and instructor?

Some of the literacy work we do is easily done in a discussion forum or facilitated through team challenges, but some is better left for a more private space where students are free to explore and write their way through the darkness (van Manen, 2002) or confines of their sometimes traditional literacy thinking. Journals, I thought, would allow them to work in their border zone, along the edge of comfort with a significant adult (i.e., instructor) who could poke, push, and prod thinking beyond taken-for-granted assumptions in a relative low-risk environment (Vygotsky, 1978). Perhaps the private space of a journal could act as a bridge between the intensely public spaces of online education, students' situated and localized life experience, and textual interpretation... Perhaps journals would make explicit emotions, life events, personal histories and stories, which could then be used for additional layers of analysis of text and self-development.

## The Assignment

Journals were facilitated through a google document shared only between student and instructor. As a tool of assessment, journals were diagnostic, formative, and summative. Worth 20% of their final grade, a high level of emphasis was placed on reflective practice, upon the melding of contextualized life experience with textual interpretations and peer interactions. Doing so, meant taking a completely individualized approach, a departure from the tradition of online discussion that is largely collaborative and public. Recognizing the complexities of researching with your own students, consent forms were signed, returned to my graduate assistant, and held until final marks were posted. I had no idea who agreed to participate in the inquiry until long after the journals were completed, thereby eliminating possible power imbalances or perceived bias.

Journals were deliberately open-ended as I am a firm believer that students need to do what it takes and take as long as necessary to work their way to understanding. For some, this would mean a poem, for others a picture, for others, a traditional paragraph, for some a page or two; some even experimented with YouTube videos, audio recordings, and web-based bulletin boards. This was all part of the plan – their journals were a way for them to experience in practice what literacy was really all about. I wanted students to see that the literacy work we do in our courses (i.e., reading, writing, speaking, listening, viewing, and representing) is inseparable from our day-to-day living, being, and working. Journaling could serve as a way of being in time and space where they could revisit thoughts, ideas, and a-has; try on new hats and new perspectives in a relatively low-risk forum. Ultimately, my goal was for them to see journaling as wilderness – wide open, only constrained by imagination and my ability to find time and space to just be in its landscape (Brady, 2005).

## The Invitation

For years, I have been a proponent of never asking your students to do something you are unwilling to do yourself. I, too, missed the face-to-face contact with students, the personal interactions, the challenge that some of what they said and did posed for my own practice. For this reason, I decided to engage in the act of writing in much the same way the students did; I made my journal available to students, but they were not required to read, comment, or engage unless of course, there was something they wanted to add to extend or broaden my thinking. One of my initial journal entries gave students a glimpse of who I am as a writer:

> I write easily. It comes from my heart and it heals my soul. Writing is therapeutic for me; it is the one time in my life that I am alone with my thoughts. For all intents and purposes, I write for me – not to be read, not to be reviewed, not to be critiqued, and not to be published. I write because I love to write and it feels good to see thoughts in black and white. I write regardless of where I am or who I am with... I have been known to be in a room full of my kids and not hear a word. Writing for me is solitude; it is a way of letting go of the seeming chaos of life for a moment or two.

In my invitation, I attempted to put students at ease by clearly articulating my expectations, while freeing them to be who they needed to be in this course and life.

## The Unanticipated

What I could not have expected was the incredible reaction I received to these journals... Marianne's 37 page journal was no exception – all students engaged – their journals became a space where they could explore intersections between readings and public spaces, where they could reflect on other readings they were doing and the connections they were making, where they could rant (as I had modeled) about some of what they had experienced in their unique contexts, trying to make sense of the seeming injustice of literacy practices in the world. As did Marianne at the end of our twelve-week block, I felt a let down. I no longer had these snapshots into my students' lives, the ongoing conversations, the insights into what was going on in their worlds. I wondered whether it had all been worth it: my time spent, students' time spent, the daily checking in, the personalized support, the prompts for editing. When I finally received my course evaluations, not only for this course, but for the one that directly followed with almost 70% overlap, one that did not include the journaling component, I saw the value and the merit. I had students talking about how this was something they would continue throughout their degrees – they would incorporate a readings and research journal that would allow them to catalogue their thoughts, ideas, musings, crystallizations, always with an eye on the gems they could use later in the graduate work. In the second course, I heard how very much missed their Meanings of Literacy journal was and how very critical they felt this personal space between faculty and instructor really was.

## The Demands

I cannot close this component without a nod and an acknowledgement of the demands of this type of an approach. I checked in with each student as often as I possibly could, typically two-three times a week. While I may not have always offered a question or comment, I did let them know that I was there, and that the work they were doing was valued. As instructor, I did my best to balance the positive and the negative and I took traditional rules of journaling to heart. I tried to rephrase or ask a question to get at the heart of meaning without marking up too much... but often the nature of graduate level work took over, and I engaged track changes to demonstrate how to fix specific errors in a paragraph. In the end, despite the incredible time commitment, with no limits except those imposed by their imagination, it was worth it. The demands were balanced by the realization of the role that I had played in in shaping and impacting broader conceptualizations of literacy in the lived experiences of these students.

## The Benefits

Although time-consuming, online interactive journaling provided a prime opportunity to bring both Dewey's (1933, 1973) and Schön's (1983, 1987) notions of reflective thought into an online classroom. The nature of the readings and the one-one interaction provided students and instructor many opportunities to feel provoked, confused, and doubtful, always within our zones of proximal development, on the edge of comfort where true learning takes place (Vygotsky, 1978). There were times where both student and instructor waited in anticipation for a response to a tentative interpretation; vulnerabilities and consequences were minimized due to the personal nature of the journal, but this freed students to be a little bolder in their online work. Their words, their thoughts, their ideas all became sites of examination, inspection, exploration, and analysis – they helped to identify various problems (in literacy, these are as diverse as we are), formulate hypotheses or reasons why, and follow up with a plan of action, something they could fix in their practice to make their literacy work more meaningful and relevant. Because the journaling was personal, the benefits were also personal. Some students took a very pragmatic approach to their journals as they used it as almost a reader response journal, whereas others, like Marianne chose to work in the metaphorical border country of theory and practice. Regardless of the purpose each established for their journal, what was very clear was that with the right conditions, interactive online journaling between students and instructor more than meets the requirements of reflective practice established by prominent thinkers in the field (Dewey, 1933, 1973; Schon, 1983, 1987). For me, I found comfort in the explorations of students, I found kindred souls in many students as they articulated their frustrations, and most importantly, I found challenge in a word, in a phrase in a response that forced me back into my own explorations and frustrations. Moving through the experience, reading the diverse responses of students, pushed me back into my own borderland between theory and practice.

## OPTIMIZING THE JOURNAL EXPERIENCE

During our twelve weeks, informed by discussions among ourselves and with other students who willingly agreed to be part of the inquiry, we have discovered some commonalities of experience that establish optimal conditions for journaling in an online course. Each is offered here with research that pulls in to online learning some of what we already know from traditional education, writing, and more recent theories of literacy learning.

## Be Mindful. Be Caring. Be Constructive.

Journaling has long been used in traditional classrooms, and in a wide array of subjects and settings (Andrusyszyn & Davie, 1997). They allow us to articulate experience, emotionality, interpretation, and subjectivity, which can then be viewed as the collective raw data of which our lives are formed (Dewey, 1933). Further, they can allow us to recursively look up, look out, look in, look around, which is ultimately how we define meaning and significance. When we revisit and mine our abstract thoughts and ideas, we can pick some up to polish into jewels of coherent concepts of understanding. In a similar vein, the way in which we curate and communicate these reflections is worthy of critical engagement; different tonal and linguistic journaled interpretations of the same event could lead to wildly divergent conclusions (Bateson, 1993). Fortunately, our musings were given a critical and caring editorial eye in the form our instructor, who could help us catch hidden gems that we may have missed in our initial mining of data.

## Be Open to Individual Differences and Broad Conceptualizations of Literacy

Using multi-literacies (The New London Group, 1996) such as music, poetry, images, and personal connections, our journaling practice was designed to reconcile the meaning in Meanings of Literacy to a grounded, supported, comprehensive theory of literacy in classrooms and the world at large. In order for our connections to be meaningful, we had to establish our own significance through our experiential schema, while laboring under the harsh conditions of solitary study and the discomfort of the border country. We began to view our journals as a way to write through the darkness (van Manen, 2002). We could tunnel our way through with the assurance that our instructor would be there to guide, prod, and expand our thinking.

## Be Vulnerable. Adopt a Spirit of Reciprocity. Never Ask Your Students to do Something You Are Unwilling To Do

Exposing our innermost thoughts, fears, emotions and insights requires a high degree of vulnerability, especially if we are putting them on display to a faceless entity hidden whose comments and suggestions spring forth mysteriously onto our computer screens. While there is a raw power in vulnerability (Brown, 2012), Michelann modeled a spirit of reciprocity, and submitted to us a copy of her journals during our first week of online learning. In openly displaying her own journaling process as a way of rescuing our personal selves from the margins of graduate studies, she made the process of layering experience with academia transparent, helping us reach new understanding on multiple planes. As we followed her example and spiraled through new knowledge before circling back to connect with our previous paradigms, we left remnants of crystallized thought behind in our journals, tracing the path through our struggles, conflicts, and reconciliations.

### Build Relationships. Be There.

Intertwined in this charting was our relationship as student and instructor. Manifested in the form of frequent comments connected to specific journaled insights, our relationship as student and instructor took on a richer, more valuable dimension. As we engaged in each others' learning beyond the public forums of the course discussion boards, our journals acted as facilitators for an authentic and mutually beneficial student-teacher relationship. Buoyed by the concept that our instructor cared about our personal, professional, and academic development, our commitment to delve deeper, both into our readings and the border country of academia, was made possible by our awareness of teacher presence (Holzweiss et al., 2014).

### Consider Logistics

Journaling can easily spiral out of control, particularly if assessment is tied to meeting a specific word limit. As well, while journals can be assessed for reflective thought, they should be viewed as draft writing whereby ideas, thoughts, attitudes, even APA and grammatical structures are being tried on, and therefore, in the spirit of reflective practice are tentative, sometimes requiring action. As instructor, I am now considering allocated specific days of the week to check in with students; this is something I recommend to my teacher candidates as a way to manage journals in the classroom, but it was an oversight in my course. Although, I do wonder whether part of the success was the just-in-time nature of feedback and authentic interaction between students and instructor that did not seem scheduled or obligatory.

### Concluding Thoughts

The success to interactive online journaling is grounded in who you are as student, and who you are as instructor. Indeed, online journaling for us, became very much like reciprocal teaching where each participant has something to add to the mix. Remaining open to new ideas, accepting divergent thoughts, challenging deeply held assumptions in the comfort of our journals opens the doors to greater collaboration in an online community. Authentic meaning-making is intensely personal and contextual; using journals as a means to crystallize significant connections, while sharing these discoveries with our instructor, is rewarding for all parties. Though the physical separation and discomfort of the *border country* is certainly lonely and intimidating work, through our mutual efforts to connect with and through the material to establish meaning and meaningfulness, we successfully mitigated many of the isolating effects of distance education.

## REFERENCES

Andrusyszyn, M., & Davie, L. (1997). Facilitating reflection through interactive journal writing in an online graduate course: A Qualitative Study. *Journal Of Distance Education, 12*(1-2), 103-26.

Armstrong, D. A. (2011). Students' perceptions of online learning and instructional tools: A qualitative study of undergraduate students use of online tools. *Turkish Online Journal Of Educational Technology, 10*(3), 222-226.

Bateson, M. (1993). Composing a life. In C. Simpkinson & A. Simpkinson (Eds.), *Sacred stories: A celebration of the power of stories to transform and heal.* (39-52). San Francisco: Harper Collins.

Boud, D. (2001). Using journal writing to enhance reflective practice. *New Directions For Adult And Continuing Education* (90), 9-17.

Brown, B. (2012). *Daring greatly: How the courage to be vulnerable transforms the way we live, love, parent, and lead.* New York, NY: Gotham Books.

Clance, P.R., & Imes, S.A. (1978). The imposter phenomenon in high achieving women: Dynamics and therapeutic intervention. *Psychotherapy: Theory, Research & Practice* (15) 241-247. doi: 10.1037/h0086006

Dewey, J. (1933). *How we think.* New York, NY: Heath and Co.

Dewey, J. (1973). *The philosophy of John Dewey* (Volumes 1 & 2). John McDermott, Editor. New York, NY: G. P.Putnam's Sons.

Holzweiss, P. C., Joyner, S. A., Fuller, M. B., Henderson, S., & Young, R. (2014). Online graduate students' perceptions of best learning experiences. *Distance Education, 35*(3), 311-323.

Janesick, V. (2000). The choreography of qualitative research design: Minuets, improvisations, and crystallization. In N.K. Denzin & Y.S. Lincoln

(Eds.) *Handbook of qualitative research* (pp. 66–81). Thousand Oaks, CA: Sage Publications.

McCormack, D. (2014). "Trína chéile": Reflections on journaling in the border country of doctoral research. *Studies In The Education Of Adults, 46*(2), 163-176.

Murakami-Ramalho, E., Militello, M., & Piert, J. (2013). A view from within: How doctoral students in educational administration develop research knowledge and identity. *Studies In Higher Education, 38*(2), 256-271.

The New London Group (1996). A pedagogy of multiliteracies: Designing social futures. *Harvard Educational Review, 66*(1), 60-91.

Pushor, D. (2011). Looking out , looking in. *Educational Leadership, 69*(1), 65-68.

Richardson, C., Parr, M., & Campbell, T.(200?). Solitary dissonance and collaborative consonance: Trialogue as a reflective practice that resonates, *Reflective Practice, 9*(2), 281-29.

Richardson, L. (1994). Writing: A method of inquiry. In N.K. Denzin & Y.S. Lincoln (Eds.) *Handbook of qualitative research* (pp. 516–529). Thousand Oaks, CA: Sage Publications.

Schön, D. A. (1983). *The reflective practitioner: How professionals think in action*. NewYork, NY: Basic Books.

Schön, D. A. (1987). *Educating the reflective practitioner*. San Francisco, CA: Jossey-Bass.

van Manen, M. (2002). *Writing in the dark: Phenomenological studies in interpretive inquiry*. London, ON: The Althouse Press.

Vygotsky, L. (1978). *Mind and society.* Cambridge, MA: Harvard University Press.

CHAPTER 8

## Digital Natives as Critically Reflexive Practitioners

*Susan Beierling and James Paul*

> He who knows others is wise; he who knows himself is enlightened.
>
> -Lao Tzu, *(GoodReads, 2015)*

### INTRODUCTION: KNOW THYSELF, REALLY!

"Know thyself" is a most demanding, almost universal, historical and contemporary invocation. The roots of such a demand are traceable both to ancient Western and Eastern thinkers, scholars and educators. Western Modernity's dictum of know thyself is perpetuated through grand narratives mediating how individual and collective knowing, doing and being might be realized. In this case, becoming and being human requires that self-awareness and self-knowledge be constructed procedurally via, more or less, prescriptive, developmental, progressive, and institutional instructive processes. Does Modernity's essential progressive design not demand all human creatures becoming human beings to truly, really and authentically, attend to the ever-present pressing call to show and tell increasing self-awareness and self-knowing? Does not Modernity use institutional schooling, along with the marketplace, culture, family, religion, war-violence, gender, ethnicity and so on, as a training rough-ground upon which evolving perfection-oriented, progressively-driven self and identity construction comes to reflect and represent what normally counts as an authentic human being? Today in a progressively determined economic-science-technological globalizing world, we seem to be evermore consumed by a post human (Hayles, 1999) desire to address our societal inheritances and exceed them in order to achieve an idealized utopian frozen future whereby body and mind, emotion and reason, male and female, and consumptive and productive are perfectly unified amalgams?

> When asked what was the most difficult thing, Thales replied, "To know thyself."
> When asked what was easiest, he replied, "To give advice."
>
> (Know Thyself, 2015)

There is seemingly a universally specific human need to explore, explain and explicate the stealthy nature of what has, is and should count as a process for knowing thyself. In context, those becoming 21$^{st}$ century teachers usually face such a requirement in most pre-service teacher preparation programs. Beginners are schooled, technically, as "reflective practitioners" (Brookfield, 1995; Dewey, 1938; Kolb, Rubin, & McIntyre, 1974; Schon, 1984). Such schooling normally proceeds formulaically by: (i) identifying an incident experienced, (ii) analyzing it via inductive or deductive critical reasoning strategies, and (iii) generating action improvements (Reason & Bradbury, 2001). This process of rule-driven reflection normally utilizes reading and writing literacies. However, in the early 21$^{st}$ century, there are challenges to traditional reflective practitioner preparation. First, most persons entering education preparation programs are Generation Y – often referred to as Cybercitizens, Netizens, Homo-digitalis, Digital Youth, Homo Zapiens, or "Digital Natives" (Prensky, 2001). Generation Y persons were born into ever-present, ever-on and ever-connected ubiquitous digital technologies. For Digital Natives there has existed, throughout their lives and schooling, a tension then between their digitally-mediated lived reality experiences and institutional schooling practices perpetuated by "Digital Immigrants" (Prensky, 2001). Second, the concept of "reflection" as a benign looking at oneself as if a reflection in a mirror is being challenged by a human sciences research requirement known as "reflexivity" (Ruby, 1982). "Reflexivity refers to circular relationships between cause and effect. A reflexive relationship is bidirectional with both the cause and the effect affecting one another in a relationship in which neither can be assigned as causes or effects" (Wikipedia, 2015).

We propose to (i) explore current teacher preparation reflective practices, (ii) open up how Digital Natives learn, and (iii) advance a 21$^{st}$ century reflexive-oriented know thyself way of engaging Digital Natives who are overwhelming multi-modal and multi-mediated visual / image, auditory / sound, and sensory / corporeal experiential beings. By reimagining Pinar's (1975) *Method of Currere*, which is a traditional textual literacy bound way of exploring one's educative past in order to understand the present and project a future, and infusing it with Brookfield's (1995) claim that critical reflection requires a multiplicity of perspectives, and adding the interpretive inquiry requirement of reflexivity, it may be possible to generate a healthy conversation regarding this question: How might Digital Natives, via a multi-modal critically reflexive know thyself inquiry process, become responsive and responsible 21$^{st}$ century education practitioners?

## Teacher Reflective Practice: An Ahistorical Approach to the History of Know Thyself

Strangely enough we begin an exploration of teacher reflective practices with Vittorio Gallese and Giacomo Rizzolatti who discovered "mirror neurons" in the cortex of monkeys (Gallese, Fadiga, Fogassi, & Rizzolatti, 1996), meaning all primate brains have mirror neurons. Interestingly, mirror neurons fire not when "some" other thing is observed, but when a specific "some" other thing *in action* is perceived. This suggests that perceived actions are represented in brain neural network systems regarding what seemingly constitutes awareness of "self" as a bounded sensory something that is different from some "other" thing by virtue of its actions. The representation of the other thing's actions within the perceiver's mirror neuron systems is direct and immediate. There are no filters; no sign system language codes to mediate the instantaneous linking from self to other and from other to self. In a survival sense, there is, in the moment, only recognition of categorical differences or similarities; therefore, all other things are threats or not, useful or not.

Early brain-based human creatures, via mirror neuron action perceiving, experienced an essential action-difference defining link between self-thing and other-thing. Since there is very limited explanatory mediation occurring when mirror neurons fire, we respond directly via perceptions of another's actions as if those actions were simply intentional. Therefore, as mirror neurons fire responding to another's perceived actions, deemed intentional acts, the brain does not attempt, in real time, to explain such perceptual events – seeing is believing. To hesitate or pause may reduce the odds of survival – he / she who hesitates is lost! So, we have a human brain, last modified when the frontal lobes were forming a hundred thousand years ago, that contemporary neuroscience evidence shows have always acted and re-acted as an (e)motion and action perceptional detector, and those workings which have become a baseline for the brain as a construction site featuring highly subjective inner and outer worlds. However, true to its survivalist nature, the brain, as a perception-perspective processing agent is quick to jump to conclusions, confidently ignorant of its mistakes, and may be easily fooled. As such, what becomes evident then that we, more or less, to this day, often see what we expect to see, hear what we expect to hear, and we act accordingly. To curb our human creature-ness an evolving social collective mind consciously and systematically develops a mediating presence – a distancing reflective perspective – a knowing, doing and being cultural set of guiding how to think, act and be protocols. Yet, the brain-based creature's mirror neuron perceiving agency still exits. Operationally it mediates how minded human beings evolve towards being rationally quick, argumentatively certain, and uncorrectable in many cases. Professedly, Sigmund Freud was correct, in that anything experienced, as far as humans are concerned, even if concealed or forgotten, never truly goes away. Western history becomes a deadly play between the impulsive human creature-beast and the perspective-distanced rational-minded human being.

Perhaps our mimetic faculty defines our human nature:

> Nature creates similarities. One need only think of mimicry. The highest capacity for producing similarities, however, is man's. His gift of seeing resemblances is nothing other than a rudiment of the powerful compulsion in former times to become and behave like something else. Perhaps there is none of his higher functions in which his mimetic faculty does not play a decisive role (Benjaman, 1986).

Aristotle viewed mimetic agency as a foundational link between nature and the human species almost always evident in most human socio-eco-politico-cultural-techno representations and expressions. Indeed, even basic representational (images, orality, performance) and/or referential (symbol letters and symbol numbers) language systems seem to have mimetic determinants (Abram, 1997). Derrida uses mimesis to illustrate how "non-disposable doubts" always seem to interpret our knowing, doing and being (Puetz, 2015). Kelly (1998) writes, "Difference is the principle of mimesis, a productive freedom, not the elimination of ambiguity; mimesis contributes to the profusion of images, words, thoughts, theories, and action, without itself becoming tangible" (p. 236). Puetz (2015) notes, citing Kelly (1998) that,

> Mimesis thus resists theory and constructs a world of illusion, appearances, aesthetics, and images in which existing worlds are appropriated, changed, and re-interpreted. Images are a part of our material existence, but also mimetically bind our experience of reality to subjectivity and connote a "sensuous experience that is beyond reference to reality" (p. 237).

Aristotle took the human action of imitation of other person or thing as not only "thinking" but as "rethinking." That is, recollections of mimetic representations understood as thinking and rethinking become essential defining features of Western humanness. Recollection as a determining inheritance becomes named as perspective, consideration and thoughtfulness, and becomes evidence of deliberate effort to search for and recapture something which was once perceived in an action moment. Recovery of that which we once experienced becomes renamed as demonstrable as learning, as teachings, and when accumulated across time, shows and tells a history foundational to a collective's cultural abilities to hold recollection as a transformative power. Recollection as initially normalized was held within a pre-textual orality – that is, layers of sounds, images and performances shown and told themselves as present, past and future inherence stories; as pedagogic narratives. This metaphysics of presence meant one had to be present to hear, see and feel the stories of how, who, when, where and why. Being present transferred a responsibility to re-tell and re-show accordingly; as embodied recollection. As scribal (read-write literacy) societies (Purves, 1990) developed, what counted as recollection, learning and teaching became defined within systems of abstract symbols – letters and numbers. Now, the requirement to participate in one's community did not depend on proximity to the telling source. Rather, community participation becomes dependent on learning encode-decode-encode literacies. Obviously, there are those with more or less measured access and capabilities to develop (learn and be taught) such literacies. Dexterity with abstract sign systems becomes "the" measurable becoming-humanness achievement, defining what must count as progress and development. Humankind's essential quest then becomes abstract mindedness – that is what we mimic towards! However, to achieve such a goal, Western societies have created regimes of misdirection and set up violently antagonistic dichotomous relationships between belief, economic, political, cultural and racial, and gendered systems.

> In the science of [humanity] and culture today there is a unilateral swerve away from anything that could be called mimicry, imitation, or mimesis. And yet there is nothing, or next to nothing, in human behavior that is not learned, and all learning is based on imitation. If human beings suddenly ceased imitating, all forms of culture would vanish. Neurologists remind us frequently that the human brain is an enormous imitating machine (Girard, 1978, p. 7).

What follows is an outline of how a contemporary scribal society defines recollection as thinking and rethinking, and how know thyself reflective practice becomes a minded inquiry. The concept and practices referred to as "reflective practice" are associated with Donald Schon (Schon 1984, 1987). However, the history of know thyself examination has a long history evolving: (i) the ancient Greek quest for Phronesis, or practical wisdom, (ii) early Protestant Reformation developmental notions of individual spiritual progress, (iii) Kant's desire to unite reason and experience, (iv) Dewey's progressivism, (v) Roger's humanistic psychology, (vi) academic research on professional practice and critical thinking, and (vi) the development of reflective learning models (Valentine, 2015). For our purposes, we focus on Schon's reflective practice concept, which has, for the most recent past 30 years, become a preparation backbone in the nursing, health, education and social care professions.

Schon (1984) regards reflection as being: (i) reflection-in-action and (ii) reflection-on-action. Reflection-in-action requires capacities to recognize and reason quickly while engaged in an action-event. Reflection-on-action requires separation from an action-event in order to facilitate in-depth review of what happened. However, both forms of reflection require a mindful empathetic stance and openness to other perspectives that may support or challenge one's practices. Also, both forms of reflection require critical analysis and critical thinking to interrogate ideas and information from a detached or objectifying positioning. To be critical, one must objectively set aside personal values and opinions, and seek other referenced evidence-based, skeptical-based, reflective perspectives. Why? Obviously, becoming and being a teacher is understood as a highly complex normative activity. It is riddled with thousands of daily decisions and, therefore, teachers are deeply implicated and as well contaminated as non-critical inquirers without any hope of being recollection or reflectively objective. So, a requirement to enable at times confused teachers in-action or on-action reflection clarity is the use of specific inquiry tools – one is taught and one learns to read and write incidents via critical analysis. That means, guidance must be provided involving making criteria-based judgments based on writing that has a critical analytical style involving clear description, well developed arguments, the exact use of evidence, and a demonstrable link between theoretical perspectives and daily practices. As such, there becomes a prescriptiveness to what counts as good reflective practice and the protocol-tools to achieve critical reflection. Reflection, as a potentially dangerous glimpse of something otherwise, must be monitored, controlled and measured. Therefore, different models of reflection emerge to guide awareness of in-action and on-action reflection.

To facilitate reflective control, several models have developed, such as: (i) Boud's triangular representation model, (ii) Gibb's reflective cycle, and (iii) the Atkins and Murphy model (Learning to Teach: Becoming a Reflective Practitioner, 2015). All these models, either stage-driven or cyclic, simple or complex, theoretical or pragmatic address the same issue; which is, how might critical reflection in-action or on-action foster transformational learning (Mezirow, 2000)? Mezirow (2000) argues that reflection has value only if it leads to transformative action. Also, Mezizow (2000) places great emphasis on conscious self-managed learning that is not experience-sensitive; experience is trickery and deceptive. Transformation only works if it is a minded action whereby one responsibly owns the critical reflection process and systemically plans and delivers a step-by-step action plan to address an identified issue. One must be seen, ironically, to be productively and properly, actively engaged in a transformative reflective act.

However, recent criticisms of critical reflection have surfaced. First, Brookfield (1995) suggests that critical reflection can be insular if self-driven, and he proposes four lenses that when engaged significantly propel teachers into a deeper process of critical reflection: (i) the autobiographical, (ii) student feedback, (iii) peer assessments, and (iv) scholarly literature. This is how Brookfield (1995) adds interruptive otherness so that multiple perspectives challenge one's self-awareness; therefore, becoming a critically reflective practitioner. For Brookfield (1995) is it data diversity understood and acted upon that enables sustained and continual transformational personal and professional improvement. Second, the human sciences research methodologies require researchers to develop "reflexivity" (Bourdieu & Wacquant, 1992; McGregor & Cartwright, 2010). Reflexivity, from the Latin, means "to turn back on oneself." If reflection is a metaphorical and literal gaze into the mirror, then to be reflexive means breaking any hedonist self-indulgent gazing and to critically expose how one's concepts, values and beliefs have already mediated what one brings to any situation and is returned to him or her. Reflexivity requires an inquirer to be self-aware as a constructed person, citizen and as self and other, and as an implicit (hidden) and explicit (overt) curriculum impacting and being impacted by every context. Reflexive critical practice, in the normative setting of schooling, requires a teacher to lay bare his or her deeply held assumptions and beliefs and question his or her implicated-ness in the cause and effect of his or her very existence never mind action-practices. Simply, critical reflexivity calls for a designated self-research to address contradictions and complexities of who one is first and foremost as an implicated set of constructed actions.

## Digital Natives: Here, There, Everywhere

As Moderns, we measure almost everything in terms of defining units, such as: now-then times, here-there spaces, and this-that relationships. It is not surprising then that we locate segments of persons in fifteen (15) to twenty (20) year herds called generations. Persons born after 1980, living lives immersed in ubiquitous digital technologies – computers, video games, digital music players, video cams, cell phones – are called Net Generation, Millennials or Generation Y (Tapscott, 1998). Prensky (2001) named this group "Digital Natives," and that name has stuck. Also, Prensky (2001) metaphorically described a "digital divide" between "Digital Natives" and "Digital Immigrants." Beginning in the early 1980s with the first online interest groups, the Digital Age gained force that stream-rolled forward with the 1980s introduction of email and the World Wide Web in 1991. However, what is different with the onset of the Digital Age, from any other technological advancement, is the hyper-speed with which digitization operates; especially via modes of communication and expression. A key difference between other ages – mechanical, electrical, nuclear – and the Digital Age is that digital social-communication-media technologies no longer arise out of user needs. Rather, we are living in a "technological driven scenario" whereby technology "catches space" and "hooks" new users (Dingli & Seychell, 2015).

As well, Digital Natives were exposed early and often to digital technologies, which Prensky (2001) claims actually seems to alter a Digital Native's brain elector-chemical networking structures. Constant digitalized connections saturate a child and come to define experiences, in turn, shaping perceptions of self, other and the world, as well as what counts as time, space, body and relationships. The constant digital connections do not have the same saturation levels with Digital Immigrants. Digital Natives function best with fast, multi and parallel processes, still and moving visual representations, being part of a networked, highly connected environment, instant gratification and rewards, and they possess short attention spans for tasks that are linear progressions or rational logic-driven processes. These characteristics are not the only differences emerging in the Digital Native population; their identity formation and self-expression are reciprocally connected with how individuals communicate and process and share information – sound-bites, eye-bites and action-bites dominate their communications. Basically all Digital Natives today who spend the majority of their time online or connected via mobile devices exhibit similar behaviors in terms of "self" construction and expression. For Digital Natives, online and offline identities are not usually that dramatically different from one another, and Digital Natives "almost never distinguish between the online and off-line versions of themselves" (Palfrey & Gasser, 2008, Introduction, para 12). Digital Natives and those mimicking them come to simultaneously and continuously create and invent and recreate and reinvent their personal and social identities over and over in both the physical and digital worlds. This new way of representing and expressing oneself offers and enables quick changes, constant revisions, and alterations to one's identity. Experimentation with online identity alterations is one of the fundamental differences between Digital Natives and Digital Immigrants. Hence, the self, or identity, for a Digital Native is a synthesis of real and online expressions of who one is moment to moment, and how they have come to know, do and be as persons and citizens is fundamentally different than that of Digital Immigrants.

Of course there are issues that come with characterizing an entire "anything" as homogenous with similar characteristics. To do so is problematic, never mind what it does to a generation of diverse persons. To establish group distinct characteristics is perhaps even more problematic as is the blanket endowment of knowledge and skills of one group over the absences of such knowledge and skills in the other. To blanket each native or immigrant polarity without acknowledging issues associated with access, skill sets, development, socioeconomic, gender, and cultural differences (Bennett, Maton, & Kervin, 2008; Guo, Dobson, & Petrina, 2008) is problematic. Simply, technological knowledge, skills and attributes vary widely amongst both Digital Natives and Digital Immigrants. As such, in 2009 Prensky, responding to questions regarding the relevancy of defining the Digital Native in contrast to the Digital Immigrant, introduced the term" digital wisdom." A digitally wise person is not age defined, but rather understands how to use digital technologies and to use them to enhance cognitive processes (Prensky, 2015).

Still, at the heart of being digital or not lives, in Prensky's (2001) original defining charge that a Digital Native's brain, once saturated with digitization, actually changes in response to significant digital media stimuli (Jonassen, 1990, cited in Guo, et al., 2008). Even though Prensky (2015) cites neuro-scientific evidence to make his case, the debate moves on, and the result, as usual with any controversy, is a call for more research to determine the effects digital media has on the human brain (Bennet, Matron, & Kervin, 2008; Guo, Dobson, & Petrina, 2008).

If being submerged in, through and across digital technologies from birth has resulted in Digital Natives becoming brain re-wired or re-engineered, and as Prensky (2001) claims, such changes may not be easily reversed, then digital technologies, and their workings, have literally opened Pandora's brain box.

Jukes and Dosaj (2003) indicate that Digital Native learners prefer (i) perceiving information quickly from multiple sources, (ii) using parallel processing to multitask, (iii) processing multi-media images – still and moving – sounds and performances, (iv) continuous, always on, always available connectivity and networking, (v) instant gratification and rewards, and (vi) learning that is fun, action-filled, instantly useful, and self-referencing relevant. Then, does engaging so not change how learning and teaching are experienced (Tapscott, 1998)? Perhaps, this is an awareness case that sensory powerful sounds, evocative images and sensory performances all manifest as action bombardments from digital inputs experienced by the young from birth has indeed modified their neuroplasticity processing speed capacities. Or, perhaps as well, have digital technologies as seemingly intentional actions returned becoming human back to its original difficulty? Digital stimuli action invokes the firing of mirror neurons in the brain and reasoning is not part of what such firing is about. Action equates to intentionality in the brain if mirror neurons are stimulated and the response is immediate – threat or not, useful or not, but never reasonable or not. Again, perhaps, knowing how the brain evolved and its mirror neuron operations, that even though having been rigorously schooled for centuries to demonstrate control of the brain-body – especially the lizard brain – as a minded rational being, digital technologies has seductively created a generation where mindless action rules – Twitter, Blogs, Facebook, "likes," selfies, and on and on. A generation topping out today at 25 years of age – a generation perhaps now just leaving teacher education programs with traditional know thyself reflective practitioner schooling. What are the chances any of that made any sense to these Digital Natives?

If, as Prensky (2012) claims, and this global digital transformation is an event of "singularity," meaning that it has changed society so fundamentally that there just is no way to return to traditional ways of knowing, doing and being, then how do we, as educators embrace, acknowledge, and alter our own ways of knowing, doing, and being in order to better serve our Digital Native students as they move towards a future where they are responsible for educating others? We would like to suggest that a reimagined 21$^{st}$ century version of Pinar's (1975) *Method of Currere* could provide a way and a means to platform modifications to the know thyself process such that Digital Natives find it user-friendly and life-relevant.

**Conceptualizing Pinar's Method of Currere**

Pinar's (1975) *Method of Currere* involves moving through four separate and distinct stages. Beginning with one's "biographic past," the Regressive Stage, one enters his or her past, but from a more informed vantage point brought on by time and experience. Using an auto-biographical free-flow writing process an inquirer opens up memories primarily regarding one's past curricula experiences. The next stage is the Progressive Stage wherein one looks forward to what may happen (Pinar, 1975). Imagining forward is guided by one's current intellectual public and private life experiences, relationships with colleagues, peers, teachers and superiors, and social and extra-curricular activities. In doing so, visions of what is not yet present are given space to manifest (Pinar, 1994). This stage also uses a free-flow form of writing to capture thoughts, ideas, dreams and hopes as one looks towards their immediate and distant futures. The third stage is the Analytical Stage. Now one takes their biographical past (Regressive Stage) and their biographical possible futures (Progressive Stage), and as if written images they are set aside so one now considers the biographical present as a focus directly on the here and now. Pinar (1975) suggests using visualization transcribed into textual notes with a particular focus on the institutional "self." The final stage is the Synthetical Stage. Here one locates past, present, and the future together, held up for contrast and comparison to realize what emerges and what know thyself insights may be attained.

Currere is a step-by-step process across three stages of one's life – the past, present, and future. Currere culminates by bringing these three life stages together in a systematic and linear progression such that one's life experiences are exposed and interrogated for understanding. However, the process of currere is grounded in a textual knowing thyself as an educational experiential being.

## Currere 2.0

Pinar's (1975) currere operates within it a specific educational focus, including one's formal and informal learning, teaching and curricular experiences and behaviors with and within past, present and possible future educational contexts. However, currere, conceptualized over forty (40) years ago, needs to be updated to respond to the 21$^{st}$ century learning know thyself needs, considering the brains and learning styles of Digital Natives. Currere 2.0 requires different understandings of what is considered formal and informal educational experience, as well as technology's role in one's past, present and future. There is great value in Pinar's (1975) essential structures of know thyself currere, but the method, as currently constituted, no longer offers a know thyself process for 21$^{st}$ century Digital Native learners. So, what would Currere 2.0 look like as a know thyself process to enable critically conscious transformational examinations of one's self-architecture?

To engage the Digital Native, generally and specifically, a multi- and parallel- and visual-oriented representational process is required. Digital Natives require the ability to consider the stages of life, past, present and future, in a networked, fast-paced and visual environment that enables free-flow between the temporal as well as the procedural. Instead of progressing through past, present and future as separate temporal / spatial stages in one's life, the Digital Native requires the ability to boarder-cross through, across and between these life stages, and to enter and return to these stages during the data collection and analysis processes.

Currere 2.0 maintains a focus on the three primary temporal / spatial life stages: the past, present and future. However, in this $21^{st}$ century version of this know thyself auto-biographical method, with a blended and enhanced focus on educational and technological experiences, the focus of each section shifts, such that:

- *Regressive* – To regress, according to Merriam-Webster's online dictionary, is "an act or the privilege of going or coming back." Being regressive for Digital Natives is difficult. Digitization seduces towards one towards moments in the here and now. The invitation to go backward needs to be located as a specific kind of quest such as being an observer of self via still and moving images with specific technologies and the curricula – again, asking what was at hand technologically and through the curricula then and how did one learn to use that technology and curricula? How did the technology at that time, in that place, inform one's way of knowing, doing and being? The intention in this stage is not to simply create lists of these educational and technological artifacts, but to consider how one's self was formed through and within a curricula of digital technologies and the experiential situations they created. Capturing the data generated by participating in this stage will rarely result in the reading and writing textual form, and if it does, it will result in a digital or online format. This stage requires the use of the technologies at hand today, to explore those of yesterday evident in one's past experiences. What results from this stage, for the Digital Native, is a representation that slows down – a slow motion – viewing / seeking /looking at the meditations of becoming hyper-engaged digitally within evolving networks of cultures of connectivity. To the Digital Native this will culminate as a private-public display, a sharing between peers, including feedback to and from peers, with a constant availability opening up how one became a knowing, doing and being digital global citizen.

- *Progressive* – Defined as "moving forward or onward," this stage considers a projecting of possible or probable futures. Digital Natives, consumed by producing experiences, living in the moment, have difficulty imagining how they have come to be and who they are becoming in a rapidly changing world. However, if digital innovation and creativity are core qualities, then this stage must invite autobiographical, creative design thinking processes to be evoked. Pinar (1975) used a textual form of visualization – journaling. However, in using design thinking, especially with digital technologies, it enables Digital Natives, via design experimentation and re-invention, utilizing networked communities and multiple forms of self-expression, to conceive of and create the future. For a generation weaned on futuristic designed media and tools and gaming, they "build" / "construct" themselves into a time / space / body / relationship future – a future riddled with robotics, nanotechnology, genomics, software, hardware and so on, that includes designs regarding assumptions about culture, economics, politics, and ethics. Perhaps there is a realization here that one is indeed a local and global curriculum in one's self-design.
- *Analytical* – Being analytical normally implies some separation of something into elements or parts. Pinar (1975) called it a "loosening-up of." For Digital Natives, analysis must engage the processes of visualization which often cannot be translated into the textual forms. Digital environments and physical environments seem to be same for Digital Natives. To study being biographically present then, requires Digital Natives to be deconstructive and engage in a process that enables them to consider digital and physical environments in parallel and from multi-focal, highly visual perspectives and expression modes.
- *Synthetical* – For Digital Natives, this stage requires a digitalized putting together of time / space / body and relationship image perspectives. However, the key is to move towards reflexivity. Brookfield (1995) notes that moving from critical reflection to becoming critically reflexive requires that one identify self-assumptions, biases, and prejudices and to do so by using multiple perspectives. Thus, utilizing Brookfield's four (4) lenses as educative feedback from multiple other sites – students, peers, self and the literature – invites one to imagine, through different lenses, the hegemonic power of digitization and the education system.

Becoming aware so enables: (i) improved pedagogic relationships, (ii) best use practices with technologies and current curricula, and (ii) self-preservation when we realize that self-other worlds are not of our making (Brookfield, 1995).

## Conclusion: Digital Knowing Thyself

Know thyself means this, that you get acquainted with what you know, and what you can do. Menander

(Manifest Your Potential, 2015)

Pinar's (1994) use of a reflexive know thyself inquiry process reminds us all that much of our life experiences are "always hidden from view, but present nonetheless" (p. 202). However, the 'us' here seems to be those 'Boomers' born into a privileging and dominating scribal – reading and writing literacy – society. Still, the need to become and be self-aware, an essential characteristic of human being, remains paramount during times of generation-to-generation transference. Even in an overwhelmingly digital $21^{st}$ century era with seemingly 24-7 limitless outgoing and incoming connectivity operating at hyper-speeds, there is a significant need for an equivalent inquiry self-aware reflexive process. Again, if there is an understanding of how today's Digital Native generation in waiting learns, then an authentic self-awareness process for such a generation cannot be analogue-driven; that is, information or data is translated into electric pulses of varying amplitude. Rather, if digital technologies mediate Digital Native ways of knowing, doing and being, then a digital-oriented reflexive self-awareness inquiry process is required; that is, a reflexive inquiry process whereby information or data is understood as a translation into a binary format, zero or one, and wherein each piece of information becomes a representative eye-bite of two distinct amplitudes.

The pedagogic point here is the current, slowly-evolving education system is ill equipped to meet the learning and development and self-awareness needs of today's and tomorrow's technologically mediated, and even perhaps brain-altered, Digital Natives. We suggest that through a reimagined, for the $21^{st}$ century, critically reflective know thyself inquiry practice, such as Currere 2.0, educators, especially those at post-secondary teacher preparation institutions, may be able to establish solid self-aware groundings so Digital Natives are not "blown about by the winds of cultural and pedagogic" and technological, "preference" (Brookfield, 1995, p. 265). Currere 2.0 as imagined here is a hyper-text inquiry process opening up a foundational space to begin building a binary bridge between Digital Native learning needs and current and future curricular and education contexts. For post-secondary educators embracing Currere 2.0, the necessary outcome is simply that Digital Native students becoming Digital Native teachers are invited imaginably, and digitally, to engage in a binary dialectic whereby they become less seduced by digital media technologies and more critically aware of self, other and world as mediated constructs. Perhaps, via critically reflexive Currere 2.0, there could be a pedagogic opportunity that requires leaders to be visible and authentic and to be able to communicate the decisions they've made and why they've made them, to be able to acknowledge when they've made a mistake and to move forward, to engage in the debate (Gail Kelly, 2015).

## REFERENCES

Abram, D. (1997). *The spell of the sensuous: Perception and language in a more-than-human world.* New York: Random House.

Benjaman, W. (1986). *"On the mimetic faculty" reflections.* New York: Schocken Books.

Bennett, S., Maton, K., & Kervin, L. (2008). The "digital natives" debate: A critical review of the evidence. *British Journal of Educational Technology, 39*(5), 775-786.

Bourdieu, P. (1989). *The state nobility: Elite schools in the field of power.* (L. C. Clough, trans.) Stanford: Stanford University Press.

Bourdieu, P., & Wacquant, L. (1992). *An invitation to reflective sociology.* Chicago: Chicago University Press.

Brookfield, S. (1995). *Becoming a critically reflective teacher.* San Francisco: John Wiley & Sons.

Dewey, J. (1938). *Experience and education.* New York: Kappa Delta Pi.

Dingli, A., & Seychell, D. (2015). *The new digital natives.* Berlin: Springer-Verlag.

Donald, M. (2001). *A mind so rare: The evolution of human consciousness.* New York: W. W. Norton and Company.

Gallese, V. (2011). Neuroscience and phenomenology. *Phenomenology and Mind*, 33-48.

Gallese, V., Fadiga, L., Fogassi, L., & Rizzolatti, G. (1996). Action recognition in the premotor cortex. *Brain, 119,* 593-609.

Girard, R. (1978). *Things hidden since the foundation of the world.* Stanford: Stanford University Press.

Guo, R., Dobson, T., & Petrina, S. (2008). Digital natives, digital immigrants: An analysis of age and ICT competency in teacher education. *Journal of Educational Computing Research, 38*(3), 235-254.

Hayles, K. N. (1999). *How we became post human: virtual bodies in cybernetics, literature, and informatics.* Chicago: Chicago University Press.

Jukes, I., & Dosaj, A. (2015, September 1). *Understanding digital children.* Retrieved from: Wikispace.com: http://edorigami.wikispaces.com/file/view/Jukes+-+Understanding+Digital+Kids.pdf

Kelly, G. (2015, September 23). Quote. Retrieved from: http://www.brainyquote.com/quotes/keywords/digital.html#pCXtXARvOVohsXls.99

Kelly, M. (Ed.). (1998). *The encyclopedia of aesthetics* (Vol. 3). Oxford: Oxford University Press.

*Know thyself.* (2015a, August 28).

Quote. Retrieved from: Ark in Time: http://www.arkintime.com/know-thyself/Knowthyself. (2015b, September 16).

Quote. Retrieved from:
http://www.manifestyourpotential.com/self_discovery/0_start_journey_self_discovery/know_thyself/know_thyself_inspirational_quotes.htm

Kolb, D. A., Rubin, I., & McIntyre, J. (1974). *Organizational psychology: A book of readings.* Englewood Cliffs: Prentice-Hall.

*Learning to teach: Becoming a reflective practitioner.* (2015, August 30). Retrieved from: The Open University: http://www.open.edu/openlearn/education/learning-teach-becoming-reflective-practitioner/content-section-6.1

McGregor, D., & Cartwright, L. (2010). *Developing reflective practice: A guide for beginning teachers.* Wolverhampton: Open University Press.

*Merriam-Webster Dictionary.com.* (2015, September 2). Definition: Analytical. Retrieved from: http://www.merriam-webster.com/dictionary/analytical

*Merriam-Webster Dictionary.com* (2015, September 2). Definition: Regressive. Retrieved from: http://www.merriam-webster.com/dictionary/regress

Mezirow, J. (2000). Learning to think like an adult: Core concepts of transformation theory. In J. Mezirow, *Learning as transformation* (pp. 3-34). San Francisco: Jossey-Bass.

Palfrey, J., & Grasser, U. (2008). *Born digital.* New York: Basic Books.

Pinar, W. (1975, April). The method of Currere. Washington, District of Columbia, United States of America. Retrieved from: http://eric.ed.gov/?id=ED104766

Pinar, W. (1985). Autobiography and an architecture of self. In W. Pinar, *Autobiography, Politics and Sexuality: Essays in curriculum theory 1972-1992* (pp. 201-222). New York: Peter Lang.

Prensky, M. (2001, October). Digital natives, digital immigrants. *On the horizon, 9*(5), 1-6.

Prensky, M. (2010). *Teaching digital natives: Partnering for real learning.* Thousand Oaks: Sage Publications.

Prensky, M. (2011). *From digital natives to digital wisdom: Hopeful essays for the 21st century education.* Thousand Oaks: Corwin.

Puetz, M. (2015, August 28). *Mimesis.* Retrieved from University of Chicago: Theories of Media: http://csmt.uchicago.edu/glossary2004/mimesis.htm#_ftn26

Purves, A. (1990). *The scribal society: An essay on literacy and schooling in the information age.* London: Longman Group.

Reason, P., & Bradbury, H. (2001). *SAGE Handbook of action research: Participatory inquiry and practice.* New York: SAGE Publications.

Ruby, J. (1982). *Crack in the mirror: Reflexivity perspectives in anthropology.* Philadelphia: University of Pennsylvania Press.

Schon, D. (1984). *The reflective practitioner: How professionals think in action.* New York: Basic Books.

Schon, D. (1987). *Educating the reflective practitioner: Toward a new design for teaching and learning in the professions.* San Francisco: Jossey-Bass.

Tapscott, D. (1998). *Growing up digital: The rise of the net generation.* New York: McGraw-Hill.

Valentine, D. (2015, August 30). *Reflective practice.* Retrieved from: Academia: http://www.academia.edu/4276897/REFLECTIVE_PRACTICE_and_THE_PROFESSIONAL_HISTORY_PRINCIPLES_and_TOOLS

*Wikipedia.* (2015, August 28). Reflexivity: Definition. Retrieved from: https://en.wikipedia.org/wiki/Reflexivity_%28social_theory%29

CHAPTER 9

# Closing the Loop: Using Reflection in Teaching Management and Leadership Subjects in Higher Education

*Zelma Bone*

My personal journey as an educator incorporating reflection into teaching and assessment design and illustrating how reflection can be used in a variety of ways to enhance the learning process.

The focus of this paper is the use of reflection by the academic in subject and assessment design within undergraduate and graduate management and leadership programs. John Dewey stated we do not learn from experience; we learn from reflecting on our experience. Despite this, with over 25 years in academia, my experience has shown that some colleagues have been reluctant to incorporate reflection into their learning and teaching. It is a challenge that many have found onerous as it required them to be introspective in order to effect change and facilitate deeper approaches to learning and teaching. It has often been a case of emphasis: colleagues have placed importance on the content (the 'what') to be learned rather than the 'how' or the 'why'. Dewey's statement has resonated with me and has greatly influenced my approach to learning and teaching. My development as an educator has required me to focus on learning from my experience through reflection informed by theory with the 'eternal' aim of improving my practice. I realized that this was not only an important process for me to improve but also for students so they could improve their learning as well. When designing subjects, I have started with the design of the assessments and reflection has always featured. This paper explores the role of experiential learning, and in particular reflection in teaching and learning and gives examples of the ways that reflection has been incorporated into assessment of subjects. It also has allowed me to reflect on this process.

## INTRODUCTION

John Dewey stated we do not learn from experience; we learn from reflecting on our experience. This statement has resonated with me during my extensive career in education and experiential learning has greatly influenced my approach to learning and teaching. Experiential learning involves the whole person, through thoughts, feelings and physical activity (Beard & Wilson 2006). Kolb (1984) talks of learning from our experiences and he sees learning as a continuous process in which we take responsibility for our own learning. I am constantly reflecting upon my learning experiences and seeking ways to improve my practice. All too often subjects are designed and developed in isolation to each other and often focus on the content. The experiential learning approach provides a thread joining many of the learning approaches together in a more unified whole. These learning theories have been a cornerstone of my subject development and as such, reflection has been an important component of my teaching and the majority of assessment tasks. Reflection, represents 'closing the loop' in learning in order to effect change and facilitate deeper approaches to learning and teaching. Learners need to develop the ability to think and reflect on previous experiences and make some sense of what has happened and then construct plans for the future (Bolton, 2010).

### A Personal Journey

> Reflection is an important human activity in which people recapture their experience, think about it, mull it over and evaluate it. It is this working with experience that is important to learning (Boud, Keogh & Walker, 1985, p. 19).

Despite being an educator for over 37 years, I find that teaching can still be a daunting prospect. A new group of students each session, new subjects, changing technological and monitoring requirements, 'will they like the subject?', 'will they learn?' Each can contribute to a level of anxiety. Over time I have found that the answers to these dilemmas are best answered by me or in consultation with my peers. Reflective practice has involved evaluating my processes of learning and teaching and questioning 'why' I do something as well as 'how' and the 'what'. My development as a teacher in higher education has required me to focus on learning from my experiences through reflection informed by the theory with the 'eternal' aim of improving my practice. I realized that this was not only an important process for me to improve but also for students so they could improve their learning as well. Thus, over time, when I have been designing subjects, I have started with the design of the assessments and some form of reflection has always featured.

Performance management reviews have meant that I am expected to demonstrate my commitment and experience in teaching as well as being broadly accountable for the learning outcomes of my students (National Tertiary Education Union, 2005). To do this, I have produced my own teaching portfolio to document and demonstrate teaching responsibilities, practices and expertise. My teaching portfolio has two components: one, a statement that outlines my teaching philosophy, practice and performance; and two, a dossier of relevant material to support the claims I make in the summary statement. It started as a paper-based document but has progressed to an ePortfolio format. The teaching portfolio has provided me with the opportunity to reflect on my own approaches to and philosophies on learning and teaching and to be used as a tool to undertake some self-evaluation of my teaching practices. However, merely reflecting was not going to improve my practice. I needed to think about how to put into practice some of these developments.

## What has Shaped my Learning and Development?

> Reflection ... may take place in isolation or in association with others. It can be done well or badly, successfully or unsuccessfully (Boud, Keogh & Walker, 1985, p. 19).

Many factors have influenced my approach to teaching and learning over the years. However, two stand out for me: the influence of experiential learning, and the opportunity to share my ideas and practice with my colleagues.

### Experiential Learning

David Kolb was writing about experiential learning when I started my academic career in higher education 25 years ago and he was emphasizing then that what you really need to acquire was the ability to learn and keep learning from your experiences. Kolb drew on early work on experiential learning by John Dewey and Kurt Lewin. Experiential learning is built on six propositions (Kolb & Kolb, 2005, p.194):

1. Learning is best conceived as a process.
2. All learning is relearning.

3. Learning requires the resolution of conflicts between dialectically opposed modes of adaptation.
4. Learning is a holistic process of adaptation to the world.
5. Learning results from synergetic transactions between the person and the environment.
6. Learning is the process of creating knowledge.

David Kolb identified that 'knowledge results from the combination of grasping and transforming experience' (Kolb, 1984, p. 41) and from there developed his experiential learning cycle. According to Kolb, learners can learn using four different styles (Adams, Openshaw & Trembath, 2006):

- Concrete Experience – likes varied experiences, specific examples and action oriented.
- Reflective observation – likes time to ponder different viewpoints; to consider and assemble knowledge;
- Abstract conceptualization – likes logical and analytical thinking, clear structure and rational evaluation;
- Active experimentation – likes to try ideas out, to apply and test them.

The Kolb Learning Cycle has been a feature of my subject design to introduce students to 'how and why they learn' and to identify their preferred learning styles and the implications of their learning style on decision-making and their approach to learning. It can be very edifying and reassuring for students to realize that people learn in different ways. Completion of the Kolb Learning Cycle would also give the students understanding of how and why they had succeeded, or not, in their education up to entering university.

Argyris and Schön (1996) have argued that while Kolb's learning cycle can be seen to depict 'single-loop' learning, it is the reflection stage at which we may venture into 'double-loop' learning (see Figure 1). Double-loop learning is an educational concept and process that involves teaching people to think more deeply about their assumptions and beliefs. It was created by Chris Argyris, a leading organizational trainer, in the mid-1980s. Double-loop learning is different from single-loop learning which involves changing methods and improving efficiency to obtain established objectives (i.e., "doing things right"). Double-loop learning concerns changing the objectives themselves (i.e., "doing the right things") and asking 'why' things happen (Cartwright, 2002).

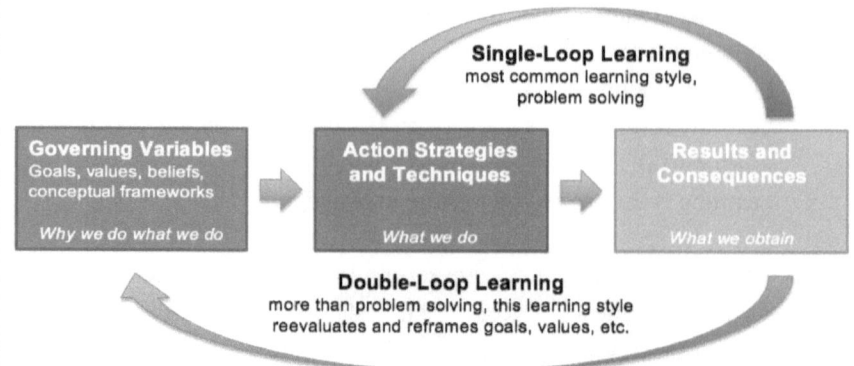

**Figure 1**: Single-loop and double-loop learning (Adapted from interpretations of Argyris's writings: http://www.infed.org/thinkers/argyris.htm and http://bsix12.com/double-loop-learning/)

*Collaborating and Reflecting with My Colleagues*

> It is the language of reflection that deepens our knowledge of who we are in relation to others in a community of learners (Miller & Saxon cited in Barrett, 2005).

Academic teaching can be a solitary pursuit for some, but the increasing demands for accountability and a more scholarly approach to teaching scholarship has encouraged teachers to share ideas, collaborate and research their teaching practice. Ramsden argued that 'the aim of teaching is simple: it is to make student learning possible' (1992, p.5). Trigwell, Martin, Benjamin and Prosser (2000, p.156) extend this idea by saying that the aim of scholarly teaching is also simple: 'it is to make transparent how we have made the learning possible'. Teachers are encouraged to communicate about what they do and how they do it. This creates not only a conversation around teaching practice; this research into teaching contributes to a body of literature that can be shared. However, 'telling' is only one part of the story. To become more scholarly, teachers need to be involved in more formal approaches of inquiry (Trigwell et al., 2000). The use or writing groups in learning and teaching provides support and a space for this inquiry. I was part of the three-person research team that facilitated a writing group with 12 academics from our School.

The practice of writing groups can be theorized in terms of peer learning and engaging in a 'community of practice' (Lave & Wenger, 1991). That is, the academics coming together in a voluntary capacity to engage in structured forms of learning through sharing teaching experiences with academic colleagues. The term community of practice refers to 'participation in an activity system about which participants share understandings concerning what they are doing and what that means in their lives and for their communities' (Lave & Wenger 1991, p.98). The community is conceptualized as a group of academics interested in understanding and improving their learning and teaching capabilities and communicating their reflections on aspects of their teaching practice to a broader audience. Learning, rather than being an individual activity, occurs through participation in the community (Bone, Jarzabkowski and Eiseman, 2000). Thus, a community of practice is based on collective expertise: it offers opportunities for participants to co-construct knowledge by inviting them to 'share, build upon, and transform what they know about effective practice' (Buysse, Sparkman & Wesley, 2003, p. 265).

Action learning was particularly relevant to this exercise as it involved reflection on teaching practice, development of capability in scholarship of teaching, and more generally, professional development through participation in peer learning in a community of practice. There were two action learning sets. While acting as facilitators of the group, the research team were also undertaking the same activities in the group as other group members, i.e. writing about a particular aspect of their own teaching practice and preparing a paper for publication (Bone, McMullen & Clarke, 2009). The research team also met on a regular basis to plan upcoming sessions and to reflect on the progress of the group. All members engaged in structured reflection on what had been achieved since last meeting; sharing stories/problems/issues; planning what the next stage of the process would be; making modifications if needed; writing in reflective diary.

One of the challenges of reflective practice is the temptation to jump from observation to resolution. The research team used the tool, the Discussion Method or ORID, developed by the Institute of Cultural Affairs (1995), to help avoid this temptation. ORID is an acronym for the four steps involved in the process: *objective, reflective, interpretive and decisional*. At each step, there is an alignment with a stage of the learning cycle (Kolb, 1984). The discussion method is a progression of questions that take the group on a journey of consciousness (Institute of Cultural Affairs, 1995). This method was useful for the participants to collectively reflect on their experiences of being part of the writing group. The ORID was conducted at a three-day writing retreat held off campus. This time was chosen because of the relaxed atmosphere of the retreat venue, most of the group were in attendance and there was time scheduled for reflection. The reflection focused on the emotional responses and associations evoked by the facts (e.g. How did you feel about being part of the writing group?), for example:

> I enjoy learning with others. I enjoy the momentum generated from spending time with peers and colleagues. I enjoy the collegiality, the cooperation and the collaboration. I enjoy the potential for sharing information and learning from colleagues – thus creating a community of practice. The regular scheduled meetings were the key to success for me – these created the momentum, the space and the time for writing and sharing our learning and teaching experiences (author's reflections from the writing group exercise).

### Incorporating Reflection into Assessment Design

1. *A learning contract in an undergraduate leadership subject.* The learning contract is a negotiated process between the learner and the academic supervisor. It is often the student's first foray into research so the staged guidelines provide supportive 'training wheels' and a detailed 'recipe' to follow. The process can be challenging for both parties as it is a scaffolded assessment with close monitoring and regular feedback. The contract has three distinct stages. The contract proposal is the first step and is where the student can choose their focus for project by articulating a learning goal and justifying why this goal is important. This is followed by the second stage of the contract which includes a literature review, reflections on readings and a detailed methodology. The final component is the learning in action (describing what they did), analysis and evaluation of their findings and a reflection on their learning. The many advantages of this assessment are it can be used in a variety of situations and with a diversity of learners; puts the students into the center of the learning process; students can choose a learning goal that is relevant to their situation; and it can stimulate deep approaches to learning.

The diagram below (Figure 2) outlines the connections between the different phases of the learning contract. These six phases must be planned for over the period of the semester. The *learning goal (1)* is the central driving force behind the contract. It is the focus. It will direct students to *the literature (2)* that will be reviewed. Students need to keep their learning goal in mind as they proceed through the contract. The *literature review (2)* in turn will influence what they write about in their *reflections on their literature (3)*. These reflections need to show what they have learned in relation to their contract goal. Here they also need to assess where they stand in relation to what they have read. For example, if their goal was to understand business ethics they would assess their strengths and weaknesses against some of the ideas found in the literature.

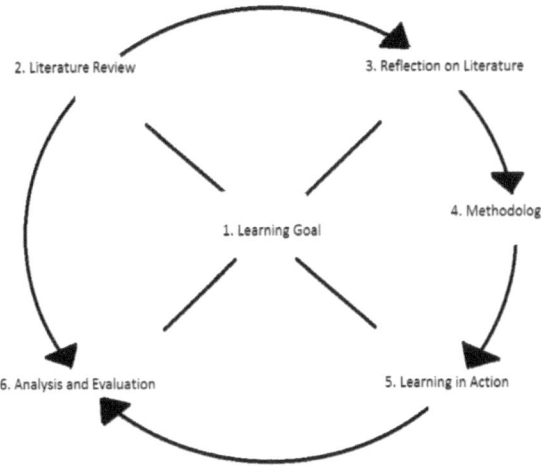

**Figure 2:** Connections between the different phases of the learning contract

After the students have completed the report there is one last phase, reflecting on their learning. Here is where they can step back from the content and think about how and why they went about doing the learning. Experiential learning readings and the Kolb Learning Cycle (Kolb, 1984) are used to assist the students in their reflections. The learning contract process 'pushed' the students to plan, act, reflect and generate ideas from analysis, which is very similar to the stages of the Kolb Cycle.

Reflective writing as well as the more traditional scientific /technical report writing is valued in the academic and business worlds (Cameron, 2007) and students to need to be good at both:

> Demonstrating development at different levels and talking about it retrospectively as well as taking it forward shows a management mentality prepared to keep learning as well as being able to constructively criticize the self (Cameron, 2007, p.16).

Duffy (2007) believed that reflective practice was an active process of critically examining practice where an individual is challenged and enabled to undertake the process of self-enquiry. Learning is derived from experience but it does not just happen (Schön, 1991). By thinking about what you are doing and why you are doing it is what turns experiences into meaningful learning.

Business graduates need to learn about professional conduct and working with customers and clients in different situations and these require particular skills. Schön (1983) referred to the uncertainty, uniqueness and conflict inherent in professional practice. As the world is ever-changing standard procedures of analysis and action may not be applicable or appropriate in all situations. There is a need for alternative strategies. 'Messy' or 'wicked' problems need subjective processes of thinking about what you know and how to find solutions to problems.

Therefore, employers want students who understand problematic situations and can do something about them (Cameron, 2007). The learning contract requires the students to respond to questions such as 'what might I do better next time?' or 'how would I do things differently?' It is the ability to effect change that makes reflective practice so fundamental to higher education and to the graduates as they progress to the business world. What gets us from experience to understanding is reflection (Schön, 1991; Kolb, 1984). Boud, Keogh and Walker (1985, p.19) described reflection in the context of learning as 'a generic term for those intellectual and affective activities in which individuals engage to explore their experiences in order to lead to new understandings and appreciation'.

2. *Learning journal associated with overseas tour*: The study abroad tour offered the challenge and the opportunity for the academics to explore different ways of teaching and learning. The tour was a different learning situation for the students and the academics. It was an intensive 21-day overseas tour to Argentina with all assessment to be completed whilst on tour. The assessment included a group oral presentation and a reflective learning journal. Effective learning is highly dependent on the relationships between students and academics and among students themselves. The challenge was to move the emphasis away from individualized model of learning towards one which emphasized that a great deal of learning takes place in groups and communities, and this learning becomes part of the process of enculturation or initiation into 'communities of practice' (Lave & Wenger, 1991).'

Travelling abroad does not necessarily create a global learner. What assists the study abroad tour's intercultural experience for both academics and students is their process of reflecting on the experience (Welikala, 2011). O'Connell and Dyment (2006, p. 672) stated that 'journals can be a useful instructional/ learning strategy that allows students to reflect critically on material, to ground their learning in their lived experience, to develop their writing skills and to demonstrate their knowledge/understanding in a non-traditional manner'. Bolton (2010, p. 126) outlines that a learning journal can ask the writer to enquire into what you:

- and others did on any particular occasion
- thought, and what others might have thought
- felt, and what others might have felt
- believe, and how these beliefs are carried out in your practice
- are prejudiced about, take for granted, and unquestioningly assume
- can do about how all of the above affects yourself and others.

Benefits also include bringing the responsibility for learning back to the student (constructivism), and getting students actively involved in the reflective process. Reflective writing is personal and thus does not need to overly formal in style. It is becoming useful for graduates to master both 'the scientific/factual approach of report writing' as well as 'the more holistic/emotional approach of reflective work' (Lee-Davies, 2007, p.16). Most students on the tour had not been required to do this style of writing before. In completing their reflective learning journals, based on their experiences of the group study tour to Argentina, students could write using their own writing style and could use their own format. Thus, the learning journal is a relatively unstructured form of reflection. Through the reflective writing exercise students were able to identify what was important to them at the time and what was relevant to them for their course and for their personal development. Trigger questions were used to stimulate thoughts and to encourage the student's reflection, for example: What happened? How did I feel about what happened? What have I learnt? How has this changed my perception of this issue? Why has this been an important experience for me? What will I do differently next time?

The study abroad tour to Argentina and the associated assessment allowed the students to discover new strengths and abilities, conquer new challenges and solve new problems. In addition, they were enhancing generic communication and problem solving skills and allowing them to develop new ideas and perspectives and a deeper understanding with respect to themselves and their chosen profession. Thus, they were engaged in 'double loop' learning.

3. *Postgraduate leadership subject.* A fully online subject, *Leadership in Teams* explores how leaders manage teams and how teams shape the requirements for effective leadership. Students examine the theory and practice of leading productive teams and facilitating groups. Through the university's virtual online learning platform and the Online Meeting tools, students have the opportunity to develop and demonstrate leadership skills. What better way to learn about leadership in teams than by doing it! With that in mind, four Leadership Challenge activities, along with the associated readings, provide the student with an ideal balance between theory and practice.

There are four students in a team and four leadership challenges. Each student has a turn of leading a challenge. Each Challenge activity has been designed to run over a two-week period. However, three weeks have been allocated in the study schedule. This allows for some flexibility and negotiation among teammates as needed. It will also prevent issues of the Challenge assessments 'running' into each other. The Challenge activity has the following format to echo the experiential nature of the subject:

1. Pre-test and pre-skill assessment (individual task) – a self-assessment exercise and short scenario with questions. This is completed without extra reading – just by exploring current knowledge and experience to get a basic idea of where they are starting from in terms of the material covered in the module.
2. The Leadership Challenge (team task) – a case study based task where the team can develop skills in applying various strategies to facilitate the functioning of a team.
3. Post-challenge reflection (individual task) – students are asked to reflect not only on the what they learned in this module but also to reflect on how and why their team behaved the way they did during the Challenge process. The students revisit their Pre-test/Pre-skill exercise to see if they would change or add to their initial responses(thus closing the loop on the experiential learning cycle)

The challenge has a particular theme of an aspect of leading and working in teams (e.g. team development, facilitation and coaching, diversity, conflict resolution and negotiation). Before each challenge the student completes a pre-test/pre-skill exercise to determine their current knowledge and attitudes on the topic. After they complete the challenge exercise they complete a Reflection-Action Sheet with questions to guide them in their reflection. The students identified the one or two areas in which they are strongest; the one or two areas in which they need more improvement; identified one thing or action to improve; identified what making this change would result in; and finally, if they did not make any change, how would it affect their personal and professional life (De Janasz et al., 2009).

In the final challenge exercise the team members reflect on their performance in the team over the four challenges. The interpersonal dynamics among team members can be a difficult process to go through, especially when assessment deadlines loom, personalities clash, and tempers flare. The students get the opportunity to reflect on and study the effects of tension in the team and to explore ways of coping with frustration. Each member is asked to complete such statements as: I feel frustrated when my teammates ........; I show my frustration by ..........; and If my teammates were frustrated with me, I would feel ......... . After the postings, the leader facilitates a discussion to process their reactions to the responses and then come up with a list of the typical reasons why people become frustrated with one and other and the best ways to deal with it (Griffith & Dunham, 2015).

## CONCLUDING REMARKS

My favorite quotes, from literature and from my students, that I turn to every now and then to keep me motivated and focused include, firstly, from the literature:

- 'Experience without reflection is like eating without digesting' (comment by a conference presenter, n.d.)
- 'We are inclined to think of reflection as something quiet and personal. My argument here is that reflection is action-oriented, social and political. Its 'product' is praxis (informed, committed action), the most eloquent and socially significant of human action (Kemmis 1985, p. 139)
- 'By three methods we may learn wisdom: First, by reflection, which is noblest; second, by imitation, which is the easiest; and third by experience, which is the bitterest' (Confucius cited in Hinnett, 2002).
- 'Reflective practice is a dialogue of thinking and doing through which I become more skilful' (Schön, 1983, p. 42).

Secondly, from my students:

- '...what I did not realize was the beauty of writing and discovering things that I have done and experienced and recording it down and sometime later reading the journal again, it gave me the pleasure to know my real self, my real feelings and thoughts.'
- 'As a reflective observation, I found that I now step back from what has happened to understand ideas and experiences from different points of view.'
- 'The one thing that I have learned from reflecting is that if I do not know myself then the capacity to learn is limited and that actually trying to make a difference to others will not eventuate!'
- 'The reflection process has opened up a whole new view for me on how I see myself and the way I behave. The outcomes that can be achieved from experiential learning are quite unique and would be hard to match in any other approach. The best part of this learning is that it allows you to be flexible and encourages you to change and improve your action theory to meet your current knowledge and experience.'

Throughout this paper I have emphasized the importance of using the concept of experiential learning, and in particular the role of reflection, as a means of drawing together theory and practice to enhance not only the deeper learning of students but of the educators as well. It is a process that takes the academic and the student on a journey that goes beyond 'single-loop' learning (Argyris & Schön, 1978). The students become actively engaged in 'double-loop' learning as this is necessary if managers and organizations are to make informed decisions in rapidly changing and often uncertain contexts (Argyris, 1990). Reflective practice is fundamental and 'closes the loop' but also encourages them to proceed to further action-reflection spirals of learning. Kolb and Kolb (2002) outline that the effective teacher builds on the exploration of what students already know and believe, on the sense they have made of previous experiences and allows the student to re-examine and modify their previous sense-making in light of the new ideas. Learning is a continual and life-long process.

## REFERENCES

Adams, P., Openshaw, R. & Trembath, V. (eds) (2006). *Score More: Essential Academic Skills for Tertiary Education.* South Melbourne Australia: Thomson Dunmore Press.

Argyris, C. (1990). *Overcoming Organizational Defenses. Facilitating organizational learning.* Boston: Allyn and Bacon.
Argyris, C., & Schön, D. (1978). *Organizational learning: A theory of action perspective.* Reading, Mass.: Addison Wesley.
Argyris, C. and Schön, D. (1996). *Organizational learning II: Theory, method and practice.* Reading Mass.: Addison Wesley.
Barrett, H.C. (2005). White Paper: The Reflect Initiative. Researching Electronic Portfolios: Learning, Engagement, Collaboration, Through Technology. *Journal of Adolescent and Adult Literacy,* March 2007.
Beard, C. & Wilson, J. P. (2006). *Experiential Learning.* 2nd ed. London: Kogan Page.
Bolton, G. (2010). *Reflective Practice. Writing & Professional Development.* 3rd ed. London: Sage.
Bone. Z., Jarzabkowski, P. & Eiseman, J. (2000). Breaking the Isolation: Academics in Action Learning Groups and Peer Appraisal. *16th EGOS Colloquium, Organisational Praxis.* Helsinki, Finland, July 24.
Bone, Z., McMullen, C. & Clarke, D. (2009). Academics Writing and Learning Together: Using Writing Groups to Promote Scholarship of Teaching. *The International Journal of Learning.* Volume 16.
Boud, D., Keogh, K. & Walker, D. (eds) (1985). *Reflection: Turning Experience into Learning.* London: Kogan Page.
Buysse, V., Sparkman, K. L., & Wesley, P. W. (2003). Communities of practice: Connecting what we know with what we do, *Exceptional Children, 69*(3), 263 -277.
Cameron, S. (2007) *The Business Student's Handbook: Learning Skills for study and employment,* Harlow, England: Financial Times Prentice Hall.
Cartwright, S. (2002). 'Double-Loop Learning: A Concept and Process for Leadership Educators'. *Journal of Leadership Education.* Vol. 1, Issue 1 – Summer.
De Janasz, S., Wood, G., Gottschalk, L., Dowd, K. & Schneider, B. (2009). *Interpersonal Skills in Organisations.* North Ryde Australia: McGraw-Hill Australia Pty Ltd.
Duffy, A. (2007) 'A concept of reflective practice: determining its value to nurses', *British Journal of Nursing,* Vol. 16, Iss. 22, 1400-1407.

Griffith, B. A. & Dunham, E. B. (2015). *Working in Teams. Moving From High Potential to High Performance.* London: Sage Publications Inc.

Hinnett, K. (2002). *Developing Reflective Practice in Legal Education.* Warwick UK: Warwick Printing Press.

Institute of Cultural Affairs. (1995). *An Introduction to Discussion Method.* Canada: Institute of Cultural Affairs.

Kemmis, S. 'Action Research and the Politics of Reflection'. In Boud, D., Keough, R. & Walker, D. Eds. (1985). *Reflections: Turning Experience into Learning.* New York: Kogan Page Ltd.

Kolb, A. Y. & Kolb, D. A. (2005). Learning Styles and Learning Spaces: Enhancing Experiential Learning in Higher Education. *Academy of Management Learning & Education.* Vol. 4, No. 2, 193-212.

Kolb, D. (1984). *Experiential learning: experience at the source of learning and development.* London: Kogan Page.

Lave, J. & Wenger, E. (1991). *Situated learning: Legitimate peripheral participation.* Cambridge: Cambridge University Press.

Lee-Davies, L. (2007). *Developing Work and Study Skills.* London: Thomson Learning.

National Tertiary Education Union. (2005). *Preparing and Presenting a Teaching Portfolio.* Melbourne: NTEU National Office, Policy & Research Unit.

O'Connell, T., & Dyment, J. (2006). Reflections on using journals in higher education: a focus group discussion with faculty. *Assessment & Evaluation in Higher Education. 31*(6), 671-691.

Ramsden,P. (1992). *Learning to teach in higher education.* London: Routledge.

Schon, D. (1983). *The Reflective Practitioner: How Professionals Think in Action.* London: Basic Books Inc.

Schon, D. (1991) *The Reflective Turn: Case Studies in and on Educational Practice.* New York: Teachers College Press.

Trigwell, K., Martin, E., Benjamin, J. & Prosser, M. (2000). Scholarship of teaching: A model. *Higher Education, Research and Development.* 19, 2,155168.

Welikala, T. (2011). Rethinking International Higher Education Curriculum: Mapping the research landscape. *Universitas 21 Teaching & Learning Position Paper.* UK: Universitas 21.

CHAPTER 10

# Reflective Practice through Reflecting Writing

*Abraham Motlhabane*

In this chapter, reflection on the classroom practices of mathematics and science teachers is used to showcase how reflective writing can be useful to improve classroom practice. Reflection on teacher's experiences in the classroom was seen as vital in improving classroom practice. To explore teacher's classroom practices, teachers were given quiet time to reflect on three questions, namely, *"What do you do in the classroom to ensure effective learning and teaching?" "Describe some areas of the teaching of Maths and Science that could be improved to ensure effective teaching and learning?" "What can we do better?"* Data was collected from their written responses and focus group interviews with teachers. Common themes were derived from the written responses and transcribed interviews. Motivation was identified as being key to achieving effective learning and teaching.

## INTRODUCTION

The study reported on here is located within reflective practice. Although the term *reflective practice* is interpreted and understood in a number of different ways, in this context it is viewed as a means by which teachers are able to develop a greater level of self-awareness about the nature and impact of their classroom practice. It is interpreted in this way in the hope of creating opportunities for professional growth and development (Osterman & Kottkamp, 1993). This is consistent with the ideas of John Dewey that reflection is "a kind of thinking that consists of turning a subject over in the mind and giving it serious thought"; it is "active, persistent and careful consideration of any belief or supposed form of knowledge in the light of the grounds that support it, and further conclusions to which it leads...it includes a conscious and voluntary effort to establish belief upon a firm basis of evidence and rationality" (Dewey, 1933).

Reflective practice is located within both the older tradition of experiential learning and the more recently articulated perspective of situated cognition. Experiential learning theorists, including Dewey, Lewin, and Piaget, maintain that learning is most effective, most likely to lead to behavioral change, when it begins with experience, and specifically problematic experience. From experience and research, we know that learning is most effective when people become personally engaged in the learning process, and engagement is most likely to take place when there is a need to learn (Osterman & Kottkamp, 1993).

Although experience is the basis for learning, learning cannot take place without reflection; moreover, as reflection is essential to the process, reflection cannot be separated from action. Teachers' reflective practice integrates theory and practice, thought and action – a process which could be described as a dialogue of thinking and doing, through which teachers become more skilful (Osterman & Kottkamp, 1993).

Teachers' reflection involved observation, discovery, and collaborative inquiry and discourse through shared experience. For that reason, classroom experience was seen as both a resource and a stimulus for learning. Through the associated processes of observation and analysis, teachers were able to see clearly the discrepancies, incongruities, and failures to reach intentions. The problem begins to emerge more clearly, and teachers begin to see their own role in the problem with greater clarity (Osterman & Kottkamp, 1993).

In the reflective practice model, the link between theory and practice is explicit rather than implicit, as it is in the traditional approach, and the developmental process begins with practice. The belief on which the study being reported on is founded is that to develop new and better methods of practice, we should begin by examining the classroom practices we want to improve. The central knowledge questions are thus much broader than in the traditional approach: "What do teachers do, and why do they do it?"; "How do their knowledge, understanding and personal theoretical framework affect their classroom practice?"; "Given new knowledge, what will they do differently?" The reflective approach integrates several kinds of knowledge: both theory *and* practice are integral and central considerations, and theory includes ideas derived from both formal research and personal experience. Attention to public knowledge and formal theory is not lost or diminished, but practice – specifically, personal practice– assumes a far greater importance (Osterman & Kottkamp, 1993).

Teachers' reflective writing therefore involved analyzing, reconsidering and questioning experiences within their own environmental context and teaching and learning theories. For example, teachers have found that the realities of their practicum experiences do not match what they may have learnt from theories about teaching and learning. Accordingly, the process of reflecting on the disparities between expectations and actual experience enables teachers to become more closely engaged with the process of their own learning (Moon, 1999). It is through reflection and analysis that the study strives to understand the teachers' experience. Furthermore, examining experience by considering both the teachers' actions and classroom outcomes becomes a means to articulate and understand espoused theories and theories-in-use. Why did events take place as they did? What ideas or feelings prompted teachers' practices? Did their practice correspond with their intentions? Did their practice lead to the outcomes as intended? (Osterman & Kottkamp, 1993).

To encourage teachers to be reflective is to encourage the development of a habit of processing cognitive material that can lead to ideas that are beyond the curriculum, beyond learning defined by learning outcomes, and beyond those of the teacher who is managing the learning. However, the context in which reflection takes place cannot be overlooked (Boud & Walker 1998). Hence the analysis of the teachers' written reflections took cognizance of their context.

It is through practice in reflection that we learn to adopt a conscious orientation toward finding the problems. Even though this step may seem difficult or feel "unnatural," the skill develops quickly, because the learning cycle begins with problematic experience. One of the initial tasks of the facilitator in a formal reflective practice setting is to enable individuals to uncover or discover problematic situations within the context of their practice (Osterman & Kottkamp, 1993).

Teachers found it difficult to identify problems. This is because people generally, and teachers in particular, want to view things positively and to be optimistic. In response to organizational problems, discussion quickly turns to solutions, while problem identification and analysis are cut short (Bolman & Deal, 1991). Identification of personal problems is even more difficult.

An assumption of the study was that finding the problem would motivate the teachers. Because reflective practice focuses on personal behavior within the professional context, the study began by gathering and analyzing rich information about the experience, and particularly about the teachers' experiences (Osterman & Kottkamp, 1993).

Reflection on the teachers' experience was harnessed because it is viewed as potentially transformative of everyone involved in the teaching and learning of mathematics and science. The approach adopted in the study entailed reflective writing because it is simple and direct. The personal pronouns *I* and *we* can be used because participants are reflecting on *their own* experiences or perceptions. Whereas most academic writing tasks require main points to be supported with references to the literature or to current practice, teachers' reflective writing involved recording their personal views, impressions or observations. However, it was more than simply a *description* of their observations or thoughts. Teachers' reflective writing involved evaluating their experiences, and thinking about both the strengths and limitations of their classroom practice.

## Research Questions

The central research questions were based on the reflection questions as indicated below:
- What do teachers do in the classroom to ensure effective learning and teaching?
- Describe some areas of the teaching of Maths and Science that could be improved to ensure effective teaching and learning?
- What can we do better?

## Methodology

Qualitative methods were used to collect and analyze data. These teachers had participated in a mathematics and science colloquium attended by 450 teachers. Those attending the colloquium were divided into smaller groups to discuss various topics related to the teaching of mathematics and science. 21 teachers participated in the study. Of these, 15 were female and 8 male teachers. 5 had an honors qualification in mathematics and science education; 1 had an honors qualification in education management; 8 had a diploma in education; and 7 had an advanced certificate in education, specializing in mathematics and science. Of the 21 participants, 6 had more than 20 years' experience, 7 had between 11 and 20 years' experience, 5 had between 6 and 10 years' experience, and only 1 had less than 5 years' experience. Only 4 of the participants were teaching higher grades (grades 10–12), while 17 were teaching grades 1 to 3.

The teachers were given a reflective writing task. They were given 45 minutes quite time in which to reflect on the following three open-ended questions: "What do you do in the classroom to ensure effective learning and teaching?"; "Describe some areas of the teaching of Maths and Science that could be improved to ensure effective teaching and learning"; and "How can we teach better?". Teachers were asked to write down their responses, and at the end of the 45 minutes allocated, all 21 submitted their written responses.

To elaborate further on the written responses, focus group interviews were conducted with the participants. The interview schedule comprised questions intended to obtain clarity on the written reflections the participants had submitted. The interviews took roughly an hour, and afforded teachers the opportunity to share ideas about classroom practice.

The written responses were collated and inspected in order to identify common themes. The phenomenographic approach was used to categorize and analyze the responses, the intention behind these categories being to capture the qualitative understanding of the phenomenon (classroom practice) (Marton & Booth, 1997). This approach was chosen because of its usefulness in representing data; the phenomenographic approach makes it possible to view the ideas as constituting an internal relation between the teacher and his or her world (Marton & Booth, 1997).

The teachers' responses were interpreted for "variation of meanings" and placed into temporary categories referred to as the "pool of meanings" (Marton & Booth, 1997). Then, through a lengthy process of iteration, the characterizations of the categories as qualitatively distinct methods of classroom practice were identified. Researcher bias in interpretation was minimized by repeating the iterative process of data analysis after a few weeks. Cross checks to improve the methodological credibility of the characterization of the categories included examining relevant literature.

## DISCUSSION OF RESULTS

The discussion of the teacher's reflections is divided into three parts. The responses to reflection question 1 will be discussed first, followed by the second reflection question and reflection question 3. The educational implication for using reflection with teachers is then discussed.

### Reflective Question 1: What Do You Do in the Classroom to Ensure Effective Learning and Teaching?

A wide body of research shows that the single most significant factor affecting learner achievement is classroom instruction. In a study, Mortimore and Sammons (1987) found classroom instruction to have more impact on student learning than any other factor. As McKinsey & Company concluded in their study of the world's best schools, "The only way to improve outcomes is to improve instruction."

It is acknowledged that there are a variety of teaching strategies, but the most crucial factor is how teachers alternate their teaching strategies. This is because the success of teaching depends mainly on the effective use of the available teaching strategies. In response to the reflective question 1 above, one of the teachers stated that, *"I use different strategies/methods of teaching and learning"*. Teachers may well alternate teaching strategies to capture the interest of learners. A variety of teaching strategies used in the classroom was identified, one of which was play, which teachers reported using to enhance learning. Play as a teaching strategy may have both advantages and disadvantages. An advantage is that many of the learners in primary and high school are at a stage where play forms part of their daily activities, and it is something they find enjoyable. However, play can be less successful as a strategy if a teacher has not planned his or her lesson properly or if the play is not controlled. It should be clear how play will benefit learning in terms of its purpose and execution in the classroom.

Some teachers reported using practical work as a teaching strategy. This requires suitable equipment, as without it, practical work can be unsuccessful; learning science in particular requires that learners touch and see during experiments. However, teachers can improvise by using existing materials for practical work. The use of practical work in teaching requires real, practical examples so that learners can see the real-life relevance of the practical work.

Teachers explained that they encouraged learners to participate actively in the classroom by creating interest in the subject. Teachers can do a variety of things to capture learners' interest. One of the teachers explained: *"When I introduce the topic, I make sure that my introduction is clear and understandable and always try to relate it with things that they familiar with, (everyday life experience)."* This teacher believed in proper lesson planning, with the main focus being on capturing the learner's interest from the beginning of the lesson. Another teacher emphasized: *"I present the subject in a well organized manner."*

Planning a lesson is critical, because when a lesson is well planned, the teacher knows what to teach, how to teach it, and when to teach it. This means ensuring that the introduction is clear and understandable, and that learners understand the relationship between what they are going to learn and everyday experience.

As part of the lesson planning, some teachers suggested group discussions. Many things can happen during group discussions. For instance, learners can discuss what they already know (pre-knowledge) about the topic to be taught, and they can be given a problem to solve. However, every learner should participate actively so that he or she realizes the benefits of a group discussion. In this context, teachers can try to encourage underperforming learners. One of the teachers explained: *"I try and help underperforming learners by giving them individual attention"*: this prevents learners who do not understand from being left unattended, as they may then lose interest in the subject. Learners are given an opportunity to participate actively in the discussions by being allowed to comment, ask questions and help each other with regard to topics of interest.

Teachers reported making every effort to treat all learners equally, and encouraging learners to take responsibility for their own learning. A teacher stated, *"I motivate learners to ask questions when they do not understand."* This shows how important it is for teachers to be approachable, so that learners feel comfortable asking questions. In addition, the classroom atmosphere should be supportive, so that learners are not afraid to ask questions, and do not fear that they will be laughed at. Teachers should therefore find ways to create a classroom environment that is conducive to effective learning and teaching.

Learners are given homework as a way of keeping them engaged. Learners should be encouraged to do their homework, and to do it at home. A way to encourage them is to let them present their work to their peers, and teachers can praise them for good performance. Homework should be interesting, and learners should not perceive it as a punishment. The aim should be for learners to be motivated to come to class the following day.

Learner motivation has been identified as instrumental in influencing the engagement of learners in the learning process. An important aim of science education is to empower learners by nurturing the belief that they have the capacity to succeed in science learning and to cultivate the adaptive learning strategies required to help to bring about that success. Research shows that poor performance in school science is attributable mainly to the inability of science curricula and classroom practices to ignite the interest of learners in learning science (Velayutham, Aldridge & Fraser 2011). Learner's self-regulation in academic settings has been identified as a pivotal construct that influences learner engagement in learning (Boekaerts & Cascallar, 2006).

It should be noted that teachers reflected on very important aspect of classroom practice and their responses can be useful to many stakeholders including teachers themselves. The ideas presented will definitely help improve how we teach maths and science. In addition, teacher trainers can learn from teacher's reflected ideas, to position their training to meet the real needs of teachers in the classroom.

## Reflective Question 2 Describe Some Areas of the Teaching of Maths and Science That Could Be Improved to Ensure Effective Teaching and Learning?

The teachers' responses to this reflection question highlighted two critical points namely, improving teacher's and learner's skills in geometry and improving learner's counting skills. The two points are discussed briefly below.

### Improving Teachers' and Learners' Skills in Geometry

Teachers suggested that in-service training in specific content areas would be helpful. The majority identified finance and geometry as areas in which they would like training. A teacher stated: "*Geometry could be improved if learners can be provided with mathematical instruments for construction,* " From the teacher's written reflections, it was apparent that there are limited skills in the teaching and learning of geometry. Their responses suggest lack of appropriate resources that can be used in the teaching of geometry. This is coupled with lack of training in the teaching of geometry on the part of the teacher. What can be learnt from this is that, education officials should constantly monitor the teachers in terms of their teaching needs, so that learners should not be disadvantaged.

### Improving Learners' Counting Skills

Many teachers observed that learners had problems counting. However, this was not surprising, as this phenomenon had already been revealed in the South African Annual National Assessment (ANA) results. The ANA results indicate that learners do not have counting skills. The fact that teachers are doing something to help learners overcome the difficulties they experience with counting is encouraging. A teacher reported: "*I start my lesson everyday by letting learners count forward and backward.*" Some learners may interpret this as a way of making fun of them, but they will later come to realise the purpose of the activity. An activity such as this can help improve the learners' concentration skills ahead of a lesson. Some teachers use this type of activity as an ice breaker. The most important thing, however, is its value in improving learners' counting skills.

## Reflective Question 3: What Can We Do Better?

With the last question, I wanted the teachers to reflect on "what can we do better" and after going through the responses of teachers, two themes came out. The themes as discussed below are: Improving the learning environment and stakeholder support.

## Improving the Learning Environment

Teachers emphasized the role of a supportive learning environment in enhancing the teaching and learning of mathematics in the classroom. A number of factors can improve the learning environment of learners in schools, including intrinsic and extrinsic motivation of learners.

Ryan and Deci (2002) describe motivation as a process in which a person's way of thinking has an important role. These authors suggest that two primary cognitive processes affect motivation, namely a change in the *perceived locus of causality* and a change in *perceived competence*. When the perceived locus of causality changes to a more internally perceived locus, the intrinsic motivation or the more self-determined forms of extrinsic motivation will be enhanced. When learners are extrinsically motivated, they perceive the locus of causality and the regulation of their studying activities to be external to themselves, whereas when students are intrinsically motivated, they perceive the locus to be within themselves. Change in perceived competence is related to the psychological need for competence. Events that increase perceived competence enhance intrinsic motivation, whereas events that reduce perceived competence tend to undermine intrinsic motivation.

Ryan and Deci (2002) define intrinsic motivation as an "inherent tendency to seek out novelty, and challenges, to extend and exercise one's capacities, to explore and to learn." Intrinsically motivated behavior is characterised by concentration and engagement; it occurs spontaneously, and people become wholly absorbed in it. Intrinsically motivated activity gives rise to interest, excitement, and enjoyment. Intrinsically motivated behaviours are based on the need to feel competent and self-determined. Teachers who support autonomy have been shown to have more intrinsically motivated students with higher levels of self-esteem compared with the students of teachers who are control oriented (Deci, Nezlek & Sheinman, 1981).

Providing choice rather than control and acknowledging students' inner experiences therefore enhances intrinsic motivation, and student learning improves (Deci& Ryan, 2000). Vallerand, Pelletier, Blais, Briere, Senecal, and Vallieres (1992) have divided intrinsic motivation (IM) into three types: IM to know, IM to accomplish things, and IM to experience stimulation. Several studies (Deci, 1975; Deci & Ryan, 1985) have shown that intrinsic motivation has a number of positive effects on learning. However, it is unrealistic to imagine that all science learning can be intrinsically motivated. That is, it is not possible to make all the goals of the curriculum intrinsically motivating, and in a classroom situation it is not always possible to give students choices in terms of what they are to learn (see Byman & Kansanen, 2008). Initially, intrinsic and extrinsic motivation were described as dichotomous, and extrinsic motivation was even said to be damaging to intrinsic motivation (Deci, 1975). However, Deci and Ryan (1985) subsequently refuted the notion that intrinsic and extrinsic motivation were mutually exclusive.

Teachers' efforts are intended to motivate learners extrinsically. This is because, through an internalization process, extrinsically motivated behaviours can become increasingly self-determined or autonomous (Byman, Lavonen, Juuti & Meisalo, 2012). When the internalization process succeeds, learners will acknowledge the importance of the aims of the curriculum, and will assimilate these into their integrated sense of self, and thus fully accept them as their own.

Similarly, self-determination theory draws distinctions between four types of extrinsic motivation based on the degree of self-determination, namely external, interjected, identified, and integrated regulation. External and interjected regulation are considered to be relatively controlled forms of extrinsic motivation, whereas identified and integrated regulation are considered to be relatively autonomous. External regulation refers to intentional behaviours engaged in to earn some expected reward or to avoid a threatened punishment. Externally regulated behaviours are the least self-determined behaviours because the underlying values have not been internalized. A learner who does his or her homework to avoid parental reproach is externally regulated. Working only if the teacher is in the vicinity is a further example. Externally regulated studying tends to be characterised by poor maintenance and transfer once the teacher's control is withdrawn.

*Stakeholder Support*

The issue of stakeholder support is becoming part of the schooling system to an increasing degree. This is because schools cannot operate solely on their own. They need the constant support of all levels of the education system, including circuit, district, provincial and national departmental levels. Teachers feel the need for support in order to optimize their performance at school level. Regular visits to offer the necessary support to schools are encouraged.

## EDUCATIONAL IMPLICATIONS

Reflection is a crucial and important aspect in the teaching and learning of any subject. It helps us to have a second thought about how we teach and learn subject content. This is because things change, for example technology improves and change every day. The challenges we had as mathematics and science teachers 20 years ago are not the same as the present challenges. The way mathematics and science was taught 20 years ago may not be the same as the present way. Hence, upon reflection we can think about better ways of improving the teaching methodologies and learning styles. This means trying out new teaching and learning styles in the classrooms. Investigating the impact of using new teaching and learning styles in the teaching and learning of mathematics and science. We can start to appreciate the challenges we experience in our pursued endeavor to improve education in general. The questions posed to the teachers to reflect on, namely, *"What do you do in the classroom to ensure effective learning and teaching?"* "Describe some areas of the teaching of Maths and Science that could be improved to ensure effective teaching and learning?" and "What can we do better?" was simply saying to the teachers, given the circumstances you find yourself in, what is the current classroom practice of teachers and what can be done to improve the situation and make it better. It called for introspection on the part of the teachers. More especially when teachers were given quite moments to deeply reflect on this questions. Quite moments helped teachers to think and come to their senses. Basically the questions related to reflecting on the present status in terms of teaching and learning, and the improvement plans aimed at making the situation better.

It remains critical that teachers should reconsider how they teach through analyzing and questioning their previous classroom practices and experiences. This then becomes a learning experience for teachers and they can begin to think about what is possible and what is not possible given the current reality. Teachers can learn enormously by reflecting on their personal views in terms of their current classroom practice. And by comparing their current views with documented literature and the reality in the classroom, fresh ideas about improving classroom practice can emerge. Of critical importance is the act of sharing of ideas in the reflected questions. This helped teachers in positioning themselves within the broader scope of challenges, diverse possibilities about the teaching of mathematics and science. Upon going back to the classrooms teachers will be fully prepared and can tackle challenges with ease.

This notion of reflection is applied to student learning as well as to teaching. Ashcroft and Foreman-Peck, 1994 argue that "the teacher's role is to facilitate the development of students as reflective practitioners of their subject. This applies within vocational courses, where students are learning to take responsibility for their actions and to look open-mindedly for ways to improve and develop their practice and understanding, but also within purely academic studies. The implication is that students learn to analyze alternative conceptions and models of their subject, its social implications and the views and perspectives on that subject of students, tutors and perhaps writers and researchers."

## CONCLUSION

A lot can be learnt from teachers' reflection on their classroom practices. Among the most important were the initiatives that teachers mentioned to make the classroom experience more enjoyable to the learners. The major contribution of the study reported on here lies in the documentation of practical initiatives employed by teachers to motivate learners in the classroom. The reflective exercise they engaged in gave them the opportunity to take stock of their actions and suggest ways to improve the teaching and learning of mathematics and science. Key in their reflection was their efforts to instil learner interest in the subject and encourage classroom participation. Their initiatives focused on the use of different teaching strategies to capture the interest of learners. Teachers mentioned four significant obstacles, namely learners' inability to count; the inadequacy of teachers' geometry teaching skills; the environment in which learners learn; and the lack of stakeholder support (departmental officials in particular were mentioned). These four obstacles should receive particular attention. In addition, teachers were shown to require training in specific content areas, such as geometry. It should be noted that the chapter does not give all the answers related to reflective writing, hence efforts to get the most from reflective writing task should continue. To sum it up *"The critical part of reflective practice is that it requires a commitment to learning from experience and from evidence, rather than to learning certain 'recipes' for action. Even if you start with recipes, they need to be explored and analyzed for their underlying assumptions and effects as you gain in confidence. This process of critical enquiry should be reflexive, that is responsive to your own needs and the context in which you work, but also critical of the existing educational provision and ideology (including your own). The analysis involves not just your own practice, but also the social, moral and political context for that practice."* Ashcroft and Foreman-Peck, 1994.

## REFERENCES

Ashcroft, K. & Foreman-Peck, L. (1994). Managing Teaching and Learning in Further and
 Higher Education. London: Falmer.

Boekaerts, M., & Cascallar, E. (2006). How far have we moved toward the integration of theory and practice in self-regulation? *Educational Psychology Review*, 18, 199–210.

Boud, D., & Walker, D. (1998). Promoting reflection in professional courses: the challenges of context. *Studies in Higher Education*, 23(2),191–206.

Bolman, L. G., & Deal, T. E. (1991). Reframing organizations. San Francisco: Jossey-Bass.

Byman, R., Lavonen, J., Juuti, K., & Meisalo, V. (2012). Motivational orientations in physics learning: a self determination theory approach. *Journal of Baltic Science Education*, 11(4).

Byman R., Kansanen, P. (2008). Pedagogical thinking in a student's mind: A conceptual clarification on the basis of self-determination and volition theories, Scandinavian Journal of Educational Research, 52 (6), pp.603-621.

Deci, E.L. (1975). *Intrinsic motivation*. New York: Plenum Press.

Deci, E.L., & Ryan, R.M. (1985). *Intrinsic motivation and self-determination in human behavior.* New York: Plenum Press.

Deci, E.L., & Ryan, R.M. (2000). The "what" and "why" of goal pursuits: human needs and self-determination of behavior. *Psychological Inquiry*, 11,227–268.

Deci, E.L., Nezlek, J., & Sheinman, L. (1981).Characteristics of the rewarder and intrinsic motivation of the rewardee.*Journal of Personality and Social Psychology*, 40,1–10.

Dewey, J. (1933). *How we think*. Boston, MA: DC Heath and Co.

Marton, F., & Booth, S. (1997). *Learning and awareness*. New Jersey: Lawrence Erlbaum Associates.

McKinsley & Company. (2007). How the world's best-performing school systems come out on top.

Moon, J. (1999).*Reflection in learning and professional development*. London: Kogan Page.

Mortimore, P., & Sammons, P. (1987). New evidence on effective elementary schools. *Educational Leadership, 45* (1), 4-8.

Osterman, K.F., & Kottkamp, R.B. (1993). *Reflective practice for educators:improving schoolingthrough professionaldevelopment.* Newbury Park, CA: Corwin Press.

Ryan, R.M., & Deci, E.L. (2002). An overview of self-determination theory: an organismic-dialectical perspective. In EL Deci & RM Ryan (Eds.), *Handbook of self-determination research* (pp. 3–33). Rochester, NY: The University of Rochester Press.

Vallerand, R.J., Pelletier, L.G., Blais, M.R., Briere, N.M., Senecal, C & Vallieres, E.F. (1992). The academic motivation scale: a measure of intrinsic, extrinsic, and amotivation in education. *Educational and Psychological Measurement*, 52, 1003–1017.

Velayutham, S., Aldridge, J., & Fraser, B. (2011). Development and validation of an instrument to measure students' motivation and self-regulation in science learning. *International Journal of Science Education*, 33(15), 2159–2179.

CHAPTER 11

# Creating Intergenerational Portraits through "Life Stories" in Communication Studies

*Marilyn J. Matelski*

> This assignment is intended to personalize and expand upon current theories and models in interpersonal, family, and cross-cultural communication. Through interviewing either family members or peers, students create cultural identity profiles, while exploring existing worldviews as well as the cultural factors that shape them. As a result, they are better able to "connect the dots" when analyzing family dynamics and intercultural encounters. They can also more skillfully explore the dynamic, ever-changing dialectic between different populations within different cultural and historical settings.

While most communication scholars include history as an integral part of culture, the "prevailing view" of society often overshadows the richness of other perspectives (or worldviews) from the multiple generations found in all communities which reflect, shape and infuse that very perspective.

Students may also find this "prevailing view" of society both somewhat dry and detached as well as unfamiliar to their own daily lives. The life story paper—a capstone project representing the assimilation and culmination of smaller assignments throughout the semester—is intended to *personalize* the literature and to create common links between multi-generational populations. By sharing family information through a prism of systems and cultural dimensions theories, students can contextualize generational differences that are both unique and universal as well as fundamental to their own "life stories," which form a solid foundation for cultural identity.

## The Concepts

**Cultural Identity**

Communication scholars Myron Lustig and Jolene Koester have defined "cultural identity" as a:

> ...sense of belonging to a particular culture or ethnic group. It is formed in a process that results from membership in a particular culture, and it involves learning about and accepting the traditions, heritage, language, religion, ancestry, aesthetics, thinking patterns and social structures of culture (1999, p. 138).

Lustig and Koester underscore the deep connection between culture and individuality as well as its propensity for constant change. They also identify three stages of identity awareness that take place:

1. The *unexamined cultural identity*: a lack of interest in cultural issues as a result of taking one's own cultural characteristics for granted.
2. *Cultural identity search:* a process of exploration and questioning about one's culture in order to learn more about it.
3. *Cultural identity achievement*: accepting oneself and internalizing one's cultural identity (Lustig & Koester).

Crucial to moving from stage 2 to stage 3 is a broad understanding of general systems and cultural dimensions theories.

**General Systems Theory**

Karl Ludwig von Bertalanffy, an Austrian-born biologist (1901-1972), is now recognized as one of the greatest minds of the twentieth century, having helped to create an interdisciplinary paradigm for the dynamic processes that take place in all parts of life. While specifically described as a biological model at first, "general systems theory" soon expanded into many other areas, including, as psychologist Thaddus E. Weckowicz once noted, "cybernetics, education, history, philosophy, psychiatry, psychology and sociology" (Weckowicz, p. 2). Weckowicz went on to describe not only von Bertalanffy's specific contributions to scholarly knowledge, but his philosophical approach to study as well:

> He was a "trail blazer." He was critical of the 'Cartesian' cult of analytical thinking which prevailed in modern science and philosophy. He suggested that it should be replaced by the holistic systems approach. In some respects, he retreated from the Cartesian-Galilean paradigm of science, which became predominant in the seventeenth century, and went back to the Neo-Platonist paradigm of the sixteenth century (p. 2).

When applied within a communication studies perspective, von Bertalanffy's definition of a "system" as a set of interactive components relates directly to the cultural elements of society (i.e., religion, economic status, geography, ethnicity, race, etc.), which continuously interconnect with each other to form a whole. Through this paradigm, then, it is easy to see how and why one's cultural identity is constantly changing, based on the volatility of each component at any given time. Also, given the reality that every person can be a part of multiple "families" (e.g., biological, professional, sports, adoptive, extended, etc.); the complexity of this dynamism is almost incomprehensible, to say the least (von Bertalanffy). And it has become further complicated with globalization and the growth of technology.

But how best to convey this profound concept to undergraduate students...and to allow them adequate time and space to reflect upon its application to their own lives? One way to "connect" theory to personal experience is through introducing simpler models found in most interpersonal textbooks, and assigning informal journal essays to apply these models to the students' daily lives. An example of one such model used in a family communication course is therapist Virginia Satir's mobile model.

Virginia Satir uses the image of a mobile to describe a family system. In this model, as one member of the family is impacted by a particular circumstance the other members must react to the change. A mobile's parts are always moving but connected in the same way that the different members of a family are always experiencing motion in their lives but are bonded together as a family system as well:

> As events touch one member of the family, other members reverberate in response to the change in the affected member… No matter what change a family experiences, all members are affected due to their interdependence Galvin, Bylund & Brommel, 2012, p. 59).

Change may come as an internal shift—e.g. a discovery, awareness, or understanding—that brings about external change; or it may simply reinforce the existing family bond. In any case, the overall dynamic has undergone some alteration.

Students who apply this model often write about "chapters" in their lives where the family dynamic was changed, either due to an added new member, a health crisis, divorce, economic change or death in the family. For them, it not only personalizes the theory, it helps them to analyze the family undercurrents from a more objective perspective.

## Cultural Dimensions Theory

While general systems theory clearly demonstrates the dynamic nature of families and communication, the element of culture is also a significant area to study. Social psychologist Geert Hofstede began to quantify and apply several key cultural elements in cross-cultural organizations in the 1970s. Several years later, he co-founded the Institute for Research on Intercultural Cooperation (IRIC). Since that time, Hofstede and others have built on his original cultural dimensions model and it now reaches far beyond the multinational corporate structure, encompassing all disciplines dealing with national identities and cultures.

Today, Hofstede's model emphasizes six specific dimensions of culture—individualism/collectivism (IDV), power distance (PDI), uncertainty avoidance (UAI), masculinity/femininity (MAS), short-term/long-term orientation (LTO) and indulgence/restraint (IVR)—as they both define society, and change through time (Hofstede, Hofstede & Minkov).

The individualism/collectivism scale measures how members of a group (or society) look at themselves in relationship to that group (i.e., individual identity within the group versus an affiliate of the group identity). Individualistic national cultures such as the United States tend to reward those who "stand out" from the crowd, whereas collectivistic societies value those who sacrifice and remain true to "the greater good" (e.g., China, Korea and Japan).

Power distance addresses hierarchical class structure, and the degree of social mobility and ease to traverse these classes. Systems with a high power distance usually have rigid class codes, making it almost impossible for one to move from one social class to another. Low power distance cultures are much more egalitarian, providing many opportunities (e.g., education, marriage, etc.) for social rise (or fall). These societies tend to be more "merit-based" than related to birth and bloodlines.

Uncertainty avoidance deals specifically with societal ambiguity and how it is resolved. National cultures with low uncertainty avoidance tend to be long established, with a rich history of custom and tradition—written contracts are not considered as important as traditional convention. Those nations with high uncertainty avoidance tend to be "younger" (either newly independent after a successful revolt against outside occupiers or victors in a decisive political coup within the country). They also may include an assembly of different ethnic, social, political and economic groups—and thus, require specific rules and laws to which everyone can agree and will follow.

Masculine and feminine societies are characterized by their policies on defense, social welfare and economics. Highly "masculine" cultures like the United States, for example, are likely to have a well-funded military, with huge arsenals of weaponry and sophisticated military intelligence. They also reward entrepreneurial enterprises and privatized initiatives; they devote comparatively little funding for health services and social welfare reform. Highly "feminine" cultures in the Nordic countries, on the other hand, emphasize community interests, tend to use minimal military force (and mostly for national concerns). Socialized medicine and free education are also often associated with these nations.

Short- and long-term orientation explores the dynamic between financial success and business relationships. Following in the tradition of Confucian thought, a long-term orientation values harmony and collective growth over short-term gain; consensus over divergence. Short-term orientation, instead, addresses the immediate goals needed for perceived "success."

Finally, indulgence/restraint (the most recent addendum to Hofstede's original dimensions) addresses the needs gratification allowance within societies. Nations with strict social codes are less likely to tolerate certain behaviors, while those with more unrestricted norms will be more lenient.

Arguably, Hofstede's cultural dimensions are very generalized and are applied on a grand scale; however, when combined with family communication models found in most communication theory texts, students' understanding of both becomes clearer and more relevant to their daily lives. For example, Koener and Fitzpatrick's work in family conversational patterns identifies a conformity orientation scale, which implies certain assumptions about hierarchy (power distance), the value of individualistic identity (individualism/collectivism), consensual versus pluralistic ways of talking (masculinity/femininity), "rules" for conversation (uncertainty avoidance) and topic censorship or lack thereof (indulgence/restraint). The Olson Circumplex Model, addressing family cohesion and adaptability, also incorporates cultural dimensions of short term/long term relationships and masculinity/femininity, as well as individualism/collectivism. The emphasis of cultural dimension elements in these (and other) models presents both continuity and clarity to an otherwise complex and sometimes confusing body of research for undergraduates.

## ACTIVITY

This research assignment explores different generational perspectives through an examination of several key cultural components—gender roles, holiday celebrations, media influences, and family relationships. Students are asked to interview representatives from three generations of their family to form a portrait of their cultural identity within the greater picture of American society.

Before collecting the data, students are asked to create a descriptive "profile" for each person they've chosen to interview. This profile should include basic demographic information such as: 1) gender; 2) age; 3) marital status; 4) education level; 5) economic class; and 6) relationship to the interviewer.

Next, students ask each person the same questions—some reflecting specific personal memories; others incorporating the family's "oral history." They then note the similarities and differences between generational perspectives on these topics. Based on this data, students begin to formulate their own "family history," or "life story," within a family systems paradigm found in their outside readings. This model should also create "links" between similar experiences across generations, thus creating a fabric of cultural identity.

Interview questions include the following:

1. How did our family came to the United States?
2. What historical moment was most memorable to you when you were a child?
3. Who was your hero as a child? Why?
4. What was your favorite holiday as a child? Why?
5. What was your first job? How did you get it?
6. Did you have many "family" dinners? What were they like?
7. What was your favorite form of entertainment?
8. Was religion an important part of your life as a child? Why or why not?
9. What was your neighborhood like?

Students' research analysis is presented in two ways: through a formal paper (8-10 pages, not including notes and bibliography); and with an in-class, 15-20-minute summary of their study (including time for questions and answers). When giving their projects in class, presenters are required to bring three family artifacts to serve as "talking points" for their family profiles. These artifacts usually include such items as maps, special plaques or trophies, jewelry/heirlooms, uniforms, hats/helmets or badges, photo albums, newspaper clippings, personal correspondence, family crests, and/or musical instruments. Favorite family foods are also a popular choice.

Implicit within these presentations are the values of older generations, and their contributions to today's worldview. This aspect of cultural identity, unfortunately, is often either ignored or marginalized. Through oral presentations and class discussions, however, "intergenerational connections" invariably become more emphasized.

## LEARNING OUTCOMES

After completing this assignment, students should be able to:

1. Articulate, integrate and apply concepts cultural identity, systems theory and cultural dimensions through a multigenerational profile of their own families.
2. Understand the differences between theories and models.
3. Improve interviewing skills and techniques.
4. Improve presentational skills.

## DEBRIEFING

Using this method of research, written and oral presentation, as well as class discussion, students are able to create a framework of family systems by adapting theories previously learned in class to their own case study examples. Included in the objectives is the improvement of open-ended interviewing techniques in a relatively comfortable setting. Students are often reluctant to conduct these interviews at first; but they soon discover pathways of conversation with relatives they've not known before. These interviews often become extended conversations with family that go far beyond the classroom experience; and students are encouraged to expand these interviews beyond the course assignment. Comments from the following student papers confirm this observation:

Student A:

> "I began this project assuming I would choose three relatives, ask them the interview questions, and get predictable responses from each of them. While most of the answers were conventional and uninteresting,

the conversations that the interviews initiated amazed and enlightened me. The resulting dialogue caused me to examine myself and the relationships within my family more deeply than I ever had."

Student B:

"Three generations of the _____ family have taken vastly different routes through the road of life. In their individual pursuits, they have all garnered some level of success and overcome a great deal of hardship. Each story offers insight into the development of the family system that exists today. The stories are also a valuable tool in discerning how each generation has adapted itself to their surroundings in different manners. In conducting primary research for this paper, I was unfortunately only able to feed on the knowledge of two generations as my grandfather and all of his siblings have passed away. Both my uncle and my father however, served to fill in the gaps in my knowledge of my grandfather's wonderful life. I consider myself lucky though to have had the ability to interview two people of the same generation. It was astounding to see the stark contrast in the way two brothers viewed notions of family and responsibility. My sister _____ offered a wonderful look into how it has been to grow up as a first generation American. Again, there were significant differences in the manner in which _____ was raised as well as in the way she viewed the world. The fabric of our family has been woven amidst love and conflict. The only thing that can be said for sure is that this fabric has only become stronger over the years."

Since this assignment is the final project of the course, all students have already been exposed to family systems theory as well as several other family structure models. In the data-gathering stage, it allows them to reflect upon, and apply this theory to their "real world" experience, creating "connections" between generations in their own families. They also begin to recognize the process of cultural cultivation through meals/food, language, religion, holiday customs, gender roles and hierarchical status. Finally, they realize that communication involves much more than fact-finding, as one student noted:

Student C:

According to the Narrative Theory explained in *Family Communication: Cohesion and Change*, a person's recollection and telling of events does not simply reveal facts, but the interpretations and personal meanings of the stories through the way they are told (Galvin, Bylund & Brommel, p. 77)."

In the presentational/class discussion phase of the assignment, students begin to extend their personal worldviews to the recognition of cultural commonalities between ethnic groups, including social mores, attitudes toward family, spiritual influences, economic pressures, first-generation immigrants, and generational identifications. And at the end of the shared oral presentations, they often see more similarities than differences between diverse cultural groups.

## APPRAISAL

First of all, it is important to note that the paper and presentation fulfill different—though related—objectives for the assignment. The paper portion is intended to emphasize a theoretical paradigm of the family structures, using the interviews as supplementary to the analysis, not as the focal point. The presentational segment of the project, however, highlights interpersonal and cultural dynamics through students' use of family artifacts as "talking points."

One of the challenges to this project has been the "special cases," including: 1) students who have little or no access to three generations of their family due to death or disenfranchisement; 2) students who come from adoptive families; or 3) students who have had difficult past relationships with their families due to alcoholism or drug abuse. In these cases, it is important to have a private conference with the affected students to determine the best way to proceed. Sometimes, the student will opt for writing a longer paper, thus avoiding the potential stress and embarrassment of presentational questions. In other circumstances, the student will choose different generational breakdowns (i.e., parent-sibling-child) instead of the more conventional choice of grandparent-parent-sibling. Both alternatives have proven relatively successful, although not optimal.

Another challenge to this assignment has been the built-in emotional component for those who may have recently lost a relative or those who have learned about a family "secret" or feud which has previously been unknown. Both of these circumstances can often be used for positive discussion in other areas of family communication or cultural identity, however.

Finally, as discussed in the next section, this exercise can be used in several settings and modified for other disciplines, including sociology, psychology and anthropology; but for large classes, it may be more appropriate to conduct small discussions among four or five student-groups, rather than including a public speaking assignment. There may be a point of diminishing returns for a large class when listening to more than 15-20 "life stories."

## PROJECT ADAPTABILITY

While originally designed for a family communication class, this exercise was later modified as an online intercultural assignment for students studying abroad. The key outcomes in this case were much the same; however, while the previous project emphasized *identity*, this paper highlights *culture*, i.e., comparing similarities and differences between the students' national identities and that of their interviewees. They include:

1. To reflect on and apply cultural identity, general systems and cultural dimensions theories to students' own cultural identity.
2. To articulate both shared cultural characteristics and unique distinctions between the students' homeland and the host country studied, applying the circumplex model of cultural dialectics.
3. To improve interviewing skills and techniques.

### Cross-Cultural Communication

The definition of intercultural communication has evolved over time, given the political, economic and technological changes since the mid-20$^{th}$ century. At that time, cultural identities were viewed more as "national identities—perspectives cultivated from the worldview of nation states. However, with the development and growth of internet communication (as well as other technologies), along with changing political borders, the rise of independent nations (and fall of colonialism), populations were no longer seen as members of certain countries but, instead, cultural groups. In addition, post-WWII reconstruction and the subsequent rise of globalization altered world economics, bringing about different worldviews from the haves and have-nots. Finally, the creation of political "partnerships" (e.g., the European Union, NAFTA, NATO, etc.) blurred the distinctions between national identities.

With this in mind, one approach that provides both flexibility and utility when addressing cross-cultural communication is dialectical—analyzing both similarities and differences between cultures. One of the benefits to this model is that it accounts for both individual and group differences, but within a relational and holistic context, rather than as distinct entities (Martin & Nakayama, p. 199). Communication scholars Judith N. Martin and Thomas K. Nakayama identify six similar, but distinct dialectics applied when studying cross-cultural communication:

1. the *cultural-individual dialectic* (recognizing the balance between individual idiosyncratic behavior and those actions representing cultural norms);
2. the *personal/social-contextual dialectic* (acknowledging differences in behavior, based on the particular social context at hand);
3. the *differences-similarities dialectic* (framing intercultural communication as an amalgamation of similarities and differences that can co-exist in harmony);
4. the *static/dynamic dialectic* (stressing the ever-changing nature of culture);
5. the *present-future/history-past dialectic* (recognizing the importance of historical context in understanding different cultures); and
6. the *privilege-disadvantage dialectic* (understanding the differentials of economic power between cultures) (Martin & Nakayama, pp. 199-203).

Not surprisingly, most students learn more about their own cultural identity when living in a different environment, subconsciously contrasting their worldviews with those in their host country, but yet then, seeing common themes within seemingly dichotomous perspectives. For example, one student, after reflecting upon the personal interview, synthesized what appeared to be dissimilar "heroes" into a pattern of mutually shared values:

Student D:

> "Growing up, _____ says her childhood hero was Daniel O'Connell, also known as "The Liberator," who achieved Catholic emancipation for the Republic of Ireland from British rule. It also helps, she said, that O'Connell himself was a Kerry man from the South of Kerry. She explained that while she would have learned about him mainly in school, she was a self-proclaimed "nerd" and was always interested in him and the history of her country. _____'s hero differs significantly from my obsession with Mia Hamm as a young girl playing soccer. The stark difference in who we idolized demonstrates how role models for young girls have changed now that more women are in positions to be such that. This emphasizes a difference in our cultures as women often, and

sometimes still do, face hard times in Ireland and struggle to get and then maintain a position of influence in society whereas in America, girls are taught from a young age that boys are not better than them, a thought echoed by Mia Hamm in advertisements in which she told Michael Jordan, 'Anything you can do I can do better.'"

## THE ASSIGNMENT

In this paper, students are asked to interview a contemporary from the host country of their academic program. The assignment is framed accordingly:

\*\*\*

## LIFE STORY PROJECT

This paper explores different cultural perspectives on such issues as gender roles, holiday celebration, media influence, and family relationships. Your job is to interview someone you have met during your study abroad. This can be a student, a member of a family where you may be living, a distant (or not so distant) relative who now lives in the country where you are studying, etc.

Before collecting your data, create a descriptive "profile" the person you've chosen to interview. This profile should include basic demographic information such as: 1) gender; 2) age; 3) marital status; 4) education level; 5) economic class; and 6) relationship to you.

Next, answer the questions below yourself; and compare those answers with your interviewee. Based on these answers, formulate the cultural similarities and differences between your national identity and that of your interviewee.

Here are the questions:

1. How many generations has your family lived in this country? Do you know the circumstances through which they came? If so, what were they?
2. What historical moment was most memorable to you when you were a child?
3. Who was your hero as a child? Why?
4. What was your favorite holiday as a child? Why?
5. What was your first job? How did you get it?
6. Do you have many "family" dinners? What are they like?
7. What is your favorite form of entertainment?

8. Is religion an important part of your life? Why or why not?
9. What is your neighborhood like?

This paper (10-12 pages in length, not including citations and interview quotes), is worth 30% of your grade.

Be sure to provide specific quotes from your interview to compare your cultural identity with that of your interviewee; and include other citations as needed, using a citation style you've identified on the cover page).

\*\*\*

While students in this exercise were not required to address different generational worldviews, the suggested research questions (and chosen interviewees) indirectly addressed this issue, especially questions 1-5. More significantly, the way these questions were interpreted by the interviewees was often a bigger surprise than the answers themselves. Here are two examples:

Student E:

> (*When discussing childhood heroes*) "\_\_\_\_ and I both chose fictional characters as our childhood heroes. That in itself says something about childhood expectations and looking up to perfection rather than reality…. \_\_\_\_'s choice was a male cartoon character that fought crime and upheld just morals and values. I chose Dorothy from the *Wizard of Oz*. I found her very beautiful and kind but strong willed. \_\_\_\_ and I chose characters that did similar things, we chose them for similar reasons, but the main difference between these characters is whether they are masculine or feminine. The U.S. has traditional gender role expectations where males are expected to have more masculine qualities and gender displays. Boys are to identify with this at a young age as females do the same but with feminine qualities and gender displays. His cultural experience was similar to mine in the U.S. \_\_\_\_ identified with a male figure who fought crime and injustice in traditional masculine, and aggressive ways, while I identified with a female figure who did the same thing but in a more feminine way, such as with emotions. This sheds light on the gender roles in France, where boys are taught to be closer to masculine than to feminine and to identify with their respective sex."

Student F:

> "When I asked her about a historical moment that she remembered well when she was a child, she responded by offering a memory of her childhood that she understood to be a historical moment: "When I was little, I went to our house in the mountains with my father. We saw a bunch of stray horses and I was very afraid of them. My father told me to not be afraid because he was there, and he was very strong and powerful. He then flexed his muscle and it ripped through his t-shirt!" After I corrected her to try and clarify the question, she took a very long time to respond and could not come up with a very certain answer. The closest thing to an answer that she came up with was the historical Man on the Moon landing, but she was not alive for the actual event, she just remembers a lot of coverage on it when she was a little child."

Interestingly, many of the answers were comparable to those in the family communication classes; however, national identity and the presence of subcultures in other countries seemed quite different that that defined by Americans, due in part to historical circumstances, as described very articulately by one student:

Student G:

> "If there has been one thing that I have learned from my cross-cultural encounters throughout my time in Italy and in school is that culture is something that is learned and practiced. Personally, I define culture as a system of values, beliefs, experiences, and ideas that are shared among a group of people. Language, religion, views on societal roles, media, their sense of time, diet and behaviors are some components of one's culture. And while we may have learned the ways of our nation's dominant culture, within our cultures, there exists sub-cultures that differentiate themselves from the larger culture of which they belong. These sub-cultures enable people from different countries to more easily connect and relate. So, while culture functions as a determinant of how humans relate to one another and how they view the world, people from two varying cultural backgrounds can share cultural perspectives on issues ranging from media to family and gender roles if they belong to the same sub-culture.

In America, sub-cultures are in abundance due to the American identity being influenced by cultures from all corners of the globe. Since its inception, the United States has been a country of immigrants bringing their native traditions and practices into the everyday lives of is citizens. Encompassing traditions from the English, Italian, French, and more recently black and Hispanic cultures, residents in the United States belong to more than one sub-culture and it is far more ethnically diverse than Italy [which] has a long history of homogeneity. However, despite America's 'w' in the diversity column, one culture seems to dominate the numerous others that are present in the US. Patriarchal, Anglo-Saxon, protestant, capitalist views are the dominant ideologies at work in American society. These principles and values triumph over the practices of other cultures and shape how the majority of American society thinks and works. However, regardless of this reigning as the dominant culture, many Americans still adhere to the practices and teachings of their ancestors and to the many recently established sub-cultures of the more technological era. So while someone may identify with the dominant ideologies in American culture, they will most likely also practice the opposing traditions.

Contrastingly, Italy has historically been a homogenous and nationalistic state that has only recently seen waves of immigration and introductions to other cultures within its confines. While Northern and Southern Italy may vocalize their cultural differences, within a region, there exists less dissimilarities among Italians than that of Americans because most Italians strongly identify with their national identity due to their family's long Italian history. Since Italy's fascist period, the country has held strong to the idea that one's ethnicity is tied to the nation state and a person's national identity. So, homogeneity and the exclusion of other cultures has resulted in Italy having less diversity and fewer sub-cultures present than that of the US, which makes it easier to generalize Italian culture. However, due to the spread of sub-cultures through global interconnectivity, younger generations may belong to more sub-cultures and share more cultural similarities with Americans than the older generation Italians. So increasing interactions with immigrants and technology's ability to spread American culture has resulted in the adoption and sharing of some American sub-cultures by many Italian young adults."

This narrative is especially noteworthy because it both clearly articulates specific components of national identity, and reflects the dynamic nature of culture. The student contemplates the *why* of different worldviews and how they interrelate. The obvious next step is to address the dialectic between similarities and differences across culture, and how this applies to one's understanding of self and others, as demonstrated in these student paper excerpts:

Student F:

" Having spent a time living another country's culture, I have gained a better sense of clarity about both who I am and what Italian people are like. Identity is something that is constructed by practices and experience that are instilled throughout someone's lifetime, combined with the various political and historical situations of the place of one's birth. Italy has its own unique background, as does Parma, and this certainly has influenced how _____, my host mom has grown up. Spending time with my Italian family has been invaluable in understanding the differences between cultures, and ultimately all that I have learned will certainly influence the way I think about myself when I return to the United States."

Student H:

" I thoroughly enjoyed this project because I learned a lot more about _____ that I would have otherwise never known since these topics do not generally come up during daily small talk conversation or in class. It was also really interesting to learn how similar we are, despite being from different countries and cultural backgrounds. I was able to gain new perspectives on such issues such as gender roles, holiday celebration and traditions, religion, and the importance of family relationships. It is fascinating that I can attribute a lot of our similarities to my Italian background, even though I live in the United States, because our cultures actually have a lot in common such as the significance of traditions, religion, and importance of food and family."

Student I:

" Being an American semester study abroad student in South Africa for the past three months inevitably influences the way in which I see and interact with my surroundings. _____ has lived in Cape Town her entire life, as did her parents before that, and probably her children will in the future. She has a connection, closeness, and understanding of her country in a way that I couldn't possibly. And yet getting to know the country and the countrymen these past three months I can't help but consider the cultural similarities between the two despite our different cultural upbringings. A mutual love of sushi and hate of cockroaches, connection to our hometowns despite problematic dynamics, and close familial ties unite our cultural identities, while political and social contexts raise us to see the world through different perspectives."

The above comments also exemplify "cross-over" cultural identity as well as vital to basic family values.

## FINAL THOUGHTS

In scholar Jin Li's book, *Cultural Foundations of Learning: East and West*, he identifies four characteristics necessary for those looking to learn about the world: 1) having a good mind and using it well; 2) possessing a natural curiosity, interest, playfulness and intrinsic enjoyment; 3) employing an open mind and free inquisitive spirit; and 4) seeing the world as an ultimate goal in learning (pp. 34-35). These characteristics cannot realize their fullest potential, however, without proper and generous reflective time, as well as a vehicle through which students can best hone their abilities and skills. One means to address this challenge is to find ways to make theory more relevant to everyday life; another is to enrich personal experience through thoughtful research projects and classroom discussion.

## REFERENCES

Bylund, C.L. (2003). Ethnic diversity and the functions of family stories. *Journal of Family Communication, 3,* 215-236.

Galvin, K.M., Bylund, C. J., & Brommel, B.J. (2012). *Family communication: Cohesion and change,* 8th ed.. Boston: Pearson.

Hofstede, G., Hofstede, G.J. & Minkov, M. (2010). *Cultures and organizations: Software of the mind,* 3rd ed. New York: McGraw-Hill.

Koerner, A.F. & Fitzpatrick, M.A. (2006). Family communication patterns theory: A social cognitive approach. In Braithwaite, D.O. & Baxter, L.A. (Eds.). *Engaging theories in family communication: Multiple perspectives.* Thousand Oaks, CA: Sage Publications, Inc., pp. 50-65.

Larkin, E., Friedlander, D., Newman, S. & Goff, R. (Eds.). (2005). *Intergenerational relationships: Conversations of practices and research across cultures*. Binghamton, NY: Haworth Press.

Li, J. (2012). *Cultural foundations of learning: East and West*. Cambridge, UK: Cambridge University Press.

Lustig, M.W. & Koester, J. (Eds.) (1999). *AmongUS: Essays on identity, belonging and intercultural competence*. Boston: Allyn & Bacon.

_____. (2013). *Intercultural competence interpersonal communication across cultures*, 7th ed. New York: Pearson.

Martin, J.N., & Nakayama, T.K. (2014). Thinking dialectically about culture and communication. In *The Global Intercultural Communication Reader*, 2$^{nd}$ ed. Asante, M.K., Yoshitaka Miike, Y., & Yin, J. (Eds.). New York: Routledge, pp. 199-203.

Olson, D. (2011). FACES IV and the circumplex model: Validation study. *Journal of Marital and Family Therapy, 37*(1), 64-80.

Student A. (2010, July 15). Final paper. Family Communication.

Student B. (2008, July 11). Final paper. Family Communication.

Student C. (2010, July 15). Final paper. Family Communication.

Student D. (2013, May3). Advanced Intercultural Communication.

Student E. (2015, April 29). Advanced Intercultural Communication.

Student F. (2014, December 10). Advanced Intercultural Communication.

Student G. (2015, April 29). Advanced Intercultural Communication.

Student H. (2014, December 10). Advanced Intercultural Communication.

Student I. (2013, May 1). Advanced Intercultural Communication.

Vangelisti, A.L., Crumley, L.P., & Baker, J.L. (1999). Family portraits: Stories as standards for family relationships. *Journal of Social and Personal Relationships, 3,* 335-368.

Von Bertalanffy, L. (1969). *General systems theory: Foundations, development, application*, rev. ed. New York: George Braziller Inc.

Weckowicz, T.E. (1989, February). *Ludwig von Bertalanffy (1901-1972): A pioneer of general systems theory*. CSR working paper 89-2, p.2. Retrieved from http://www.richardjung.cz/bert1.pdf

Wood, B., & Talmon, M. (1983). Family boundaries in transition: A search for alternatives. *Family Process, 22,* 347-357.

CHAPTER 12

# Interactive Reflection in a Photomedia Participatory e-Feed Learning Culture

*Kathryn Meyer Grushka and Aaron Bellette*

This chapter focuses on the affordances of social media to address online learner identities and support the development of critical self-reflective and creative dispositions in student-directed on-line learning. It reports on an aspect of an ethics approved study titled Photographic Participatory Inquiry, researching the participatory pedagogies of photomedia students in the blended e-learning environment. It elaborates on how the students use social media tools within an e-feed journal that employs arts-inquiry strategies and how it facilitates the development of reflective dispositions for higher education introductory photomedia students. It will describe the underpinnings of an arts based and interactive aesthetic pedagogical philosophy, discuss the blended studio/e-learning framework and through the analysis of two case study students provide insights into how the students through enaction actively shape their own critical creative and self-reflective skills taking advantage of being interconnected learners in their local and global social media learning communities. Discussion of the findings reveals how a connected space emerged that goes beyond the idea of an ePortfolio as a repository and reflective self-assessment tool to an e-feed personal pedagogy.

## INTRODUCTION

The rhetoric of new media learning is its potential to be flexible and accommodate students' different modes of thinking and communication platforms (Jenkins, Walker, & Voce, n.d.; Johnson et al., 2014). In addition, educators need to focus on learner participation and creativity as students build their online learner identities (Greenhow, Robelia, & Hughes, 2009). While many advocate for the affordances offered by new technologies to empower student-directed learning, little research exists into how social media pedagogies build critical and creative self-reflection, particularly in photomedia (K. M. Grushka, Bellette, & Holbrook, 2015).

This chapter considers the findings of an ethics approved study titled Photographic Participatory Inquiry (PPI), researching the participatory pedagogies of photomedia students in the blended e-learning environment. It elaborates on how the students use social media tools within an e-feed journal that employs arts-inquiry strategies and how it facilitates the development of reflective dispositions for higher education introductory photomedia students. It will describe the underpinnings of an arts based and interactive aesthetic pedagogical philosophy, discuss the blended studio/e-learning framework and through the analysis of two case study students provide insights into how the students through enaction actively shape their own critical creative and self-reflective skills taking advantage of being interconnected self-directed learners in their local and global social media learning communities. Discussion of the findings reveals how a connected space emerged that goes beyond the idea of an ePortfolio as a repository and reflective self-assessment tool to an e-feed interconnected socially reflective personal pedagogy.

## THE PHOTOMEDIA LEARNER CYBORG

The art and design tertiary students now see visibility as identity. Creating and communicating with images actively constructs the learner self (Grushka, 2010) and is rapidly shifting the photograph away from photography as a memory device (Barthes, 2000; Harrison, 2002; Schiano, Chen, & Isaacs, 2002; Sontag, 1990), replacing it with the interconnected communicative imperative facilitated by the Camera Phone. The invention of the Camera Phone finds us all communicating within web-linked communal spatial flows. The Camera Phone is one of many techno-social objects that make possible the 'low-tech cyborg' and brings forth many questions about how students now prefer to learn. The networked student has an interconnected imperative (Drexler, 2010) to instantly record and communicate life world experiences unimpeded by the distance or size of the targeted audience. The affordances of such techno-social objects and the learners associated engagement with their new social media representational capabilities are shaping 'knowledge' (Kress, 2009). Knowledge is no longer fixed, but shifting daily or even hourly, and the cyborg-learner feeds off this constant and interconnected knowledge stream. The popularity of these social media devices has profound implications for our understanding of experience. More importantly multimodal communications supported by Web 2.0 tools are shaping how we now learn and how we reflect (K. Grushka, Donnelly, & Clement, 2014).

This leaves many educators pondering what the self-reflective capacities of the next generation of ocular centric learners looks like. More importantly what form this reflective knowledge will take, how stable it is and how e-learning is addressed in their own contemporary reflexive inquiry into their teaching practice (Mockler & Sachs, 2011).

In Figure 1: *Media Life Span of Aaron Bellett's Instagram Feed*, the immediacy of the image and the shrinking life span of the knowledge it contains is evidenced when we start to measure the life of an image in hours. Media Life Span of Aaron Bellette's Instagram Feed. Data provided by IconSquare

In the study *Coming of Age (Digitally): An Ecological View of Social Media Use among College Students* in America (Wang et al., 2015) it was identified that students engaged with a median of 90.5 visits per day on social media with a mean visit time being 1:04 (p. 575). The social media access was shared between mobile devices and computers and researchers now speculate that such quick interactions and constant checking could impact the quality of learner engagement such as concentration spans and reflective capabilities. It may also build particular communicative preferences, such as images, video and short text rather than the more accepted practice of critical analysis as writing. Cochran and Rhodes (2013) argue that this unpredicted shift in our preferences for how we communicate and access knowledge will bring about pedagogical transformation driven by a student-directed imperative to learn within a mobile learning (mlearning) framework they prefer (McLoughlin & Lee, 2008a).

## THE INTERCONNECTED IMPERATIVE AND PARTICIPATORY CULTURE OF SOCIAL MEDIA

Tertiary learning is increasingly driven by both productivity and cost effectiveness and this finds educators investigating heavily in consideration of the potential benefits of learning through the hyperlinked social media and the networks of knowledge supported in participatory scholarship cultures (Abbott, Donaghey, Hare, & Hopkins, 2014; Cho & Trent, 2006, Veletsianos & Kimmons, 2011). These participatory cultures find the learner connecting to a range of virtual multimodal platforms beyond the traditional photomedia studio-learning environment. Increasingly they learn by accessing online content through social media forms such as, blogs, wikis, twitter, forums, YouTube, Tumblr, apps, and email to name a few current platforms. The flows between these participatory platforms, produces new communities of learners as each student creatively builds new online learner identities (Cochrane & Rhodes, 2013; Greenhow et al., 2009). Students describe these online learning cultures as personalized, participatory and productive (Cochrane & Rhodes, 2013; McLoughlin & Lee, 2008b) within these communities the students are seeking more self-regulated learning approaches (Dabbagh & Kitsantas, 2012, 2013). It is therefore not surprising that photomedia curriculum is now seeking to respond to the online cultural and social learning capital of students while making them vocationally ready (Edge, 2009; K. M. Grushka et al., 2015; Kennedy, 2009; Williams, 2009). In the case of photomedia students their culturally organized practices as digital photographers are increasingly bound by the ubiquitous nature of the digital photographic image and the related social media communication skills, including visual adaptive thinking (Gauthier, 2015) which are seen as critical and core knowledge for their future working life.

The affordances of online participatory learning, applied in the context of a blended learning environment for photomedia students, is that these communities mirror many of the qualities of studio learning which allows for informal dialectic knowledge generation and which tolerates risk taking, problem-solving and the generation of new ideas (Hetland, 2007). Knowledge is generated in an artistic community through shared epistemological positions and through a shared understanding about the cognitive technologies that scaffold their learning, this this case the making of digital images and writing about their artistic intentions through what can be described as critical and hermeneutic reflection (Grushka, 2005). It could be argued that these online and networked communities offer a form of virtual studio where the learning is student-driven and the online cultures nurture informal kinds of mentorships where experts and novices communicate online. As the contribution to the participatory culture is informal and dependent on a willingness to contribute it produces a fluid and flux driven learning environment or e-feed learning culture in which the educator contributes as a facilitator. In participatory cultures all contributions matter and the collective participating membership affords all members a degree of social connection, including the educator.

## INTERACTIVE REFLECTION IN NEW LEARNING DIRECTIONS: E-FEED PORTFOLIO

Increasingly higher education mlearning in photomedia courses are shaped by emergent participatory e-feed cultures of social media. The complexity and multiplicity of this e-feed visual culture (video, photography, film, the web and the camera phone) finds the student simultaneously interacting with and making meaning across different modes and settings. There is now an imperative for educators to consider the ways in which the multimodal platforms of Web 2.0 tools are impacting on student-directed learning as increasingly students are choosing to access, photographic images, didactic video clips and moving or animated pictures over extended reading and writing.

Learning or enaction is the development of cognitive skills as a result of embodied experience and our actions in the world. Learning involves perception and memory and is multimodal, with memory being a composite of interactivity between self and the perceived and experienced object (Damasio, 2012). Enaction focuses on the autonomy of each individual, the embodiment of experience and how sense-making is emergent from the interactive spaces between self, others and the world (Varela, Thompson & Rosch, 1991). These interactive spaces shape who we are, how we learning and direct us to multiple options about how we may choose to represent knowledge and communicate it an audience. The increasing use of new participatory learning cultures supported by Web 2.0 tools is facilitating new virtual interactive spaces across online communities extending creativity (Greenhow et al., 2009). This learning is not only multimodal but it is multi-temporal, as memories are shaped by the past, the present and our actions as embodied cognition are future oriented. It is these multimodal and embodied experiences and their cultural forms, which are now seen as saturated with affect and key in the enactment of insight and creativity (Hutchins, (2010). The challenge for the educator is how will this e-feed enaction and the affordances of the extending array of techno-objects be harnessed to build both intuitive and reflective capabilities when making meaning.

The traditional way art educators have chosen to access and evaluate student creative and reflective learning has been through the analysis of the traditional artist diary and/or the presentation of a portfolio or exhibition of works and an oral account of their ideas and intensions. Within this new media learning space these traditional assessment tools and the teacher/student learning spaces are being reshaped/ replaced. The potential of the ePortfolios described as a user-generated content that encourages self -reflective participation through the use of social media tools is presented as a more appropriate learning tool (Wenger, 2010). EPortfolios focus on the learning, appraisal, assessment and promotion journey (Klenowski, Askew, & Carnell, 2006). The ePortfolio becomes a highly curated showcase designed for assessment or for an audience rather than for the critical and hermeneutic reflection to the creator/artist. EPortfolios in higher education are used mainly for summative purposes (Baume & Yorke, 2002; Brown, 2003; Kim, Ng, & Lim, 2010; Nystrand, Cohen, & Dowling, 1993). While reflection occurs in the ePortfolio the writers argue that it is shaped by its need to present refined and resolved artefactual evidence of learning usually accompanied by concise and audience targeted writing about their intensions such as artist statements. As these ePortfolios fulfil an audience driven imperative and the learning evidence they generally will not contain critical and self-reflective insights about the learning journey. Nor do they demonstrate to the assessor how the students' critical reflective skills have emerged during the learning event. These are presented as limitations of the ePortfolio journals functionality as a critical and reflective process thinking assessment tool.

The chapter seeks to demonstrate that the affordances of the participatory culture and the habits and experiences of the cyborg-learner are driving different performative acts and reshaping the self-reflexivity of the learner. This self-reflective space is increasingly occupied by multiple flows both internal and external and is filled with liminal possibilities that trigger our thinking, our actions and our learning. As events or experience in the virtual world contain learning at the borders of the past and future how self-reflexivity and learner insight is measured must increasingly respond to the flows generated by our new media realities and through the materiality of the photographic images and its e-feed productive processes. In this space the educational rhetoric of a curriculum that seeks uniformity is resisted and uncertainty and reflection are ever present (Sameshima & Irwin, 2008).

It is therefore important to reflect on the new richness of the experiences provided by new media technologies and the digital networked society to complement reality and extend multimodal learning in the first instance. Secondly how it shapes the way we think about reconceptualizing traditional material learning objects such as the portfolio or its new digital form, the ePortfolio. More significantly, how the cyborgs' web-based knowledge acquisition and social communicative practices are shifting learner behaviors and defining the role of reflection in the new e-learning spaces. Thirdly, how can a new iteration of the ePortfolio, the e-feed journal a real-time, interactive and participatory space that accommodates multimedia and web platforms build intuitive and creative reflective capabilities for the cyborg learner? What kind of reflective learning is present in these e-spaces and is an e-feed journal designed to respond to photomedia education shifting online (Edge, 2009; Kennedy, 2009; Rubinstein, 2009) an effective pedagogical tool?

## THE STUDY

The ethics approved study sought to investigate the quality of the e-feed participatory learning of photomedia tertiary students working in a blended studio and e-learning context in an introductory photomedia course. The course used a variety of screen capture tools that would support self-reflection when both pre-visualizing an image (before they take the shot) using GoPro software and in the post-visualization digital manipulation process, using screen capture software. The study sought to identify whether the e-learning pedagogical innovations, an e-feed journal (a blog format) informed by reflective practices found in arts-inquiry strategies (Butler-Kisber & Poldma, 2011) would develop in the photomedia students interactive reflective dispositions that responded to what Xenakis, I., & Arnellos, A. (2013) call and interactive aesthetic. Applying a participatory self-study methodology, the educator takes a critical and emancipatory position towards learning (Gallagher & Kim, 2008; Kemmis, 2008; McTaggart, 1997; Mockler & Sachs, 2011). The methodology differs from traditional teacher/educator action research methods as it draws on self-study approaches including narrative inquiry, reflective e-feed journals, memory work and arts-based approaches to understanding student thinking processes and the appropriateness of the educators associated pedagogies (Lunenberg & Samaras,

2011). In this chapter analysis focuses on the students e- feed learning journals in combination with visual qualitative analysis methods (Pink, 2004, 2007; Prosser & Schwartz, 1998; Rose, 2007) and a dialogue with the students using photo and video elicitation interview approaches (Grushka, Bellette & Holbrook, 2015). The analysis of the e-feed interactions together with the interviews were managed and analyzed using the qualitative data managements tool NVivo. The coding of the data sort to ascertain the level of critical and reflective engagement of the students in relation to the concepts of interactional aesthetics, the development of formalist language and critical audience insights as they build their own photomedia practices. The analysis and the reporting focuses on the evidence that reveals whether e-feed participatory pedagogies were able to build critical self-reflective skills in the students. The findings are illuminated through the case studies of Felicity and Kate.

## FINDINGS

The findings report on the critical self-reflective learning of photomedia students Kate and Felicity and are enriched through the reflective insights the photomedia educator.

### Blog Culture and Students Writing in their e-Feed Journal

The current media usage trends show university age students access social media content in micro-bursts almost constantly through out the day. These factors affect how students engage with the post-visualization photographic reflective thinking as process when blogging and writing about their learning.

In the e-learning blogs of Kate and Felicity the analysis identified that their writing about their photographic visualization processes were regularly accompanied by a limited vocabulary associated with affective response.

'Love' and 'like' were used to describe both their own work and the images of other artists and their techniques. NVivo word cloud findings for both their e-feed blogging and their interviews showed that in these spaces provided clear and fluid descriptions about their aesthetic choices. The writing style was one of a self reflective narrative posted regularly on their e-feed journal using a blogging genre.

> "I like it. I think it's really interest[ing], like all through here, these bits and all the cracks and stuff like that, but I knew I didn't like it as it was".
> (K)

## The e-Feed: Researching,

Traditional art journaling and the associated recorded and illustrated aesthetic and conceptual thinking has been critiqued for its inability to capture the non-linear, connected and associated thinking and memory work of the artist in active thinking and performative mode. This work occurs as thinking when making and can't be separated out as words or text (Grushka, 2005). This thinking has traditionally been captured using the post reflective and rational construction of a written linear artist statement. The time between the action, research or making can be critical in the accurate recording of reflections. The e-learning blog, because of its open accessibility and in-time functionality may well be a learning tool closer to capturing research, reflection and artist practice as a cognitive phenomenon.

Felicity talking about her blogging

> 'It's a bit tedious I do a lot of research online.... I'll save some and I'll move on from some, and then I'm like, oh I should be documenting this.... But as far as putting my process and my reflections and that sort of stuff up, I've really really liked it. It hasn't been a task at all." (F)

> 'Yeah. I was rating them by stars so that when I finished I could just really easily sort them. I could filter them by three stars or (F)

> "I did a lot of research on how I was going to light it, and how I was going to position and everything,...I definitely went in with a plan (F)

This blogging activity was in-time and a chronological reflective process.

In addition, the blog structures and layout appear to appeal to the students;

> ' Yeh I like the logical step by step/ I enjoy that I don't have to physically stand there and layout my page, which I really enjoy but when you have stacks to get through...[the blog] orders for you easily and simply." (K)

> 'I like having stuff up there that I can show other people.... I just send the link... I liked the blog". (K)

For Felicity when she was asked to reflect on the benefits of using screen capture and recording tools to help her refine her imagery she states:

'[I] watched it back, I go, why did I do that?. I should have done that a bit different.... I ended up with 350 images, about 100 were unusable... next time I will spend my time looking back.'(F)

### e-Feed Clarifying Processes and Refining Ideas

The extracts from Kate's e-learning journal are able to demonstrate how she works seamlessly between her traditional visual drawn conceptualization processes and her e-feed uploads. Her written texts as reflective critical conversations punctuate her visual journaling (Figure 2, below).

Figure 2: Kate's e-learning journal compilation of visual Conceptualization and critical reflection

'I had it! What would happen if I shot images of shattered glass, then in Photoshop superimposed the florals I had already shot over the top, editing it to look as though the flowers themselves had fallen and shattered?' (K)

And *'Setting up the rig'* (Figure 3, below) demonstrates a compilation of e-feed entries image and technical notes in a chronological order from Kate's e-learning journal.

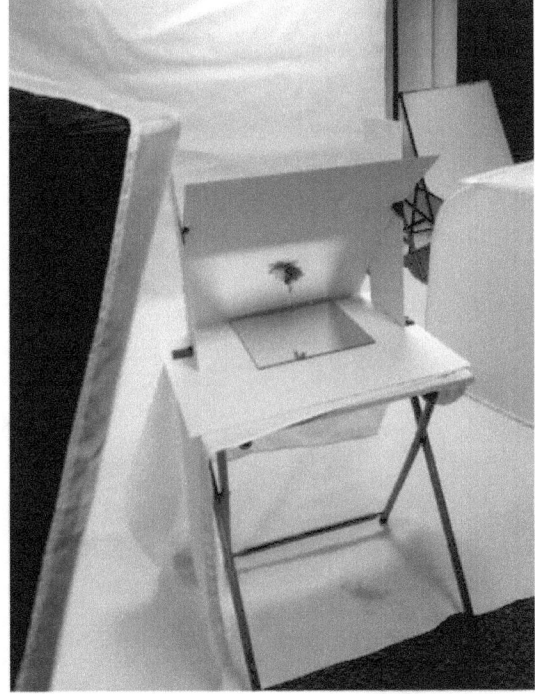

Figure 3: 'Setting up the rig' Katie's Blog, Detail of the photographic apparatus;

> 'White chip board for the back, sides and bottom, held together with duct tape. The back was curved slightly, held by the sidepieces to conduct the light. The mirror was placed in the centre. The flashes were placed to the front of the set up, but to the sides…. I must confess that I was quite excited by this point.'(K)

Significantly both students used their blogging to reflect on their technical skills development and their emergent autonomy in critical decision-making.

Felicity in her reflection of her final project in her blog (below) states:

> "The technical side of editing and photography is something I love to learn about, and I want to obtain the most skill I can in those areas...
>
> I learned a lot from both my successes and failures." (F)

Building new conceptual and technical skills can open the possibilities that will push the boundaries of ideas to strengthen artistic intentions, technical and aesthetic pointers to help encode an effective message in their images. There is evidence of critical self-reflection related to technical research and application, conceptual experimentation and insights into her developing interactional aesthetic seen in Figure 4 : *'Fractured Florals' Kate Langbein , e-learning journal entry.*

> '...The bottom image was my answer I loved the effect, though was annoyed by the fuzzy edges of the glass piece.
>
> One problem I encountered with this set was that some of the images were just slightly out of focus, which meant I couldn't use them, however, I was very happy with the rest of these images, and was particular pleased at some of the striking/slightly edgy glass forms, (for example, the first image).' (K)

Figure 4: 'Fractured Florals' Kate , e-learning journal entry

The potential failure of the e-feed blog to loose their information looms on the horizon for many students and some are caught between the potential duplication of their learning as it may impact on their study time and on their assessment. Felicity reflects;

> 'I was frustrated... things were dropping out and it was bugging me...but I love that it structures it all for me'

**E-feed Towards Artistic Intentionality**

In the final blog entry by Felicity you can see the coming together of all the learning tools offered in the e-learning blog environment and her curatorial skill development. In Figure 5 (below) " *The sum or our parts*", Felicity is able to take significant control over how she chooses to present her concepts and her thinking. This is a layout of Felicity's body of work accompanied by her poetic insights.

> My world is built of unassuming parts, which have been strung together to make something "more"...I believe I am more than a sum of my parts.(F)

Figure 5 " *The sum or our parts*" Felicity e-learning journal entry

My world is built of unassuming parts, which have been strung together to make something "more"...I believe I am more than a sum of my parts.(F)

## Discussion: e-Feed Photographic Practice

The findings identified that the extensive use of words such as 'like' may well come from a heavy immersion in social media interactions. Social media sights demand interaction and quick responses. These feeds and updates occur at a high rate and affective behaviors written as 'like' or 'love' demand less contemplative and composed written responses and are ingrained habits and an acceptable part of social media. However, 'Like' and 'Love 'appear to be affective text entry points that link technical and artist research sites and these can be rated and ranked sites. In addition, a level of critical reflection has already been employed before images are 'liked' and then uploaded to the e-feed journal. Text analysis reveals that 'Like' is linked to 'Make' demonstrating an increase focus by the students on being meaning makers with the creation of imagery (Lowy, 2015).

The structures of blogging and the use of related software such as Photoshop and screen capture video software, like the blog sites record in order uploads, text and/or versions of images in process, often dated as well as timed. The structures draw down on this information to talk about why and how they have captured the image in such a way, and it affords them the opportunity to validate their decisions by comparing multiple digital files. Student thinking when reflecting, undoing, and redoing is now a documented multiple imaging process. At any point in the development process, images can be digitally saved and students can question the technical and interactional aesthetic of their image by comparing digital images in conversation with self and others. Different file sets can be shared and reflective conversations had between peers and the educator.

Reflective language permeates the e-learning journal and both Kate and Felicity, have blog entries that link aesthetic qualities and visual aesthetic language with conceptual understanding: *My world is built of unassuming parts, which have been strung together to make something "more" (F)*. E-feed written reflections draw down on the wide range of images generated, located and stored in the accompanying learning tool box made up of GoPro video files, Photoshop image files and Screen Capture tools. These in effect chronologically map the 'doing in action' so that the "in between space", the creative moments that emerge from this space can become more visual to the student, and the educator. The student can now mine this reflection trail in order locate the intersection between concepts, technical innovation and creative outcomes providing them with evidence of the cognitive and liminal moments between old and new ideas that emerge when rendering new image possibilities (Grushka, 2008).

The pedagogies facilitated by the e-learning journal may also be able to capture and sustain the techno-cyborg generation who have digital devices at the center of their lives (Valkenburg & Peter, 2011). It may well be that the features of the e-feed learning journal as a blog can better respond to a poetics of inquiry approach (Prendergast, Leggo, & Sameshima, 2009) capturing the liminal spaces (Sameshima & Irwin, 2008) and rendering the learners self- reflective practice visible demonstrated in Figure 7: Image and words from the series "Fractured Florals" (below). This continuous flow or feed of images and associated narrative forms in the e-learning journal may offer the perfect pedagogical tool for cyborg learner agency.

Figure 7. Images and words from series "Fractured Florals", Kate

> the tangible side of fragility
> things can be shattered
> life is fragile
> Fragility brings beauty

Learning behaviours emerge both from experiences as both past and future actions that arise from the external and internal responses and these, in turn, shape our cognitive styles. Events, and in this case the new photomedia tools, mobile devices and blended learning environments are active in informing the way we make sense of the world and how we act in the world. To build new concepts or to make meaning requires adaption based on the students own internal reasoning informed by research and feedback from peers or the photographic educator as their critical friends.

Entries both of images and texts were nonlinear in placement, and iterative, broken or fragmented in the emergence of concepts. It would not be possible to argue that the students working in their e-learning journals in a continuous blogging style maintained a consistent retrospective journaling process. What can be affirmed is that the entries were in-time and connected, mirroring the way our brains connect and our memories shift images, words and ideas over time.

The e-feed journal provides a personal, participatory and interactive communicative platform (Grushka et al., 2014). It connects decoding and encoding skills for students, and the continuous feed of reflections about artistic ideas, different photographers' works and technical processes may well encourage students to expand their vocabulary and critical analytical skills. The fluid, interweaving of practices, theory and making, between knowing, doing and making, can be seen in Figure 5. *Image from Series "The Sum of Our Parts"* and Figure 7. *"Image from Series "Fractured Florals"*, both demonstrate this cognitive work. The representations found in this form of e-feed learning could be described as a poetics of inquiry able to demonstrate both inter and intra-connected learning.

Synthesising the findings on the case study students learning within the blended studio/e-learning framework has brought into focus the interconnected activity between the three areas of research, creation and reflection. These three cognitive areas work in a cyclical, iterative and concurrent fashion with each containing self-reflective critical cycles. Research is broken down into cognitive reflection related to both technical and conceptual artistic practice of other artists and their own techniques. The knowledge was documented as ongoing refinement of technical notes and related conceptual ideas. Students revisited the cycle of research as critical reflection across all the stages of the evolution of the body of work or set of photographic images. Creation was fluid and included actions and reflections related to image capture and digital image experimentation. Reflection when making images occurred between on-line research; between conversations with peers, as blog entries; between dated iterations of each image shift; between consideration of their artistic intensions and as a refinement of their ideas towards consideration of their intended audience. These reflections shaped the form of the final body of work as a set of images and related words. The learning in these interactional spaces was both in-time and across time. Recorded as dated and sequenced evidence of evolving image changes that mapped clearly the evolution of the photographic image and its conceptual refinement over time. It also included the final images and refined statements about artistic intentions that could be used for summative assessment purposes. The complexity and multiplicity of all of the reflective acts could be referred to as mirroring virtual and global connectivity skills an increasingly important aspect of contemporary photographic design teams.

In addition the e-feed journals it could be argued, best accommodate the multimodal realities of human perception and memory (Damasio, 2012). Blogging acts and the personally designed layout of the e-learning journal allows for the modeling of constructive learning and self-reflective practice best suited to each individual student. It involves opportunities to download, reflect and record as images and text fragments as cognation. If cognition involves moving between independent states of external focus on experience, information, internal constructive, and reflective thought generated from what is perceived as personally significant to the learner (Immordino-Yang, Christodoulou, & Singh, 2012), then the e-feed journal is able to accommodate this form of self-reflective meaning making. The in-time digital technologies are an agenic force connecting the lifeworld of the learner (K. Grushka et al., 2014).

There are clear limitations of this paper to make larger claims about the benefits of the e-feed journal as representative on the overall quality and benefit of blended online photomedia pedagogies for all students or for the photomedia educator. Such claims will require the synthesis of other aspects of the larger research project. There are, however, positive findings from the in-depth analysis of the two case studies students that point to the e-feed journal's capacity to accommodate personalized learning while allowing for exploring, creating, self-regulation and peer-to-peer collaboration as critical aspects of contemporary teaching practices and professional environments.

## Conclusion

The analysis of the two case study students critical and reflective photomedia learning provides opportunities for the educator to examine: i) the kinds of interactive thinking that this blended and e-feed journal can develop in their photomedia students and ii) how the educator can use this wealth of digital learning data to inform their own reflexive inquiry (Mockler & Sachs, 2011). More importantly it reveals own the e-feed journal is able to accommodate an array of personalized techno-behaviours and engage the students in multi-temporal processing of their reflective memories. The e-feed journal is able to connect the inter-related fields of artistic practice, artistic and technical research and reflection about their photographic processes and artistic intensions. Most significantly for the educator, it can reveal the effectiveness of teaching and learning strategies as they inform "knowing when doing," both when taking an image with the camera and when working within the e-feed blog environment.

In particular, the e-feed journal actively supported becoming self-reflexive learners, with rich and inter-connected links between ideas, feelings and emergent concepts as revealed through an embodied poetics of inquiry. The e-feed journal was also able to accommodate the online, open and learning anytime cyborg learner seeking a personalized, participatory and productive a networked learning environment. Building a more inter and intra connected critical reflective learner and critical writer within the social media-learning environment remains a challenge. As art and design education shifts towards a stronger interactional aesthetic, emergent between the artist/designer and their audience/consumer pedagogies will require stronger critical intra-connectability.

## REFERENCES

Abbott, W., Donaghey, J., Hare, J., & Hopkins, P. (2014). The perfect storm: The convergence of social, mobile and photo technologies in libraries. *VALA 2014*. Retrieved from http://epublications.bond.edu.au/library_pubs/34

Lenhart. A. (n.d.). Teens, Social Media & Technology Overview 2015. Retrieved from http://www.pewinternet.org/2015/04/09/teens-social-media-technology-2015/

Barthes, R. (2000). *Camera lucida: reflections on photography*. London: Vintage.

Baume, D., & Yorke, M. (2002). The reliability of assessment by portfolio on a course to develop and accredit teachers in higher education. *Studies in Higher Education, 27*(1), 7–25.

Brown, S. (2003). Assessment that Works at Work. *The Newsletter for the Institute for Learning and Teaching in Higher Education, Summer*(11), 6–7.

Butler-Kisber, L., & Poldma, T. (2011). The Power of Visual Approaches in Qualitative Inquiry: The Use of Collage Making and Concept Mapping in Experiential Research. *Journal of Research Practice, 6*(2), Article M18.

Cho, J., & Trent, A. (2006). Validity in qualitative research revisited. *Qualitative Research, 6*(3), 319–340. http://doi.org/10.1177/1468794106065006

Cochrane, T., & Rhodes, D. (2013). iArchi [tech] ture: Developing a mobile social media framework for pedagogical transformation. *Australasian Journal of Educational Technology, 29*(3). Retrieved from http://www.ascilite.org.au/ajet/submission/index.php/AJET/article/view/191

Dabbagh, N., & Kitsantas, A. (2012). Personal Learning Environments, social media, and self-regulated learning: A natural formula for connecting formal and informal learning. *The Internet and Higher Education*, *15*(1), 3–8.

Dabbagh, N., & Kitsantas, A. (2013). The role of social media in self-regulated learning. *International Journal of Web Based Communities*, *9*(2), 256–273.

Damasio, A. (2012). *Self Comes to Mind: Constructing the Conscious Brain* (Reprint edition). Vintage.

Drexler, W. (2010). The networked student model for construction of personal learning environments: Balancing teacher control and student autonomy. *Australasian Journal of Educational Technology*, *26*(3). Retrieved from http://ascilite.org.au/ajet/submission/index.php/AJET/article/view/1081

Edge, S. (2009). Photography, Higher Education and the Skills Agenda. *Photographies*, *2*(2), 203–214.
http://doi.org/10.1080/17540760903116663

Freeman, M., deMarrais, K., Preissle, J., Roulston, K., & Pierre, E. A. S. (2007). Standards of Evidence in Qualitative Research: An Incitement to Discourse. *Educational Researcher*, *36*(1), 25–32. http://doi.org/10.3102/0013189X06298009

Gallagher, K., & Kim, I. (2008). Moving Towards Postcolonical, digtial methods in qualitative resarch. In *The Methodological Dilemma Creative, Critical and Collaborative Approaches to Qualitative Research*. Hoboken: Taylor & Francis. Retrieved from
http://0www.newcastle.eblib.com.library.newcastle.edu.au/patron/FullRecord.aspx?p=342367

Gauthier, C. (2015). Photography Confidential: Educators Speak. In M. Bogre (Ed.), *Photography 4.0: a teaching guide for the 21st century :educators share thoughts and assignments*. Burlington, MA: Focal Press.

Greenhow, C., Robelia, B., & Hughes, J. E. (2009). Learning, teaching, and scholarship in a digital age Web 2.0 and classroom research: What path should we take now? *Educational Researcher*, *38*(4), 246–259.

Grushka, K. (2005). Artists as reflective self-learners and cultural communicators: an exploration of the qualitative aesthetic dimension of knowing self through reflective practice in art-making. *Reflective Practice*, *6*(3), 353–366.

Grushka, K. (2010). Montage as visual art research: identities, images and meanings | NOVA. The University of Newcastle's Digital Repository, Montage as visual art research: identities, images and meanings. Retrieved from http://novaprd-lb.newcastle.edu.au:8080/vital/access/manager/Repository/uon:9520;jsessionid=7BF462FB29C8C6B59A250B83B0E8193F?f0=sm_subject%3A%22montage%22

Grushka, K., Donnelly, D., & Clement, N. (2014). Digital Culture And Neuroscience: A Conversation With Learning And Curriculum. *Digital Culture & Education*, *6*(4).

Grushka, K. M., Bellette, A., & Holbrook, A. (2015). Researching Photographic Participatory Inquiry In An E-Learning Environment. *McGill Journal of Education / Revue Des Sciences de L'éducation de McGill*, *49*(3). Retrieved from http://mje.mcgill.ca/article/view/9060

Harrison, B. (2002). Photographic visions and narrative inquiry. *Narrative Inquiry*, *12*(1), 87–111. http://doi.org/10.1075/ni.12.1.14har

Hetland, L. (2007). *Studio thinking: the real benefits of visual arts education*. New York: Teachers College Press.

Hight, C., Khoo, E., Cowie, B., & Torrens, R. (n.d.). Software literacies in the tertiary environment. Retrieved from http://ascilite.org/conferences/dunedin2014/files/concisepapers/65-Hight.pdf

Hutchins, E. (2010). Imagination and Insight. In J. G. Stewart, O & DiPaola, E. (Ed.), Enaction: towards a new paradigm for Cognitive Science (pp. 425-450). Massachusettes: Massachusettes Institutue.

Immordino-Yang, M. H., Christodoulou, J. A., & Singh, V. (2012). Rest is not idleness implications of the brain's default mode for human development and education. *Perspectives on Psychological Science*, *7*(4), 352–364.

Jenkins, M., Walker, R., & Voce, J. (n.d.). Achieving flexibility? The rhetoric and reality of the role of learning technologies in UK higher education. Retrieved from https://vle.york.ac.uk/bbcswebdav/institution/E-Learning%20Development%20Team/External/Conference%20Pres%20and%20Papers/ascilite%202014/ascilite2014_paper.pdf

Johnson, L., Becker, S., Estrada, V., Freeman, A., Johnson, L., Becker, S., ... Freeman, A. (2014). *Horizon Report: 2014 Higher Education*. Retrieved from /p/130341/

Kemmis, S. (2008). Critical theory and participatory action research. *The SAGE Handbook of Action Research: Participative Inquiry and Practice, 2*, 121–138.

Kennedy, B. (2009). Print on Demand: Developing New Curriculum for Photographic Education. *International Journal of the Book, 7*(1), 91–101.

Kim, P., Ng, C. K., & Lim, G. (2010). When cloud computing meets with Semantic Web: A new design for ePortfolio systems in the social media era. *British Journal of Educational Technology, 41*(6), 1018–1028.

Kitsantas, A., & Dabbagh, N. (2011). The role of Web 2.0 technologies in self-regulated learning. *New Directions for Teaching and Learning, 2011*(126), 99–106.

Klenowski, V., Askew, S., & Carnell, E. (2006). Portfolios for learning, assessment and professional development in higher education. *Assessment & Evaluation in Higher Education, 31*(3), 267–286. http://doi.org/10.1080/02602930500352816

Kress, G. (2009). *Multimodality: A social semiotic approach to contemporary communication*. Routledge. Retrieved from https://books.google.com.au/books?hl=en&lr=&id=jzMGc75jcXEC&oi=fnd&pg=PT21&dq=kress+2009&ots=U8jZSDCvIE&sig=B3apy9ezhCvgTb_xifhyNj0DyqQ

Lowy, B. (2015, May). *Benjamin Lowy Award winning Photographer*. Presented at the Adobe Amplify, Roslyn Packer Theatre. Retrieved from https://twitter.com/Adobe_aus/status/598761764788932609

Lunenberg, M., & Samaras, A. P. (2011). Developing a pedagogy for teaching self-study research: Lessons learned across the Atlantic. *Teaching and Teacher Education, 27*(5), 841–850.

McLoughlin, C., & Lee, M. J. (2008a). Mapping the digital terrain: New media and social software as catalysts for pedagogical change. *Ascilite Melbourne*. Retrieved from http://cms.ascilite.org.au/conferences/melbourne08/procs/mcloughlin.pdf

McLoughlin, C., & Lee, M. J. (2008b). The three p's of pedagogy for the networked society: Personalization, participation, and productivity. *International Journal of Teaching and Learning in Higher Education*, *20*(1), 10–27.

McTaggart, R. (1997). *Participatory action research: international contexts and consequences*. SUNY Press.

Mockler, N., & Sachs, J. (2011). *Rethinking educational practice through reflexive inquiry: Essays in honour of susan groundwater-smith* (Vol. 7). Springer Science & Business Media. Retrieved from https://books.google.com.au/books?hl=en&lr=&id=J08v9IEctZgC&oi=fnd&pg=PR7&dq=self-reflective+participatory+Mockler,+2011+&ots=uVu7C22RWH&sig=4W6gmmIizBgXs0LYYmWHds0Y4Vc

Newbury, D. (1996). Photography in Schools: Current Trends in Theory and Practice. *Journal of Art & Design Education*, *15*(1), 17–22. http://doi.org/10.1111/j.1476-8070.1996.tb00644.x

Nystrand, M., Cohen, A. S., & Dowling, N. M. (1993). Addressing reliability problems in the portfolio assessment of college writing. *Educational Assessment*, *1*(1), 53–70.

Pink, S. (2004). Visual Methods. In *Qualitative Research Practice*. SAGE.

Pink, S. (2007). *Doing Visual Ethnography*. SAGE.

Prendergast, M., Leggo, C., & Sameshima, P. (2009). Poetic inquiry. *Educational Insights*, *13*(3), 743–744.

Prosser, J., & Schwartz, D. (1998). Photographs within the Sociological resarch Process. In *Image-based Research: A Sourcebook for Qualitative Researchers*. Routledge.

Ribbens, A. (Editor). (1989). *The Other Side of Photography: Profiles of Education*. De Balie and Gerrit Rietveld Academy.

Rose, G. (2007). *Visual methodologies: an introduction to the interpretation of visual materials* (2nd ed). London ; Thousand Oaks, Calif: SAGE Publications.

Rubinstein, D. (2009). Towards Photographic Education. *Photographies*, *2*(2), 135–142. http://doi.org/10.1080/17540760903116598

Sameshima, P., & Irwin, R. L. (2009). Rendering dimensions of a liminal currere. *TCI (Transnational Curriculum Inquiry)*, *5*(2), 1–15.

Schiano, D. J., Chen, C. P., & Isaacs, E. (2002). *How Teens Take, View, Share, and Store Photos'*. CSCW Interactive Poster presented at the Proceedings of the Conference on Computer-Supported Co-operative Work (CSCW).

Sontag, S. (1990). *On photography* (1st Anchor Books ed). New York: Anchor Books.

Valkenburg, P. M., & Peter, J. (2011). Online communication among adolescents: An integrated model of its attraction, opportunities, and risks. *Journal of Adolescent Health*, *48*(2), 121–127.

Varela, F. Thompson, E., & Rosch, E. (1991). *The Embodied Mind, Cognitive Science & Human Experience.* London: MIT Press

Wang, Y., Niiya, M., Mark, G., Reich, S. M., & Warschauer, M. (2015). Coming of Age (Digitally): An Ecological View of Social Media Use among College Students. In *Proceedings of the 18th ACM Conference on Computer Supported Cooperative Work & Social Computing* (pp. 571–582). ACM. Retrieved from http://dl.acm.org/citation.cfm?id=2675271

Wenger, E. (2010). Communities of Practice and Social Learning Systems: the Career of a Concept. In C. Blackmore (Ed.), *Social Learning Systems and Communities of Practice* (pp. 179–198). Springer London. Retrieved from http://link.springer.com/chapter/10.1007/978-1-84996-133-2_11

Williams, A. (2009). Identity Crisis. *Photographies*, *2*(2), 125–133. http://doi.org/10.1080/17540760903116572

Xenakis, I., & Arnellos, A. (2013). The relation between interaction aesthetics and affordances. *Design Studies*, *34*(1), 57–73. doi:10.1016/j.destud.2012.05.004

CHAPTER 13

# Reflective Practice: A Way of Life

*Gabriel Julien*

In some organizations reflective practice plays a pivotal role in the development of practitioners. Reflective practice when carried out properly and effectively can certainly assist to motivate, encourage and energize practitioners. Moreover, it molds and builds character. In this regard, the chapter tries to underscore the purpose and significance of this discipline as well as offer some practical guidelines for practitioners in the area of reflective practice. It strongly advocates that practitioners should be unafraid to engage in the process of reflective practice so that they can become more competent in their respective fields. Some important guidelines of this discipline are offered since these demonstrate how reflective practice complements relationship-based practice. The chapter concludes by laying noticeable emphasis on the importance of practitioners being afforded the opportunities to practice in reflective ways and thus improve their overall relational experiences.

## INTRODUCTION

If reflective practice is to be meaningful, it ought to be a continuous process. This chapter begins by suggesting that reflective practice ought to be a way of life. Some guidelines on the reflective learning process are offered and the difference between reflection-in-action and reflection-on-action is discussed. The author addresses some difficulties that may arise during the process and he offers some suggestions in decision making; additionally, the use of the reflective diary is presented. The chapter concludes with the hope that practitioners will value and appreciate the importance of reflective practice.

## Reflective Practice: A Life-long Process

The term reflective practice derives from the enlightening and outstanding work of Dewey and Schön. Dewey (1910) refers to reflective practice as: "The active, persistent and careful consideration of any belief or supposed form of knowledge in the light of the grounds that support it." Dewey (1933 a) further states that it transforms a scenario: "In which there is experienced obscurity, doubt, conflict, disturbance of some sort, into a situation that is clear, coherent, settled, and harmonious." Once practitioners get into the habit of reflective practice, they will find it very useful. Echoing Dewey's understanding, Schön (1987), Gagastis & Patronis (1990), Lee (2005), Rodgers (2002) and several other scholars propose similar views on reflective practice. Lyons (2010) puts forward that: "The challenge of learning is learning to think," and MacNaughton (2003) describes reflective practice as: "An intellectually engaged activity geared to changing practices by transforming knowledge".

To this end, Lindon (2010) firmly believes that: "Accuracy is an important basis for reflecting on events and experiences. Sometimes it will be on your return to a written account that you can tease out the separate strands." She further states that: "Reflection upon the accuracy of your description, and wondering about possible gaps, can help move you toward thoughtfulness about what is happening." Additionally, Lindon (2010) affirms that reflective practice is not exclusively intellectual but it also involves emotions and incorporates values and principles. Osterman et al (1993) support this view of reflective practice that includes the emotional as well as the rational.

The above-mentioned perspectives seem to suggest that there are some practitioners who, because of their inquisitive minds may consider why things are in a particular way, and how they could be different, and this is not unusual. Indeed, according to York-Barr et al (2006), reflective practice requires a conscious effort to think deeply about situations, and develop insights into them. Louise et al (2010) state that reflective practice affords professionals with avenues to develop a good understanding of their own practice because it further develops the necessary skills, knowledge and approaches to achieve the best outcomes in their practices. Similarly, MacNaughton, (2003), and Raban et al (2007), strongly affirm that professionals who regularly and consistently engage in the reflective process achieve the best outcomes in their practice.

Reflective practice, according to Osterman et al (1993): "…is neither a solitary nor a relaxed meditative process." It is rather: "…a challenging, demanding, and often trying process that is most successful as a collaborative effort." Lindon (2010) states that reflective practice also includes self-evaluation and self-assessment. By doing so practitioners can analyze their decision making, draw on theory and relate this process to their own practice. Thus, critical analysis and evaluation can help them to refocus on their existing philosophy and thus generate new knowledge and ideas. Osterman et al (1993) offer a similar view:

> Awareness is essential for behavioral change. To gain a new level of insight into personal behavior, the reflective practitioner assumes a dual stance, being, on one hand, the actor in a drama and, on the other hand, the critic who sits in the audience watching and analyzing the entire performance. To achieve this perspective, individuals must come to an understanding of their own behavior; they must develop a conscious awareness of their own actions and effects and the ideas or theories-in-use that shape their action strategies. Achieving this level of conscious awareness, however, is not an easy task.

From the above-mentioned perspectives it can be observed that reflective practice is a life-long process which not only allows practitioners to think critically about their careers but it also allows them to enhance their own awareness, energize their thoughts and thus, to be able to approach issues from a different perspective. While this process is difficult and demanding practitioners ought not to be punitive, rather they should seek to highlight strengths as well as their capacities for improvement. Dewey (1933 c), Schön, (1983 a), and MacNaughton (2003), offer that the catalyst for reflection can be either internal or external, that is, it can be self-reflective or involve others. Sometimes reflection can be spontaneous, and at times, it can be deliberately planned. What is interesting is that reflection can often provide both the basis and the motivation for further inquiry which in turn serve as a guide for future improvement in practice.

Chitpin & Simon (2009), Deans et al (2007), and Kinsella (2009), in noting that there are several interpretations of what constitutes reflective practice, concede that the fundamentals of reflective thinking involve the following: Practitioners ought to clearly identify and state the problem which is then analyzed. Solutions will present themselves, therefore, they should analyze these solutions which will eventually engage them in decision making. Dewey (1933 b), Schön (1983 b), Lee (2005) and Rodgers (2002) contend that problems emerge naturally when individuals communicate and Gagastis & Patronis (1990) believe that they can be solved.

Listed below are some basic guidelines that assist practitioners to become more reflective. As stated above, they should try to identify a situation in their work or personal life that they believe could be dealt with more effectively, Jasper (2003). Thus, an accurate and honest description of the setting can be achieved by using the following stages.

1. What really happened?
2. When and where did it occur?
3. What thoughts did you have about the particular situation?
4. Did you reflect honestly on how you behaved?
5. How did it make you feel?
6. Were there other factors that influenced the situation?
7. What lessons have you learned from the experience?

It is important to note that because reflective practice is a process it is normal that sometimes practitioners may not be able to address all the questions. However, the use of the following questions, may assist to formulate how the experience matches with preconceived ideas, Leitch & Day (2000).

1. Was the outcome expected or unexpected?
2. How did it relate to any formal theories that you know?
3. What behaviours do you think might have changed the outcome?
4. What changes can be made for the future?
5. What behaviours can you alter?

Reflective practice assumes the centrality of emotion along with cognition. It strives to recognize, work with, and support the emotional aspect of behavioral change Osterman et al (1993). As practitioners develop the habit of reflection they often become more insightful about self, although this knowledge could bring some level of discomfort. Through reflecting on past events, practitioners gain practical insights about their own assumptions. In this way they could be guided to make more productive decisions and avoid less prudent choices of behavior. Mention must be made that reflection does not engage in unproductive fault finding in self or in co-workers, Lindon (2010). This approach is unhelpful. Reflection is a personal and shared enterprise, Lindon (2010) which enables practitioners to become brutally honest with themselves and others. Moreover, it is a continuous learning process and practitioners should be willing to engage in spite of the challenges they will encounter.

In his book, The Reflective Practitioner, Donald Schön (1983 b), who coined the term reflective practice asserts that it is dynamic and progressive. When done as suggested, or in a similar manner it offers indisputable benefits. This is an absolutely necessary component of emotional intelligence and it certainly assists in developing a better understanding of both self and others. Donald Schön (1983 b), also introduced two concepts: reflection-in-action that is, thinking spontaneously, and reflection-on-action that is, thinking after the event.

## REFLECTION-IN-ACTION AND REFLECTION-ON-ACTION

Schön (1991) makes a distinction between reflection-in-action and reflection-on-action He states that reflection-in-action is concerned with practicing critically. For example, physiotherapy initially designs an exercise programme for a client, makes decisions about its suitability, frequently judges the success of the exercises, considers the next step and simultaneously continues the course of therapy. Reflection-on-action occurs after the activity has taken place when you are thinking about what you did, judging how successful you were and whether any changes to what you did could have resulted in different outcomes.

Smith (2001, 2011) affirms that reflection-in-action and reflection-on-action was one of the major themes of the scholarly work of Donald Schön. Reflection-in-action could be synonymous with what is called quick thinking. This refers to the spontaneous thinking and reaction by practitioners. For example, in the classroom the teacher may be teaching a given topic and notes that students are not actively engaged and perhaps not understanding. The reflection-in-action allows the teacher to carefully note this setting and consider why it is happening and respond by spontaneously taking a different course of action. This could involve rethinking, reshaping and so, explaining the topic from a completely different approach. Lindon (2010) considers reflection-in-action as: "Professional thoughtfulness, keeping key values to the front of your mind, recognizing choice point and using the limited time to make the best decision for the moment."

Smith (2001, 2011) suggests that: "It involves looking to our experiences, connecting with our feelings, and attending to our theories in use. It also entails building new understandings to inform our actions in the situation that is unfolding." Atherton (2013) posits that: "The cultivation of the capacity to reflect-in-action (while doing something) and on-action (after you have done it) has become an important feature of professional training programmes in many disciplines, and its encouragement is seen as a particularly important aspect of the role of the mentor of the beginning professional." To put it differently Ghaye & Ghaye (1998) use the term knowing-in-action and offer two perspectives. One element involves what one does to have a knowledge base that rests on practice.

The other involves using this understanding to make this knowledge more apparent in the workforce.

Reflection-on-action is a direct continuation of reflection-in-action which occurs outside the classroom or workplace when the situation is reconsidered. This time the teacher may think more deeply about why the students did not understand, what caused the situation, what choices were available and why one option was preferred to another. Responses will depend on existing levels of knowledge and experience, and the understanding of theories and values. Dewey (1933) has explained that being reflective: "Enables us to direct our actions with foresight because…It enables us to know what we are about when we act." He further adds that this is of paramount significance in teaching because: "What you do in the classroom and how you behave should have been carefully planned, informed by theory and experience, and be purposeful."

Thus reflection-on-action which often includes academic, social or professional parameters deepens the personal beliefs and self-awareness of practitioners. This understanding of self can assist practitioners to perform their functions more competently since it makes them more aware of the assumptions that they might make automatically or uncritically as a result of their view of issues.

Schön (1983 b), was acutely aware that practitioners are confronted with daily challenges. Thus, he argues that the most effective practitioners use their previous experiences and knowledge to better comprehend how and why things happen. It is not surprising that the scholarly work of Schön has been instrumental in influencing practice globally. It also motivates and encourages practitioners to assume full responsibility for improvements in and on practice. Practitioners ought to bear in mind that reflective practice is not an easy activity. The next segment highlights some of the difficulties that individuals may encounter during the reflective process.

## DIFFICULTIES: A NORMAL PART OF REFLECTIVE PRACTICE

When practitioners engage in reflective practice it is only natural that problems and difficulties will surface and this ought not to be viewed as totally negative. Some problems are easy to solve while others may be more complex. For example, some senior practitioners may be very reluctant to engage in reflective practice. Others may be vulnerable to criticisms, while still others may be unfamiliar with the true notion of reflective practice. Lindon (2010) points out that the: "Experienced practitioners, in any profession, may resist significant change because of the perceived, negative implications...Thus, it can be stated that reflective practice does not always lead to change."

Osterman et al (1993) suggest that: "In other situations, the problem emerges from one's own experience. In whatever form, problems arise out of a sense of discomfort or a desire to change. There is a discrepancy between what we perceive to be and what we consider desirable and in some way, the situation falls short of the ideal." Osterman et al (1993) are of the firm opinion that: "A relevant problem rivets attention and arouses the need to learn. Thus, it is useful to examine the nature of the problem and try as best as possible to address it with new knowledge, fresh insight and competency gained as a consequence of deep reflection. Hence, practitioners could confront problems with better awareness of the situation and with more effective strategies. "With practice in reflection, we learn to take a conscious orientation toward problem finding." Osterman et al (1993).

## Problem Solving and Decision Making

Problem solving, according to Nolan (1989), is the means of finding ways to get from the present situation to where you ought to be. The problem, therefore, is the gap between the current situation and a more desirable one. Hicks (2005) states that to make this transition, practitioners must first of all recognize that there is a problem. This recognition is not simply mentioning that a problem exists. It means defining precisely and as accurately as possible the presenting scenario. Decision making is using the most prudent choice among several types of action. In this regard, Hicks (2005) offers three main approaches to problem solving and decision making.

We live in a complex world and we are often faced with problems to solve some of these problems Hicks (2005) suggests the following. The creative approach uses the assumption that some individuals possess the knowledge and the experience to address a certain situation but most times they do not recognize the approach. Creative problem solving means using this knowledge to address the presenting problem. Another is the rational or logical approach which requires a careful examining and analyzing of the situation. In this way individuals approach the problem in a careful and methodical manner. Hicks (2005) suggests that the use of the creative and rational often complement each other.

Adair (2007) offers five stages in decision making: define the object, collect relevant data, generate feasible options, make decision, and implement and evaluate. It is strongly recommended, according to Adair (2007), that practitioners begin to document events since this often serves to clarify problems and assist in the process of decision making. In addition to documenting information practitioners need to ensure that all the data is available, relevant and necessary. The generating of feasible options allows practitioners to move systematically from a range of possibilities. For example, individuals could begin by evaluating the results of imaginative thinking in order to arrive at a number of options that emanate from the resources that are available. In making decisions individuals need to assess the possible risks that may be involved. Adair (2007) emphasizes that implementing and evaluating the decision is an integral part of the entire decision-making process. In this regard, the use of the reflective diary could be useful in assisting practitioners to minimize problems and maintain objectivity throughout the decision-making process.

## THE USE OF A REFLECTIVE DIARY

Julien (2002), during field work made successful use of the reflective diary. What is a reflective diary, and what kind of information is documented? The reflective diary is similar to the actual daily journal that some individuals have as a means of noting personal information, appointments, meetings of organizations or even names, addresses and telephone numbers of friends. Thus, Julien (2002) kept an autobiographical detailed account outlining the social situations of his fieldwork. The diary of Julien (2002) contained an analytical account that raised questions and difficulties that were encountered while doing research. The notes in the diary were organized around a series of questions: Who?, What?, When?, Where?, Why and How? Keeping these questions in perspective literally forced him to document details that at times seemed mundane. Such tasks, though mundane, often sharpened his thinking. For example, Julien (2002) could vividly remembered documenting the date, time and experience, when he first conducted an interview with a group of street children on the streets of Port of Spain, the capital of Trinidad and Tobago. A valid consequence arising from keeping a reflective diary was the fact that such an interview made an indelible impression on his mind. Subsequent reading of the diary on the events of that first interview created a graphic image in mind. When Julien (2002), began to analyze data from fieldwork, information on interviews and observation noted in his reflective diary often helped him to elaborate scenarios. Issues which Julien (2002) could not immediately comprehend and which might have been easily dismissed as trivial, were carefully noted in the diary.

Julien (2002) added that the diary helped to clarify certain methodological questions. For example, the different kinds of circumstances under which observation and interviews were conducted, his personal feelings at a given moment, his reactions to what he thought the informants were experiencing were all noted carefully in the reflective diary. Words and phrases that the children used among themselves were also carefully documented. That type of information provided Julien (2002) with first hand data and such documentation was used as a resource. It was also used to query and provide further data.

Thus, the use of a reflective diary, according to Julien (2002), can assist practitioners to maintain their focus and thereby maximize objectivity. Because it is used to record personal information as well as field notes it can sometimes monitor the progress of practitioners. This latter use is extremely helpful because it can help safeguard them from becoming manipulative, dominating and controlling while conducting their work. Information from the reflective diary can generate further data and can assist to cross check inconsistencies, Julien (2002).

Furthermore, the reflective diary can help practitioners to make that necessary and apt connection between theory and practice. It can also assist in deepening that sense of self which heighten critical thinking skills and promotes professional growth and development. The following authors attest to this fact: Asselin (2011), Bulman (2008), Dunfee et al (2008), Eckroth-Bucher (2004), Idczak (2007), Kennison & Misselwitz (2002), Ruland & Ahern (2007), and Padden (2013). The literature affirms that practitioners can maximize the use of the reflective diary when they begin to reflect and thus allow growth-promoting changes to take place.

Luidens (1997) and Crowe et al (1986) share a similar view and add that writing facilitates learning because it encourages practitioners to think deeply which results in increased clarity of ideas. Yinger et al (1981) further add that practitioners sometimes need to re-present knowledge that was gathered in a different form. This process can offer new understanding and learning as practitioners perceive information from a completely different perspective.

This lends credence to the use of the reflective diary according to Ong (2015). In encountering different concepts in varying contexts the reflective diary becomes the vehicle in getting practitioners to actively make their own connections between new and prior situations, Ong (2015). When they make entries in the reflective diary they sometimes build bridges and thereby expand their own experiences. They build on their understanding of the knowledge, through a blending between old and new knowledge, and they extend it by reflecting on how they can further use the skill in their other courses and in their everyday life, Woods (1995).

Making entries in the reflective diary, according to Crowe et al (1986), is like a distillation process. It gets the learner to filter, to reconstruct, to organize, to gather, to process, and to feel the experiences. Hence, the reflective diary provides an apt avenue where practitioners can closely monitor their own thoughts and reflections, Crowe et al (1986).

Lindon (2010) and Moon (2003) underscore the significance of a reflective diary. They add that in work situations, keeping the diary, and consistently using reflective practice, will enhance personal development and support more meaningful discussions about life in general. Moon (2003) suggests that although no single correct format is given, practitioners must always try, as far as possible, to maintain professionalism when documenting events. Some may prefer a free-style approach while others may like a more guided structure. In the early stages, it may be useful to have some guiding questions to clarify the process of diary making. McKay & Fanning (2000) offer some guidelines as to how practitioners could make proper documentation.

McKay & Fanning (2000) state that it is extremely important to try to eliminate negative ways of describing things or events and to try no to exaggerate nor embellish them. It may be helpful for practitioners to list some of their limitations and corresponding strengths. The next stage is to try to blend weaknesses and strengths into a self-description that is accurate, objective and supportive. Through this process practitioners minimize the negatives and focus on the positives. McKay & Fanning (2000) encourage practitioners to use specific rather than general language in describing issues, and to eliminate negatives in favor of positives. Practitioners can document their thoughts using complete sentences, synonyms, adjectives and adverbs. This step is very essential since it fosters honesty and clarity that underscore the reflective process, McKay & Fanning (2000).

## Conclusion

This chapter began by emphasizing that because reflective practice is important, it ought to be inculcated in the life of practitioners. It has tried to explain the true and real significance of reflective practice and has attempted to present some effective guidelines to assist practitioners to become more reflective. It has acknowledged that difficulty is part of the process and suggestions have been offered concerning decision making. It has recommended that the proper use of the reflective diary could be valuable in maintaining integrity and objectivity during the reflective process. This process will assist practitioners to become more conscience of self and the inevitable interaction between self and humanity and the environment as they maximize their individual and collective potential.

## REFERENCES

Adair, John (2007) Decision Making and Problem Solving Strategies. London: Kogan Page Limited.

Asselin, M. E., (2011) Using reflection strategies to link course knowledge to clinical practice: The RN-to-BSN student experience. Journal of Nursing Education, 50, 125-133.

Atherton J. S., (2013) Learning and Teaching; Reflection and Reflective Practice. Online: UK retrieved 2 June 2015 from http://www.learningandteaching.info/learning/reflecti.htm

Bulman, C., (2008) An introduction to reflection. In C. Bulman & S. Schutz (eds.) Reflective practice in nursing (4th ed., pp. 1-24). Oxford, United Kingdom: Wiley-Blackwell.

Chitpin, S., & Simon, M., (2009) "Even if no-one looked at it, it was important for my own development": Pre-service teacher perceptions of professional portfolios. Australian Journal of Education, 53(3), 277.

Crowe, D. & Youga, J., (Summer 1986) (p. 218-222) "Using Writing as a Tool for Learning Economics", Journal of Economic Education.

Deans, J., Brown, R., & Young, S., (2007) The possum story. Australian Journal of Early Childhood, 32(4), 1.

Dewey, J., (1910) How We Think. New York, N.Y.: D.C. Heath.

Dewey, J., (1933 a) How We Think. Buffalo, New York: Prometheus Books.

Dewey, J., (1933 b) How We Think. Boston, D. C. Heath & Co.

Dewey, J., (1933 c) How we think: A re-statement of the Relation of Reflective Thinking in the Education Process. Chicago: Henry Regnery.

Dunfee, H., Rindflesch, A., Driscoll, M., Hollman, J., & Plack, M., M., (2008). Assessing reflection and higher-order thinking in the clinical setting using electronic discussion threads. Journal of Physical Therapy Education, 22, 60-67.

Eckroth-Bucher, M., (2004) The process of self-awareness development in female BSN students within the context of nursing education (Doctoral dissertation, Widener University).

Gagastis, A., & Patronis, T., (1990) Using Geometrical Models in a Process of Reflective Thinking in Learning and Teaching Mathematics. Educational Studies in Mathematics, 21(1), 29-54.

Ghaye, Anthony & Ghaye, Kay (1998) Teaching and Learning through Critical Reflective Practice. London: David Fulton.

Hicks, Michael, J., (2005) (2$^{nd}$, ed.) Problem Solving and Decision Making: Hard, Soft and Creative Approaches. United Kingdom: Thomas Learning.

Idczak, S. E., (2007). I am a nurse: Nursing students learn the art and science of nursing. Nursing Education Perspectives, 28, 66-71.

Jasper, Melanie (2003) Beginning Reflective Practice United Kingdom: Nelson Thomas. https://books.google.tt/books?hl=en&lr=&id=FKroWQSJ7z4C&oi=fnd&pg=PR5&dq=reflective+practice+definition&ots=vmRLF3FokH&sig=YQdsd4MWxNhpPvAHRvi-qb1zecc&redir_esc=y#v=onepage&q=reflective%20practice%20definition&f=false

Julien, Gabriel (2002) 'Street Children' in Trinidad and Tobago: Insights from a Case Study. Unpublished Thesis.

Lee, H. J., (2005) Understanding and Assessing Pre-service Teachers' Reflective Thinking. Teaching and teacher education, 21(6), 699-715.

Kennison, M., M., & Misselwitz, S., (2002) Evaluating reflective writing for appropriateness, fairness, and consistency. Nursing Education Perspectives, 23, 238-242.

Kinsella, E., (2009) Professional knowledge and the epistemology of reflective practice. Nursing Philosophy, 11(1), 3-14.

Leitch, Ruth & Day, Christopher (2000) Action research and reflective practice: towards a holistic view, Educational Action Research, 8:1, 179-193, DOI http://www.tandfonline.com/action/showCitFormats?doi=10.1080/09650790000200108 http://dx.doi.org/10.1080/09650790000200108

Lindon, Jennie (2010) Reflective Practice and Early Years Professionalism Linking Theory and Practice. London: Holder Education.

Louise Marbina, Amelia Church & Collette Tayler (2010) Victorian Early Years Learning and Development Framework Evidence Paper Practice Principle 8: Reflective Practice. Marbina, Church & Tayler.

Luidens, P. M., (1997 "Paper Thinking: The Process of Writing", in Costa, A. L. & Lineman, R.M. (ed.) 'Envisioning Process an Content: Towards a Renaissance Curriculum', Corwin Press, USA.

Lyons, N., (2010) Handbook of Reflection and Reflective Inquiry. New York, N.Y., Springer.

MacNaughton, G., (2003) Reflecting on early childhood curriculum In G. MacNaughton Shaping Early Childhood (pp. 113-120) England: Open University Press.

McKay, Matthew & Fanning, Patrick (2000) Self-Esteem (3rd, ed.) Oakland: New Harbinger Publications, Inc.

Moon, Jennifer (2003) Learning Journals and Logs, Reflective Diaries. Dublin: Centre for Teaching and Learning, University College Dublin.

Nolan, Vincent (1998) The Innovator's Handbook: The Skills of Innovative Management – Problem Solving, Communication and Teamwork. London: Sphere Books.

Ong, Rachel (2015) The role of reflection in student learning: a study of its effectiveness in complementing problem-based learning environments. Centre for Educational Development Republic Polytechnic 1 Kay Siang Road, Singapore 248922 retrieved 02 June 2015 from http://www.myrp.sg/ced/research/papers/role_of_reflection_in_student_l earning.pdf

Osterman, Karen, F. & Kottkamp, Robert, B. (1993) Reflective Practice for Educators
Improving Schooling Through Professional Development California: A Sage Publications Company. retrieved from http://www.tandfonline.com/action/showCitFormats?doi=10.1080/09650 790000200108

Padden, Mary L., (2013) "A pilot study to determine the validity and reliability of the Level of Reflection-on-Action Assessment." The Journal of Nursing Education, 52(7), pp.410-5.

Raban, B., Nolan, A., Waniganayake, M., Ure, C., Brown, R., & Deans, J., (2007) Building Capacity Strategic professional development for early childhood practitioners. Melbourne: Thomson Social Science Press.

Rodgers, C., (2002) Defining reflection: Another look at John Dewey and Reflective Thinking. The Teachers' College Record, 104: 842-866.

Ruland, J. P., & Ahern, N. R., (2007) Transforming student perspectives through reflective writing. Nurse Educator, 32, 81-88.

Schön, Donald (1983 a) The Reflective Practitioner: How Professionals Think in Action. London: Routledge.

Schön, D. A., (1983 b) The structure of Reflection -In- Action. The reflective practitioner. New York: Basic Books.

Schön D. A., (1987) Educating the Reflective Practitioner. San Francisco: Jossey-Bass.

Schön, D., (1991) The Reflective Practitioner. Aldershot: Ashgate Publishing Ltd. Learning Development at Plymouth is a partner in Learn Higher www.plymouth.ac.uk/learn learn@plymouth.ac.uk Learning Gateway, RLB 011 01752 587676 Tutorials Drop-in Zone Taught sessions Peer Assisted Learning Schem.

Smith, M. K., (2001, 2011) 'Donald Schön: learning, reflection and change', the encyclopaedia of informal education. retrieved 02 June 2015 from www.infed.org/thinkers/et-schon.htm

Woods, Donald, R., (1995) Problem-based Learning: Helping your students gain the most from PBL, Woods, McMaster University.

Yinger, R., J & Clark, C. M., (1981) "Reflective Journal Writing: Theory and Practice", Occasional Paper No. 50, Institute for Research on Teaching, Michigan State University.

York-Barr, Jennifer, Sommers, William, A., S. Ghere, Gail & Montie Jo (2006) (eds.) Reflective Practice to Improve Schools: An Action Guide for Educators United Kingdom: A Sage Publishing Company. retrieved from
https://books.google.tt/books?hl=en&lr=&id=v7VyAwAAQBAJ&oi=fnd&pg=PP1&dq=reflective+practice+definition&ots=LTV7YNybdB&sig=_T8djCZP3tVB5JnMMxUfgPLR11U&redir_esc=y#v=onepage&q=reflective%20practice%20definition&f=false

CHAPTER 14

# The Effects of an Intervention Program Based on Metacognitive Strategies on Young Students' Writing

*Konstantinos Mastrothanasis and Athina Geladari*

The development of cognitive psychology brought to light metacognition, alongside with a new perspective in the field of teaching writing. The present study pursuits to explore the possible effects of a 15-week metacognitive strategies-based instruction intervention program on young learners' writing performance. 445 pupils attending the 5th and 6th grade of primary school and their 26 teachers participated in the program, separated into experimental and control group. Educational material and several activities were designed for the experimental group, aiming to foster pupils' metacognitive awareness and enrich their metacognitive strategies armory with the goal to gradually develop writing autonomy, based on the teaching model of CALLA (Cognitive Academic Language Learning Approach).

Pupils' writing performance was measured with standardized pre-tests and post-tests before and after the completion of the teaching intervention. Data were analyzed using the non-parametrical Mann-Whitney U-Test and Wilcoxon Signed-Ranks Test revealing the positive effects of the intervention on pupils' writing performance and more specifically, in terms of textual organization, text cohesion and coherence. Moreover, at the end of the program pupils made more accurate use of their vocabulary and the errors were reduced. Benefits extend to students' engagement level, creativity and motivation which were increased. The study concludes with some practical suggestions for teachers, who wish to develop metacognition in their writing class.

## INTRODUCTION

Writing is a communicative skill that arises in a specific sociocultural environment (Clark & Ivanic, 2013) and is influenced by structural conventions and stylistic choices made by the author, as well as the textual content determined for each text genre (Kostouli, 2009). Composing a written text is largely dependent on the conversational roles and communicative situations and is related to social, historical, ideological and cultural practices (Prior, 2008; Graham, 2006a).

The composition of a communicatively appropriate and coherent text requires the acquisition of a variety of skills and mental organization: production skills, organizing ideas, writing and assessment skills. In modern language teaching, communicative suitability focuses on three dimensions of knowledge that contribute to this effect (Mousiou-Mylona, 2004). Linguistic knowledge involves the acquisition of the written code, the phonology and morphology, vocabulary and syntax rules. Textual knowledge includes the acquisition of connectives, organizational forms, relation between semantics, while the sociolinguistic knowledge includes the awareness of style to be adopted in a text depending on the situation of communication (Grabe & Kaplan, 1996).

The latest theoretical models of studying and development of writing production consider writing as an event consisting of three non-linear and repetitive phases where organization, transfer and review concurrently coincide (Tribble, 1997). In the phase of organization, the author sets the text by generating ideas, checking their relevance and significance and organizing them into a plan designed by them. During the transfer phase, the author selects the proper vocabulary to form sentences, paragraphs and text in order to convey their organized ideas in the written code, following the rules of writing. Finally, in the phase of the review the author revises and corrects errors in both the micro and the macro level of the text that has already been produced in order to produce its final version (Graham, 2006a; White & Arndt, 1991).

The above mentioned phases require the activation of sub-skills and higher-order cognitive functions, the activation of pre-writing, writing and review writing strategies, all of which result to the final text (Mastrothanasis, Geladari & Griva, 2010; Gavriilidou & Psaltou-Joycey, 2010; McCutchen, 2006) and are unlikely to be excluded from the area of metacognition (Sitko, 1998). The term "metacognition" is adopted to describe our knowledge of the way we perceive, remember, think and act (Kostaridou - Euclides, 2005). Metacognitive processes occur when we consider the acquisition of the knowledge of something (metacognitive knowledge), the steps we need to follow to acquire the knowledge (metacognitive activities), and what is the current state of knowledge (metacognitive experience). According to Pintrich (1999), the concept of metacognition focuses on the regulation and control of a person's actions using three strategies: planning, monitoring and self-regulation.

During the writing process, metacognition affects students' efficiency directly, thus, determining to a large extent their performance (Harris, Graham, Brindle & Sandmel, 2009, Hacker, Keener & Kircher, 2009; Stern, 1992). Some field researches have underlined that the productive use of metacognitive strategies (organization, monitoring and control procedures) contribute to successful writing (Wenden, 1998; Graham & Harris, 1994; Cohen, 1990), forming a framework for the author's effective supervision of their followed processes and autonomy.

Previous studies have revealed that good writers of school age are flexible in their strategy employment when composing a text and acquire greater metacognitive awareness, hence, they select appropriate strategies for specific activities and are capable of interpreting their choices (Mastrothanasis, Geladari & Griva, 2010; Baroudy, 2008; Ferrari, Bouffard & Rainville, 1998). Conversely, students of low linguistic backgrounds are confronted with difficulties in organizing and controlling the processes of writing texts, are usually reluctant to get involved in the processes of total control and evaluation of the final text and are unlikely to make effective use of metacognitive strategies (Geladari & Mastrothanasis, 2014; Griva, Tsakiridou, & Nihoritou, 2009; Goddard & Sendi, 2008).

Further studies in the domain of metacognition in writing have demonstrated that practice in selecting and adopting certain metacognitive strategies may contribute to successful completion of writing, reinforcing the perception that the way the writing process is accomplished have the potential to be taught (Griva, Alevriadou & Gountouras, 2011; Yanyan, 2010; Lane et al, 2008; Graham, 2006b; Graham, Harris & Mason, 2005; Keith & Frese, 2005). Alongside with the improvement of performance in writing, a positive correlation is noted between the development of students' metacognition and their performance in written evaluation (Rose & Kasper, 2001; Kasper, 1997; Welch, 1992), while there is a qualitative improvement in content, textual organization, consistency and reduction of errors (Reshadi & Aidinlou, 2012; Goddard & Sendi, 2008; Lu, 2006; Xu & Tang, 2005; Biedenbach, 2004; De La Daz & Graham, 2002; Yarrow & Topping, 2001; Wilkinson, 1992). Finally, the development of metacognition contributes to the autonomy of writing (Graham, Harris & Olinghouse, 2007; Hsiao & Oxford, 2002; Graham & Harris, 2000; Graham & Harris, 1993; Graham, Harris & Reid, 1992; Harris & Pressley, 1991).

Metacognitive strategies can be taught and consciously guide the thinking of individuals performing writing. An educational aim should be to teach students and develop a repertoire of thinking processes which will be available to withdraw whenever they need to. Students' thought is directed to the process (process goal) and not just the content (content goal), as the process and understanding are the components of learning.

One of the most popular models regarding teaching employing strategies is considered the CALLA (Cognitive Academic Language Learning Approach). According to this model, the strategies that facilitate learning are systematically added in the context of teaching. The five components that also comprise the phases of teaching strategies of CALLA model are preparation, presentation, practice, evaluation and expansion. More specifically (Zaga, 2005: 75-76; Chamot, 2005; Oxford, 2001):

*Preparation of the teaching content:* At this stage, the teacher detects students' prior knowledge on the theme content, the already acquired effective strategies and identifies the level of students and gaps in prior knowledge.

*Presentation of Content*: At this stage the teacher selects and uses a range of metacognitive strategies in order to assure that the students have successfully comprehended the new strategies. The strategies transferred are chosen based on the age of the students and the subject, including planning, self-monitoring, self-evaluation. Then, various applications of the strategies are provided within explicit examples so that students can apply the strategies during the next stage.

*Students' practice*: During this stage the students are encouraged to practice and recycle their knowledge in strategies. Practice is achieved by adopting certain strategies in several activities designed to help them easily take in the new information received during course.

*Evaluation of the course*: This phase involves teacher's estimation/self-evaluation whether the learning objectives were sufficiently covered in aspects of content, language and strategies used by both the teacher and the students themselves. Students check their level of writing achievement and review the new strategies.

*Expansion*: This phase is estimated as a crucial one for the generalization of what students have learned in other fields of knowledge (interdisciplinary approach), considering that the conversion of declarative knowledge into procedural is very important (Anderson, 1983). Students are inspired to transfer the new strategies to different contexts. Furthermore, students have the chance to consolidate, automate and internalize the strategies.

Generally, teaching based on strategies is considered a student-centered approach in the teaching of writing, aiming at the adoption of effective techniques, activation of sub-skills in the content of the course.

## THE STUDY

Throughout this research, an effort is made to investigate the effect of metacognitive strategies in writing. More specifically, the main hypothesis was focused on whether the implementation of an intervention program of development and use of metacognitive strategies, in the last two grades of primary school (5$^{th}$ and 6$^{th}$), will have a positive effect on student performance on writing. The research questions raised by this case were defined as follows:

1. What is the effect of direct instruction of metacognitive strategies in the characteristics of the generated texts by the students?
2. What is the effect of direct instruction of metacognitive strategies in the writing of students?
3. What is the impact of direct instruction of metacognitive strategies in the processes followed by students in writing?

These questions form the null and alternative hypotheses of the research.

## THE EXPERIMENTAL DESIGN

In order to investigate the above research questions an experimental intervention program was designed. The teaching intervention program can also be considered as a field research, since it was conducted in the natural environment of the participants where they do not feel their participation in the experimental procedure (Argyle, 1996). The sample of the experimental group (EG) and control group (CG) was formed during the first month of the program, according to the schedule (see Table 1). In addition, this first month all participants were evaluated using standardized essays in the production and processing of written speech. Furthermore, the cognitive, metacognitive, social and affective strategies that were employed by the students in the production of the writing were detected, recorded and evaluated (Petric & Czarl, 2003), in order to get an insight on the use of effective strategies on writing.

Table 1: The schedule of the teaching intervention

| Week | Action | Team |
|---|---|---|
| 1st-3rd | Outlining and coding the general profile of students. Identify the strategies that students already make use of. Evaluate the characteristics of pupils' writing and production. | Experimental Control |
| 4th-13rd | Teaching metacognitive strategies and practice the new strategies in class (2 hours / week) | Experimental |
| 14th-15th | Reassessment of the strategies that students use. Reassessment of the production and features of writing. | Experimental Control |

Then, a set of ten-week duration was determined for the teaching intervention with the participation of the students enrolling the experimental group in the activities for the development of metacognitive writing strategies, for two teaching hours per week during the language class. Only the experimental group received explicit instruction on metacognitive writing strategies while the students of the control group were taught writing, as required by the curriculum and in accordance with the course book, receiving no intervention.

The teachers who would teach the experimental group voluntarily joined in the process. They were provided with educational material by the program's scientific team on a weekly basis. The material consisted of instructions and worksheets designed to support them in their direct teaching of metacognitive strategies. The activities were aiming in raising students' metacognitive knowledge and awareness, enriching students' metacognitive strategies armory and experience, with the ideal to gradually develop students' writing autonomy, according to the model of teaching strategies CALLA (Cognitive Academic Language Learning Approach). The implementation of the program by the class teacher, contributed to the maintenance of the established psychological and social interactions in the school context as well as the positive climate in the class team (Kontos & Keyes, 1999). The themes and text genres of the material designed for the experimental group, varied and were in accordance with the purposes and objectives of the curriculum for the language course of the 5th and 6th grade. In addition, the distributed worksheets were based on the reason of creating material that promotes teaching strategies (Wenden, 1986). The worksheet themes, text genres introduced and the metacognitive strategies selected to be taught by the participant teachers are presented in the following table (see Table 2).

Table 2: Themes, text genres and metacognitive strategies targeted through the intervention

| Theme | Text genre | Metacognitive strategies |
|---|---|---|
| A school excursion | Narrative | Subject organization<br>Peer evaluation |
| Guess who | Expository | Self-monitoring<br>Peer improvement |
| Setting the table | Procedural | Local organization<br>Self-evaluation |
| Children's rights | Expository | Defining the aim of writing<br>Self-monitoring<br>Peer evaluation<br>Peer improvement |
| The story of a paper sheet | Informational | Full & thematic organization<br>Peer evaluation<br>Peer improvement |
| Cooking spaghetti | Procedural | Local organization<br>Peer evaluation<br>Peer improvemet |
| Illustrated stories- Pirate's Treasure/Myths from Aesop | Narrative | Defining the aim of writing<br>Full organization<br>Self-evaluation |
| Classified advertisements- Missing dog/house rent etc. | Persuasive | Message adaptation<br>Defining the aim of writing<br>Full organization<br>Peer evaluation |
| The research of our class- Accidents in our class | Expository | Defining the aim of writing<br>Full organization<br>Self-evaluation |
| Trying to persuade uncle Paul to buy me a bike for my birthday | Persuasive | Defining the aim of writing<br>Full & thematic organization<br>Self-evaluation |

The post-test of both groups, experimental and control, took place at the end of the program, in order to collect data that would allow comparison of the two groups.

## SAMPLE

The survey involved 445 fifth and sixth graders who attended the school year 2013-2014 of primary schools in Central Greece. 222 of these (49.9%) comprised the experimental group and 223 (50.1%) the control group. In particular, the composition of the two groups is shown in the following table (see Table 3).

Table 3: Composition of research groups

| Group | Grade | Gender | | Total |
|---|---|---|---|---|
| | | Boys | Girls | |
| Experimental Group (EG) | 5th | 77 (50,7%) | 75 (49,3%) | 152 (68,5%) |
| | 6th | 42 (60,0%) | 28 (40,0%) | 70 (31,5%) |
| *Total* | | 119 (53,6%) | 103 (46,4%) | 222 (100%) |
| Control Group (CG) | 5th | 66 (47,1%) | 74 (52,9%) | 140 (62,8%) |
| | 6th | 52 (62,7%) | 31 (37,3%) | 83 (37,2%) |
| *Total* | | 118 (52,9%) | 105 (47,1%) | 223 (100%) |

## METHODOLOGY

All participants from the experimental and control group were required to take a pre-test and a post-test to determine whether there were benefits in the writing performance after their training in metacognitive writing strategies. The pre-test was carried out before the intervention so as to confirm that the writing abilities of these two classes were at the same level. In order to measure and evaluate students' abilities, participants were asked to write a descriptive text, in accordance with a standardized test (Porpodas, Diakogiorgis, Dimakos & Karantzis, 2007) of granted validity and reliability.

Texts and their features were analyzed according to the indicators of analytical evaluation of texts (Matsagouras, 2009). The dependent quantitative variables that emerged are the following: a) number of words of produced text, b) number of sentences of generated text c) number of errors in punctuation, d) number of syntax errors and e) number of errors in vocabulary use.

In addition to these variables, students' texts were checked for their spelling correctness, consistency, coherence and textual organization, according to the criteria defined by the standardized test (Porpodas, Diakogiorgis, Dimakos & Karantzis, 2007). These criteria formed, additional to the above mentioned quantitative dependent variables, the following indexes: a) spelling accuracy index, b) text cohesion index, c) text consistency index and d) textual organization index.

Finally, with regard to evaluate the process of writing by the students, we employed a standardized test that contained tasks of varied and gradual difficulty. Part of it was the restoration of destructurized sentences by the students in order to form meaningful sentences (Porpodas, Diakogiorgis, Dimakos & Karantzis, 2007). The indexes that emerged as dependent quantitative variables are: a) restoring deconstructed sentence index (RDS) and b) restoring deconstructed text index (RDP). For the restoration of the destructurized sentence (words of a sentence that are given with a wrong grammatical order), students have to replace the words in the right order in the sentence so that it makes sense. Accordingly, students have to place the sentences in the correct order so that they form a meaningful paragraph, and eventually, a whole text.

The data collected from the initial (pre-test) and final assessment (post-test) were transferred to a linear array of subjects' tables using the statistical package SPSS 18 and, then, were analyzed quantitatively. The regularity of the sample was checked with the Kolmogorov-Smirnov test, yielding values smaller than 0.05 ($z<0,05$). The non-parametric Mann-Whitney U-Test and the Wilcoxon Signed-Ranks Test were selected to determine differences between the variables. The level of statistical significance (p) was set at 5% while the findings with value $p <0,05$ were considered statistically significant. The descriptive characteristics will be presented using the average (mean) and standard deviation (SD).

## RESULTS

### Pre-test

In order to estimate the comparisons regarding writing performance between the participants of both groups, the criterion Mann-Whitney U in independent groups was employed. More specifically, we explored potential differences between the mean score in the evaluation of performance concerning the characteristics of the produced text, the indices of writing and indices of processing writing in the pre-test.

As shown in Table 4, the two groups show no statistically significant differences in the characteristics of the produced text in the pre-test.

Table 4: Comparison of EG and CG based on the assessed characteristics of the pre-test's generated text.

| Assessment of the characteristics of the generated text | Group | M.S. | T.D. | Z | P |
|---|---|---|---|---|---|
| Number of words | Experimental | 135,03 | 49,653 | -1,520 | 0,129 |
| | Control | 127,11 | 39,868 | | |
| Number of sentences | Experimental | 9,91 | 4,250 | -0,140 | 0,889 |
| | Control | 10,26 | 5,037 | | |
| Number of punctuation mistakes | Experimental | 1,59 | 1,650 | -0,406 | 0,685 |
| | Control | 1,52 | 1,671 | | |
| Number of syntax mistakes | Experimental | 1,27 | 1,336 | -1,897 | 0,580 |
| | Control | 1,52 | 1,454 | | |
| Number of vocabulary mistakes | Experimental | 1,59 | 1,650 | -0,406 | 0,685 |
| | Control | 1,52 | 1,671 | | |

As displayed on Table 4, there are found no statistically significant differences between the control group and the experimental group regarding the number of words used in their text (z=-1,520, p=0,129), the number of sentences (z=-0,140, p=0,889), the number punctuation mistakes (z=-0,406, p = 0,685), the number of errors in syntax (z=-1,897, p=0,580) and the number of the mistakes in vocabulary use (z=-0,406, p=0,685).

Similarly, no statistically significant differences are noticed comparing the indicators on writing (see Table 5) in the pre-test process.

Table 5: Comparison of the EG and CG pre-test performance on the indices of assessment in writing.

| Assessment of writing | Group | M.S. | S.D. | Z | P |
|---|---|---|---|---|---|
| Spelling accuracy index | Experimental | 91,16 | 10,856 | -1,815 | 0,070 |
| | Control | 92,67 | 8,713 | | |
| Text cohesion index | Experimental | 14,42 | 4,465 | -1,830 | 0,067 |
| | Control | 15,21 | 4,072 | | |
| Text consistency index | Experimental | 21,75 | 4,354 | -0,207 | 0,836 |
| | Control | 21,85 | 4,074 | | |
| Textual organization index | Experimental | 36,17 | 8,025 | -0,982 | 0,326 |
| | Control | 37,06 | 7,418 | | |

There are not shown any statistically significant differences concerning the indices of spelling accuracy ($z = -1,81520$, $p=0,070$), text cohesion text ($z = -1,830$, $p = 0,067$), text consistency ($z = -0,207$, $p = -0,836$), and textual organization ($z = -0,982$, $p = 0,326$), between the control and the experimental group.

Also, the comparison between the mean scores in the indices of the processing of writing, between the participants of the two groups showed no statistically significant differences (see: Table 6) in the pre-test.

Table 6: Comparison of EG and CG based on the pre-test in the assessment of indices of processing writing.

| Indices of processing writing | Group | M.S. | S.D. | Z | P |
|---|---|---|---|---|---|
| Restoring deconstructed sentence index | Experimental | 8,38 | 3,106 | -1,574 | 0,115 |
| | Control | 8,92 | 2,710 | | |
| Restoring deconstructed text index | Experimental | 24,86 | 10,310 | -0,251 | 0,801 |
| | Control | 25,83 | 8,198 | | |

Differences in restoring deconstructed sentences index ($z = -1,574$, $p = 0,115$) and text ($z = -0,251$, $p = 0,801$) are not at the significance level of 5%.

The absence of statistically significant differences demonstrates that at the beginning of the research, the experimental and the control group appear to obtain similar performance characteristics of the individual evaluation, and in particular the characteristics of texts produced, the writing process indicators and indicators of processing written language.

## POST-TEST RESULTS

After the completion of the intervention program, which lasted for 15 weeks, students completed the same test again. The data were undergone the Wilcoxon Signed-Ranks Test, in order to estimate and compare the performance in the pre-test and the post test for each of the two groups separately. This instrument allowed the analysis of the impact of teaching metacognitive strategies in the characteristics of the texts, the indices of the writing production and indices of writing process. Furthermore, using the Mann-Whitney U criterion, the comparisons among participants of the two groups in the post-test were assessed, as to investigate possible differences between the means scores in the performance in the assessment of the above components of writing.

Regarding the assessment of the characteristics of the produced texts by the control group, there are no statistically significant differences found in the number of words of the texts ($z = -0,664$, $p = 0,507$) and the number of sentences ($z = -0,240$, $p = 0,215$) that students formed at the beginning and in the end of the intervention (see table 7). As for the experimental group, statistically significant difference is noticed in the number of sentences of the produced texts ($z = -2,069$, $p = 0,039$) at the end of the intervention (mean = $10,42 \pm 4,318$) compared with those of the beginning of the intervention (m v = $9,91 \pm 4,250$). On the contrary, there is no significant difference in the number of words used in the text ($z = -0,619$, $p = 0,536$).

Table 7: Comparison of the two groups' mean scores regarding the characteristics of generated texts in the pre- and post-test.

| Assessment of the characteristics of the generated text | Group | Pre-test | | Post-test | | Z | P |
|---|---|---|---|---|---|---|---|
| | | M.S. | S.D. | M.S. | S.D. | | |
| Number of words | EG | 135,03 | 49,653 | 137,45 | 50,580 | -0,619* | 0,536 |
| | CG | 127,11 | 39,868 | 126,13 | 40,976 | -0,664* | 0,507 |
| Number of sentences | EG | 9,91 | 4,250 | 10,42 | 4,318 | -2,069* | 0,039 |
| | CG | 10,26 | 5,037 | 10,55 | 4,902 | -0,240** | 0,215 |
| Number of | EG | 1,59 | 1,650 | 1,03 | 1,234 | - | 0,000 |

| | | | | | | | | |
|---|---|---|---|---|---|---|---|---|
| spelling mistakes | | | | | | 7,183** | | |
| | CG | 1,52 | 1,671 | 1,31 | 1,593 | -2,654* | 0,008 | |
| Number of syntax mistakes | EG | 1,27 | 1,336 | 0,74 | 1,115 | -5,605** | 0,000 | |
| | CG | 1,52 | 1,454 | 1,29 | 1,321 | -3,362* | 0,001 | |
| Number of vocabulary mistakes | EG | 1,59 | 1,650 | 0,90 | 1,304 | -6,585** | 0,000 | |
| | CG | 1,52 | 1,671 | 1,31 | 1,593 | -0,932* | 0,003 | |

\* Based on negative rankings.
\*\* Based on positive rankings.

However, the experimental group showed statistically significant improvement (see Table 8) compared with the control group ($z = -2,229$, $p = 0,026$), with respect to the number of words used in the text generated in the post-test (mean = 137, 45 ± 50,580). No differences are detected between the experimental and the control group in relation to the number of sentences in the text in the post-test ($z = -2,229$, $p = 0,026$).

Table 8: Comparison of the two groups regarding the assessment of the characteristics of the generated texts.

| Assessment of the characteristics of the generated text | Group | M.S. | S.D. | Z | P |
|---|---|---|---|---|---|
| Number of words | Experimental | 137,45 | 50,580 | -2,229 | 0,026 |
| | Control | 126,13 | 40,976 | | |
| Number of sentences | Experimental | 10,42 | 4,318 | 0,108 | 0,914 |
| | Control | 10,55 | 4,902 | | |
| Number of spelling mistakes | Experimental | 1,03 | 1,234 | -7,881 | 0,000 |
| | Control | 1,31 | 1,593 | | |
| Number of syntax mistakes | Experimental | 0,74 | 1,115 | -5,162 | 0,000 |
| | Control | 1,29 | 1,321 | | |
| Number of vocabulary mistakes | Experimental | 0,90 | 1,304 | -2,871 | 0,004 |
| | Control | 1,31 | 1,593 | | |

Comparing the generated texts in the pre-test and the post-test for both groups, In relation to the number of punctuation mistakes, number of syntax mistakes and the number of wrong vocabulary use, mistakes appear reduced for both groups, with a statistically significant difference (see Table 7). Moreover, this reduction is greater in the experimental group than in the control group and is statistically significant (see: Table 8). In particular, the participants in the experimental group made fewer punctuation mistakes (z = -7,881, p = 0,000), syntax (z = -5,162, p = 0,000) and vocabulary mistakes (z = -2,871, p = 0,004) compared to the control group at the end of the intervention.

Regarding the assessment indices of writing production, both the control group and the experimental group showed statistically significant improvements regarding the spelling accuracy index, consistency, coherence and textual organization indices at a significance level of 5% (see Table 9).

Table 9: Two groups' mean scores differences in the assessment of writing.

| Assessment of writing | Group | Pre-test | | Post-test | | Z | P |
|---|---|---|---|---|---|---|---|
| | | M.S. | S.D. | M.S. | S.D. | | |
| Spelling accuracy index | EG | 91,16 | 10,856 | 92,65 | 9,713 | -4,323* | 0,000 |
| | CG | 92,67 | 8,713 | 92,88 | 8,504 | -2,017* | 0,044 |
| Text cohesion index | EG | 14,42 | 4,465 | 16,05 | 3,756 | -6,421* | 0,000 |
| | CG | 15,21 | 4,072 | 15,46 | 3,926 | -3,157* | 0,002 |
| Text consistency index | EG | 21,75 | 4,354 | 23,46 | 3,542 | -6,706* | 0,000 |
| | CG | 21,85 | 4,074 | 22,52 | 4,225 | -6,422* | 0,000 |
| Textual organization index | EG | 36,17 | 8,025 | 39,51 | 6,660 | -7,624* | 0,000 |
| | CG | 37,06 | 7,418 | 37,98 | 7,480 | -5,124* | 0,000 |

* Based on negative rankings.

The data collected by the post-test essay were analyzed under the statistical criterion of Mann-Whitney. As seen on Table 10, the experimental and control group do not differ concerning the indices of spelling accuracy (z = -0,506, p = 0,613) and cohesion of the text (z = -1,623, p = 0,104). However, a statistically significant difference is observed regarding the index of consistency of the text (z = -2,397, p = 0,017). Moreover, findings indicate that the score on this index was higher in the experimental group (mean = 23,46 ± 3,542) compared to the control group (mean = 22,52 ± 4,225).

Table 10: Comparison of EG and CG on post-test's assessment of writing characteristics.

| Assessment of writing | Group | M.S. | S.D. | Z | P |
|---|---|---|---|---|---|
| Spelling accuracy index | Experimental | 92,65 | 9,713 | -0,506 | 0,613 |
| | Control | 92,88 | 8,504 | | |
| Text cohesion index | Experimental | 16,05 | 3,756 | -1,623 | 0,104 |
| | Control | 15,46 | 3,926 | | |
| Text consistency index | Experimental | 23,46 | 3,542 | -2,397 | 0,017 |
| | Control | 22,52 | 4,225 | | |
| Textual organization index | Experimental | 39,51 | 6,660 | -2,051 | 0,040 |
| | Control | 37,98 | 7,480 | | |

A statistically significant difference was also observed in the index of textual organization (z = -2,051, p = 0,040) in the post-test. The score on this index was higher in the experimental group (mean = 39,51 ± 6,660) in comparison to the control group (mean = 37,98 ± 7,480).

In relation to the writing process indices, both groups showed statistically significant improvement in the restoration of sentences index, while no differences were observed in the index of restoration of a destructurised text at a statistical significance of 5% (see Table 11).

Table 11: Comparison of the mean scores of the pre-test and the post-test of experimental and control group.

| Indices of processing writing | Group | Pre-test | | Post-test | | Z | P |
| | | M.S. | S.D. | M.D. | S.D. | | |
|---|---|---|---|---|---|---|---|
| Restoring deconstructed sentence index | EG | 8,38 | 3,106 | 9,14 | 2,776 | -4,399* | 0,000 |
| | CG | 8,92 | 2,710 | 9,33 | 2,462 | -3,968* | 0,000 |
| Restoring deconstructed text index | EG | 24,86 | 10,310 | 24,95 | 9,907 | -0,511* | -,609 |
| | CG | 25,83 | 8,198 | 26,11 | 8,028 | -0,673* | 0,501 |

* Based on negative rankings.

No statistically significant differences were observed in the restoration of deconstructed sentences (z = -0,310, p = 0,756) as part of the post-test between the experimental group and the control group (see Table 12).

Table 12: Comparison of the mean scores of the EG and the CG in the indices of processing writing.

| Indices of processing writing | Group | M.S. | S.D. | Z | P |
|---|---|---|---|---|---|
| Restoring deconstructed sentence index | Experimental | 9,14 | 2,776 | -0,310 | 0,756 |
| | Control | 9,33 | 2,462 | | |
| Restoring deconstructed text index | Experimental | 24,95 | 9,907 | -0,679 | 0,497 |
| | Control | 26,11 | 8,028 | | |

Furthermore, there was no statistically significant difference in marker recovery destructurised text (z = -0,679, p = 0,497) between the two groups in the post-test.

## CONCLUSIONS

Through this research we made an attempt both to detect the effect of teaching metacognitive strategies in writing class and to investigate its impact to the characteristics of the produced texts and student performance in the production of the writing.

According to our findings, the systematic teaching, exposure and employment of metacognitive strategies on behalf of the students, result to the production of more accurate writings. More specifically, direct teaching of metacognitive strategies contributes towards the reduction of errors in punctuation and syntax, while assisting the employment of appropriate vocabulary. Likewise, students increased the number of words in their post writing, making their essays more expressive and vivid. At the same time, the textual organization and coherence of the text indices were affected positively, engaging students in the adaption of pre-writing processes, and therefore, more coherent content.

The results reinforce previous studies proving that the adoption and practice in metacognitive strategies contribute to enhanced performance in writing (Rose & Kasper, 2001; Kasper, 1997), and improvement in the content, textual organization, coherence and reduced errors (Lu, 2006; Xu & Tang, 2005; Biedenbach, 2004; De La Daz & Graham, 2002; Yarrow & Topping, 2001; Wilkinsin, 1992).

## RECOMMENDATIONS

The results of the study indicate some directions to the teachers who are willing to integrate the metacognitive strategies in their teaching routine and provide their students the benefits of planning, monitoring, self-regulation and self-assessment. The employment of metacognitive strategies in writing may increase students' awareness about the process of writing, leading to better performance. By offering students the opportunities to practice on metacognitive strategies, they are gradually led towards autonomy and enabled to accomplish various activities, of diverse levels of difficulty without guidance.

Considering the above, we suggest that teaching is focused on exploring and recording procedures and strategies that students use while writing a text, as well as adopting teaching techniques for empowering writing strategies and sub-skills. Generally, when teaching, it is useful to take into consideration some factors that aid the development of strategies and the skill of writing, such as reading awareness, support, training and feedback. With respect to the development of cognitive awareness, which is necessary to the progress of reading, the students are oriented to discover the specific characteristics of different text genres, spot elements of proper written language and oral expression in diverse communicative situations. As far as teachers are concerned, they should support their students in terms of providing them with information, examples and instructions about the organization and the specific characteristics of each genre, while trying to activate their critical thinking.

On the following stage, while students practice on strategies, teachers offer to the development of the writing skill. This technique can be divided into two levels: those of focused and total practice. During the processes of focused practice attention is centered on the micro-processing activities of the writing, for example activities of restoration of deconstructed sentences and paragraphs, synthesis of complex sentences etc. On the other hand, the processes of total exercise activities focus on the macro processing of writing. It is necessary that the teaching and practice provide opportunities for students to interact with their text and their peers' texts, to set goals and strive to achieve them through the composition of a specific text genre.

Finally, it is essential to provide feedback throughout the activities. The concept of feedback is not only related to the correction process but relies on identifying the weaknesses of a student in writing and the effort of the student to overcome difficulties and to discuss possible ways of improvement. In such an educational context, students are inspired and internally motivated to practice their synthesis sub-skills, restoration, correction, and production skills as well as the review and evaluation of their writings, thus constructing their metacognitive awareness.

## REFERENCES

Anderson, J. (1983). *The Architecture of Cognition*. Cambridge: Harvard University Press.

Argyle, A. (1996). The experimental study of relationships. In D. Miell & R. Dallos (Eds.), *Social Interaction and Personal Relationships* (pp. 343-355). Milton Keynes: Open University Press.

Baroudy, I. (2008). Process writing: successful and unsuccessful writers. *International Journal of English Studies*, 8(2), 43-63.

Chamot, A. U. (2005). Language Learning Strategy Instruction: Current Issues and Research. *Annual Review of Applied Linguistics*, 25, 112-130.

Clark, R. & Ivanic, R. (2013). *The politics of writing*. New York: Routledge.

Cohen, A. D. (1990). *Language learning: insights for learners, teachers and researchers*. USA: Newburry House Publishers.

De La Paz, S. & Graham, S. (2002). Explicitly teaching strategies, skills, and knowledge: Writing instruction in middle school classrooms. *Journal of Educational Psychology*, 94, 291–304.

Ferrari, M., Bouffard, T. & Rainville, L. (1998). What makes a good writer? Differences in good and poor writers' self-regulation of writing. *Instructional Science*. 26 (6), 473-488.

Gavriilidou, Z. & Psaltou Joycey, A. (2010). Language learning strategies: an overview. *Journal of Applied Linguistics*, 25, 11-25.

Geladari, A. & Mastrothanasis, K. (2014). The employment of cognitive and metacognitive strategies in bilingual pupils' creative writing. In N. Lavidas, Th. Alexiou & A. M. Sougari (Eds.), *Selected Papers from the 20th International Symposium on Theoretical and Applied Linguistics (ISTAL 20)*, Vol.3, (pp.97-113), Poland: Versita.

Goddard, Y. L. & Sendi, C. (2008). Effects of self-monitoring on the narrative and expository writing of four Fourth-Grade Students with Learning Disabilities. *Reading & Writing Quarterly*, 24(4), 408-433.

Grabe, W. & Kaplan, R. B. (1996). *Theory and practice of writing: An applied linguistic perspective*. New York: Longman.

Graham, S. & Harris, K. & Reid, R. (1992). Developing self-regulated learners. *Focus on Exceptional Children*, 24, 1-16.

Graham, S. & Harris, K. (1993). Self-regulated strategy development: Helping students with learning problems develop as writers. *The Elementary School Journal,* 94 (2), 169-181.

Graham, S. & Harris, K. (1994). The role and development of self-regulation in the writing process. In D. Schunk & B. Zimmerman (Eds.), *Self-regulation of learning and performance: Issues and educational applications* (p.p. 203-228). New York: Lawrence Erlbaum.

Graham, S. & Perin, D. (2007). *Writing next: Effictive strategies to improve writing of adolescent middle and high school*. Washington, DC: Alliance for Excellence in Education.

Graham, S. (2006a). Writing. In P. Alexander & P. Winne (Eds.), *Handbook of educational psychology* (pp. 457-478). Manhawah, New York: Erbaum.

Graham, S. (2006b). Strategy instruction and the teaching of writing: A meta-analysis. In Ch. MacArthur, S. Graham & J. Fitzgerald (Eds.), *Handbook of writing research* (pp. 187-207). New York: Guiford press.

Graham, S., Harris, K. & Mason, L. (2005). Improving the writing performance, knowledge and self-efficacy of struggling young writers: The effects of self-regulated strategy development. *Contemporary Educational Psychology,* 30, 207-241.

Graham, S., Harris, K. & Olinghouse, N. (2007). Addressing executive function difficulties in writing: An example from the Self-Regulated Strategy Development model. In L. Meltzer (Ed.), *Executive functioning in education: from theory to practice* (pp. 216-236). New York: Guilford.

Graham, S. & Harris, K. (2000). The role of self-regulation and transcription skills in writing and writing development. *Educational Psychologist*, 35, 3–12.

Griva, E., Alevriadou,A. & Goudouras, N. (2011). Intervention program on direct and indirect language strategies to bilingual students with difficulties in writing: Targets and description. In G. Papadatos, A. S. Antoniou, A. Bastea & P. Trakadas (Eds.), *Proceedings of the 2nd National Conference in Education*, 27-30 May 2010, Vol. 2 (pp. 69-78). Athens: Kissos. In Greek.

Griva, E., Tsakiridou, E. & Nihoritou, I. (2009). Study of FL composing process and writing strategies employed by young learners. In M. Nikolov (Ed.),

*Early Learning of Modern Foreign Languages* (pp. 132-148). Bristol: Multilingual Matters.

Hacker, D., Keener, M. & Kircher, J. (2009). Writing is Applied Metacognition. In D. Hacker, J. Dunlosky & A. Graesser (Eds.), *Handbook of Metacognition in Education* (pp. 154-172). New York: Routledge.

Harris, K. & Pressley, M. (1991). The nature of cognitive strategy instruction: Interactive strategy construction. *Exceptional Children*, 57, 392-405.

Harris, K., Graham, S., Brindle, M. & Sandmel, K. (2009). Metacognition and children's writing. In D. Hacker, J. Dunlosky & A. Graesser (Eds.), *Handbook of Metacognition in Education* (pp. 131-153). New York: Routledge.

Harris, K., Graham, S., Mason, L. & Friedlander, B. (2008). *Powerful writing strategies for all students*. Baltimore: Brookes.

Hsiao, T. Y. & Oxford, R. L. (2002). Comparing theories of language learning strategies: A confirmatory factor analysis. *Modern Language Journal*, 86(3), 368-383.

Kasper, L. F. (1997). Assessing the metacognitive growth of ESL student writers. *TESL EJ*, 3(1), 1-20.

Keith, N. & Frese, M. (2005). Self-regulation in error management training: Emotion, control and metacognition as mediators of performance effects. *Journal of Applied Psychology*, 90, 677-691.

Kontos, S. & Keyes, L. (1999). An ecobehavioral analysis of early childhood classrooms. *Early Childhood Research Quarterly*, 14 (1), 35-50.

Kostaridou Eukleides, A. (2005). *Metacognitive processes and self-regulation*. Athens: Greek Letters. In Greek.

Kostouli, T. (2009). A sociocultural flamework: Writing as social practice. In R. Beard, D. Myhill, J. Riley & M. Nystrand (Eds.), *The sage handbook of writing development* (pp. 98-116). California: Sage publication Inc.

Lane, K. L., Harris, K. R., Graham, S., Weisenbach, J. L., Brindle, M. & Morphy, P. (2008). The effects of self-regulated strategy development on the writing performance of second-grade students with behavioral and writing difficulties. *Journal of Special Education*, 41 (4), 234-253.

Lu, W. J. (2006). Relationship between metacognitive strategies and English writing. *Foreign Languages and Their Teaching*, (9), 25-27.

Manchón, R. M., Roca de Larios, J. & Murphy, L. (2007). *A review of writing strategies: Focus on conceptualizations and impact of first language*.

(p.p. 229-250). In A. D. Cohen, E. Macaro (Eds.), *Language learner strategies*. Oxford: Oxford University Press.

McCutchen, D. (2006). Cognitive factors in the development of children's writing. In Ch. MacArthur, S. Graham & J. Fitzgerald (Eds.), *Handbook of writing research* (pp. 115-130). New York: Guiford press.

Mastrothanasis, K., Geladari, A. & Griva, E. (2010). Writing processes and strategies employed by elementary school students in first language (L1). *Scientific Yearbook of Primary Education of University of Ioannina*, 22, pp. 25-48. In Greek.

Matsagouras, I. (2009). Text-Centered approach of writing. Athens: Grigoris. In Greek.

Mousiou-Mylona, Ol. (2004). *Linguistics education and teaching of first reading and writing*. Thessaloniki: A. Stamoulis. In Greek.

Oxford, R. L. (2001). Language learning strategies. In R. Carter, D. Nunan (eds.), *The Cambridge guide to speakers of other languages* (pp. 166.-172). Cambridge: Cambridge University Press.

Petric, B. & Czarl, B. (2003). Validating a Writing. Strategy Questionnaire. *System*, 31(2), 187-215.

Pintrich, P. R. (1999). The role of motivation in promoting and sustaining self-regulated learning, *International. Journal of Educational Research*, 31, 459-470.

Porpodas, K., Diakogiorgis, Cl, Dimakou, I. & Karantzi, I. (2007). *Diagnostic tool for the investigation of difficulties students' writing of $3^{rd}$- $6^{th}$ grade*. Ministry of Education-EPEAEK. In Greek.

Prior, P. (2008). A sociocultural theory of writing. In Ch. MacArthur, S. Graham & J. Fitzgerald (Eds.), *Handbook of writing research* (pp. 54-66). New York: Guiford press.

Psaltou Joycey, A. (2010). *Language learning strategies in the foreign language classroom*. Thessaloniki: Studio University Press.

Reshadi, E. & Aidinlou, N. A. (2012). Investigating the relationship between writing metacognitive awareness and use of cohesiveties in Iranian EFL context. *Journal of Basic and Applied Scientific Research*, 2 (5), 4699-4705.

Rose, K. & Kasper, G. (2001). *Pragmatics in language teaching*. Cambridge: Cambridge University Press.

Sitko, B. M. (1998). Knowing how to write: Metacognition in writing instruction. In D. J. Hacker, J. Dunlosky & C. Graesser (Eds.), *Metacognition in educational theory and practice* (pp. 93-116). Hillsdale, New York: Erlbaum.

Stern, H. H. (1992). *Issues and options in language teaching.* Oxford: Oxford University Press.

Tribble, Ch. (1997). *Writing.* Oxford: Oxford University Press.

Welch, M. (1992). The PLEASE strategy: A metacognitive learning strategy for improving the paragraph writing of students with mild disabilities. *Learning Disability Quarterly*, 15, 119–128.

Wenden, A. (1986). Helping language learners think about learning. *English Language Teaching Journal*, 40(1), 3-9.

Wenden, A. (1998). Metacognitive knowledge and language learning. *Applied Linguistics*, 19, 515-537.

Wenden, A. (1999). An introduction to metacognitive knowledge and beliefs in language learning beyond the basics. *System*, 27 (4), 435-441.

White, R. & Arndt, V. (1991). *Process writing.* Harlow, Essex: Longman.

Xu, J. F. & Tang F. (2005). Review of previous research on English writing metacognition in China and abroad. *Foreign Language World*, (5), 17-23.

Yanyan, Z. (2010). Investigating the role of metacognitive knowledge in english writing. *HKBU Papers in Applied Language Studies*, 14, 25-46.

Yarrow, F. & Topping, K. J. (2001). Collaborative writing: The effects of metacognitive prompting and structured peer interaction. *British Journal of Educational Psychology*, 71, 261–282.

Zaga, E. (2005). Learning and teaching of a second language: From "content-based" teaching models to "focus on content" approaches with the use of strategies. *Science Education*, 3, 70-77. In Greek.

CHAPTER 15

# Facilitating Collaborative Reflection: Researching with College Students with Intellectual Disabilities

*John Kubiak*

This chapter reports on the findings of a research project - conducted in one higher education institution in Ireland - which provides a Post-Secondary Education (PSE) programme for people with intellectual disabilities (ID). This study was undertaken by this author with six co-researchers with ID and outlines how reflective practice was used to navigate the journey from initially learning about research, through to collecting and analyzing data. The chapter is presented in three main parts: (1) 'Before research' (Exploring co-researchers' pre-understandings of research and researchers), (2) 'During research' (Engaging with the reflective learning cycle; data collection and analysis), and (3) 'After research' (A model of learning). All of these three stages of the research aim to capture the scope, depth, richness and flexibility that reflective analysis offered to this author, the individual co-researcher and the collective research group. Finally, some tentative findings are offered on reflection in research with people with ID. These are: (i) reflection is shared active learning; (ii) reflection involves awareness of an identity shift; (iii) reflection needs a skilled supporter, and (iv), reflection is emancipatory.

## INTRODUCTION

The activity of reflection is so familiar that, as teachers, students or researchers, we often use reflection without really defining how and why we are using it. Sometimes we make assumptions about the fact that reflection is occurring effectively, even though our definition of it can be somewhat nebulous and imprecise. However, as practitioners, if we can refine our awareness of what reflection involves, we may then be in a position to improve our own professional practice *with* the support of those who are learning with us. In this way, reflection progresses from being an individual undertaking to becoming a group activity, and if it is done well, it has the potential to teach and spur individuals towards a more radical consciousness. Reflection ultimately is a political act that should possess a structure which allows equal power relationships between group members (Grundy, 1982); such relationships not only promote meaningful learning, but can also be emancipatory (Kemmis, 1985). Eliciting 'voice' through reflective practice can enhance the understandings of both researcher and participant and has the potential to empower people who are normally researched *on*, for example, those with intellectual disabilities (ID), considered one of the most marginalized groups in society and in higher education (Newman, Wagner, Cameto & Knokey, 2009). Going some way to address this omission however, this chapter reports on the findings of a research project, conducted in one higher education institution in Ireland, which provides a Post-Secondary education (PSE) programme for people with ID. This study, undertaken by this current author with co-researchers with ID, outlines how reflective practice was used to navigate the journey from initially learning about research, through to collecting and analyzing data. The chapter is presented in three main parts: (1) 'Before research' (Exploring co-researchers' pre-understandings of research and researchers), (2)'During research' (The reflective learning cycle; Data collection; Data analysis), and (3) 'After research' (A model of learning). All of these three stages aim to capture the scope, depth, richness and flexibility that reflective analysis offered to this author, the individual co- researcher and the collective group. Finally, some tentative findings are offered on reflection in research with people with ID. These are: (i) reflection is shared active learning; (ii) reflection involves awareness of an identity shift; (iii) reflection needs a skilled supporter, and (iv) reflection is emancipatory.

## DEFINING REFLECTION IN RESEARCH

It has been argued by Pillow (2003) that most qualitative researchers use reflection and reflexivity without defining how they are using it, as if it is something "we all commonly understand and accept as standard methodological practice for critical qualitative research" (p. 176). In this chapter, for the purposes of clarification, a definition of the term 'reflection' is defined as an in-depth subjective activity that involves reliving and rendering. The reflector attempts to work out practical problems, such as: what happened, what I thought or felt about it, why, who was involved and when, what others might have experienced and thought and felt about it, and how can I do it better next time?

The work of Boud, Keogh and Walker (1985) emphasizes the attention to feelings and the role of emotions in reflection; for them reflection is an activity in which people "recapture their experience, think about it, mull over it and evaluate it" (p. 19). Schön (1987) added a further layer to our understandings of reflection by introducing the ideas of reflecting 'in' and 'on' action where "the practitioner allows himself to experience surprise, puzzlement, or confusion in a situation which he finds uncertain or unique (p. 69).

Reflection has also been described as more than an individual or solitary activity: it can also occur in group settings. For Thorpe & Barsky (2001), even the best self-reflective strategies are inadequate unless they translate into "presence with another" (p. 767). In her description of the nature of reflection Grundy (1982) emphasized the importance of a shared relationship, for example, the relationship between teacher and students and among students. Grundy argues that there must be a structure which allows equal power relationships between group members, if the freedom of choice is to be a valid one.

One possible structure - co-operative inquiry (Heron 1985) – aims to facilitate more equal power relationships between group members and is described as primarily a way of undertaking research *with* people rather than *on* people (Heron & Reason 2001). Heron (1985) states that co-operative inquiry is a way of breaking down the distinction between researcher and the subject: the researchers are also co-subjects and the subjects are also co- researchers; everyone involved moves between both roles. In this way, the subjects of research become co-researchers, and are empowered to participate in the thinking that "generates, manages and draws conclusions from the research" (p. 128).

Kemmis (1985) added a further level to our understandings of reflection by defining it as "action-oriented and historically embedded" (p. 140). He argues that because reflection is a political act, any research programme for the improvement of reflection, "must be conducted through self-reflection (and) it must engage specific individuals and groups in ideology- critique and participatory, collaborative and emancipatory action research" (p. 152). This definition of reflection by Kemmis foregrounds the importance of the emancipatory element of reflection and the role participants can play in their own critical self-reflection; insights resulting from these practices can potentially lead to the expansion of people's understandings and the development of a course of practical action.

## RESEARCHING WITH PEOPLE WITH DISABILITIES

Over the last decade disabled people have increasingly become involved in research projects with an aim to create a more balanced partnership between non-disabled researchers and research participants with disabilities (Traustadóttir, 2006). Because of the influence of the Disability Studies movement, new approaches to research have begun to appear under the rubric of inclusive research (Walmsley & Johnson, 2003), which is closely related to participatory and emancipatory influences (Barnes, 2004; Chappell, 2000; Reason & Bradbury, 2001). These approaches denote research in which people with disabilities are active shapers of the research rather than passive research subjects.

Disability Studies academics have criticized the myth of objectivity that has characterized a lot of traditional disability research and have proposed an emancipatory paradigm for its development (Priestly, 1997). One (of six) of the core principle of emancipatory disability research is "the devolution of control over research production to ensure full accountability to disabled people" (p. 91). Traditional research has involved unequal power relationships with 'expert' researchers viewing people with disabilities as the subjects of research. For Cameron (2014) however, there is a need for researchers to put their experience and skills in the hands of people with disabilities, "identifying them as participants and collaborators, actively involved in determining the aims, methods and uses of research" (p. 35).

Consequently, the 'voices' of people with disabilities are fundamental to understanding how disabling barriers are experienced both personally and collectively. Furthermore, the methods used for data collection in response to the changing needs of people with disabilities need much consideration; for example, the importance of accessibility replaces a responsibility on the researcher to be creative and inventive in research design (Mercer, 2002).

## BACKGROUND—HIGHER EDUCATION AND PEOPLE WITH INTELLECTUAL DISABILITIES

Inclusive research projects are an unusual occurrence within the context of higher education. Indeed, it has even been argued that the active engagement of *any* student in research collaborations in higher education remain "under-theorized and under-utilized" (Kirshner & O'Donoghue, 2001, p.4). Although higher education is frequently seen as a pathway towards better employment outcomes and better life outcomes, students with ID have the least inclusive educational experiences, the lowest level of academic achievement, and the fewest postsecondary educational goals reflected on their transition plans (Grigal, Hart &Migliore, 2011). Consequently, people with ID have the poorest college access and employment outcomes of all disability groups (Newman, Wagner, Cameto & Knokey, 2009).

However, a number of countries have responded to this deplorable state of affairs (i.e. see University of Alberta 2006; Flinders University 2011;

Stefánsdóttir 2010). In the US, the Higher Education Act was reauthorized in 2008 as the Higher Education Opportunities Act (HEOA), and contained several new provisions aimed at increasing access to higher education for people with ID. At this time of writing there are 27 Transition and Postsecondary Programs for Students with Intellectual Disability (TPSID) being implemented on 50 colleges or university campuses in the US. The goal of these TPSID programs is to create and expand high-quality, inclusive higher education experiences to support positive outcomes for individuals with ID.

In Ireland, the location of this current study, efforts to provide access to a mainstream college education for individuals with ID has been the core mission of **The Trinity Centre for People with Intellectual Disabilities** (formally The National Institute for Intellectual Disability), Trinity College Dublin which has a prestigious and high-ranking reputation for academic excellence. Since the pilot of the two-year Post-Secondary Education program (PSE), entitled the Certificate in Contemporary Living (CCL) (see O'Keeffe, Iriarte-Garcia, Kubiak, O'Donoghue & Murphy, 2015) began in 2005, the course has provided and continues to provide a varied curriculum for people with ID. The CCL now contains 11 modules covering transferrable skills, the expressive arts, sports and recreation and the humanities, and aims to promote full citizenship for its students through the development of learning networks (Kubiak & Espiner, 2009; O'Connor, Kubiak, Espiner & O'Brien, 2012)) and career opportunities.

The ambition of providing access to a mainstream college education for individuals with ID is both ambitious and ground-breaking in terms of challenging models of learning and promoting the inclusion of individuals with ID. There is a real need therefore to advance our current understandings of how this group of individuals experience learning in PSE programs. European studies that have explored learning in higher education for mainstream students from a phenomenographic perspective (Marton, 1986; Marton & Booth, 1997) have produced descriptive conceptions of learning that initially seem universal and hierarchically organized (Boulton–Lewis 1994; Boulton-Lewis, Marton, Lewis, & Wilss, 2000). However, other phenomenographic studies undertaken outside Europe have found somewhat different results (see Watkins & Regmi, 1992; Marton, Dall'Alba &Tse, 1996). Consequently, there are clear messages that learning varies across different cultures and systems of higher education. It can be reasonably argued therefore, that professionals teaching people with ID in higher education do not possess adequate knowledge of how this group of adult learners experience learning. For this reason, the views students with ID in tertiary (post-secondary) education deserve to be closely examined and a fresh perspective sought on understanding the dynamics of their learning processes. A specific intention in this chapter is to outline the role of reflection from the perspective of six CCL students who trained as co-researchers, and to engage in an explicit, meta-analysis of the research process.

## THE STUDY

This chapter forms part of a larger phenomenographic study which described how college students with ID learn (see Kubiak, 2015a; Kubiak, 2015b). The purpose of this section is to describe how co-operative reflection was used as a methodological lens to enable students with ID to have some agency in the process of research. The research group consisted of six co-researchers, all of whom were undertaking the CCL program. Cognisant of Kemmis's (1985) definition of reflection as being action-oriented, a co-operative enquiry (Reason & Rowan, 1981a) was adopted where co-researchers systematically refined and modified an experiential learning cycle which subsequently informed how they collected qualitative data from eighteen of their peers. The reflective accounting presented in this chapter makes explicit how the current researcher and co-researchers collected and analyzed the research data, ultimately presenting a model of how people with ID learn.

The following section outlines the three main parts of the research (Figure 1):

1. Before research: Exploring co-researchers' pre-understandings of research and researchers
2. During research: the reflective learning cycle; data collection and analysis
3. After research: A model of learning

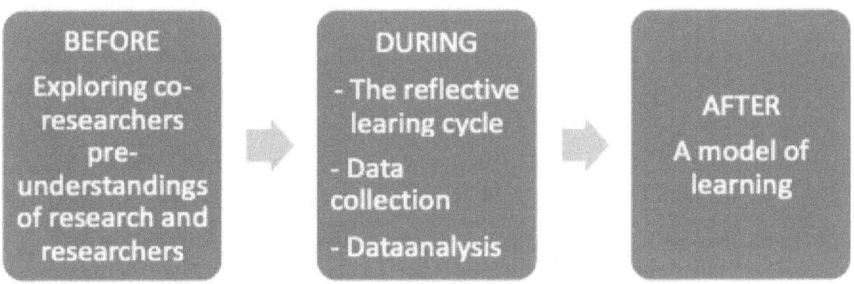

Figure 1: The three main stages of the research

## Before Research: Exploring Co-Researchers' Pre- Understandings of Research

Ideally, the process if reflection should start from the moment the research is conceived (Finlay, 2002). For van Manen (1990), our common-sense "pre- understandings, our suppositions, assumptions, and the existing bodies of scientific knowledge, predispose us to interpret the nature of the phenomenon before we have even come to grips with the significance of the... question" (p. 46).

In the context of this current research, one of my first objectives was to set out to understand how the individuals I was researching with understood the concept of research and the role of researchers. I needed to discover our shared understandings and how we diverged in our understandings of this topic. In this pre-research stage, I was careful to nurture a 'new' relationship between myself and the co-researchers: we were no longer teacher and student working in a familiar classroom environment. Instead, my role was that of a fellow (albeit lead) researcher and I was conscious of the need to enter carefully and sympathetically into the alternative and possibly rival perspectives of the co-researchers. Consequently, it was important for me to acknowledge my own values in relation to this research by recognizing that people with ID are experts by their experience regarding their knowledge and awareness of their impairment; consequently, they already possess a voice, but may not have had the opportunity to vocalize it more formally as part of a research project.

For this reason, I carried out an exercise so I could come to a better understanding of the pre-conceptions co-researchers had of the research community. Informed by Heron's (1985) concept of "Presentational Construing... (for example) making sense of experience in non- verbal ways, by drawing and graphics..." (p. 136), I was able to loosen up creative and divergent verbal thinking to good effect. I gave co-researchers a worksheet that posed the question using a visual prompt: "When you think of research and researchers, what do you see?" Using a blank page, co-researchers were then invited to draw an image of themselves as a researcher. The responses of co-researchers helped me understand how they understood the topic in question and also helped me clarify the impact of my own position and perspective in future discussions with them. Co-researchers are identified in the following section as CR1- CR6.

## Co-researchers Preconceptions of Researchers

In speaking about the role of researchers, CR1 outlined that they are informed individuals who also seek out information from printed sources as well as other people. She said: *Researchers use computers and look up books so that they can get students to talk out ideas...they take notes or use a (Dictaphone) to record what people are saying. They also give advice on research.* CR2 also saw the role of researcher as someone who *"looks up books"* to find out information. He also stated that researchers carry out interviews and can also work as a team. He said: *By working as a team you help each other out... then you type up the research on the computer and do a PowerPoint presentation... this can be written out and you need to add pictures because a picture tells a thousand words.* (CR2)

One of the key skills for a researcher to have, according to CR4, was the ability to listen. For him a researcher should possess good listening skills because *"you can retain what people say to you. (A researcher) should also be able to interact well with people"*. However, this co-researcher spoke about his memory of being researched *on* and the feeling of being uncomfortable when these researchers were observing him. For him, what was unusual about this research project as that it was done by students themselves and not by *"people in suits and coats"* (CR2). Another co-researcher agreed that she felt "O.K." about carrying out this research because *"it is very interesting that we are doing it. It makes us feel like teachers – nervous as well.* (CR5)

Table 1 presents co-researchers responses to the question: 'What is a researcher?'

| | |
|---|---|
| CR1 | *A researcher* - uses the internet and computer / types up research / has interview skills and presentation skills / uses brainstorming / does not ask personal questions. Research is done for coursework |
| CR2 | *A researcher* -uses a computer / looks up books in the library / works in groups / gives presentations / informs others and gets feedback / helps people / speaks up for people with disabilities |
| CR3 | *A researcher* - looks up information on the internet / works in groups / looks up books / gives PowerPoint presentations / Research is something done by lecturers to gather information |
| CR4 | *A researcher* – gives PowerPoint Presentation / takes notes / finds out information that's useful / listens and has good listening skills / interacts with people |

| CR5 | *A researcher* - Uses the internet/ Computer / asks questions / looks up books / works in teams / interviews people / finds out information / helps people |
|---|---|
| CR6 | *A researcher* - works in teams / takes notes / helps students / passes on information and helps learning |

**During Research: The Reflective Learning Cycle; Data Collection and Analysis**

In the above exercise co-researchers describe a number of components of research that include method (interviewing), purpose (asking questions / finding out information), dissemination (passing on information) and learning. Applying this information to my own understanding of this current qualitative study allowed me to appreciate the common understandings we shared of research, as well as the view that reflection is part of learning and is essential to decision making, particularly with regard to changing one's behavior.

According to Boud, Keogh and Walker (1985), one of the most important ways to enhance learning is to strengthen the link between the learning experience and the reflective activity that follows it. This link can be formed by incorporating a specific allocation of time that can be used for reflection into the learning activity. In the context of this current study, a specific period was set aside for: (1) co-researchers to individually keep a journal of events and (2), to collectively react to the experience. Starting from the position that is was useful for co- researchers to have a model of reflection which points to the importance of the stages in the reflective activity, we were informed by the experiential learning cycle made popular by Honey and Mumford, (2000) (Figure 2).

*Facilitating Collaborative Reflection* 279

Figure 2 Honey and Mumford's (2000) reflective learning cycle

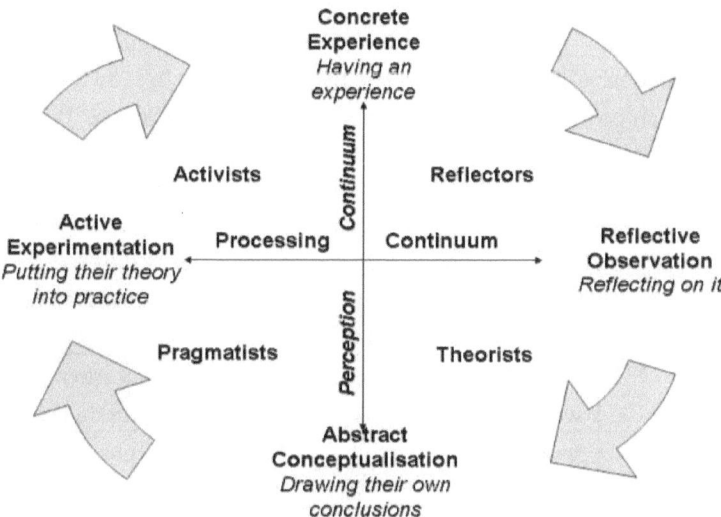

This model takes the cyclical form of:

1. Describing the experience
2. Reflecting on the experience
3. Abstract conceptualization (engaging with the theory presented), and
4. Actions to be taken to inform future learning – putting theory into practice.

The following sub-sections describe how Honey and Mumford's reflective learning cycle informed three stages of reflection; these are: (i) co-researchers' engagement with the reflective learning cycle, (ii) data collection and (iii) data analysis. These stages are now presented in turn.

### (i) Co-researchers' Engagement with the Reflective Learning Cycle

In this study, the research group (i.e. this current author and six co-researchers) started the co- operative inquiry process by collectively agreeing on an eleven-week plan that covered a total of nine stages of the project: (1) Exploring co-researchers' pre-understandings of research and researchers; (2) Stages of the research project; (3) Addressing the research question:

'What are we researching and why are we carrying out this research?'; (4) The theory and application of inclusive research; (5) Designing the consent form / exploring ways to share information of the project with the sample / gaining consent; (6) Interview techniques and exploring facilitation; (7) Role play: practicing interview skills; (8) Presenting the research project to the sample, and (9), Data collection (see Table 2).

Table 2 Timetable for co-researchers' training

| Week 1 | Establishing a baseline: Exploring co-researchers' understanding of research and the role of the researcher |
|---|---|
| Week 2 | Stages of the research: Introducing the stages involved in a research project and the meaning of keywords. |
| Week 3 | The research question: Addressing the question: 'What are we researching and why are we carrying out this research'? |
| Week 4 | Inclusive research: Understanding the theory and application of inclusive research. |
| Week 5 | Designing the consent form; exploring ways to share information of the project with CCL students; signing up; getting consent; ensuring that students know they are signing up for. |
| Week 6 | Interview techniques: Exploring facilitation; looking at ways of asking questions. |
| Week 7 | Role play: practicing interview skills. |
| Week 8 | Presentation: Presenting the research project to CCL students, gaining consent. |
| Weeks 9, 10 and 11 | Data collection: Interviewing the research sample. |

*Stage One of the Learning Cycle—Concrete Experience/Having the Experience*

Individual co-researcher's reflections of the training period were completed by each co- researcher after each of each training sessions and were informed by the Honey & Mumford reflective learning cycle. In the first stage–'Describing the experience' - co-researcher's made the following comments on: (1), group-work *"We talked about the research and howwe would work it all out together in a group"* (CR2); (2) informing the sample about the research: *"we spoke about "giving out the information", why are we carrying out this project... information on "inclusive research...and what questions we will ask the group"* (CR2); (3), active listening: *"We spoke about the different listening process in the session"* (CR2), and(4), ways of questioning: *"We talked about open and closed questions. How to start an interview by saying: How are you today?"* (CR6).

### Stage Two of the Learning Cycle—Reflective Observation / Reflecting on it

For stage 2 of the cycle – 'Reflective on the experience'- co-researchers wrote about their feelings regarding the acquisition of new knowledge: *"I feel very well. I'm learning new things about research... and I gave out good information in the session today"* (CR5), and *"I feel good because I learned a bit more about researching and what it means and I am looking forward to looking up stuff about it"* (CR1), while another co-researcher commented on the importance of sharing ideas with other co-researchers: "This session went very well...because it was very good to hear other people's ideas and ways of putting it together for the research" (CR1).

### Stage Three of the Learning Cycle—Abstract Conceptualization /Drawing Their Own Conclusions

The third stage of Honey and Mumford's cyclical model -'Abstract conceptualization' – looks at individual's experience in relation to the theory presented. As the main concepts in relation to this current research included 'inclusive research' and 'qualitative research methods', this author was aware of the potential difficulty for co-researchers to understand the more abstract elements of this material. In an effort to make the demands of this cycle more accessible, the term "Abstract conceptualization" was changed to the question: "What, in your opinion, were the main thoughts and ideas of this session?"

In responding to this request, CR2 understood that the main idea of stage three of the learning cycle was *"the different stages of the research and the questions we could to ask the students"*. CR1 responded by focusing on the methods used in qualitative research: *"we'll do a few interviews with each other... we'll ask open questions and closed questions too* (CR1). CR2 spoke about the topic of inclusive research and the need to explain this concept to the CCL students: *"We'll give out information on inclusive research... and making sure they understand what it is."*

However, follow up conversations and further reflections with co-researchers revealed that there was an element of confusion on their part in understanding the third stage of the reflective cycle. All co-researchers felt that it was tricky to distinguish between the first stage ("Having the experience") and the third stage; they considered it a complex task to include new ideas in stage three, and often found they were repeating themselves for the sake of completing the reflection exercise. In an effort to resolve this issue, co-researchers suggested a revised reflective cycle that consists of a more understandable word structure taking the following form (see Figure 1):

1. What was the class about?
2. Think about what was discussed in class. What are your feelings?
3. Can you describe / understand these ideas in a different way?
4. Next steps – how can we use these ideas?

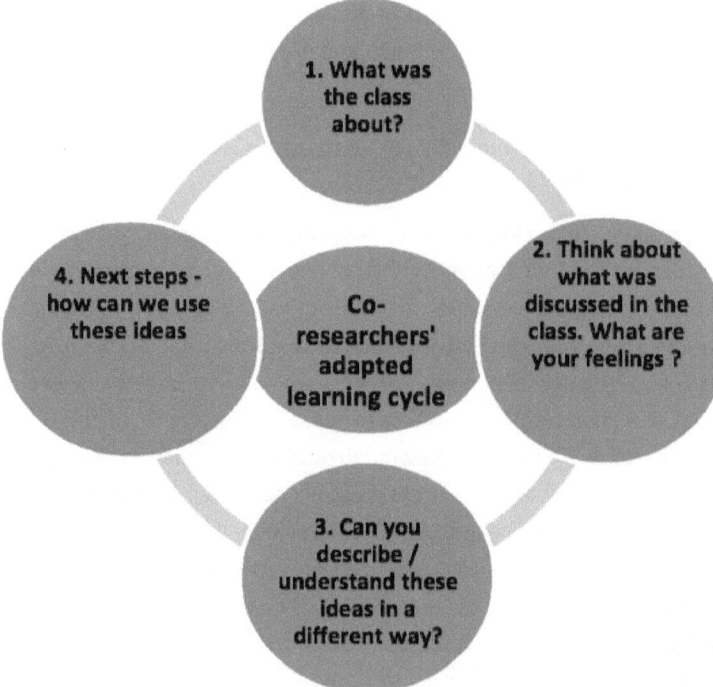

Figure 1 Adapted learning cycle – co-researchers' version

## Co-researchers' Variation of Kolb's Learning Cycle

The above reflection highlights the problems co-researchers had in engaging with stage 3 of the reflective learning cycle; however, it also highlights how the group resolved these difficulties by creating an alternative re-wording to the cycle. Making variations of Kolb's learning cycle is not unusual: indeed, Mackeracher (2004) describes how adaptations of Kolb learning cycle can be used to expand learning strategies and encompass more styles. For Brown (1987), such metacognitive processes improve achievement and can ultimately lead to an increased awareness of a person's knowledge of their own cognition, i.e. the ability to consciously reflect on one's cognitive abilities and activities. In the above passage, co- researchers demonstrated that they can step back and consider their own cognitive processes as objects of thought and reflection. As CR2 stated: *"I was writing the same things (in stage 3 of the reflection)... I found it hard to write new things down... we needed to make this easier for us... and we've made our brains more active and more knowledgeable".*

## Data Collection

While reflection itself is an experience, it is not an end in itself (More, 1974). The outcome of reflection makes us ready for new experiences which may be the resolution of a problem or the development of an original skill or perspective. These outcomes can be (1) cognitive in nature – in the case of this current study it may be an increased knowledge by co-researchers of the skills of interviewing and the process of questioning, or (2) affective – co-researchers may have changed their attitudes regarding researching and may now possess an enhanced sense of their personal capacity through having engaged in the process of interviewing and reflection.

Gaining confidence in the practice of interviewing is imperative for people with ID for two main reasons: among this group there is evidence that they have low levels of responsiveness during interviews which might vary as a consequence of the characteristics of the interviewer (e.g. Perry & Felce, 2002). However, it is also stated that conducting interviews is one aspect of the research process which is readily amenable to the active involvement of people with an ID, at least for those people with adequate cognitive and language ability (Perry & Felce 2004).

This current project aimed to minimize the possibility of achieving a low level of responsiveness from the study sample (i.e. eighteen CCL students) by actively involving their peers (i.e. six co-researchers) in the interview process. It is argued here that training co-researchers minimized the perceived imbalance in the status of the interviewer and the interviewee, and increased the level of responsiveness of the interviewees. Maintaining a positive attitude towards people with ID as researchers is a necessary prerequisite for us to overcome the problems that Perry and Felce have identified. CR2 encapsulated this by stating: *"I will use these ideas to find out how CCL students learn... talking to students and interviewing them... will help me learn how other CCL students learn."* This individual clearly saw his role as a researcher who could use his skills to find answers, build knowledge and inform others.

Some benefits of reflection may be lost if they are not linked to action (Boud, Keogh & Walker (1985). Action may precipitate a new phase of reflective activity; in this current study co-researchers put Stage 4 ('Next steps, how we can use these ideas') of the learning cycle into practice by initially using role-play – alternating between the role of interviewer and interviewee - and subsequently by undertaking one-to-one semi-structured interviews with their peers. Using this method, co-researchers practiced their facilitation and interviewing skills during weeks 7 and 8 of their training. Undertaking these sessions allowed them to learn in a safe environment where they could take risks and seek advice and guidance from each other and *"take everything at our own pace"* (CR6). For the interviewing procedure, co-researchers were informed by Bull (1996) who recommended a phased approach to interviewing people with ID; these were: 1) building rapport, 2) free narrative, 3) questioning, and 4) closure. During role-play however, this approach proved problematic for co-researchers who found it difficult to conform to the rigidity of the structure. In reflecting on how they could adapt Bull's version, the following solution was offered by co-researchers – a three-part adaption of Bull's version that addressed the following:

i. Building rapport
ii. Using a visual stimulus, and
iii. Questioning (introducing, follow-up and probing questions).

*Undertaking the Interviews*

Using this adapted method of interviewing, co-researchers undertook one-to-one interviews with eighteen of their peers during weeks 9, 10 and 11 of the training period. At the start of each interview, the group agreed that the interviewer would recapitulate the purpose of the research to each interviewee and explicate the objective and purpose of the interview. Before each interview ethical issues were discussed and each participant was assured of confidentiality. Each participant was also informed that the interview would be recorded and if needed that they could take a break or stop the recording anytime during the interview.

*Using a Visual Stimulus*

Co-researchers did not have any questions prepared beforehand; participants were asked instead to produce a drawing of "How I learn in college" and were informed that this would be the focus of the interview. Heron (1985) describes this technique as "Presentational Construing" (p. 136), a way of reflection that makes sense of past experiences in non-verbal ways; in the current study participant drawings served as a catalyst for co-researchers to elicit information on the research topic. This took the form of a semi-structured interview where no written notes were made by the interviewer during this process.

*Building Rapport and Questioning*

Before the conversation became centered onto the topic of learning, some dialogue was initiated between interviewer and interviewee in order to create a relaxed and calming atmosphere. Because of this, a more conversational style of interview was encouraged which stimulated participants to talk more freely about their experience of the research topic, i.e. how they learn in college. This strategy allowed all interviews to get off to a good start and gave the interviewee the choice of what area of the topic they were most comfortable to talk about. Follow-up questions were asked when it was thought necessary for the participant to reflect further on a topic or to ensure that the interviewees' expressions were properly understood. However, during these questions it was also necessary for the co-researchers to be aware that the responses of the interviewee were not been manipulated in any way by the interviewer placing words in the mouth of the participant (Francis, 1996). Consequently, leading questions were avoided and every effort was made to use terms that were uttered by the participants (D'Eath, 2005).

Occasionally however, for some co-researchers, the skill of following up on participants' utterances proved to be a difficult task. For all co-researchers asking the opening questions was straightforward and frequently this author prompted co-researchers to use follow-up questions. This sequence of co-researchers asking introductory open questions and getting support from this author when a topic needed to be elaborated or explored was repeated for all co-researchers throughout the initial interviews. Gradually however, after a number of efforts, co-researchers started to gain more confidence in asking follow-up questions using the words or expressions uttered by participants, thus requiring gradual less support from this author. If support was needed by the interviewer, it usually took the form of a non-verbal nod by this author to which the co-researcher quickly picked up on as an indication to continue probing the participant with more direct questions.

In summary, during this data collection phase, co-researchers used both individual and group reflective procedures to work out their own ways of engaging with the process of interviewing and questioning. By adapting recognized techniques of the qualitative interview (i.e. Kvale 1996) co-researchers demonstrated that there is no one right way to approach questioning in inclusive research. The message from this stage of the study is that through reflective processing, adjustments can be successfully made with regard to the research methods, and the skills and abilities of the co-researchers.

## Data Analysis

For this third section – the data analysis stage - both my own (and co-researchers') reflective accounting disclosed a degree of uncertainty and slight apprehension. In one way I felt swamped by the enormity of the task of analyzing the data collected, and whether I would be able to make sense of it at all; however, in another way, I was quietly confident that with the support of co-researchers we could make something emerge if we kept our reflective discussions open.

This process of dialogue was important for me to maintain: to fail at this would have compromised what I stood for as an inclusive researcher and educator. I was keen to make my role and co-researchers' roles transparent in order to avoid "using people with intellectual disabilities in tokenistic ways" (Williams 2011, p. 172). I also heeded the warnings of Walmsley (2004) who stated that the lessons from research practice suggest that people with ID should not be asked to carry out tasks relating to research for which that have no training or preparation.

In the context of this project, it was an unreasonable expectation within the limited time- frame I had, to expect co-researchers to carry out training in research, *and* gain an understanding of phenomenographic analysis and write up. For me, it made eminently good sense that these individuals could make a valuable contribution to this research, firstly, by reflecting on their role as co-researchers, and secondly as contributors to the analysis stage.

This need for co-operacy and discussion is in keeping with the recommendations of Bowden and Green (2005) who stated that phenomenographic analysis should be carried out as a team. This process, called 'interjudge reliability' (Marton, 1986) involves the formulation of 'categories of description' arising from transcripts of interviews, and for Marton (1986) it "must be possible to reach a high degree of intersubjective agreement concerning their presence or absence" (p. 35).

## A Model of Learning

Four categories of description that describe how CCL students experience learning in college were formed from the data, namely:

- The cognitive stages of learning
- Self-regulation of learning
- Learning as collective meaning making
- The supportive environment and learning.

I presented these categories in an accessible format to the co-researchers (Figure 4) going into considerable detail to describe each category by using supporting visual imagery. In undertaking this process I hoped that co-researchers would serve as 'devil's advocates' who would raise questions, provide critical insights, and possibly bring up different ways of seeing the data, bearing in mind that all data must be critically considered and debated (Green, 2005b).

In keeping with the techniques of phenomenographic analysis, I invited co-researchers to arrange the categories in order of a hierarchy - in other words, which categories did they think were the most important, the second most important, third most important and the least important. Upon completion of this exercise a group discussion followed in which individuals spoke about their choices - what they viewed as the simplest way of experiencing learning to what they viewed as the most sophisticated.

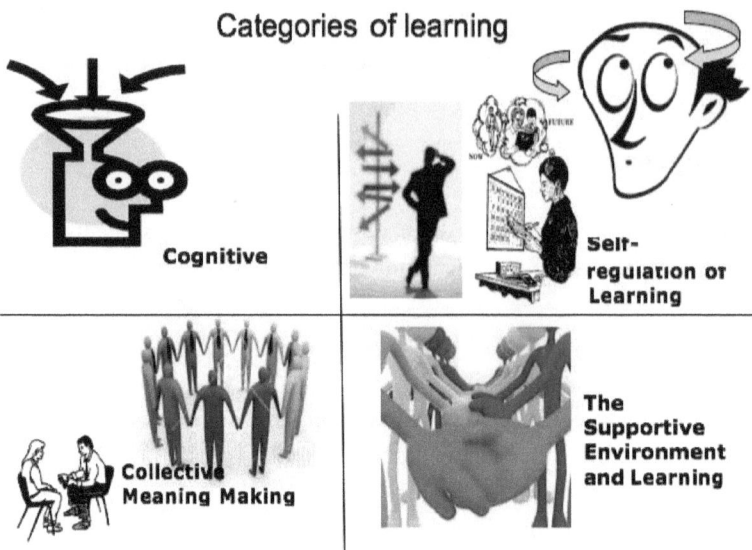

Figure 4: Categories of description for CCL students' experiences of learning – accessible version

*Hierarchy of Categories*

In the opinion of all co-researchers, the *most important* category was the category entitled "The Supportive Environment and Learning". For example, CR1 felt that *"feeling safe in the space you learn in is highly important"*. The second most important category (*very important*) was "Self-regulation of Learning", (i.e. planning, monitoring and reflecting on the work that you're undertaking); for CR2 this meant a gain in self-knowledge: *"it's good to plan... and it's o.k. if I want to work in silence"* (CR2).

The category that was considered as *important* by co-researchers was "Collective Meaning Making". For example, the process of learning collectively, either in groups or in pairs, was considered by CR3 to be *"good, as you can help others out... and be there for each other"*.

Finally, the category considered to be *least important* was the "Cognitive Stages of Learning". Although this category was seen by one co-researcher (CR6) as most important - *"you need to get stuff into the head... and use this information"*, the five other members of the group thought that taking in information was best placed at the bottom of the hierarchy; as CR4 said: "your head can get filled with too much information". Figure 5 offers a visual representation of a model of learning according to co-researchers.

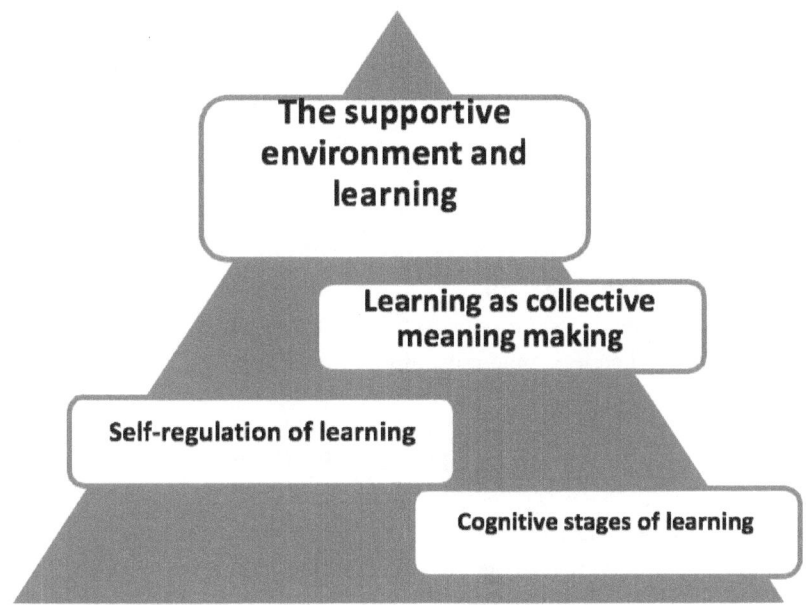

Figure 5: A model of learning

## Discussion

This chapter reports on a research project which was conducted by the current author with co- researchers with ID. The main purpose of the study was to explore how co-operative reflection could be used as a methodological lens to enable students with ID to have some agency in the process of research. Cognisant of the inherent limitation of this study's sample, some tentative findings on the use of reflective process for people with ID in research can be offered.

## Reflection is Shared Active Learning

"Reflecting on what you do in research is like learning in a different way ... I'm a person with a mild (intellectual) disability but at the end of the day I am the only one that can say what's inside my mind, and I can speak up for other people with disabilities... Everybody should be doing reflection... and people need to listen to what we say" (CR4)As a starting point, a number of important characteristics about reflection are present in the above co-researcher's comment: firstly, when pursued with intent, reflection is a way of learning; in this study it was learning about how to become a co-researcher. Secondly, reflection is both internal - something that goes on inside the head of the reflecting individual– *and* external, a shared relationship - in this instance, the relationship between teacher and students and among students. Thirdly, reflection also has an active element – it advances human thoughts into action. By looking inward at our thought processes, and outwards at the situation in which we find ourselves, our reflections consider this internal / external interaction through 'meta-thinking' and points us in the direction of further thought. The co- researcher quoted above, rethinking her identity and role, now considered herself an advocate who *"can speak up for other people with disabilities"*. Fourthly, the actions that result from these reflective thoughts have an end product – praxis, described by Kemmis (1985) as "informed, committed action... the most eloquent and socially significant form of human action" (p. 141).

## Reflection Involves Awareness of an Identity Shift

In this study, co-researchers had to negotiate the uncertain shift that came from being a student to becoming a researcher. As their teacher (and lead researcher), I was keen to redress the power imbalance between myself – the "active doer of research" and the "passive subjects of research" (Milne & Bull, 2001, p. 66), i.e. the people I was working with. My intention was to put my skills and experience at the disposal of students so that they might take their rightful place as co-researchers and through the process of co-reflection, have a meaningful, yet realistic role.

However, during the course of this research, I noted that inequalities were reflected and re-enacted mainly through my verbal interventions in the interview process between co- researchers and their peers. Consequently, it is vital to analyze how disempowerment occurred in the talk that unfolded in these interviews, so that it can be challenged and changed. However, in defense of this intervention, allowing co-researchers to speak with no, or minimum verbal intrusions may - or may not - have resulted in a more authentic set of findings. Williams (2011) notes that the right to speak is often weakened by the presence of others, and in particular by the presence of others who are familiar to people with ID. An analysis of the interviews shows how often I 'supported' co-researchers by prompts and verbal instructions; while the intentions were good, there is however a very narrow dividing line between providing support to the talk, and threatening to take it over. A key implication for further research practice in this area is to explore what can be gained by saying less and stepping back while supporting people with ID.

## Reflection Needs a Skilled Supporter

The role of those who assist the learner is to provide a context and a space for them to learn; in this way they may also give them support and encouragement and help clarify the learner's intentions and assist them in setting goals. Perhaps one of the most important roles, according to Boud, Keogh and Walker (1985), is to alert people to the nature of reflection in the learning process and provide ways whereby others can assist it at its various stages. Such support is essential as a skilled supporter is "as vital as a wheelchair is to a person who is unable to walk" (Walmsley, 2004, p. 68). Walmsley also argued for more transparency about the role of the non-disabled researcher in order to highlight the challenges of working inclusively on research projects. For the current researcher, it was vital to document how the reflective process worked in this inclusive research project, because without some honest reporting on exactly what roles people played, the inclusive research agenda could become trapped in a "cycle of sentimental biography or individual anecdotes" (p. 65).

## Reflection is Emancipatory

Doing the "self-advocacy talk" (Williams 2011, p. 141), i.e. *"speaking up for people with disabilities* (CR4), allowed these individuals to articulate their own concerns so they can begin to instigate change. Ultimately this type of informed reflection has the potential to challenge the dominant orders of discourse relating to people with ID and research. The collective power that people possess when they come together to express their own ideas has enormous potential to challenge the status quo (Beresford 2001) and ultimately change policy and practice. In the words of Kemmis (1985), reflection undertaken through emancipatory research has the potential to "assist in the transformation of this social world towards a world which is more rational, just, fulfilling and safe, not only for us but also for those who will inherit the history we are making today" (p. 162).

ACKNOWLEDGEMENT

The author wishes to acknowledge the eighteen students on the Certificate in Contemporary Living and the six co-researchers whose participation made this study possible.

REFERENCES

Barnes, C. (2004). Reflections on doing emancipatory disability research. In: J. Swain, S.

French, C. Barnes , & C. Thomas (Eds.), *Disabling barriers – enabling environments.* London: Sage Publications.

Bersford, P. (2001). Service users, social policy and the future of welfare. *Crtitial Social Policy, 21*(469), 494-512.

Boulton-Lewis, G. (1994). Tertiary Students' Knowledge of Their Own Learning and a SOLO Taxonomy. *Higher Education 28* (3), 387–402.

Boulton-Lewis, G., Marton, F,. Lewis, & Wilss, L. (2000). Learning in formal and informal contexts: Conceptions and strategies of Aboriginal and Torres Strait Islander university students. *Learning and Instruction, 10,* 393–414.

Boud, D., Keogh, R. & Walker, D. (1985). Promoting Rejection in Learning: a Model. In D.

Boud, R. Keogh, & D. Walker (Eds.), *Reflection: Turning Experience into Learning* (pp. 18-41) London: Kogan Page.

Bowden, J. & Green, P. (2005). *Doing Developmental Phenomenography.* Melbourne: RMIT University Press.

Brown, A. (1987). Metacognition, executive control, self-regulation, and other more mysterious mechanisms. In (Eds.) F.E. Weinert & R.H. Kluwe *Metacognition, motivation, and understanding* (pp. 65-116). Hillsdale, New Jersey: Lawrence Erlbaum Associates.

Bull, R. (1996). Good practice from video recorded interviews with child witnesses for use in criminal proceedings. In (Eds.) G. Davies, S. Lloyd-Bostock, M. McMurran, & C. Wilson (pp. 100–17).*Psychology, law and criminal justice*. Berlin, de Gruyter.

Chappell, A.L. (2000). The emergence of participatory methodology in learning disability research: Understanding the context. *British Journal of Learning Disabilities 28*(1): 38–43.

Chiseri-Strater, E. (1996). Turning in upon ourselves: Positionality, subjectivity, and reflexivity in case study and ethnographic research. In (Eds.) P. Mortensen &G.E. Kirsch, *Ethics and responsibility in qualitative studies of literacy* (pp. 115–133). Urbana, IL: NCTE.

D'Eath, M. (2005). *Guidelines for Researchers when Interviewing People with an Intellectual Disability.* Retrieved from: http://www.fedvol.ie/_fileupload/File/Interviewing%20Guidelines(1).pdf

Finlay, L. (2002). "Outing" the Researcher: The Provenance, Process, and Practice of Reflexivity, *Qualitative Health Research, 12*(4): 531-545.

Flinders University (2011) *'Up the hill project'*. Retrieved from: http://www.flinders.edu.au/sohs/sites/disability-studies/associated-programs/up- thehill-project---flinders -university.cfm (Retrieved 5 December 2015).

Francis, H. (1996). Advancing phenomenography: Questions of method. In (Eds.) G.

Dall'Alba & B. Hasselgren, Reflections on phenomenography: Toward a methodology? (pp. 35-47). Göteborg, Sweden: Acta Universitatis Gothoburgensis.

Green, P. (2005b). A rigorous journey into phenomenography: From naturalistic inquirer viewpoint. In (Eds.) J. A. Bowden & P. Green, *Doing developmental phenomenography* (pp. 32-46). Melbourne: RMIT University Press.

Grigal, M, Hart, D. & Migliore, A. (2011). Comparing the Transition Planning, Postsecondary Education, and Employment Outcomes of Students with Intellectual and Other Disabilities. *Career Development and Transition for Exceptional Individuals 34* (1): 4–17.

Grundy, S. (1982). Three modes of action research, *Curriculum Perspectives, 2* (3): 23-34. Habermas, J. (1974). *Knowledge and Human Interests.* London: Heinemann.

Heron, J. (1985). The Role of Reflection in a Co-operative Inquiry. In (Eds.) D. Boud, R.

Keogh, & D. Walker, *Reflection: Turning Experience into Learning* (pp. 128-138) London: Kogan Page.

Heron, J. & Reason, P. (2001). The practice of co-operative inquiry: Research with rather than on people. In (Eds.) P. Reason & H. Bradbury, *Handbook of Action Research: Participative Inquiry and Practice* (pp. 179–188) London: Sage, London.

Honey, P. & Mumford, A. (2000). *The learning styles helper's guide.* Maidenhead: Peter Honey Publications Ltd.

Kemmis, S. (1985). Action Research and the Politics of Reflection. In (Eds.) D. Boud, R. Keogh, & D. Walker, *Reflection: Turning Experience into Learning* (pp. 139-162) London: Kogan Page.

Kirshner, B & O'Donoghue, J. (2001). *Youth – Adult Research Collaborations: Bringing Youth Voice and Development to the Research Process*. Paper presented at the Annual Meeting of the American Educational Research Association, Seattle, WA, April 10–14.

Kubiak, J. & Espiner, D. (2009). Pushing the Boundaries of Inclusion Within Third Level Education. *The Frontline of Learning Disability 74*: 8–9.

Kubiak, J. (2015a). How students with intellectual disabilities experience learning in one Irish university.*Irish Educational Studies.* DOI: 10.1080/03323315.2015.1025532

Kubiak, J. (2015b). Using 'voice' to understand what college students with intellectual disabilities say about the teaching and learning process, *Journal of Research in Special Education Needs.* DOI: 10.1111/1471-3802.12098

Kvale, S. (1996). *Interviews: An Introduction to Qualitative Research Interviewing.* Thousand Oaks, CA: Sage.

Larkin, M, Watts, S. & Clifton, E. (2006). Giving voice and making sense in interpretative phenomenological analysis. *Qualitative Research in Psychology 3:* 102-120.

Milne, R. & Bull, R. (2001). Interviewing witnesses with learning disabilities for legal purposes. *British Journal of Learning Disabilities, 29:* 93-97.

Mackeracher, D. (2004). *Making Sense of Adult Learning.* Canada: University of Toronto Press.

Marton, F. (1986). Phenomenography – A Research Approach to Investigating Different Understandings of Reality. *Journal of Thought 21* (3): 28–49.

Marton, F. & Booth, S. 1997. *Learning and Awareness.* Mahwah, MJ: Lawrence Erlbaum.

Marton, F, Dall'Alba, G. & Tse, L. K. (1996). "Memorizing and Understanding: The Keys to the Paradox?" In *The Chinese Learner: Cultural, Psychological and Contextual Influences,* (Eds.) D.A. Watkins, & J.B. Biggs, (pp. 69–83). Hong Kong: University of Hong Kong, Comparative Education Research Centre.

Mercer, G. (2002). "Emancipatory Disability Research", in (Eds.) C. Barnes, M. Oliver & L. Barton, *Disability Studies Today.* Polity; London.

More, W.S. (1974). *Emotions and Adult Learning.* Farnborough: Saxon House. Newman, L. Wagner, M. Cameto, R. & Knokey, A. M. (2009). *The Post-High School Outcomes of Youth With Disabilities up to 4 Years After High School.* A Report From the National Longitudinal Transition Study-2 (NLTS2) (NCSER 2009-3017). Menlo Park, CA: SRI International.

O'Connor, B. Kubiak, J. Espiner, D. & O'Brien, P.( 2012). Lecturer Responses to the Inclusion of Students with Intellectually Disabilities Auditing Undergraduate Classes. *Journal of Policy and Practice in Intellectual Disability 9* (4): 247–256.

O'Keeffe, M. Iriarte Garcia, E. Kubiak, J. O'Doherty, S. Murphy, T & Lally, N. The impact and journey of the Certificate in Contemporary Living, a third level course for adults with intellectual disabilities at Trinity College, Dublin, Ireland. in (Eds.) T. Buchner, O. Koenig & S. Schuppener, *Inclusive Research*, Germany (in press).

Perry, J. & Felce, D. (2002). Subjective and objective quality of life assessment: Responsiveness, response bias and agreement between the responses of people being supported and those of staff responding on their behalf. *Mental Retardation, 40*(6): 445-456.

Perry, J. & Felce, D. (2004). Initial findings on the involvement of people with an intellectual disability in interviewing their peers about quality of life. *Journal of Intellectual and Developmental Disability, 29*(2):164-171.

Pillow, W. (2003). Confession, catharsis, or cure? Rethinking the uses of reflexivity as methodological power in qualitative research, *International Journal of Qualitative Studies in Education. 16*(2): 175-196.

Priestly, M. (1997). 'Whose research? A personal audit', in (Eds.) C. Barnes, C. & G. Mercer (Eds.), (pp. 88-107) *Doing Disability research.* Leeds: The Disability Press.

Reason, P. & Bradbury, H. (2001). *Handbook of Action Research: Participative Inquiry and Practice.* London: Sage Publications.

Reason, P. & Rowan, J. (1981a). *Human Inquiry: A Sourcebook of New Paradigm Research,* Chichester: Wiley.

Schön, D. (1987). *Educating the reflective practitioner.* San Francisco: Jossey-Bass. Sinason, V. (1992). *Mental Handicap and the Human Condition.* London: Free Association Books.

Stefánsdóttir, G. (2010). *University Program for People with Intellectual Disabilities at the University of Iceland.* Retrieved from: http://ec.europa.eu/education/grundtvig/doc/conf10/w7/empowerment.pdf

Thorpe, K. & Barsky, J. (2001). Healing through self-refection. *Journal of Advanced Nursing 35*(5): 760-768.

Traustadóttir, R. (2006). Fötlunarrannsóknir: Á herslur óg alitamal í rannsóknum með fötluðu fólki [Disability research: New emphasis and challenges in researching with disabled people], cited in K. Björnsdóttir & A.S. Svensdóttir (2008), Gambling for capital: learning disability, inclusive research and collaborative life histories. *British Journal of Learning Disabilities, 36:* 263–270. University of Alberta. 2006. *On Campus Program.* Retrieved from: http://www.uofaweb.ualberta.ca/oncampus/nav01.cfm?nav01=33356

van Manen, M. (1990). *Researching lived experience: Human science for an action sensitive pedagogy.* New York: State University of New York Press.

Walmsley, J. & Johnson, K. (2003). *Inclusive Research with People with Intellectual Disabilities: Past, Present and Futures.* London: Jessica Kingsley.

Walmsley, J. (2004). Involving users with learning difficulties in health improvement: lessons from inclusive learning disability research, *Nursing Inquiry, 11*(1): 54-64. Watkins, D. & Regmi, M. (1992). How Universal Are Student Conceptions of Learning? A Nepalese Investigation. *Psychologia 35:* 101–110.

Williams, V. (2011). *Disability and Discourse: Analysing Inclusive Conversation with People with Intellectual Disabilities.* Wiley-Blackwell: UK.

CHAPTER 16

# Students as Bricoleurs: Eliciting Creativity in a Cluttered World

*Gail Matthews-DeNatale and Amy Cozart-Lundin*

THE THEORETICAL BACKDROP

What is creativity and how is it related to learning? This question is central to educators who value creativity, because it helps us consider the pedagogical purpose of eliciting it in our students.

Claude Lévi-Strauss authored some of the earliest work on the relationship between creativity and culture. He discussed the difference that he perceived between enlightened and "primitive" thinking (1962). Within his schema, enlightened creativity is a scientific process that involves completely original work and abstract interpretation. In contrast, primitive creativity involves the development of new things out of found objects. The tinkerer, or bricoleur, improvises with the materials at hand and this concrete approach is inherently limited because it takes place within the confines of the pre-existing world.

Preferential treatment of "original" work is also embedded in the culture of higher education. For example, research-based publications carry more weight for tenure than reviews of the literature. Some professors decry the use of master syllabi and designated competencies, which they claim will limit creativity. Yet Brian Massumi admonishes us to not "think of the creativity of expression as if it brought something into being from nothing. There is no tabula rasa of expression. It always takes place in a cluttered world" (Massumi 2002, p.29, as quoted in Pigrum, 2009, p. 1).

In the landmark book *How People Learn*, the authors state:

> It is especially important to understand the kinds of learning experiences that lead to transfer, defined as the ability to extend what has been learned in one context to new contexts ... Educators hope that students will transfer learning from one problem to another within a course, from

one year in school to another, between school and home, and from school to workplace" (2000, p.51).

Recent research on the science of learning also identifies the activation of prior knowledge as central to the formation of new understanding (Ambrose et al, 2010, p. 10). Tapping into the interior "cluttered world" of prior knowledge is a precondition for learning because learners cannot leverage or question experiences that they haven't surfaced.

Learning how to access and make meaning of external clutter is also critical to learning. According to George Siemens

> Personal knowledge is comprised of a network, which feeds into organizations and institutions, which in turn feed back into the network, and then continue to provide learning to [the] individual. This cycle of knowledge development (personal to network to organization) allows learners to remain current in their field through the connections they have formed (2004).

The ability to "transfer," or make connections across domains, is an indicator that learning has taken place. Far transfer, the ability to draw upon a set of skills and concepts in a completely different context, is one of the characteristics of expertise (Bransford et al, 2000, p. 31).

With the exponential growth of web-based resources, Siemens proclaims Connectivism as a "Learning Theory for a Digital Age," yet the process he describes bears many similarities to the concept of bricolage that Lévi-Strauss articulated more than 50 years ago. Messy piles of material do not overwhelm bricoleurs because they can perceive opportunities in situations where others might only see broken or disparate parts. As opposed to "primitive," the capacity to tinker is a critical competency in the present-day digitally saturated and global landscape.

This case study presents the story of a course that embraces clutter, that helps students become bricoleurs who know how to search, evaluate, curate and stitch together learning experiences for themselves and for others. It positions the process of curation as creative and transformational bricolage.

This case study is also about the fluid relationship that develops between student and teachers when bricolage becomes the primary mode of learning. The first goal for the educator in this case was to help students learn skills and concepts that are central to successful tinkering. But all tinkerers need test subjects who are willing to try out their creations, and over time the educator became a pilot user of the resources created by her students. That portion of our story will be told through a dialogue between one of the students and her instructor.

NOTE: The authors have created a companion website for this case study that includes links to course materials and work samples. It is located at https://northeastern.digication.com/open_learning

## THE COURSE AND ITS CONTEXT

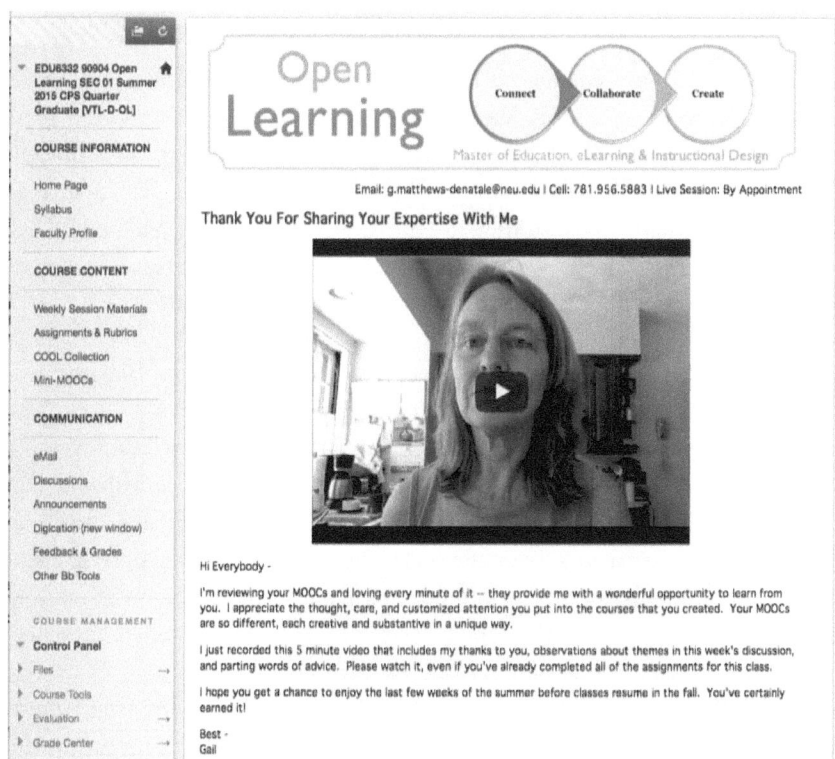

EDU 6332 Open Learning is an elective within the Master of Education in eLearning and Instructional Design program at Northeastern University. The program is fully online and aims to prepare its graduates to "shape the future of any learning-driven organization [and] respond innovatively to the opportunities and challenges that are revolutionizing all sectors of education."

The Masters curriculum was developed with a strong commitment to connected learning. Each course includes one or more "signature assignments"— authentic work that maps to program-level outcomes and competencies that faculty envision for their students. Students work within a personal ePortfolio throughout the program. They are expected to use their ePortfolios as a space to collect signature assignments, reflect upon their growth in relationship to competencies, and make connections across coursework. The ePortfolio reflection is a significant component of the final grade for each course (2013).

In the video "Success in a MOOC," Dave Cormier lists five steps to success: Orient, Declare, Network, Cluster, and Focus (2010). The modules in Open Learning were structured according to this sequence. In his essay on Open Pedagogy, David Wiley makes the distinction between disposable and renewable assignments, stating

> The defining characteristic of a disposable assignment is the tacit understanding that as soon as the faculty member returns the graded assignment to the student, the student will promptly throw it away ... The value that [renewable assignments] add to the world increases exponentially because they are all openly licensed. In addition to being viewed and used by countless people, they will also be extended, revised, and improved by future students and others (2015).

While it is ironic that the course takes place within the confines of Blackboard, all of the major assignments were designed to be open and renewable.

One of the challenges of connected learning is helping novices develop the ability to find and evaluate sources, to distinguish between wheat and chaff. According to Bansford et al, experts "experts notice features and meaningful patterns of information that are not noticed by novices" (2000, p. 31). Experts have developed an ability to spot the deep structure of a source, which makes it easier for them to determine if a substance is germane to their interests and needs, while novices tend to focus on surface elements. Novice learners can quickly become overwhelmed by the lack of explicit direction because the cognitive load is too great (Brennan, 2013; Mayer and Moreno, 2003). As beginners, they don't know how to begin because they haven't developed the requisite skills to make meaning of the clutter. But self-directed learning is central to the philosophy of connected pedagogy and so instructors who want to ground their courses in this approach need to also take on the responsibility for helping learners develop self-efficacy.

Bricoleurs have the ability to perceive opportunities for connecting seemingly disparate elements in new ways in order to solve problems. In other words, they need to learn how to tinker before they can be truly creative. They also need to identify a purpose or problem that they want to solve. The Open

Learning assignments were carefully sequenced with students' developmental needs in mind:

> **Phase 1.** A Multimodal Timeline assignment designed to equip students with the background knowledge and skills related to open learning. A COOL Collection assignment (Crowd-sourced Open Online Learning) in which students identified and evaluated open learning resources relevant to their interests.
>
> **Phase 2.** A Mini-MOOC assignment in which students developed a two-week online learning experience about one of their interests. The assignment guidelines mandated that the MOOC contain at least three high quality open online resources and at least two pieces of work authored by the student.
>
> **Phase 3.** A Mini-MOOC pilot in which they role played running their MOOC, with peers and the instructor serving as students, followed by a round of revision on the MOOC.

## THE MULTIMODAL TIMELINE

The goal of this assignment was to help students broaden their understanding of Open Learning as a concept and deepen their knowledge about the many ways that this idea has been enacted over time. Most people perceive open learning to be a new idea, limited to the xMOOCs developed by organizations such as EdX. A second, yet equally important goal was to help students consider the relevance and positionality of Internet sources related to the topic.

In the second week of the course students used David Wiley's excellent MOOC on Openness in Education as the reading (2013). They divided up into groups, and each group was expected to view one of Wiley's course modules and report on the big ideas in a threaded discussion.

Then they were given a list of search terms and asked to identify, log, and evaluate 18 online sources. In the book *Situated Learning: Legitimate Peripheral Participation*, Lave and Wenger describe an apprenticeship process in which beginners are given defined, simplified tasks so that they have an opportunity to contribute to the community even before they develop the capacity to work independently (1991). What are the opportunities for legitimate participation in a context in which almost all participants are novices, with the exception of the instructor? The pre-identified list of search terms helped bridge the gap between students' prior knowledge so that they could have a successful first experience in sifting through the clutter. It also helped establish the importance of keyword selection in search queries. The difference between the number of sources logged and the number of timeline nodes required them to weigh the relevance and quality of their resources.

In the third week they each created a multi-modal Open Learning timeline that included at least 15 nodes. Students created their timelines with the online tool Tiki-Toki. Tool features included the ability to create categories of nodes, embed images and video, and annotate entries. Martin and Schwartz have identified four cognitive mechanisms of creativity that are fostered in the process of authoring a visualization: reinterpretation (letting go of old assumptions), abstraction (the omission of details and, as a result, improve the odds of discovering higher-order relations), combination (combining previously uncombined mental representations), and borrowing (drawing on other forms of visual representation) (2014). While their work focuses on the creation of graphic visualizations, these four elements also present in the timeline assignment.

Live timeline at http://www.tiki-toki.com/timeline/entry/481948/Stefs-Open-Learning-Timeline

Each student's multi-modal timeline emphasized the aspect of Open Learning that was most relevant to that individual, which allowed them to connect the new subject matter with their prior knowledge and expand their thinking in the process. For example, one person with a background in early childhood education placed Montessori on her timeline, while another person with a technical background included Richard Stallman's GNU project and his founding of the Free Software Foundation. When they compared timelines, it helped them see the many tributaries of influence that converge in the Open Learning movement. Because the assignment took place in the earliest weeks of the course, the assignment also conveyed the value that the instructor placed on individuality and creativity, making thinking visible, and co-constructed understanding.

## THE COOL COLLECTION

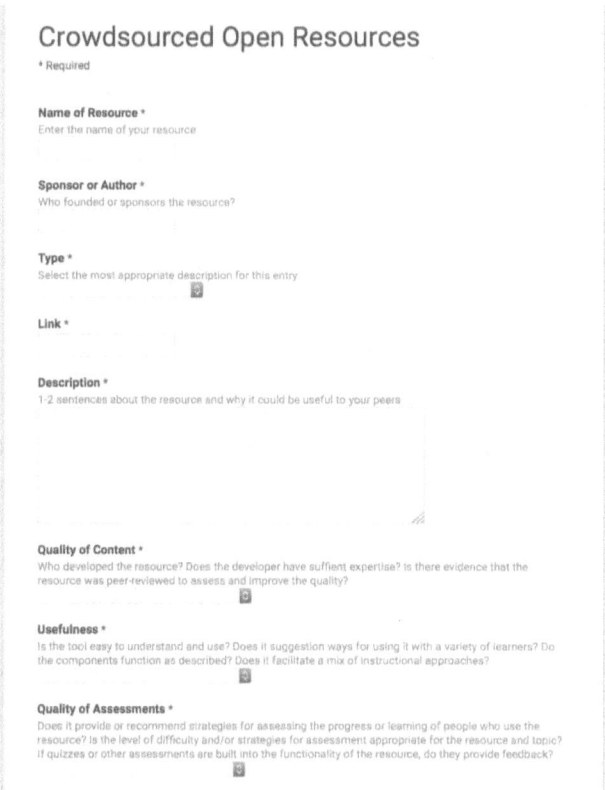

The goal of this assignment was to increase student proficiency with resource evaluation and curation. The first few weeks of the course were heavily scaffolded to support students in their development. In the COOL Collection assignment, the instructor began to fade those supports, transferring more responsibility to the learner.

The students were asked to identify a topic in which they would like to teach a course. They also had an opportunity to view courses created by previous students, which helped them see the rich diversity of topics (from dog training to financial aid advising) and reassure them that the assignment would be possible. They were then expected to identify at least five resources relevant to their topic and evaluate them using a Google doc form that was based on the TEMOA rubric for assessing the quality of Open Education Resources (2011). The class had access to the results spreadsheet so that they could discuss results and benefit from each other's work.

## Mini-MOOC

The goal of this assignment was to help students learn how to curate, combine, repurpose, and augment Open Education Resources to create something new, to become bricoleurs, and to complete the cycle of Open Learning by giving something back to the world. The culminating signature assignment for the Open Learning course was the development of a two-week Mini-MOOC on a topic of the student's choosing. They were required to make their MOOCs open and accessible to the general public, and to assign Creative Commons licensing to their work.

Creativity is a capability that needs to be cultivated, and each form of creativity involves fundamental skills and techniques. The painter learns how to mix color and the qualities of different paint media. The printer learns how to prepare a plate, use different tools to gouge out a pattern, and even prepare chemicals to etch the metal. The COOL Collection assignment was designed to equip students with essential resource identification and evaluation skills, and to help them begin to identify promising resources related to their interests. Wiggins and McTighe refer to this approach as "backward design," in which course authors first identify desired outcomes and then design the learning sequence to help students develop the competencies and knowledge they will need to attain those outcomes (2003).

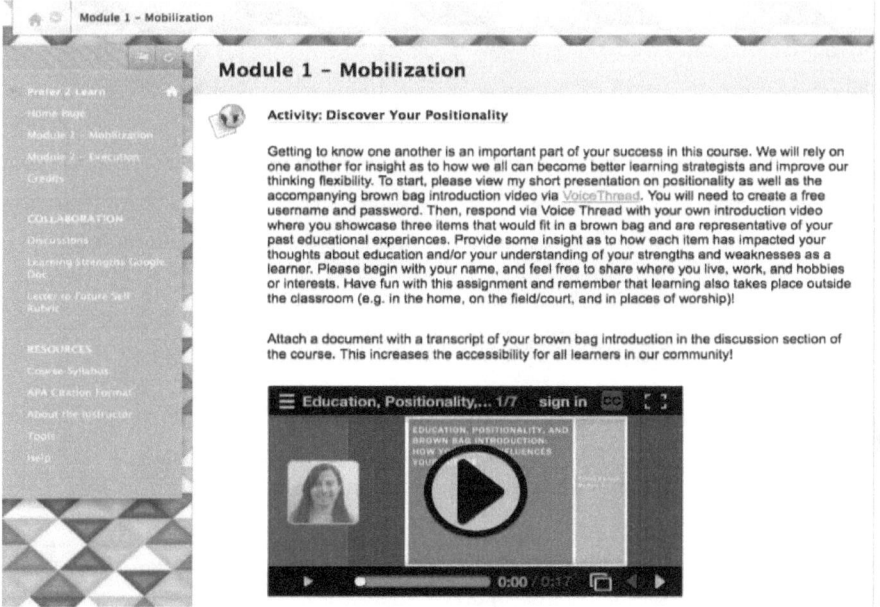

Open Education Resources are ingredients but they are not the same thing as a "course" that includes a vision for student learning, course narrative, and carefully designed sequence of experiences that foster a community of inquiry, engage learners in their development, and yield evidence of learning (COI, n.d.). The MOOC assignment also called upon students to imagine how their topic could be taught to a heterogeneous group of learners, and that thought exercise helped them grapple with challenges that are fundamental to education such as engagement and motivation.

The students used a MOOC planner to outline and receive feedback on their ideas. This helped guide their backward design process of identifying outcomes and designing a learning sequence that would help students develop the competencies to attain and demonstrate those outcomes. The planner also supported the content curation process, in which they finalized decisions about the open education resources that they would use and identified the original content that they would need to develop for their MOOC to be a success.

Students had the option of developing their MOOC in a Digication template (project portfolio), or to use a learning management system set to be publicly available. This created a pathway for both the people who wanted to experiment with technology and the less technically proficient or adventurous people who preferred to focus solely on course content.

In the last third of the course the tables were turned. Each student ran her or his MOOC, classmates each selected a MOOC to take, and the instructor role-played being a student in all of the courses. This made it possible for students to experience the role of online instructor, which included fielding questions for clarification, facilitating discussions, and seeing the work produced by those who took the course. They had one week to revise their MOOC before submitting the link for evaluation, and all made major improvements to the collateral materials, assignment directions, and user interface.

## REFLECTIONS AND STUDENT-INSTRUCTOR DIALOG

How did students and the instructor experience the Open Learning course? In this section we tackle that phenomenological question through a dialogue between one of the Open Learning students and her instructor.

Amy Cozart-Lundin was a student in Open Learning during the spring term of 2015. Gail Matthews-DeNatale, the professor who also designed the course, taught the Open Learning. Gail and Amy met online for an interview in August 2015. First Gail interviewed Amy, and then Amy interviewed Gail

The following quotes are taken from the interview verbatim transcripts. Unedited versions of the transcripts and interview questions are located in the companion website for this article. That site also includes a reflective journal entry written by Amy.

Amy's MOOC was on the topic of Visual Merchandizing. In an interview with Gail, Amy provided the following description of this work:

> Amy: I was a merchandiser for a long time. I chose that because I was well-versed in it. It's outside of academia, but it's something that applies to everywhere you go. In stores, you see those pretty displays. But how are they made? Why are they made that way? The title of it was *Visual Merchandising and the Psychology of Consumer Behavior*.
>
> The first week was more about the 'why' of the reasons for how to merchandise, how the brain looks at things, what elicits spending, what elicits impulse buying. There is a lot of psychology and reasoning behind why something looks the way it does. I had the students study eye patterns, how your eyes move onto a display and how color stories go together and how that can be important. With the use of props, are they overdone? Are they applicable, an enhancement to the display, instead of taking away from it and being too cluttered?

Then the second week was more about structure and the how-to. The signature assignment was for everybody to make their own displays. I did the same format kind of with our final assignment in Open Learning. I said, 'Make it your own.' I didn't give a lot of parameters. I think it was a little daunting to some people at first, because some of the feedback I got was, 'I didn't know exactly how to make it look or how to do it.' But then I said, 'It doesn't have to be a window at Bergdorf's. It just needs to be something that is eye-catching and important to you. Use your own creative license.' So the things that they came up with were awesome — really, really cool."

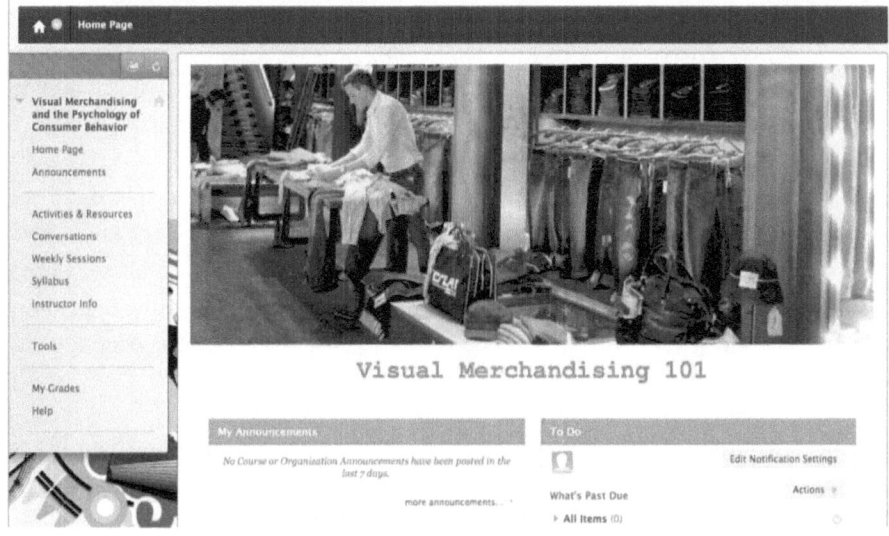

Amy was also enrolled in a course on social media during the spring term. The majority of the course was staged in Blackboard Coursesites, but she decided to draw upon what she was learning in the social media class to use Pinterest as a space for the sharing and discussion of student work.

In the first week students were asked to find pictures of store windows that they liked and that they thought demonstrated the cognitive concepts discussed in the week's readings. They pinned these images to a Pinterest board, along with an explanation, and then commented on each other's pins. In the second week each person was asked to create several configurations of a merchandise display with a set of found objects, take pictures of the displays, and pin them to the board with an explanation of the course principles that informed their design decisions. The students viewed the displays and again commented on each other's work.

Note that both of these assignments align with the bricolage approach to creativity, creating something new with the materials at hand, and Amy perceived her assignments to be in the "same format" of assignments in the Open Learning course. This indicates that the form of creativity that is modeled by the instructor influences the student's creative decision-making and pathway.

Amy was both thrilled and challenged by the experience of running her course. During the first week some of Amy's students, including the professor, had difficulty understanding the assignment directions. The way that the course was staged in Coursesites also made some of the materials difficult to find, and her students also recommended that she embed instead of link to outside media. However, Amy experienced these challenges as part of the creative process.

> Amy: There's a lot to it, I found out, because I had to be there to be responsive to discussions or posts and to be responsive to adding comments, giving clarification, grading, and things like that.
>
> But I loved it. I loved every minute of it. I think it was hard to do. Your job is still hard. I didn't find it overwhelming or, "Oh, I don't know how to do this. How do I give good feedback?" Because I've already been given good feedback by students and by instructors, to know that's how you do it. That's how you encourage. That's how you help people grow or learn better what you're trying to teach them.

The most exciting aspect of Amy's teaching experience was to discover the many different ways that her students responded to her creative assignments. The assignments were grounded in the course readings, but also open-ended enough to allow for different interpretations.

> Amy: The things that they came up with were awesome, really, really cool. My professor was my student as well, which was intimidating, to say the least, to teach my teacher. She came up with a graduation display because her daughter had just graduated. So that was something that was important to her, that she could put her personal touch on to it. She did a couple different structures of it to get opinions about it, and everybody shared their opinions like, "Oh, I like it in this. I like the little displays in this little grouping, as a circle, as opposed to scattered." Other people said, 'Well, I like the scattered look.' So everybody has their own opinion on how something can look. I liked that they each gave their input. Merchandising is such a subjective career.

The MOOC pilot phase of Open Learning required participants to play multiple roles. They were instructors for the MOOCs that they created, while simultaneously serving as students in their peer's courses, and also debriefing and providing peer feedback in their role as Open Learning students. The Open Learning instructor played two roles, as student and course instructor. During Gail's interview she observed

> Gail: I had also taken on this separate self, a second self. For the assignment to work, I needed to stay in character as a student and experience the vulnerability of being a student. So there is the vulnerability of really not being able to find the Pinterest board the first week and going hat-in-hand to the help board to ask a clarifying question. It was a risk, because maybe I hadn't read the directions carefully. Maybe when you pointed it out, it was going to all make sense. I was lucky in that there was a piece missing in your assignment, and that was okay, which happens with any assignments.

One of the classmates developed a MOOC on Financial Aid Advising for graduating students. She developed a simulation in which MOOC students selected one of two fictitious advisees, viewed mock videos of the character explaining his goals and family circumstance, and accessed spreadsheets with information on the debt incurred by the student. The culminating assignment was to calculate the cost of several loan repayment strategies, compare that data with the student's obligations and prospective income, and make recommendations for loan repayment. According to Amy

> Amy: One of my classmates did her MOOC on the financial aid system, which included a lot of math problems that we had to work out. That was daunting for me because that's not my strength, because there is a right and wrong answer.
>
> So it was interesting to take her course. She has a very different personality than I do. I think I was able to learn from her, as my classmate. I also think she was able to step outside of her comfort zone and do the creative thing. So that's how we learned from each other.

Gail also experienced this challenge when Amy interviewed her about her experience

Gail: When I was in Jillian's course about financial aid I all of a sudden felt like I was hanging out all over the place. I had to submit math work. I'm doing these calculations. I'm running these numbers and I'm just about to post and then I realized I've made a major error. I've made a major mistake. So I go back and I run them again and then I've got myself all turned around and I'm thinking, 'I'm going to be hanging out all over the place in front of my students, making maybe major mathematical errors. How am I going to feel about that?' So there was a huge vulnerability. My peers, my students who were now my peers when I stepped into that role, and my student who was now my teacher were going to be looking at that with an evaluative lens.

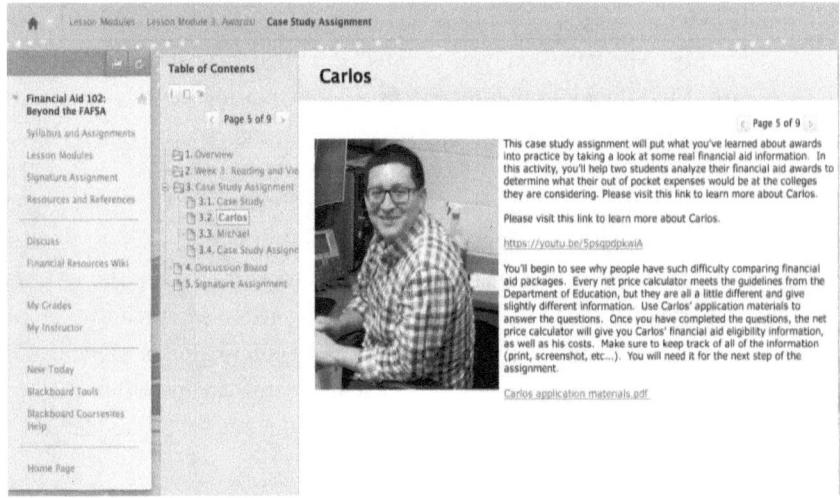

Note that Amy experienced the financial aid MOOC as valuable, even though it took her outside her comfort zone, because Open Learning course experiences leading up to the pilot emphasized the importance of co-learning. Co-learning supports intellectual risk.

During the interview Gail asked Amy to describe other aspects of the Open Learning course design that contributed to her perceived success. Many themes emerged, but the most prominent were the importance of embracing vulnerability to gain competence, guided creativity, multiple opportunities to share and represent ideas, public and authentic work, iterative design, and honest and substantive feedback.

## Embracing Vulnerability to Gain Competence

At the outset of the course, Amy reported feeling unsure of her capabilities. However, the assignments scaffolded her skills development. She also gained insight into open learning concepts that would help her make the assignments more manageable, such as the notions of combining and adapting pre-existing resources.

> Amy: I really didn't know what to expect. You can get only so much from the course description, but it did say what the final project was, that you're going to be making a full course, and it will be public online. I was kind of thinking, 'I can't do that. That's too much.' So I thought, 'Well, when I get in the class, I'll have step-by-step instruction how to do it. So I'll be fine.' Then when that wasn't there, it was, 'Oh, no. I'm going to have to ask a bunch of questions and look kind of ridiculous because I don't know what's going on.'

> But as the course went on, I got a better picture of what Open Learning really was, and that these are the open educational resources, and you get to use those in your MOOC, as opposed to, 'Pick this textbook and write out the lessons and write all these things.' You can have these resources and supplements to help you teach the course. So when I got a SlideShare, some YouTubes and different articles, it just helped give the meatiness to the course. So what I wrote was just supplemental to it, as opposed to writing a whole course.

> So I became a lot less overwhelmed when I learned about that part. Because I didn't have as much instruction about the project and how to do it, it was better, not only because of the creativity, but because I think I needed that to prove my research skills and to prove that I really can do this and figure it out for myself, because the working world is not going to give you a rubric.

## Guided Creativity

The elicitation of creativity is a lot like Jazz. The pre-determined chord progression and agreed upon sequence of measures makes it possible for musicians to engage in wild improvisation. Learning designs that elicit creativity are also a lot like Jazz. If there is not enough structure the learners can flounder, but too much structure discourages the learners from taking the risk of making the assignment their own.

## Gail: How did the course's design elicit creativity in you?

> Amy: [In] courses before it said, 'Follow this rubric. Write this paper, this many words, this many pages.' I did it. It's cool. I tried to make it as creative as possible ... But in this course it was, 'Make it look nice. Make it fun.' You know? It was such a different opportunity and a welcome opportunity to be able to jump in and put my own stamp on something that made it my own thing ...

> I'd call it a guided creativity. It wasn't, 'These are the five learning resources that you're supposed to put in your MOOC and put them in a certain order.' ... It was just so much more than that. There are parameters that you gave to not only give structure, but they were broad enough that I had free reign, especially because we could pick our own topic. It wasn't like, 'Pick from these five topics and make it yours, not mine.'

### Multiple Opportunities to Share and Represent Ideas

Amy noted that the Timeline assignment helped establish the expectation that each person would have an opportunity to communicate their individual understanding in a unique manner, and that also included how they presented their work.

> Amy: I think it was perfect to start with the timeline assignment. I've never done anything like that before. It was new. It was fun. Even though we all worked on the same topic, the history of open learning, everybody came up with different resources. I don't think anybody had any two articles or things like that alike. Everybody's looked different, our own background and colors, but the content and the ideas were also different.

> So there were more resources out there than you could ever put on a timeline without it being crammed. I came up with like 20 or 30 [possible nodes], and I selected the 15 that I thought fit the best. The great part of it was that nobody else in the class matched anybody else's ... My timeline background included the Creative Commons logo. Other

people included videos. They focused on concepts that were important and influential to them. It grows the education in all of us to share our own perspective.

That's what I love about learning in a class where everybody brings their own different perspective to the same idea. So I think the structure of that was great because it set the tone for [the rest of the class], that you're going to be able to put your own stamp on what you do in this course.

## Public and Authentic Work

Another theme was the impact that making their work public and the authenticity of assignments had on the quality of feedback, and on how she perceived the importance of the feedback she received.

Amy: In all the classes prior to this [my peers didn't want] to offend anybody by saying, 'You have a very blatant spelling error.' They'd rather be polite and say, 'Great job. Looks awesome,' then go do their own thing and make sure that their thing is right.

This time there was a lot more at stake. When you submit a paper the professor is the only one who's going to check it. If post it in an online discussion you might get a little bit of peer feedback, but it stays in Blackboard. I think the MOOC feedback was important to all of us to make sure that we were not going to trip over ourselves in front of the world.

## Honest and Substantive Feedback

The quote from Amy above references the importance of feedback, but it's important to note that the feedback took many forms. During the pilot phase the students and instructor took on several personas, and each identity allowed them to take a different stance in relation to the feedback process.

Gail: When I became student in your course and I could see that there was a Pinterest assignment, I think it's really cool, but I'm not sure which of the two secret boards I should be getting into. And so when I'm giving you feedback about that and role-playing as a student I'm not filling out a feedback form and sending it to you. I'm going onto the help board and saying, 'Dear Professor Cozart-Lundin, I'm so excited to be in this class.

> I'm a little confused about the Pinterest assignment. Could you please help me clarify?' Well, that is constructive feedback. That is feedback that improves the class, but it's so different because it's somebody who's in the learner role. You had the chance to really see what happens when people actually try to use your work. And so, you had a third round of feedback that wasn't just in the abstract. It was really grounded in, 'Oh, I really need to fix this.'
>
> So I've really come to believe that doing effective learning, really the last third of the course should always be involved in some form of application, seeing the reality of it and opportunities for improving it that are based on that, not just on some abstract 'I'm correcting your typos' thing, although we do want you to correct your typos. It doesn't help when it's your final grade, and in the comments you're being told that there's a typo.

**Iterative Design**

In the book *Art and Fear*, David Bayles and Ted Orland note "The seed for your next artwork lies embedded in the imperfections in your current piece ... It is precisely this interaction between the ideal and the real that locks your art into the real world, and gives meaning to both" (1993). Teaching that elicits creativity supports iterative cycles of feedback that alternate between idealistic dreaming, experiencing the reality of the work, and critique for the purpose of improvement. The more opportunities to "fail," the better. This has tremendous implications for course design.

> Gail: It was a relief to me that I had the gift of time to experience [the MOOCs], to give that user experience feedback. And it was also a relief to me to know that the final thing could be a celebration. The grading was really the culmination and the celebration, as opposed to the first time there was an evaluation, and so it was okay to say, 'Great job.'
>
> There'd been all these cycles of formative leading up to it. And I think that that's the preferable way to structure it. But that means you need to really rethink your course design and build in those cycles. A lot of people think they don't have the time to do that, but if you want students to do original work, you really have to have those iterations.

## Epilog to the Experience

In fall 2015 Amy took her Capstone course. The Capstone's two signature assignments included the authoring of a showcase portfolio and a multimodal online "problem of practice" case, in which students document a piece of professional work and use the program's concepts as a lens for analysis.

Amy decided to do her case study on the MOOC that she created for Open Learning. She noted that the majority of students in MOOCs are male, and she wondered if her choice of tool (Pinterest) and assignment design was gendered and therefore slanted toward females. She also wondered if those decisions should be revisited, and if so how. The production of authentic work in the Open Learning course made it possible for her to tackle the challenge of "scholarship of teaching and learning" in her Capstone experience, taking a research-based approach to the analysis and evaluation of her own work (Bass, 1999). Like a true bricoleur, she drew upon the readings from every course in the program to select only the most relevant works and integrate them into her analysis.

In the 1980s Lee Shulman proposed a framework for pedagogical content knowledge that is essential to effective teaching (1986). Koehler and Mishra later adapted this model to include technology, giving it the acronym TPACK (Mishra & Koehler 2006, Koehler & Mishra 2008). Amy came to the eLearning Design program with prior knowledge about visual merchandizing (content) the Social Media course helped her gain proficiency with Pinterest (technology) and the Open Learning course provided guidance in online course design (pedagogy). All of these proficiencies are exhibited in Amy's showcase portfolio, and by leveraging the learning experiences from four courses in order to produce original work she exhibits all the characteristics of a connected learner.

## References

Ambrose, S. A., Bridges, M. W., DiPietro, M., Lovett, M. C., & Norman, M. K. (2010). *How learning works: Seven research-based principles for smart teaching* (1st ed.). San Francisco: Jossey-Bass.

Bass, R. (1999). The scholarship of teaching: What is the problem?. *Creative Thinking about Learning and Teaching* 1(1).

Bayles, D., Orland, T. (1993). *Art and Fear: Observations on the Perils (and Rewards) of Artmaking*. Santa Barbara, CA: Capra Press.

Bransford,, J. D., Brown, A. L., & Cocking (Eds.). (2000). *How people learn: Brain, mind, experience, and school*. Washington, DC: National

Academy Press. Retrieved November 11, 2015 from http://www.nap.edu/read/9853.

Brennan, K. (2013). In Connectivism, No One Can Hear You Scream: a Guide to Understanding the MOOC Novice. Retrieved November 11, 2015 from http://www.hybridpedagogy.com/journal/in-connectivism-no-one-can-hear-you-scream-a-guide-to-understanding-the-mooc-novice.

COI (n.d.). Community of Inquiry Model. Retrieved November 11, 2015 from https://coi.athabascau.ca/coi-model.

Cormier, D. (2010). Success in a MOOC. Retrieved November 11, 2015 from https://www.youtube.com/watch?v=r8avYQ5ZqM0.

Koehler, M. J., & Mishra, P. (2008). Introducing TPCK. In J. A. Colbert, K. E. Boyd, K. A. Clark, S. Guan, J. B. Harris, M. A. Kelly & A. D. Thompson (Eds.), *Handbook of Technological Pedagogical Content Knowledge for Educators* (pp. 1–29). New York: Routledge.

Lave, J., Wenger, E. (1991). *Situated Learning: Legitimate Peripheral Participation*. Cambridge, UK: Cambridge University Press.

Lévi-Strauss, Claude. (1962). *The savage mind*. Chicago, IL: University of Chicago Press.

Martin, L. Schwartz, D. (2014). A pragmatic perspective on visualization and creative thinking. *Visual Studies*, (28)9. http://dx.doi.org/10.1080/1472586X.2014.862997.

Massumi, B. (2002). *A shock to thought: Expression after Deleuze and Guattari*. New York, NY: Routledge.

Matthews-DeNatale, G. (2015). Master of education ePortfolio resources. Retrieved November 11, 2015, from https://northeastern.digication.com/2013_master_of_education_ePortfolio_resources.

Mayer, R. E., & Moreno, R. (2003). Nine Ways to Reduce Cognitive Load in Multimedia Learning. *Educational Psychologist*, 38(1), 43–52.

McTighe, J., & Thomas, R.S. (2003). Backward design for forward action. *Educational Leadership*, 60(5), 52–55.

Mishra, P., & Koehler, M. J. (2006). Technological pedagogical content knowledge: A framework for teacher knowledge. *Teachers College Record*, 108(6), 1017-1054.

Pigrum, D. (2009). *Teaching creativity: Multi-mode transitional practices*. New York, NY: Continuum Press.

Shulman, L. S. (1986). Those who understand: Knowledge growth in teaching. *Educational Researcher*, 15(4).

Siemens, G. (2004). Connectivism: A learning theory for the digital age. Retrieved November 11, 2015 from http://www.elearnspace.org/Articles/connectivism.htm.

TEMOA open education resources portal: Rubrics to evaluate OER. (2011). Retrieved November 11, 2015 from http://www.temoa.info/rubric.

Wiley, D. (2015). An obstacle to the ubiquitous adoption of OER in US higher education. Retrieved November 11, 2015 from http://opencontent.org/blog/archives/3941.

Wiley, D. (2013). Openness in Education. Retrieved November 11, 2015 from https://learn.canvas.net/courses/4.

CHAPTER 17

## Developing Mindfulness, Reflection and Transformative Learning with Diverse College Students

*Hedva Lewittes*

The course Introduction to Mindfulness uses meditation, journals, reflective essays and small group work to foster engagement and mindfulness. Mindfulness, the awareness of present moment experience, develops creativity by opening up alternative ways of perceiving and knowing. Taught at SUNY Old Westbury a campus nationally recognized for diversity, the course integrates students' life stories. Guided through sitting meditations focusing on breathing, students gain somatosensory and emotional awareness, observe the flow of their thoughts and explore their inner lives. Mindfulness attitudes delineated by Jon Kabat-Zinn (2013) are discussed and applied in insight journals. Many choose the class because of stress. The students learn about the physiology of stress and new perspectives on how to respond. Bringing an intentional approach to learning, students write about educational choices and identity in relation to families. They reflect on the challenges they face in the context of gender, race and ethnicity and socio-economic background. Research suggests that meditation builds compassion and students examine empathy as it relates to the self and suffering. Social justice activism is explored as a way to address suffering caused by inequity. The civil rights movement based on love and non-violence exemplifies a mindful approach to social change. The environmental justice movement recognizing the interconnectedness of life, draws attention to how environmental degradation contributes to inequality. The students' backgrounds make the discussion of social justice particularly meaningful. Selections from journals and essays provide examples of student engagement in a process of transformative learning about themselves and the world.

### INTRODUCTION

Introduction to Mindfulness, a Psychology course that I teach at the State University of New York (*SUNY*), Old Westbury guides students in contemplative inquiry using brief meditations, journals and reflective essays to guide students in contemplative inquiry. These reflective practices foster mindfulness, defined as awareness of moment to moment experience (Kabat-Zinn, 2013). Contemplative practices encourage the discovery and exploration of an inner dimension and "develop insight and creativity" (Barbezat and Bush, 2014, p.8). Mindfulness is linked to the creative process of breaking set. Ellen Langer (2000, p. 220) describes mindful learning, as " a flexible state of mind in which we are actively engaged in the present, noticing new things and sensitive to context". It involves "drawing new distinctions" and understanding that there are "alternative ways of knowing". The course pedagogy integrates contemplative practices with small group collaboration and nurtures a classroom environment that is safer for sharing personal experience. This helps build connection between students and promotes active and engaged learning (Lewittes, 2009) two key characteristics of creative education (Flood and Coleman, 2015).

Meditation that involves full breathing and sitting in a calm, alert position opens up new somatosensory and emotional awareness. In journals students articulate insights gleaned from meditation. They learn about mindfulness attitudes which provide a foundation for and are enhanced by meditation. While meditation and a mindfulness perspective come out of the Buddhist tradition, neither requires religious affiliation. There is substantial evidence that meditation reduces stress (Hoffman et al, 2010). Examining the underlying physiological and psychological mechanisms and practicing meditation and mindfulness introduces an approach that can be used to change stress reactivity. In the course, essays entail reflection and analysis. Writing about Adrienne Rich's "Claiming an Education" (2013 ) students apply the mindfulness lens to their educational experiences. They articulate a process defined by the Association for American Colleges and Universities (AACU) as intentional learning (2002) and reflect on their responses to educational challenges. Discussing their identities in relationship to family engages them in self-authorship (Kegan, 1994). The students consider their stories in the context of gender, race and ethnicity and socio-economic background.

Increasingly, research suggests that meditation opens one up to compassion (Desteno, 2015; Ricard et al, 2014) and the course goes on to explore the cultivation of empathy towards oneself and others (Salzberg, 2005). Empathy includes cognitive perspective taking, a connection to ones' own and others emotions and suffering and caring actions (Goleman, 2013 ). There are scholars and practitioners who see caring actions as a natural outgrowth of empathy for suffering caused by injustice (*Wapner 2010; Glassman 1998*). Further, the

Association for Contemplative Mind in Higher Education's recent conference addressed the issue of building just communities (2015). Thus the course's last unit examines examples of mindful activism for social justice focusing on the civil rights and environmental movements.

Contemplative practices and mindfulness can change consciousness and lead to a more flexible, improvisational approach to living. According to Allen "transformative learning is related to a disposition for creativity" (2015, p.26). In essays about their educational journeys students reflect on a process that Allen identifies as creative becoming. However, transformative learning goes beyond the individual and involves a shift in how one views being in the world (O'Sullivan, 2003). Thus the final unit also examines how an awareness of injustice and social justice activism contribute to transformative learning.

## The Educational Context

Obtaining General Education (GE) social science status for Introduction to Mindfulness enables students to take this "out of the box" course while fulfilling a requirement (SUNY Old Westbury, 2015 b). As part of SUNY GE critical thinking, a mandated outcome is incorporated into reflective essay assignments. (Research methodology another required outcome is addressed in an assignment not discussed here). However rather than the traditional text book, survey approach the curriculum uses original readings which model reflective writing and critical analysis. Writing journals and essays encourage students to find or perhaps even embrace their own voice before it is lost (Belenkey et al, 1986). The College at Old Westbury offers a unique environment for teaching mindful and reflective practices. Part of a public University system, the College with an historic mission to the educationally underserved is recognized by *U.S. News & World Report* as one of the most diverse in the United States (SUNY Old Westbury, 2014-2016, p. 9-10). As of 2015 the undergraduate population is 29% African-American, 22% Latino, 11% Asian-American, 58% women; 82% are commuters (SUNY Old Westbury, 2015a). A survey conducted in several of my classes found that approximately 70% work from 15 to 40 hours a week. Many are from recent immigrant backgrounds, the first in their families to attend college. Thus the course encourages self-awareness in the context of the real life educational and economic challenges faced by the students. Introduction to Mindfulness provides access to the emerging discipline of Contemplative Studies (Roth, 2006) and by integrating the students' firsthand experience of inequities contributes to the College's social justice mission. Offered in spring 2014 and 2015 the classes had a combined enrollment of about fifty that mirrored the

College's diversity. The course's perspective and learning process are illustrated by examples of student writing from the 2015 spring semester class.

## MINDFULNESS AND STRESS

**Meditation**

During the first week students take a "Mindfulness Test" (Braza, 1977, p.19-20), discuss their answers in small groups and then report back to the full class. Pressured rushing turns out to be common and sharing everyday stresses begins a process of reflection and interaction that is central to the course's pedagogy. Meditations can also be a method for engaging students by putting them in touch with the information from their body and senses, feelings, personal histories, values and beliefs that they bring to learning and into the classroom. Meditations ranging from 5 to 20 minutes guided by myself and on CDs take place throughout the semester. The CD presenters, course readings and internet sources introduce contemporary practitioners, writers, scholars and researchers and a variety of perspectives drawn from Contemplative Studies and the community. This provides information that can be used to further explore and develop a regular practice for those who want to although this is not a course requirement. In class, students can choose to follow the meditation protocols or sit quietly and are asked to refrain from using electronic devices.

During the second week, students take part in a raisin eating meditation which is the initial track on Jon Kabat-Zinn's Mindfulness for beginners CD (2012). After I distribute raisins, they listen to the CD that instructs them to touch its textures, and notice colors, structures and smell. In a guided process of bringing it to their lips, putting it in their mouths, tasting and swallowing, they are asked to note their feelings and thoughts about the raisin and eating. Kabat-Zinn describes this exercise as a "surprise" because it breaks set with expectations about meditation, about a food we routinely take for granted and with the habit of eating. Following this and all subsequent meditations students take a few minutes to write down their immediate responses. One student's insight journal recognizes how this exercise sparked her imagination.

> I liked how he (the speaker on the CD) made us think about how the raisin is made, how the wrinkled ridges look like mountains and valleys which help the mind think outside the box. For instance, not just look at the raisin as food, but imagine through your own creative mind about what it looks similar to. This mediation helped me relate to the raisin not

> just simply as food, but to think about where it came from. For example, the raisin was a grape, and then was set in the sun to dry and came to the markets for people to buy and consume; it made me think about how I would've felt if I was a raisin left out in the sun to dry.

The course draws on the practices of the Insight Mediation tradition which involves sustained attention to and awareness of internal and external stimuli in the present moment (Goldstein and Kornfield, 1987). Students read about two fundamental elements of this form of meditation, breathing and sitting. *According to* Kabat-Zinn breathing is a force that is "connected to the experience of being alive" and "tuning into it brings us right into the here and now" (2013, p.41). Sitting involves an alert posture with head, neck and back vertically aligned but not rigid in the shoulders and comfortable so that one does not feel compelled to move. This facilitates watching and feeling the breath as it flows through the nostrils, expands the chest and reaches down into the belly on the in-breath and encourages a slow, relaxing process of breathing out. It encourages a mental spaciousness that attends to sensations and allows thoughts to come and go. Students discuss this method and then as part of the unit listen to Kabat-Zinn's track on mindfulness of breathing and another CD which leads them in a breathing and sitting meditation (Laverack, 2013). One student captures the essence of this technique.

> One of the reasons why I liked both meditations was because I had the chance to realize the need for my body to breath. Breathing slowly made me feel relaxed, forget about my problems for a while and focus on how my body felt at the moment. I just concentrated on every breath I took and felt how it made me feel so much better. I felt as if I was breathing for the first time. I tend to forget that as a human, I make mistakes and have the power to fix them. Just like everyone I need a break from time to time to breathe and relax.

**Mindfulness Attitudes**

Kabat-Zinn (2013, p. 21-30) identifies mindfulness attitudes as described in Table I. Drawn from Buddhist philosophy these attitudes can also provide a basis for a secular alternative world-view.

Table I: Mindfulness Attitudes

| Attitude | Description |
|---|---|
| Non-judging | Adopting stance or impartial observer towards feelings and thoughts<br>Stepping back from mechanically labeling as bad of good and intense likes and dislikes |
| Patience | Sitting in the moment whether frustrating, boring, painful or joyful<br>Allowing for beings and intentions to unfold in their own time |
| Beginner's Mind | Opening up to new knowledge<br>Taking a fresh perspective on the ordinary or accustomed<br>Adopting stance of not-knowing |
| Trust | Honoring one's own felt sense of experience<br>Recognizing others' felt sense of experience |
| Non-striving | Attending to the present moment of a process rather than fixating on future goal |
| Acceptance | Seeing things as they are in the present: Doesn't mean affirming current circumstances as positive, may entail sitting with pain |
| Letting Go | Watching and allowing feelings and thoughts to move in and out of awareness |

The various facets are distinct but also an interacting whole. Non-judging, beginners mind, non-striving, letting go and patience are relevant to creative curiosity and courage (Coleman and Flood, 2015). They illuminate an approach that can flexibly respond to change, get un-stuck from past preconceptions, behavioral patterns and prescribed expectations and express an understanding that self-knowledge and self-direction underlie reaching future goals. Tuning into and trusting the information from one's body or clearly facing troubling current realities can provide the grounding and confidence to question widely assumed beliefs. The ability to recognize that others also have their own subjective experience is part of perspective taking.

These ideas frame the rest of the course. After reading this material, students form small groups that choose, discuss and apply one of the attitudes to their lives. Re-assembling into the full class they explain and share examples. The collaborative work offers an opportunity to more comfortably engage with each other and the material. As part of this unit students listen to Kabat-Zinn's (2012) guided meditations on mindfulness of the body a whole and another on sounds, thoughts and emotions which refer to the mindfulness attitudes. An Insight

Journal is the first full writing assignment based on readings, discussions and meditations. Class time is spent on defining and understanding insight as a new awareness, involving emotional and bodily awareness as well an analytic component and is expressed in one's own voice. In the following example, a student uses the mindfulness attitudes to re-define her identity in relation to family.

> As a freshman I am still trying to understand college. I am not used to the amount of variation and diversity of each class which is why Intro Mindfulness is unfamiliar to me. When I read the word meditation in the syllabus I didn't know what to expect. I expected to be part of the class but not really involved. However, the exercises and discussions have made me discover some things about myself. I gathered that with a beginners mind we are supposed to approach a person new and fresh. If we do this we will be able to let go of the hurt or pain that we associated, take blinders off that we had because of our love. The only way we can do this is by letting go of our beliefs that prevent us from seeing things as they really are. The discussion on beginners mind made me analyze my relationship with my grandparents who moved down south. I was hurt and upset but couldn't fully move on. Yes it hurts me to remember when I would see my grandparents every day because they lived with me. Although it has been a few years I am still very family oriented. The discussion made me realize that if I am able to let go of what once was, of comparing how it used to be and how it is now, I will be able to enjoy the time we do have to spend together.

## STRESS: REACTING AND RESPONDING

During the first class students share and then write about their intention in taking the course. Dealing with stress is a common objective. One student explains,

> I am taking Introduction to Mindfulness to help combat stress in a psychological fashion so the world doesn't become too overwhelming. I consider myself a very stressed out person with only a few outlets such as swimming, exercise or music but even these are not enough. With this class I hope to gain more insight into healthy ways to relieve some stress.

In line with this interest, *Full catastrophe living* (Kabat-Zinn, 2013), a primary "text" describes Mindfulness Based Stress Relief (MBSR) a program developed at the University of Massachusetts Medical Center. The course does not require the substantial time, commitment and regular meditation practice essential for this program. Overcoming one's anxiety was not a realistic learning outcome. However, instruction in the method of the sitting/breathing meditation combined with a mindfulness perspective offered an approach to dealing with stress. One student reported that she took a meditation break while working on a paper. Another recounted how she led her friends in meditation while awaiting rescue in the snowy isolated area where their car broke down. Students most often wrote about school related stress.

It was during the sitting meditation that I realized why mediation is so beneficial for me.

> This exercise forced me to sit still for a while. For the time being I didn't feel rushed, like I usually do. I normally feel like I'm always in a hurry to get something done. For the few minutes I stopped thinking about school, work or anything else that usually keeps me busy. It was like my brain was in neutral; no positives or negatives thoughts, just a clear mind. After the sitting exercise ended I felt calm. Usually my upper body gets very tense when I'm stressed and I often suffer from severe tension headaches. During the sitting mediation I didn't feel as tense, my body felt more relaxed. Being that my mind didn't feel as cluttered anymore as it usually does, I was able to focus better in my next class. I didn't have a million thoughts running through my head that could distract from focus in class.

The course examines stress' biological and psychological roots. According to Selye (1956) stress is unavoidable and adapting to it is essential for survival. He distinguishes between stressors and the response to those stressors. It is not just the stressors but their meaning to you, how you perceive and handle them that determine their effect. Kabat-Zinn describes the fight or flight reaction which involves increased adrenalin, muscle tension and strong emotions. Reactivity to stress, he argues is automatic and unconscious. People who are stuck in reactivity are in a state of hyper-arousal that continues when the external threat has diminished. Holding on to anger or fear prolongs this hyperarousal. Kabat-Zinn contrasts reacting and responding to stress. With responsivity, a person adopts the stance of an observer, is aware of the stressors and being stressed and realizes that they have a choice to be calm instead of panicked. The practice of meditation can increase the possibility of choosing to respond rather than react. Breathing helps you to gain some distance and awareness and particularly for those with a regular practice brings a meditative approach to mind. The difficulty of responding is being able to do so at the moment when the stress is occurring. Following the discussion about the information on stress the class participated in a body scan meditation (New Mindful Life, 2013)

The assignment for the unit on stress was a reflective essay which also involved the SUNY (2015) GE critical thinking learning outcomes to identify develop arguments (Lewittes, 2009). The biological content was difficult for some without background in this area. To aid mastery, instructions stated the critical thinking components and provided scaffolding questions (Burke and Meyers, 2016, p. 324) which directed students in identifying the key concepts and constructing knowledge. This pedagogy builds on Vygotsky's (1978) theory about the zone of proximal development that involves guided learning. The following student applied the main ideas in a reflection on the present moment stress, writing the essay.

> Automatic responses to stressors are considered to be reactive. We are unaware in the moment but these initial reactions can intensify the actual stress. Our reactions can take something that was a minor problem and turn them into something greater. Since taking this course I've become more aware of my body and its reactions. I can feel my heart beating faster and I notice my muscles beginning to tense up but I'm trying to practice mindfulness practice and choose better, healthier responses, realizing that 'I am not my thoughts' not letting the stress define who we are. You are then able to take a deep breath and choose more proactively. As I wrote this essay my mind wondered off at times, worrying about the next things I had to do, three other papers, work, a group project meeting, the list goes on. With this challenge I decided to make a choice on how I would respond and take control. I was able to take a step back, give myself some space to consider and then ultimately trust that I would be able to come up with a constructive response.

## REFLECTING ON EDUCATIONAL CHALLENGES AND IDENTITY

According to Kabat-Zinn (2013) mindfulness supports the development of intentionality which involves a personal vision clear and flexible enough to sustain continuity and commitment towards an unpredictable outcome (Lewittes, 2015b). For the AACU intentional learning involves using knowledge and modes of inquiry, analytical skills and creativity; it is "self- directed and purposeful" and "develops self-awareness about the reasons for study" (2002, p. 21). This conceptualization augments mindfulness' focus on developing inner clarity by placing it in an educational context. In the next unit students reflect on their educational journeys. They read Adrienne Rich's "Claiming an Education" (2010). A speech made in the 1970's for an event at a college for women, it relates personal aspirations to broader social issues. The following excerpts concepts relevant to the course's perspective.

> The first thing I want to say to you who are students is that you cannot afford to think of being here to receive an education, you will do much better to think of yourselves as being here to claim one. One of the dictionary definitions of the verb to claim is to take as the rightful owner, to assert in the face of possible contradiction. To receive is to come into possession of; to act as a receptacle or container for; to accept as authoritative or true. The difference is that between acting and being acted-upon.......Responsibility for your self means refusing to let others do your thinking.....You demand to be taken seriously so that you can also go on taking yourself seriously (p. 347-350).

The next reflective writing assignment was based on Rich's article and the concept of intentionality. One student explained the link as follows:

> One step in order to claim and education is to become an intentional learner which requires self-motivation and a persistent energy applied to the learning process. When I decided to go back to school I now see that through taking charge of my future I became an intentional learner. Once I felt like I had enough confidence in and respected myself enough to trust my own instinct and not rely on other people for confirmation I was able to develop a vison for my life. Despite how many things might get in the way of my achieving my goals, my vision is so strong that it keeps me fighting through.

In their essays student identify with Rich's message. The following quote can be seen as an example of Allen's (2015) concept of creative becoming.

> Claiming an education means taking responsibility for my actions and life. I had been a receptacle of events occurring and for feeling bad about them especially if they were negative. I no longer wanted to feel this

way. The solution: I became an active human being. I explored options and my mind and decided I wanted to be the type of human being that left an imprint instead of the one who simply lived life being the imprint of others.

Although women's position in the academy has changed, students still resonated with the obstacles to claiming their education. Some faced cultural challenges.

> Claiming an education to me has to do with family history. My mother comes from India and in the traditional culture a women's purpose in life is just to get married and start a family. My mother has been just another immigrant in this country trying to live the American dream. Most of the women in my family aren't accomplished outside of the home. I know I have the ability to make something of myself through an education and am often told by my parents to do so. This motivates me because of how challenging it is to change the traditions of women in my family.

As in the example above, some of the stories involve several generations and intertwine education, family and economic circumstances.

> Both my parents did not go to college. They worked blue-collar, laborious jobs and for most of my life I remember them working multiple jobs at a time. I appreciate this but also feel an overwhelming amount of pressure to succeed and make their investment worth it.

Another expands on the stress of family expectations.

> I face the most pressure from my family. Their expectations are so high; sometimes it gets overwhelming. I am only one person and the weight on me to finish school and go on to getting a Master's degree is a lot when they aren't the ones doing it. I try my hardest to please my family. They look forward for me to making it. Nobody has gotten as far as me and I'm the one about to pave the way and show a great example to my younger ones. I feel like I have so much on my shoulders and many people look up to me so failure isn't an option. I just have to remain focused.

This student not only feels pressure to succeed from her family but implies a sentiment that was expressed by many in the class. Their families have high aspirations but don't understand and thus are unable to take seriously the school demands. One student explains that she was expected to take care of her younger siblings and distracted by them while she was trying to finish her paper. The following reflection details the mental stress of economic insecurity and acknowledges the difficulty of being responsible.

> The one thing that never leaves my mind is money. How I am going to make more? How much do I have to spend? How much and how I am going to pay tuition? It is a constant stressor. There are a lot of obstacles. Your family depends on you although I cannot really help them now. It is hard to reach your goals if you are not taking yourself seriously. An example, you have all week to study for a test and wait until the last minute but then something comes up such as hanging out, other homework, anything to distract. Now it's harder to focus because you are rushing to get everything done at once. This is when you realize only you can makes changes. You need to take responsibility. Once you start taking yourself seriously, you will find yourself becoming more productive.

In the next quote, the student also taps into the courage of creative becoming, realizing that she may have to change her family relationships.

> At this point in my life, claiming an education means that I will take on another job to make tuition, sacrifice social time and even assert my needs over the needs of my parents to pursue what I feel is best. I take more take more responsibility and initiative when it comes to orchestrating my courses. I credit this to my new attitude of taking myself seriously. This means that I value my choices more and I take nothing for granted. I genuinely try to extract as much as possible from every course. Claiming an education has become synonymous with taking responsibility. I am the only one who reaps the rewards or suffers for the choices I make. I fulfill three main 'disadvantages' in society. I am black, a woman and poor. The opportunities available for poor black women are slim to none in many instances, and those who have made it have had to take responsibility for their lives and learning and change.

The above examples were chosen because they best articulate the course's concepts. However, an assessment suggests that the majority of students discussed key ideas and applied them to relevant experiences. My colleague, Dr.

Laurette Morris and I developed a rubric which included the following learning outcomes:

- Addresses issues of purpose, responsibility and seriousness;
- Discusses the impact of social factors on own development

For these two items on a 4-point scale, 91% of the students were scored as meeting or exceeding standards. In a process to establish inter-rater reliability, we agreed on 65% of the scores, assigned the lower score 35% of the time and conferenced to agreement differences of more than 1 point on 4% of the items (Lewittes and Morris, 2015).

## EMPATHY AND SOCIAL JUSTICE

Building on the students' stories, the course goes on to consider how to create change both of internal beliefs and values and in the social arena. The class discussed some important concepts based on the work of Sharon Salzberg a leading theorist in the contemporary western Buddhist Insight Meditation tradition and listened to a loving kindness meditation CD that she guided (2005). She describes loving kindness as an action that confronts human suffering. Loving kindness, she posits, begins with and can transform how we view ourselves.

> When we keep opening past any version of who we are that is crafted by others, when we see that we are far bigger than the person that is delineated by family or cultural expectation we realize that we are capable of so much more than we usually dare to imagine (p. 19).

Kindness is "compassion in action" and comes from empathy. It is "through the quality of empathy we understand that suffering hurts others in just the same way that it hurts us " (p. 31). Cruelty comes from viewing the other as an object, a commodity.

> If others are seen as objects, rather than as feeling beings, it becomes quite easy to harm them, even in awful ways. Our lack of empathy reflects an inability to truly relate to other beings, to respect their boundaries or accept their feelings their needs, their hopes and dreams as viable, alive and *theirs*. This is the misapprehension that allows a person to exploit and abuse others (p. 32).

In response to these ideas in the final reflective essay a student wrote,

> A person can be made so cold and heartless that they continue to be cruel. But when someone is abused they have two choices. One choice is to inflict pain on others because a person is in pain. The other choice is not to inflict pain because a person knows what the pain already feels like and does not want to put that on others.

Although Salzberg does not directly frame cruelty in terms of injustice, her conceptualization provides a framework for considering activism for social change that embodies loving kindness (Lewittes, 2015a). The class watched Bill Moyers interview with Congressman John Lewis (Moyers, 2013), who was a student leader in the civil rights movement. Moyers asks Lewis about his 1965 march across the Edmund Pettus Bridge in Selma, Alabama.

> Bill Moyers: And when you were attacked by the police when you were beaten, when you were almost killed you didn't think for a moment of responding, replying violently?

> John Lewis: No, never because we studied the way of peace, the way of love, the way of non-violence. One of the people that beat me on the Freedom Ride in 1961 in South Carolina came to my office later with his son. His son had been encouraging his father to do it. And he said "Mr. Lewis, I'm one of the people that beat you and left you bloody. Will you forgive me? I want to apologize." His son started crying. I stared crying. He hugged me. I hugged him. He called me brother I called him brother.

For Lewis, involvement in the movement was not just political protest but rooted in a different set of values and way of relating. "We accepted nonviolence not simply as teaching or as a tactic but as a way of life...We wanted to build what we called the beloved community, a community at peace with itself. " The class also discussed an account of another participant in the movement, Jan Willis (2008) a practicing Buddhist and college professor who as a girl marched with her father in Birmingham Alabama.

> The Spring of 1963 changed me fundamentally not just because I had marched with King and Abernathy....It was also that I had stood with and therefore up for myself and for my people. White people no longer held my spirit in chains.

Thus Willis describes a transformation in her awareness and identity. One student's reflective essay recognizes that the civil rights movement changed the consciousness of its participants and empathizes with the choices activists faced.

> I imagine that many people had to make long hard decisions about risking their lives and lives of their families to fight for a better tomorrow that they may never live to enjoy. Despite the risks, both Jan Willis and Jon Lewis describe feeling proud that they fought back....Slavery and white supremacy were fundamental beliefs for centuries and will take more than 60 years to change. Each generation should remember to fight peacefully and to remember forgiveness and love when facing our enemies.

Salzberg's ideas about the roots of cruelty and interconnectedness were also relevant to the course readings on environmentalism. The article Whales are People Too (2012) recounts a history based on the commodification of whales and develops arguments for a current rights movement based on empathy for cetaceans social and emotional lives. The concept of environmental justice as explained by Professor and activist Robert Bullard emphasizes human interconnectedness with the environment and the impact on people of global warming's extreme weather events like Hurricane Katrina. He recounts how protests led to the first national studies which then created the awareness that race was the most strongly related factor in predicting those who lived near toxic sites. He writes,

> Environmental racism refers to any policy, practice or directive that differentially affects or disadvantages (whether intended or unintended) individuals, groups or communities based on race or color. Environmental racism combines with public policies and industry practices to provide benefits for whites while shifting costs to people of color.

Given the students backgrounds', for many Bullard's definitions were not abstract. One student shares her experience.

> The town I live in is located near water and a storm caused severe flooding. The town failed to make sure that all of the water would be drained. It was no coincidence that the people in that area were primarily Black and Hispanic. My friend's grandmother lived in this neighborhood

> with her son and 90-year-old father. They were forced to leave everything behind and quickly evacuate. The storm destroyed their home and all of their personal belongings. They lost everything. Most of the residents did not have flood insurance.

Students also recognized human interconnectedness with the environment and described a change in the public's consciousness about how nature and public policy affects people.

> Although one often thinks that environmental justice is related specifically to nature, it is also related to us, our surroundings and our life. In fact, every decision that affects the environment affects us directly as we depend on our surroundings. As we look back in time we can see that many natural disasters served as eye openers for many of us because they showed the truth about environmental racism.

Finally, a student incorporated a poem by Thich Nhat Hahn (2013) read in class. In her response she acknowledges the impact that protest, the government and individuals can have.

> We have to make sure we are mindful of our environment and surroundings. We have to be aware of the social structure to understand what is going on. It is important that we come together and make sure to push the government to enforce environmental regulation in all communities, even the poor ones. The poem "Please Call Me by My True Names" relates to environmental justice. "I am a member of the politburo, with plenty of power in my hands and I am the man who has to pay his debt of blood to my people, dying slowly in a forced labor camp." That can mean that if we are ever able to reach a powerful position in life we should make it meaningful and help people. If anyone is lucky enough to get a job working for the government, they could use their position to make sure that every community is granted environmental justice.

For the final reflective essay students were able to choose from several questions which in addition to the topics of empathy and the political movements discussed above covered the following: reconciliation in Rwanda (Hugo, 2014) mindfulness in relationships (Lucas, 2010); the Dalai Lama on happiness (2013). On the last day of class and right before exams I led a walking meditation based on Thich

Nhat Hahn's writing (1992). In journals students reflected that they found the slow paced walking relaxing, felt open to the surrounding spring environment and some even tried it on their own.

## DISCUSSION

Meditating the course's most innovative reflective practice was the focus in the beginning of the semester. Meditation engaged students in an awareness of bodily sensations and emotional reactions as sources of knowledge. While the impact on individuals varied, integrating meditation with journaling, reflective essays, small group work and guided questions reinforced meaningful learning. Thus, for the unit on mindfulness attitudes, small groups discussed concepts and personal examples. In journals students wrote about insights gleaned from meditations and the mindfulness perspective. They became conscious of behaviors such as breathing and emotional reactions which had been automatic or unquestioned and used mindfulness attitudes to re-think family relationships. Indeed, awareness of the affective dimension contributes to both reflective and critical thinking (Mezirow, 1998). Choice was a common theme. Students wrote about choice in responding to stress or family needs or to become more intentional learners or more serious students or to change careers and about choices made by civil rights activists to take risks. Students continued to apply mindfulness concepts throughout the semester.

The first reflective essay covered material on stress and involved critical as well as reflective thinking. Some students had not previously taken college biology and concentrated more on explaining major ideas than on applying them to personal experiences. However, for the next reflective essay students wrote both about the concepts and gave examples from their lives. They were aided by further class discussion about the guiding questions which provided a better understanding of how to use the scaffolding. Based on "Claiming an Education" (Rich, 2013) they addressed their own intentional learning and reflected on their challenges and stresses. Assessment results provide evidence that the majority of the class successfully addressed key learning outcomes. Their thoughtful and honest reflections suggest that the assignment encouraged creative thinking regarding their educational journeys. Several students wrote about courageous past decisions, such as switching from more "practical" majors favored by their parents or leaving a secure job to become a helping professional. Many used the concepts to think about themselves in new ways and articulated their intentions to become more serious and responsible students. Some followed through, others did not. This assignment engaged students in self- authoring (Kegan, 1994) and related to Erik Erikson's (1968, p.8) concept of identity development which he describes as matching one's sense of inner continuity with the continuity in one's meaning for others. While the students were at different points along their career paths, they all defined themselves in regard to educational goals. Further, framing life choices in the context of family history, needs and expectations was a recurrent theme. Many described their identities not in opposition to but rather in relation to their families. The concept of relational identity is central both to Kegan's conceptualization of contemporary adulthood and to feminist theory (Lewittes, 2011; Chodorow, 1979). However, the process of becoming autonomous is shaped by the background of these young adults many of whom come from working class families and are still connected to and receive support from their traditional, collectivist cultures (Markus and Kitiyama, 1991). Both the stresses and strengths resulting from coping with inequality and injustice need further study (Lewittes, 2015b).

The internal process of creative becoming is illuminated by Salzberg's (2005) ideas which describe a change in consciousness that unfolds with loving kindness towards oneself. Empathy entails an expanded awareness of others' suffering. Increasingly the field of Contemplative Studies is engaging in dialogue about social justice (Dayley, 2015). Recognizing the potential impact on our psyches and on others' of violent or unprincipled political acts, the final course unit considers mindful social actions that address injustice. John Lewis exemplifies loving kindness in his commitment to non-violence and his willingness to forgive. The environmental movement is built on the understanding that humans and the natural world are inextricably intertwined. In reflective essays students go beyond self and family and recognize that an involvement in social justice issues can change one's consciousness. This unit is also relevant to the AACU's (2002) conception of intentional learning which includes civic responsibility and posits that the goal of higher education is to enable students to adapt and thrive in a complex, global culture.

Finally, O'Sullivan's (2003) holistic perspective (Allen, 2015) of creative education as transformation sums up the course's perspective as follows:

> (A) shift of consciousness that....involves our understanding of ourselves and our self- locations, relationships with other humans and with the natural world, our understanding of relations of power in interlocking structures of class, race and gender, our body awareness, our visons of alternative approaches to living and our sense of possibilities for social justice and peace and personal joy.

Contemplative practices opened students up to thinking differently about their bodies, themselves and their relationships. Students developed and articulated their intentions regarding their educational careers. Because of their backgrounds the discussion of social justice was personally meaningful and contributed to a dynamic educational exchange. In journals and essays students reflected on an engaged in a process of transformative learning.

## REFERENCES

Allen, B. (2015) Creative becoming: Transformative learning for creative teaching in higher education. In K. Coleman, A. Flood (Eds.) *Capturing creativity through creative teaching (pp. 11-34).* Champaign, IL: Common Ground Publishing

Association for Contemplative Mind in Higher Education. (2015). B*uilding just communities, 7th annual conference.* Washington, D.C.: Howard University

Association of American Colleges and Universities. (2002) *Greater expectations.* Washington, DC

Barbezat, D., Bush, M. (2014) *Contemplative practices in higher education.* San Francisco, CA: Jossey-Bass

Belenky, M.F., Clinchy, B. M., Goldberger, N.R.,Tarule, J. M. (1986) *Women's ways of knowing.* NY: Basic Books, Inc.

Braza, J. (1997) *Moment by moment.* North Clarendon, VT: Tuttle Publishing

Bullard, R. (2013) Assuring environmental justice for all. In A. Anker, M. Feder-Marcus (Eds.) T*he ethics of engagement*: *Educating leaders for a just world* (pp. 708-717). Acton MA: Copley Press

Burke, L.E., Meyers, A.B. (2016) *Infants, children and adolescents. 8th edition.* NY: Pearson

Center for Contemplative Mind in Society. (2008) *Contemplative practices in higher education: A handbook of classroom practices.* Northampton, MA

Chodorow, N. (1978) Feminism and difference: Gender, relation and difference in psychoanalytic perspective. *Socialist review,* 9(14) 51-70

Coleman, K. & Flood, A. (2015) Introduction: Thinking about creativiety. In K. Coleman, A. Flood (Eds.) *Capturing creativity through Creative teaching,* (pp.1-9). Champaign IL: Common Ground Publishing.

The Dalai Lama. (2013) Modern society and the quest for human happiness. In A. Anker, M. Feder-Marcus (Eds.) T*he ethics of engagement: Educating leaders for a just world* (pp. 402- 410). Acton MA: Copley Press

Dayley, G. (2015) The arrow: A journal of wakeful society, culture and politics.

Desteno, D. (2015) How meditation builds compassion. http://www.theatlantic.com/health/archive/2015/07/mindfulness-meditation-empathy- compassion/398867

Erikson, E. (1968). Life cycle. In (Eds.) D.Sills, R. Merton, *International encyclopedia of the social sciences*, vol. 9, (pp. 286-292). Greenwich CT: Crowell, Collier and Macmillan

Glassman, B. (1998) *Bearing witness*. New York: Bell Tower

Goldstein, J., Kornfield, J. (1987) *Seeking the heart of wisdom: The path of Insight Mediation*. Boston,MA: Shambala Publications

Goleman, D. (2013) Empathy 101. http://danielgoleman.info/empahty-101

Hoffman, S.G., Sawyer, A.T., Witt, A. P, Oh, D. (2010) The effect of mindfulness-based therapy on anxiety and depression: A meta-analytic review. *Journal of consulting and clinical psychology,* 78(2), 169-183

Hugo, P. Dominus, S. (2014) Portraits of reconciliation. New York Times

Kabat-Zinn, J. (2013) *Full catastrophe living*. NY: Random House

Kabat-Zinn, J. (2012) *Mindfulness for beginners*. Boulder, CO: Sounds True, Inc.

Kegan, R. (1994) *In over our heads*. Cambridge, MA: Harvard University Press

Langer, E. (2000) Mindful learning. *Current direction in psychological science, 9:6, 220-223.*

Laverack, M. (2013) Sitting meditation. Dartmouth, NH: Dartmouth Hospital Chaplaincy.

Lewittes, H. (2009) A critical thinking rubric as the basis of assessment and curriculum. In C. Shreiner (Ed.) *Handbook on assessment technologies, methods, and application in higher education.* (pp. 22-46) Hershey, PA: IGI Global.

Lewittes, H (2015a) Social justice and mindfulness. Building just communities: 7th Annual conference, Association for contemplative mind in higher education. Washington DC: Howard University.

Lewittes, H. (2015b) The identity Interview project: Integrating critical thinking, contemplative inquiry and the curriculum of modern life. *International Journal of Higher Education*, 21(2), 1-14.

Lewittes, H. (2011) Identity revisited. Association for contemplative mind In higher education conference, Amherst College, MA.

Lewittes, H. (2009) A critical thinking rubric as the basis of assessment and curriculum. In C. Shreiner (Ed.) *Handbook on assessment technologies, methods, and application in higher education.* (pp. 22-46) Hershey, PA: IGI Global

Lewittes, H., Morris, L. (2015) Intentional learning, mindfulness and mindset. 22nd International conference on learning. What counts as learning? Big data, little data, evidence and assessment. Madrid, Spain

Lucas, M. (2010) Rewire your brain for love. http://www.psychologytoday.com/blog/rewire-your-brain-love/201001

Markus, H, Kitiyama, S. (1991) Culture and the self: Implications for cognition, emotion, and motivation. *Psychological Review,* 98(2), 224-253

Mezirow, J. (1978) Perspective transformation, *Adult education quarterly. Vol. 28, no 2, 100-110*

Moyers, B. (2013) John Lewis marches on. BillMoyers.com/video

New Mindful Life. (2013) 20 minute body scan-mindfulness meditation. www.newmindfullife.com Ricard, M. Lutz, A. and Davidson, R. (2014) Mind of the meditator. *Scientific American,* November, 39-45

O'Sullivan, E. (2003) Bringing a perspective of transformative learning to globalized consumption.*International Journal of Consumer Studies*, 27(4), 326-330

Rich, A. (2013) Claiming an education. In A. Anker, M. Feder- Marcus (Eds.) T*he ethics of engagement*: *Educating leaders for a just world* (pp. 350-354). Acton MA: Copley Press

Roth, H (2006). Contemplative studies: Prospects for new field. *Teachers college record*, 108 #9, 1787-1815

Salzberg, S. (2005) *The force of kindness.* Boulder CO*:* Sounds True, Inc.

Selye, H. (1956) The stress of life. NY: Mc Graw Hill

SUNY Old Westbury. (2015a) Office of institutional research. Old Westbury, NY: College at Old Westbury, State University of New York

SUNY Old Westbury. (2015b) *Approved general education courses.* Old Westbury, NY: College at Old Westbury, State University of New York

*SUNY Old Westbury (2014-2016) Undergraduate catalogue.* New York. Old Westbury, NY: College at Old Westbury, State University of New York

Thich Nhat Hahn. (2013) Please call me by my true names. In A. Anker, M. Feder- Marcus (Eds.) T*he ethics of engagement*: *Educating leaders for a just world* (pp. 94-95). Acton MA: Copley Press

Thich Nhat Hahn. (1992) *Peace is in every step*. NY: Bantam Books

Vygotsy, L. (1978) *Mind in society: The development of higher psychological processes*. Cambridge MA: Harvard University Press

Wapner, P. (2010) *Living through the end of nature*. Cambridge Massachusetts: Massachusetts Institute of Technology Press

Warren, J. (2012) Why whales are people too. www.readersdigest.ca/magazine.

Willis, J. (2008). *Dreaming me: Black, Baptist and Buddhist*. Somerville, MA: Wisdom Publications, Inc

CHAPTER 18

## Design Thinking, Universal Design, & Distance/Mobile Education: Impact on Learning

*Barbara Schwartz-Bechet, Roelien Bos-Wierda and Ron Barendsen*

Prospective service providers in education require an active understanding of Design Thinking (DT) and Universal Design for Learning (UDL)/Universal Instructional Design (UID) to be successful practitioners. As DT encourages empathetic understanding and actualization to solve problems through group collaboration and individualization within the group, implementation of UDL principles, through UID principles, enables DT to occur in a supportive and empathetically designed environment. Creative aspects of teaching and learning need to be identified, modeled, and understood to affect the behaviors of educators. Instructional practices are presented, analyzed, and reflected upon as exemplars of learning are identified through expressions of knowledge presented through a variety of approaches and in various formats and contexts. Discussion of how the uses of the information and communication technologies (ICT) of distance education (DE) and mobile learning (m-learning) pedagogies can support DT are presented via investigations of problems and opportunities in a case study format (Elias, 2011).

### INTRODUCTION TO UNIVERSAL DESIGN FOR LEARNING, DESIGN THINKING, AND MOBILE TECHNOLOGIES

The theoretical intersection between Design Thinking and Universal Design for Learning should be direct, yet, there are limited materials published demonstrating the linkage and/or practice resulting from the integration of both theoretical ideas, especially the combination of the two with the integration of mobile learning. Creative techniques for supporting inclusion and empathy through distance education practices are discussed in relation to the design of courses/programs and the design acceptance of responses and assignments. As many of our service providers will receive their training through distance education, breaking down the barriers that lead to creative empathetic teaching and learning in online and hybrid classes will be identified. In order to provide direct insight on the merge of the two concepts, clear definitions are provided to allow for a better understanding. A case study approach will be used to present the integration of the principles associated with Universal Design for Learning and Design Thinking with mobile technologies.

## UNIVERSAL DESIGN FOR LEARNING (UDL)

The definition of Universal Design for Learning is a framework whereby the design of the environment, which includes materials, human resources, curriculum, and space, along with the design of the pedagogy is developed to support academic achievement for any and all students through ensuring equal access. The term UDL was created by Ronald Mace in 1989. His premise was to create environments that supported individuals with disabilities that would allow for maximum opportunities. His idea, stemming from the field of architecture, guided instruction and instructional designers to develop products and services for both face to face and online instruction (Burgstahler, 2002). And, while the concept of UDL is widely known and familiar with educators in the US, its application in the US has been lagging (Rose, Harbour, Johnston, Daley, & Abarbanell, 2006). However, the concept and application of UDL has been highly embraced in the European Union through the support of an Erasmus Project to develop a unified system of practice ( http://www.udlnet-project.eu/, 2015). UDL theory encompasses the access of knowledge for all individuals but it also must include the need to have an available accessible pedagogy. The UDL principles of accessible pedagogy incorporates three processes of teaching and learning: representation, expression, and engagement (CAST, 2003).

## DESIGN THINKING (DT)

The definition of Design Thinking (DT) in education, as a concept, is of moving thoughts and actions forward to find a solution to a problem or question in an empathetic, creative, and innovative manner. It is a way to find answers to complex, unique problems with multiple solutions, where there is not only one result or correct answer. The process develops pupils' and teachers', students' and instructors' ability to act as change agents. It is a concept that is counter to the American and European established competitive model of learning; empathy through active engagement is fostered within groups or teams to work collaboratively to accomplish a task. While working in groups is most often the way that DT is implemented, it also enables the individual to develop insights about oneself and the processes of collaborative self-reflection. It is a concept that can be assistive to the enhancement of teaching practices (Alrubail, 2015). It is not problem based instruction (PBI) as PBI is often focused on coming to one clear point or development of one solution (McIntosh, 2012). Design thinking seeks to develop multiple solutions, and to allow for individuals to collectively think and act tangentially to create related or new experiences that enmesh and engage the learners in a dynamic endeavor.

## Mobile and Distance Education

Pedagogical application as applied to online teaching and learning have and continue to be in the process of development for over 20 years, with mobile devices recently identified as an educational practice technology. It is at this point in time that the institutions of higher education and local school systems have identified that the need to integrate technologies for more interactive teaching and learning, rather than merely as a tool to learn. Mcloughlin and Lee (2011) have indicated that the time is right to move the technology facilitation to a more personalized pedagogy. Network and mobile technologies (NMT's), as teaching and learning devices, need to be integrated by first identifying key variables that will be associated with successful implementation. Trentin, 2013, has identified three necessary caveat's that must be adhered to for NMT's to be effective in teaching: a clear definition of the purpose of the NMT to meet a specific educational outcome, activities identified by educators that can be implemented more effectively by the use of an NMT, and that sufficient training is provided for instructors to successfully integrate the instruction with the system. The use of NMT's may be used as an enhancement to instructional pedagogy (Beetham & Sharpe, 2013). Use of mobile devices, including but not limited to phones, iPads, tablets, digital pens, increases the opportunity to develop and adopt flexible instruction and pedagogy that embraces UDL principles. Accessible technology implementation for learning that follows the three caveats listed above, can be vetted through DT to achieve a desired student centered approach to meeting goals and objectives of a course (Izzo, 2012). As students typically select to learn on their own mobile learning devices (Bradely et. al., 2009), the variability of devices may constitute a dilemma if ideation of how to effectively utilize each device is not determined ahead of instructional design. Portability is an integral to allowing opportunities for all individuals to have access to content and learning opportunities and provides flexible use in a choice in presentation to the individual.

## INTEGRATION OF UDL AND DT AND MT'S: AN EXAMPLE IN PRACTICE

Since Design Thinking (DT) is a set of processes which involves an understanding of the concept to engage in creation through empathy while working with others, it requires the ability to acquire the dispositions to work effectively in a collaborative manner. So, working on or solving a problem, i.e.: construction of accessible teaching and learning for all in a college or a university, Universal Design for Learning (UDL) (and teaching), would be best developed through use of DT processes. The overall outcome of design thinking is to be able to collectively problem solve through innovation and creativity. It also involves iteration of different outcomes with the ability to recognize a problem, and apply an empathetic understanding to the definition and ideate solutions to the problem. Universal Design for Learning is a theory that was devised to meet the challenges of a problem, the problem being primarily equal access to educational opportunities in the form of instruction, content, and understanding of knowledge and skills and through the use of mobile technologies as an optional platform. The audience for whom the design is geared is all, in terms of UDL, to enable anyone to be able to take part in learning. Adding DT which includes empathy, the ability to put oneself in another's shoes and 'feel' how that individual can and will be able to learn, the essence of UDL, enables the problem to be vetted and redefined in operationally effective terms. Not one person is responsible for a definition but a group, as in a school board, an editorial board, a research & development (R&D) group, or any interested members of an organization that provides a service that informs clients/learners in the form of new knowledge sharing, generation, and acquisition. The discovery of a need for change is the first step in design thinking. The change to mobile devices is part of the identified 'problem' that would be addressed. The next step is to define through empathy and interpret what has been learned by recognizing that change is needed (Simon, 1969). Many corporations and companies that developed learning management systems (LMS) were familiar with, understood the value of, and tried to integrate UDL principles into their systems.

Many school systems and institutions of higher education have recognized that need to apply UDL principles and have integrated some of those practices both successfully and some not so successfully. Both United States and European institutions are now starting the process of ideating towards the integration of DT, UDL and mobile learning. Part one of the process is the DT. First, understanding that the problem is to create an environment that is fluid, can accommodate any and all participants, and will allow for equal means of representation, expression and engagement in an online system. The next step in the DT process would bring a group together to empathize with the problem through discourse and actual engagement through experiencing what a lack of vision, lack of hearing, lack of integrative sensory inputs, and lack of cognitive association would be like within the learning management system. So to identify a methodology for applying a systematic form of creativity/innovation, as identified by Papanek, to the selection and the use of, or creation of, e-pedagogy that can be combined through the use of design must facilitate all learners. The planning and developing of a creation that results in an achievable outcome constitutes the design process (Kress, Schar, 2012). Understanding unique ways to view a situation often elicits greater imagination, critical thinking and the development of more than one solution (Cross, 2006). To illustrate the process, a model of how this process can occur is presented below.

**Example of Process**

Initially, the introduction of a question/topic is presented by a person who has had some experience with the perspective or the situation or the need for a problem to be solved. Or, an individual has worked with or for persons who have been effected by, in this case, the lack of adequate service (a problem) in an online course, and have indicated what they would want in the best of all possible worlds.

- Empathize: Empathy would be with, not for, individuals who learn via alternative modes of delivery and engagement and who need to demonstrate their learning and knowledge through non-standard methods of representation. and for those who require
- Define the specific problems through an empathetic lens. Use of positive language to define a problem provides for greater openness to choices of possible solutions. Recognize that technology can be used pedagogically rather than just as a tool to learn. As such, the mobile devices that can be utilized as empathetic mechanisms that enable face to face engagement through VIOP, ensure that the processes involved that include the three concepts works seamlessly.
- Use brainstorming to generate multiple ideas from multiple sources. This can include the use of face to face meetings of multiple constituents and/or virtual discourse by practitioners as well as the possibility of using survey groups, and/or review of data and data sources on hand held devices. In this case, the college in the university, departments

within the college of the university, both individually and collectively, have identified a greater need to include all individuals in instructional practices. As aligned with UDL, the environment and the instruction and the representation of learned material must be accessible without knowing who will be participating in the class.
- Begin to ideate and provide models for successful integration of all three concepts. Look outside higher education for successful innovations and think about how they might apply in context. The use of multidisciplinary teams to collaborate and determine flexible prototyping, in this case, would include a learning management system administrator, consumers, instructors/teachers/preceptors, educators, parents.
- In the best of all possible worlds... "creation of the impossible can become reality with multiple minds, resources, and supports available. All ideas are put into practice through prototypes. Prototypes can include the use of real time, tactile deliverables or can be through the use of technology assisted computer simulations on multiple platforms. By utilizing the later, members from multiple sites can jointly develop meaningful collaborative integration of knowledge, tools, and communication. The groups internalizes the process and takes ownership of their discovery and applications of their understandings.
- Expression of knowledge enables usefulness of instructional practices. Application as essential to the development/understanding and integration through ideation to prototyping.
- Delivery of content, instruction and learning – assess the accessibility of the prototypes through implementation and data collection
- Develop new prototypes or implement with different populations and re-assess

## CASE STUDIES THAT INCORPORATE UDL, DESIGN THINKING & DISTANCE LEARNING

In recent years, schools and Universities in Europe have started to embrace Design Thinking and Universal Design for Learning to replace more traditional views on teaching and learning.

The following case studies are practices that have been developed, implemented and evaluated at and in collaboration with NHL University of Applied Sciences in the Netherlands, and, in some cases, with Universities abroad. NHL University is one of approximately 10 Institutes of Higher

Education offering Teacher Training Programs for Lower and Higher Secondary Education and Primary Education in the Netherlands.

Most Universities and Colleges in the Netherlands have implemented some form of Competency Based learning or Problem Based Learning, combined with more traditional teacher-centered approaches. There is, however, a growing demand for more personalized forms of learning and a more holistic and design-based approach to of curriculum development. Blended or Hybrid learning in combination with the UDL Guidelines and Design Thinking principles seems to go a long way providing the answers.

The first case study describes a pilot carried out collaboratively in the spring of 2013 by a University in Maryland and NHL University.

## Case Study 1

Lecturers and student-teachers of NHL University have developed the educational social network platform MySchoolsNetwork.com to facilitate international communication and collaboration between pupils in elementary and secondary education. Student teachers act as moderators, content developers and e-mentors. Although the platform is a Dutch initiative the language of communication is English. In 2013 a pilot was initiated, involving a group of Master's level graduate students from University of Maryland University College's Master of Arts in teaching program and approximately 50 14-year old secondary school pupils in the Netherlands. The US students were to work on their intercultural and e-mentoring skills while the young Dutch students were expected to benefit from the authentic English communication with native speakers.

The preparation for the project came about by following the theoretical guidelines of UDL and DT. The process began with ideation between faculty members from both universities. The problem identified was the needs of the university students to embrace global understandings through direct international experience and for pupils of English in the Netherlands to engage with pre-service teachers in an authentic use of English language. The ideation process determined that the use of the www.myschoolsnetwork.com platform would be a stellar vehicle to employ for both groups as it is a safe, UDL friendly operating system. The joint understanding of the project promoted the eight UID principles (Elias, 2010) of equitable and friendly use in an instructional climate that had supports and was user friendly for a community of practice.

Although there were some individual successes the pilot on the whole showed many weak points.

Here is a quote from the communication between a US Master student and a Dutch pupil (14)

> Hi Janneke,
>
> As promised, there is now a chart for you to review. I understand that English is not your first language, so please don't be afraid to ask questions, as both the introductory article and the chart are written for a native English speaker. What I'd like you to do is develop a similar chart. What Knowledge, Skills, Abilities, and Dispositions (beliefs, values, attitudes) do you think are essential for a good teacher? I'll be looking to compare and contrast your thoughts with mine.
>
> Best,
>
> N...(www.myschoolsnetwork.com)

Two schools participated in the pilot with a total of 50 students between the ages of 13-15 years. The younger pupils were attending lower vocational education and had a poor command of English. The older group were in high school and had a reasonable command of English as a second language. The first group were so overwhelmed with the academic level of the communication that they didn't respond at all. The second group tried but their teacher had to step in to inform the US students about the effect their mentoring attempts had:

> Hi Nathaniel,
>
> I'm Jelmer's English teacher. I am currently sending a message to all the American students with the request to not overwhelm my students with questions that are almost on an academic level. Please be aware that you are chatting with a 14/15 year old and if you want them to respond to your questions then you have to present it in small chunks and in language that is appropriate to their age group and proficiency level. I can see that Jelmer has really enjoyed some of your conversations and that he is more than willing to continue contact with you. I feel he can benefit so much from having contact with you ( and already has) just don't frighten him off!
>
> Kind regards,

Jeanine (www.myschoolsnetwork.com)

Here is a response from one of the US students to the teacher:

Hi Jeanine,

I am sorry that my questions have been so broad. Unfortunately, our course is structured in such a way that we are asked to have our mentee comment on our version of teaching and various questions related to that. I've tried to tone it down but will refrain from asking more then 2 questions in the future. I think that since this is the first time this is being done the curriculum is not in the best shape. I can delete some of my posts from Frank's page and then recraft my questions.

Best,

Marla

An analysis of this pilot, using the concepts of DT and UDL, will bring out the following points for improvement:

1. UDL assumes firm goals through flexible means. In this case there were very firm goals for the Maryland students (as described in a rubric); the learning outcomes for the Dutch pupils, however, were quite vague. (Benefiting from authentic communication with native speakers). The US students indicated that they did not feel any freedom in the way they were to achieve the desired learning outcomes.
2. The empathy phase was largely lacking in this pilot; the US student were assuming much more language proficiency and metacognitive competencies than the Dutch students actually possessed. Since the current methodological approach at the time did not include the empathy phase the US students went straight for the indicators in the rubric, whereas most Dutch students just backed off and did not respond.
3. Develop an ongoing method to create new prototypes and have the flexibility to utilize different mobile devices as supports throughout the implementation of the project

Conclusion: To improve the course's success and feeling of autonomy and competence with students in this online course it will be helpful

1. to apply the principles of UDL i.e. firm learning outcomes for both parties, to such an extent that :
2. the Design of the learning environment for both parties is an essential part of the learning process on both sides, preceded by
3. a phase in which Empathy and definition of the problem or issue is reached through empathy.

**Case Study 2:**

Two European Universities (NHL University Netherlands and Odisee University Belgium/Brussels) have worked together in a 2 European Credit Program for third-year students in the respective teacher training departments. Until 2013 the program consisted of a mutual exchange program, Belgian students visiting the Netherlands for one week and Dutch students visiting Brussels. Staff delegations from both universities used to design the programs for the two weeks, which invariably resulted in complaining students with a consumer attitude. In 2013 it was decided to try and introduce DT, UDL and DL into the concept. Groups were formed at the start of the academic year, consisting of 3 Brussels and 3 Dutch student teachers. Learning outcomes were clearly formulated and published on a specially designed Community of Practice Online Platform that could be accessed by multiple mobile technologies. The groups were responsible for the design of an attractive and educational program both in the Netherlands and in Belgium that would suit the needs and preferences of all participants. The Empathy and Ideation phases would take place through the online social platform www.myschoolsnetwork.com Students have to put themselves in the position of a foreign professional visiting their country (empathy) after which the draft program is posted online in the form of a wiki. The online rubric for this program establishes the necessary firm goals. It is up to the individual groups how these goals are reached (UDL). All of the preparation for the cultural-educational programs the students develop takes places though DT. On the final day of their one-week visit to Belgium and the Netherlands students present their "week" and everything they have learned and discovered about one another's culture in a creative and entertaining presentation.

Figure 1: The two images show the websites created by two of eleven mixed groups to present the respective programs and budgets for the week in The Netherlands and the week in Brussels. The websites are created collaboratively through DT.

**Exercise:** Online barriers for individuals with disabilities - Ideate
Problem: Images online do not have text equivalents

> Step1; bring together an effective work group made up of experts from the areas of IT, individuals with vision impairments
>
> Step 2: (What would the next step be?)

Problem: Documents are not posted in an accessible format
(What would you do next?)

## CONCLUSION & RECOMMENDATIONS

As new mobile technologies and tools continue to be developed, it is necessary to ensure that all are able to not only be accessible but engage effectively with the technology. By including multiple participants in the creation/ideation, development, through integration of DT and UDL principles, allows for greater inclusion with newly developing pedagogies of content and technology. Disintermediation lends itself to creating instructional formats that are space-free and timeless, to allow for personalization and individualized assessment of learning through a technology of choice. It is clear that data focused research which defines the best uses of the principles in practice is necessary. The future of on demand education that is accessible and empathetic in delivery and output is a consideration that is both ongoing and will allow for even greater viability and use as it continues to develops. Multi-platform relationship across students and teachers is current but fluid in development in continuous and situated learning. But, it is important to remember that ideation is limitless and ideation will guide the future successful integration of UDL, DT, and m-learning.

## REFERENCES

Alrubail, R. (2015). Teaching empathy through design thinking. From a blog pos at: http://www.edutopia.org/blog/teaching-empathy-through-design-thinking-rusul-alrubail

Beetham, H., & Sharpe, R. (Eds.) (2013). *Rethinking Pedagogy for Digital Age*. New York, NY: Routledge.

Bradley, C., Haynes, R., Cook, J., Boyle, T., & Smith, C. (2009). Design and development of multimedia learning objects for mobile phones. In M.

Ally (Ed.) *Mobile learning: Transforming the delivery of education and training* (pp. 157-182). Edmonton, AB: Athabasca University Press.

Burgstahler, S. (2002). Distance learning: Universal design, universal access. *AACE Journal, 10*, 32-61.

Cross, N. (2006). *Designerly ways of knowing*. London: Springer-Verlag.

Elias, T. (2011). Universal instructional design principles for mobile learning. *International Review of Research in Open and Distance Learning, 12.2*, 143-156.

Gregson, J., & Jordaan, D. (2009). Exploring the challenges and opportunities of m-learning within an international distance education programme. In M. Ally (Ed.) *Mobile learning: Transforming the delivery of education and training* (pp. 215-246). Edmonton, AB: Athabasca University Press.

Higher Education Opportunity Act (2008). http://www.gpo.gov/fdsys/pkg/PLAW-110publ315/pdf/PLAW-110publ315.pdf

Graves, L.M., Asunda, P. A., Plant, S., & Goad, C. (2012). Asynchronous online access as an accommodation on students with learning disabilities and/or Attention Deficit Hyperactivity Disorders in postsecondary STEM courses. *Journal of Postsecondary Education and Disability, 24*, 317-330. gsucre.edublogs.org

Izzo, M.V. (2012). Universal design for learning: Enhancing achievement of students with disabilities. *Procedia Computer Science, 14*, 343-350.

Kress, G.L., & Schar, M. 2012. Teamology - the art and science of design team formation. In: Plattner, H., Meinel, C. Leifer, L. (eds) *Design Thinking Research: Measuring Performance in Context*. Springer, London, pp. 189-209.

McIntosh, E. (2012). http://edu.blogs.com/edublogs/2012/08/whats-the-difference-between-pbl-and-design-thinking.html

Mcloughlin, C., & Lee, J.W.(Eds.) (2011). Web 2.0 based e-learning: applying social informatics for tertiary teaching. Hersey, PA: Information Science Reference.

Papanek, Victor. (1971). *Design for the real world*. New York: Pantheon B

Plattner, H., et al. (eds.),(2014) *Design Thinking Research, Understanding Innovation*, DOI 10.1007/978-3--319--01303-9_2, Springer International Publishing Switzerland

Pittman, C.N., & Heiselt, A.K. (2014). Increasing accessibility: Using universal design principles to address disability impairments in the online learning environment. Online Journal of Distance Learning Administration, 17 (3) 1-11.

Rose, D., Harbour, W., S., Johnston, C.S., Daley, S.G., & Abarbanell, L (2006). Universal design for learning in postsecondary education: Reflections on principles and there application. *Journal of Postsecondary Education and Disability, 19*(2), 135-151.

Rose, D., & Meyer, A. (2002). Teaching Every Student in the Digital Age. *ASCD*.

Scott, S. McGuire, J., Shaw, S. (2003). Universal Design for instruction: A new paradigm for adult instruction in post-secondary education. *Remedial and Special Education, 24*(6), 369- 379.

Simon (1969). *The Sciences of the Artificial*. MIT Press, Cambridge, Mass, 1st edition.

Scatligg, A.,K, & Meier, A. (2012). Holistic learner engagement for success in the innovation age: Portfolio, Strengths based and collaborative learning strategies. In *Increasing Student Engagement and Retention using Social Technologies: Facebook, ePortfolios and other Social Networking Services. Cutting Edge Technologies in Higher Education*, 6B, 17-55.

Trentin, G. (2013). Network and mobile technologies in education: A call for e-teachers. In G. Trentin & M. Repetto (Eds). *Using Network and Mobile Technology to Bridge Formal and iNformatl Learning* (pp. 153-182). Oxford, UK: Woodhead/Chandos Publishing Limited.

CHAPTER 19

# Developing Self-management Capacity in Student Learning: A Pilot Implementation of Blended Learning Strategies in the Study of Business Law

*Jacquelyn Cranney, Leela Cejnar and Vik Nithy*

## ABSTRACT

In recent years, the education sector has become increasingly cognisant of the need to provide students with opportunities to acquire not just discipline knowledge, but also self-management skills. Such skills would be beneficial to students dealing with "stressors" while they are studying and ultimately, in the workplace—a workplace which is constantly changing and reflective of the new knowledge economy (Curtis & McKenzie, 2001). Indeed, low levels of distress and high levels of well-being are considered prerequisites to high levels of cognitive functioning such as the capacity for synthesis, which is foundational to creativity.

This chapter discusses a pilot implementation of an Academic Self-management Program (ASMP), trialed within a higher education setting in a large, first-year undergraduate business law course during 2015. It defines self-management and then provides an overview of the approach employed and the range of blended strategies adopted to integrate opportunities for the development of self-management capacity into the curriculum of that particular course. Reflections on the process and outcomes are given, with recommendations for future implementations.

## INTRODUCTION

Students across the education spectrum experience numerous stressors, which if not appropriately self-managed, can lead to anxiety, distress, poor academic performance, withdrawal, and a range of other health, well-being and performance-related issues (Stallman, 2011). Self-management is the capacity to work effectively toward achieving meaningful goals, and to be flexible in the face of setbacks (Cranney & Nithy, 2015; Cranney et al., in prep). This definition encompasses the capacities for goal-directed behavior and for resilience, both of which are reliant on an underlying capacity for psychological flexibility. Clearly, self-management is essential to the successful completion of higher education studies and to the later, ongoing success of the graduate in the workplace (Field, Duffey, & Huggins, 2014). Indeed, self-management is specified by some disciplines (e.g., Law: Huggins, 2011) as a threshold learning outcome, and by some universities (e.g., Deakin University, n.d.) as a university-wide graduate capability, and is related to the concept of psychological literacy (Cranney & Dunn, 2011; Cranney, Andrews, & Morris, 2016; Cranney, Botwood, & Morris, 2012).

Specifically, one of the aims of university education is to produce *"...professionals capable of ethical and sustained self-directed practice and independent lifelong learning"* (University of New South Wales Learning and Teaching Strategy 2014, p.1). This intended graduate capability has several elements that go beyond the acquisition of content knowledge and professional skills specific to the particular discipline/profession. To acquire *"sustained self-directed practice and independent lifelong learning"* skills, graduates must be trained to engage in self-development, which in turn ensures longer-term professional development (Tano & Vines, 2009) and career success. Self-development is one aspect of self-management.

Indeed, self-management is sometimes conceptualized as "self-leadership" (Neck & Houghton, 2006). Future leaders, including those of the business community, require a high level of resilience/self-leadership capacity, in order to effectively manage stress, change and new learning. These "non technical" skills are regarded as characteristic of successful mangers; however, business graduates often struggle with these "non-technical" skills in the workplace, irrespective of excellent academic records (Andrews & Higson, 2008; Bennett, 2002; Jackson & Chapman, 2012; Kavagnah & Drennan, 2008; Tempone, Kavanagh, Segal, Hancock, Howieson, & Kent, 2012; Wilton, 2008). To develop/improve these skills in employees, employers often need to create special training. Higher education institutions can address this gap in the "career readiness" of their graduates by embedding self-management skills in education programs and accreditation requirements, especially as these skills are considered as managerial best practice (Bridgstock, 2009; Harvey, 2001; McQuaid & Lindsay, 2005).

In addition, with increasing pressure on students to perform well (Andrews & Chong, 2011; Stallman & Shochet, 2009), the capacity to self-manage in the face of multiple stressors is even more important. This is particularly the case for students in large first-year courses, where compared to high school, there is less structure, less support, and greater likelihood of social isolation, leaving the student more vulnerable to distress (Kift, 2008). For business students, reported distress levels have been high, associated with maladaptive behaviours such as alcohol abuse (e.g., Dahlin, Nilsson, Stotzer, & Runeson, 2011). With additional stressors resulting from language, cultural and educational differences, this distress is compounded in international students, who constitute a large proportion of the business student cohort (Rosenthal et al., 2006; Zhou, Willis, & Chen, 2010).

During 2015, the use of evidence-based blended learning strategies was trialed within a large first year undergraduate business law course. The intent was to ascertain whether the students would perceive as useful the implementation of a set of self-management resources into the curriculum, and thus drive further improvements to the implementation. The strategies included topics students commonly considered of interest, such as time-management, procrastination and study strategies. Although extracurricular resources to support students in these areas are available on a university-wide level to students, these resources are often not used by time-poor students.

The resources included tasks that would take relatively short amounts of time to cover the essential information but that required students to actively engage (e.g., through watching short videos, involving themselves in question and answer activities, engaging in self-reflection and self-evaluation exercises, setting personal goals and plans and discussing these with peers). In other words, the approach attempted to be personalized, providing students with opportunities to develop self-management skills that they could apply within and beyond the particular target course.

The next section provides an overview of the theoretical framework that underpins the need for self-management. The chapter continues with a discussion of the pilot implementation—the approach, findings and in particular what was learnt across two semesters regarding the appropriateness of the design and procedure from the student and instructor perspectives.

## THEORETICAL RATIONALE FOR THE NEED TO EMBED SELF-MANAGEMENT INTO THE CURRICULUM

The theoretical framework underpinning both the approach and method adopted to implement the self-management strategies, emphasizes evidence-based behavioral change strategies derived from psychological science. In relation to the definition of self-management, the concept of resilience is first considered, as this is essential to "being flexible in the face of setbacks". We then briefly consider theory relevant to the precursor of the "setback", that is, the motivational concepts underlying goal pursuit.

The American Psychological Association's (APA) "Road to Resilience" approach defines resilience as "…the process of adapting well in the face of… significant sources of stress -- such as family and relationship problems, serious health problems, or workplace and financial stressors. It means "bouncing back" from difficult experiences". The APA argues that there are five primary factors in resilience: "having caring and supportive relationships within and outside the family… capacity to make realistic plans and take steps to carry them out… positive view of yourself and confidence in your strengths and abilities… skills in communication and problem solving… capacity to manage strong feelings and impulses".

Crucially, the APA argues that resilience skills can be learned by anyone, and this provides the rationale for integration of self-management learning strategies into the curriculum. They state a number of ways in which resilience can be built: establishing connections with others, avoiding the perception that obstacles are insurmountable, accepting that change is a part of living, moving towards personal goals, acting decisively, seeking opportunities for self-discovery, nurturing a positive self-image, keeping things in perspective and looking after oneself. Many of these empirically validated behavioral change strategies were purposefully integrated into the design of the curricular and co-curricular innovations of the present initiative.

One example of previous work in this area is that of Stallman (2011) who integrated a *"Keeping on Track"* seminar into a first year psychology course. Tapping into six of the APA's suggested methods to increase resilience, the program was rated as highly satisfying, useful and a catalyst for changes in their own behavior. Resilience-building programs such as that of Stallman (2011) are increasingly being built into curriculum programs in a number of different disciplines (e.g., Field, 2014).

Considered as either a concept or a strategy, "resilience" features strongly within the positive psychology literature. Furthermore, it should be noted that whole-school positive education approaches at the primary and secondary level (particularly those utilizing strengths-based strategies) have been shown to decrease rates of depression and increase well-being and academic performance (e.g., Luiselli et al., 2005). Despite the advances of positive education in the school sector and the expectations these experiences generate in students transitioning from school to university, the implementation of positive psychology approaches at the tertiary education level has been less common. Unfortunately, those that are implemented at the tertiary level tend to be "one-off" and isolated strategies rather than a sustained set of complementary strategies (Seligman et al., 2005; Vella-Broderick, 2011).

A theoretical framework that dovetails nicely with resilience and positive psychology is self-determination theory (SDT), which has been applied successfully within educational, organizational, and clinical psychology subfields (Deci & Ryan, 2000; see http://www.selfdeterminationtheory.org/). Indeed, SDT is most relevant to the first half of the self-management definition, that is, goal-striving behavior. According to SDT, well-being is achieved when the basic psychological needs of autonomy, competence and relatedness are met. Autonomy is particularly relevant to the meaningfulness of goals, as Sheldon and Elliott (1999) have argued that self-concordant goals (goals aligned with one's values, emerging interests, and strengths) are more likely to be achieved and are more likely to lead to well-being.

A concept that is integral to both the goal-striving and resilience aspects of self-management is psychological flexibility, which is defined as *"the ability to contact the present moment more fully as a conscious human being, and to change or persist in behavior when doing so serves valued ends"* (Hayes, Luoma, Bond, Masuda, & Lillis, 2006, p.7). Although goal-pursuit persistence is often "all" that is required, during the average goal-striving sequence, it is highly likely that the situation deviates from that which one expected or desired. It is therefore essential that one is willing to modify the strategies that one employs to achieve sub-goals, or even be prepared to change the goal to varying extents. Even then, if one fails to achieve the original or modified goal or sub-goal (i.e., one experiences a set-back), one must be capable of regulating the emotional and cognitive reactions to that failure, and discover ways to continue to take actions toward "valued ends". Hence, psychological flexibility is inherent in both components of self-management.

In a rapidly evolving global digital economy, innovative leaders will require greater levels of entrepreneurial and creative thinking (Wagner, 2012). It is argued that self-management forms a foundation for young people to build the capacity for creative and innovative thinking. For example, there is an established neuropsychological connection between various forms of meditation and creativity (Horan, 2009), as well as the relationship between time management and creativity (Zampetakis, Bouranta, & Moustakis, 2010). Further, individuals with greater well-being overall also demonstrate greater creativity (Wright & Walton, 2003). Since repeated challenges and setbacks are an integral part of creative and entrepreneurial processes, resilience (one component of self-management) is critical for innovative leaders (Envick, 2004). The increasing role of creativity and innovation in the 21$^{st}$ century workplace adds credence to the integration of self-management capabilities in tertiary education.

Finally, the concept of identity negotiation during the university student lifecycle (Lizzio, 2006, 2012) is a critical psychological concept from the student perspective, whereby in the first year the student's task is to become a successful student, while in the final year the student's task is to prepare to be a successful graduate. The positive psychology, SDT and self-identity theory and research informs the position that the beginning student's explicit awareness and application of psychological knowledge should result in more adaptive goal-directed behavior, and therefore, more successful goal attainment and consequent consolidation of the self-concept of a "successful student" (Lizzio, 2006, 2012; Sheldon & Elliott, 1999).

In summary, the opportunity to acquire greater self-management skills within the tertiary curriculum, particularly during the critical first-year courses, may lead to more effective management of multiple stressors, and thus greater academic success. These self-management skills can be adapted and built upon as the student makes the transition from the final year into the workplace, where employers often complain that students do not have the kind of self-management skills that are necessary to be successful in this new and challenging environment (Lizzio & Wilson, 2004). Universities should promote broader career management competence in students (Bridgstock, 2009), and the starting point should be opportunities for self-management capacity building in core first-year courses—which is the focus of this pilot program.

## Academic Self-Management Program (ASMP): Implementation, Approach and Findings

This section reports on implementations across the two semesters of the 2015 academic year in the first-year business and law course at the University of New South Wales, Australia.

In Semester 1 of 2015, self-management resources (videos, worksheets) on the topics of time, motivation, study and well-being management, were developed and integrated into the learning, teaching and assessment strategies of several courses to varying extents, depending on the context. For the business and law course, Semester 1 was a very light implementation, whereas Semester 2 was a more targeted implementation. Indeed, as the year unfolded, the team identified five sequential topics relevant to effective self-management: meaningful goal definition; time management and planning; psychological flexibility through mindfulness; goal-striving visualizations; and metacognitive thinking about values and well-being (Cranney & Nithy, 2015). The in-class activities were usually presented within the first 5-10 minutes of tutorials (unless otherwise stated). Table 1 sets out the sequence of activities for both semesters, with brief explanations of the materials and the rationale. The strategies also included placing the tutorial materials, as well as extra video links and worksheets, on the online learning management system (LMS; i.e., this was the blended component). A manual describing in more detail some of these activities is now available (Cranney & Nithy, 2015).

Table 1. Weekly In-class and Supportive Online ASMP Activities: Semesters 1 & 2.

| WEEK | In-class Activity | Description & Rationale | Online/co-curricular component |
|---|---|---|---|
| | **SEMESTER 1** | | |
| 3 | Introduction to ASMP & Defining Goals video, in lectures | Project officer introduced ASMP. 5-min video presented the importance of goal setting and some key steps. *Rationale*: Introduction required; defining goal = first step in planning. | Intro. to ASMP on LMS, including invitation to join co-curricular program & complete survey. |
| 4 | Defining Goals worksheet in tutorials | Asked students to select meaningful goal, then go through planning steps. Occurred in tutorials at the tutor's discretion. *Rationale*: Defining goals is the first step in planning. | Defining Goals video and worksheet on LMS. *Rationale*: reinforce in-class activities. |
| 5, mid-semester break | Time-management worksheet in tutorials | Asked students to schedule their time in order to achieve their goals. This activity occurred in tutorials at the tutor's discretion. *Rationale*: once goals chosen, scheduling goal-striving behavior is the next step. | Growth mindset video on LMS. *Rationale*: Bolster motivation to strive for goals. Study strategies video on LMS. *Rationale*: Reexamine strategies to achieve goals. |
| 6 | | | Mindfulness video & procrastination worksheet on LMS. *Rationale:* Reexamine strategies to deal with barriers to goals. |

| 12 | Post-survey via co-curricular program & some tutorials | | |
|---|---|---|---|
| | **SEMESTER 2** | | |
| 1 | | | LMS intro to ASMP and *www.thefridge.org.au* |
| 3 | Pre-survey | 5-10 min survey | Goal selection video and worksheet. |
| 4 | Assessment Time Management worksheet | Brief explanation, with a few minutes to start filling in worksheet. Asked to break down assessments into sub-tasks. *Rationale*: This worksheet allowed students to personalize goal-striving in relation to course assessments. | Assessment Time Management worksheet; Student time management video; Covey task on prioritization; video on procrastination. |
| 6 | Well-being Audit worksheet. | Brief explanation, with a few minutes to start completing. Asked to think critically about their well-being using worksheet. *Rationale*: Balancing competing demands forms the foundation for effective academic performance. | Well-being Audit worksheet. |
| 7 | Procrastination and Mindfulness | Brief procrastination and mindfulness activity led by project officer. *Rationale*: procrastination is a common issue for students, and mindfulness is an effective strategy. | Procrastination and Mindfulness worksheet. |
| 9 | Contrasting worksheet. | Students asked to visualize achieving the goal, then barriers, contingency strategies and implementation intentions. *Rationale*: Re-examines planning and implementation. | Contrasting Exercise worksheet. Stressor Management worksheet. |

| 10 | Mindfulness For Stress | Mindful Relaxation Techniques. *Rationale*: Deep breathing stimulates parasympathetic nervous system activity. | |
|---|---|---|---|
| 11 | Post-survey | 5-10 min survey. | |
| 13 | Reminder by tutor. | *Rationale*: As students prepared for exams, the resources (all on LMS) could be re-used. | |

In Semester 1, in addition to the in-class activities, an optional co-curricular program was developed to allow student pre-post surveying. This also involved the construction of a student-centered website with modules on goal and time management, motivation management, work and study management, and well-being management: www.thefridge.org.au. There was insufficient take-up of the co-curricular program to allow reliable within or cross-course comparison, however the qualitative responses from the course-coordinator and the students was encouraging. In the interview at the end of Semester 1 (July, 2015) the course coordinator made the following comments:

> "Of course we all know that if you're organized, you're less likely to be stressed etc. So that aspect of it – getting students into the right framework for the longer term and not just for their studies... but if you get the right skills these are habits that we are talking about... then you are set up for life. Working life";

> "... the course is being used as an exemplar of how to be mindful of student wellbeing instead of just imparting knowledge"; "I think this is something that should be implemented at all first year level courses"; "I think that it has been a very worthwhile partnership."

In response to the question during the Week 12 co-curricular post-survey, of whether and how (if yes) they would recommend the co-curricular program to others, these are some student responses:
*"It's useful but you have to commit to letting it be useful for you".*

> "It's a good way to get yourself into good habits and learn how to better manage yourself."

> "Informative and is a good reminder to reinforce aspects of managed that may prove valuable in life."

Semester 2 involved the development of new materials, and pre-post paper surveys were administered in a total of eight tutorials—four where there were no in-class activities, and four where there were regular in-class activities. Initial analysis of variables such as well-being and resilience revealed no differences between the two conditions. In addition, the students in the classes with in-class activities on average rated the activities as neutral, with some variability, indicating that while some students appreciated the activities, others did not. When asked which activity/resource was most or least valuable, there was heterogeneity in the responses. That is, significant numbers indicated the time-management activity as most useful, but significant numbers indicated it as least useful—similarly with the mindfulness exercises. This outcome suggests that students come into the course with different needs, and so will respond differently to the different exercises.

## Conclusion—The Way Forward

Over two semesters, this pilot project attempted to integrate self-management strategies into the curriculum of a first year business law course. From the Semester 1 program, it was clear that tutor buy-in was low and hence student engagement was minimal, so that there was no attempt to persist in later weeks.

In Semester 2, a professional relationship was formed with the most interested tutor from the previous semester. While she contributed to the choice of the activities delivered in her classes, it is clear that staff development and engagement is essential in any endeavors to change curriculum practice.

The impact of the Academic Self-Management Program in this course was also limited by the lack of opportunity to have the material assessed. This proposition is often challenging in non-psychology disciplines, but it is not impossible (e.g., multiple choice questions in quizzes). Local constraints often mitigate against assessment, but nevertheless, engaging in-class activities does appear to have a substantial impact, given the right conditions.

In particular, it is recommended that future implementations in courses such as these include the following:

1. The selection of some key activities that course coordinators and tutors feel comfortable delivering themselves (e.g., video in lecture; assessment

time-management worksheets in tutorial classes), and which are well-timed in relation to course assessments;
2. The related professional development that would allow tutors to feel comfortable delivering these activities;
3. Reference by the course coordinators and tutors to useful materials that they might not themselves feel comfortable in delivering (e.g., mindfulness meditation materials on the learning management system);
4. The appointment of a senior tutor to hold regular consultation hours, during which students are encouraged to pose not just discipline-related queries, but also more generic self-management queries related to effective completion of assessments (Cranney et al., in prep). This tutor would be well-trained to reinforce the student's use of the materials mentioned above.
5. Given the increasing momentum of this field, course coordinators should be cognisant of developments in curriculum-integrated self-management approaches (e.g., engagement strategies, peer mentoring), possibly through participation in relevant communities of practice.
6. Adoption of a university-wide approach to curricular integration of the graduate capability of self-management.

The initiatives reported in this chapter represents an initial attempt to gauge the receptivity of students and staff to the integration of evidence-based self-management strategies into the curriculum of a large first-year (non-psychology) course. Several lessons were learned and there has been sufficient encouragement from interested staff and students to stimulate continued attempts to provide students with the knowledge and skills to better manage their studies, and ultimately, their careers.

## REFERENCES

American Psychological Association (n.d.). *The Road to Resilience*. Retrieved from http://www.apa.org/helpcenter/road-resilience.aspx#

Andrews, A., & Chong J. L. Y. (2011). Exploring the wellbeing of students studying at an Australian university. *JANZSSA*, *37*, 9-38.

Andrews, J., & Higson, H. (2008). Graduate employability, 'soft skills' versus 'hard' business knowledge: A European study. *Higher Education in Europe*, 33, 411-422. doi: 10.1080/037977208025226

Bennett, R. (2002). Employers' demands for personal transferable skills in graduates: A content analysis of 1000 job advertisements and an associated empirical study. *Journal of Vocational Education & Training, 54,* 457-476. doi: 10.1080/1363682020020020

Bridgstock, R. (2009). The graduate attributes we've overlooked: Enhancing graduate employability through career management skills. *Higher Education Research and Development, 28,* 31-44. doi: 10.1080/07294360802444434

Cranney, J., Andrews, A., & Morris, S. (2016, under revision). Curriculum renewal to build student resilience and success: Phase 1 [ID12-2381]. OLT Final report.

Cranney, J., Botwood, L., & Morris, S. (2012). National standards for psychological literacy and global citizenship: Outcomes of undergraduate psychology education. [2012 National Teaching Fellowship Final report]. Sydney. ISBN 978-1-922125-97-1. Retrieved from https://groups.psychology.org.au/Assets/Files/Cranney_NTF_Final_Report_231112_Final_pdf.pdf

Cranney, J., & Dunn, D. (Eds.) (2011). *The psychologically literate citizen: Foundations and global perspectives.* New York, NY: Oxford University Press. ISBN- 13: 978-0-19-979494-2

Cranney, J., & Nithy, V. (2015). Academic Self-Management Program Manual. Retrieved from www.unistudentsuccess.com/the-fridge

Cranney, J., Nithy, V...... (in prep). Collaborative Perspectives on Self-management. The University of New South Wales.

Curtis, D., & McKenzie, P. (2001). *Employability skills for Australian industry: Literature review and framework development.* Melbourne: Report to Australian Council for Educational Research.

Dahlin, M., Nilsson, C., Stotzer, E., & Runeson, B. (2011). Mental distress, alcohol use and help-seeking among medical and business students: A cross-sectional comparative study. *BMC Medical Education, 11,* 92-100. http://www.biomedcentral.com/1472-6920/11/9

Deakin University (n.d.). *Deakin Graduate Learning Outcomes.* Retrieved from http://www.deakin.edu.au/learning/designing-assessing-and-evaluating-learning/deakin-graduate-learning-outcomes)

Deci, E. L., & Ryan, R. M. (2000). The "what" and "why" of goal pursuits: Human needs and the self-determination of behavior. *Psychological Inquiry, 11*, 227-268. doi: 10.1207/s15327965pli1104_01

Envick, B. R. (2004). Beyond human and social capital: The importance of positive psychological capital for entrepreneurial success. *Academy of Entrepreneurship*, 10 (2), 13.

Field, R. (2014). Promoting law student well-being through the curriculum. Office for Teaching and Learning Final Fellowship Report. Retrieved from http://www.olt.gov.au/resource-promoting-law-student-well-being-through-curriculum

Field, R., Duffy, J., & Huggins, A. (2014). *Lawyering and positive professional identities*. Chatswood: LexisNexis Butterworths.

Harvey, L. (2001). Defining and measuring employability. *Quality in Higher Education, 7*(2), 97-109.

Hayes, S. C., Luoma, J. B., Bond, F. W., Masuda, A., & Lillis, J. (2006). Acceptance and commitment therapy: Model, processes and outcomes. *Behaviour Research and Therapy, 44*, 1-25.

Horan, R. (2009). The neuropsychological connection between creativity and meditation. *Creativity Research Journal,* 21(2-3), 199-222.

Huggins, A. (2011). The threshold learning outcome of self-management for the Bachelor of Laws degree: A proposed focus for teaching strategies in the first year law curriculum. *The International Journal of the First Year in Higher Education, 2*(2), 23-44. doi: 10.5204/intjfyhe.v2i2.82

Jackson, D. A., & Chapman, E. (2012). Non-technical skill gaps in Australian business graduates. *Education &Training, 54(2-3)*, 95-113.

Kavagnah, M. H., & Drennan, L. (2008). What skills and attributes does an accounting graduate need? Evidence from student perceptions and employer expectations. *Accounting and Finance, 48*, 279-300.

Kift, S. (2008). The next, great, first year challenge: Sustaining, coordinating and embedding coherent institution–wide approaches to enact the FYE as "everybody's business". In 11th International Pacific Rim First Year in Higher Education Conference, An Apple for the Learner: Celebrating the First Year Experience, 2008, Hobart, 16. Retrieved August 14, 2008.

Lizzio, A. (2006). Designing an orientation and transition strategy for commencing students. Downloaded from http://www.griffith.edu.au/__data/assets/pdf_file/0008/51875/Alfs-5-Senors-Paper-FYE-Project,-2006.pdf Retrieved 23/09/2014.

Lizzio, A. (2012). *The student lifecycle: An integrative framework for next-generation student-centered practice*. Manuscript in preparation, Griffith University.

Lizzo, A., & Wilson, K. (2004). Action learning in higher education: An investigation of its potential to develop professional capability. *Studies in Higher Education, 29*, 469-488.

Luiselli, J. K., Putnam, R. F., Handler, M. W., & Feinberg, A. B. (2005). Whole-school positive behavior support: Effects on student discipline problems and academic performance. *Educational Psychology, 25*, 183-198.

McQuaid, R. W., & Lindsay, C. (2005). The concept of employability. *Urban Studies, 42*(2), 197-219.

Neck, C. P., & Houghton, J. D. (2006). Two decades of self-leadership theory and research: Past developments, present trends, and future possibilities. *Journal of Managerial Psychology, 21*, 270-295.

Rosenthal, D. A., Russell, V. J., & Thomson, G. D. (2006). *Growing experience: The health and wellbeing of international students at the University of Melbourne*. Downloaded on January 31, 2012 from http://cms.unimelb.edu.au/__data/assets/pdf_file/0011/358436/GrowingExperience.pdf

Seligman, M. E. P., Steen, T. A., Park, N., & Peterson, C. (2005). Positive psychology progress: Empirical validation of interventions. *American Psychologist, 60*, 410-421.

Sheldon, K. M., & Elliot, A. J. (1999). Goal striving, need satisfaction, and longitudinal well-being: The self-concordance model. *Journal of Personality and Social Psychology, 76*, 482.

Stallman, H.M. (2011). Embedding resilience within the tertiary curriculum: A feasibility study. *Higher Education Research & Development, 30*, 121-133.

Stallman, H.M., & Shochet, I.M. (2009). Prevalence of mental health problems in university general practices. *Australian Psychologist, 44*, 122-127.

Tano, M., & Vines, P. (2009). Law students' attitudes to education: Pointer to depression in the legal academy and the profession? *Legal Education Review, 3*, 3-39.

Tempone, I., Kavanagh, M., Segal, N., Hancock, P., Howieson, B. & Kent, J. (2012). Desirable generic attributes for accounting graduates into the twenty-first century: The views of employers. *Accounting Research Journal, 25*(1), 41-55.

The University of New South Wales (2014). *Learning and Teaching Strategy 2014-2018*. Retrieved from https://teaching.unsw.edu.au/sites/default/files/upload-files/UNSW%20Learning%20and%20Teaching%20Strategy%202014%20-%202018.pdfThe

Vella-Brodrick, D. A. (2011) Positive psychology: Reflecting on the past and projecting into the future. *InPsych, 33(2)*. Retrieved from http://www.psychology.org.au/publications/inpsych/2011/april/vella-brodrick/#s1

Wagner, T., & Compton, R. A. (2015). *Creating innovators: The making of young people who will change the world.* Simon & Schuster.

Wilton, N. (2008). Business graduates and management jobs: An employability match made in heaven?, *Journal of Education and Work, 21*, 143-158. doi:10.1080/13639080802080949

University of New South Wales (2014) *Learning and Teaching Strategy 2014-2018*. See: https://teaching.unsw.edu.au/strategy

Zampetakis, L. A., Bouranta, N., & Moustakis, V. S. (2010). On the relationship between individual creativity and time management. *Thinking Skills and Creativity, 5*(1), 23-32.

Zhou, C., Willis, P., & Chen, G. (2010). The price of learning: A study of Chinese students' psychological challenges in South Australia (ISANA Conference Presentation). Retrieved on 31/1/2012 from: http://www.cdesign.com.au/proceedings_isana2010/PDF/paper_zhou.pdf?id=254&file=P:/Eventwin/docs/pdf/isana2010Abstract00066.pdf

ACKNOWLEDGEMENTS

Support for this project was provided by UNSW Australia, and support for some of the resources referred to in this chapter was provided by the Australian Government Office for Learning and Teaching. The views expressed in this publication do not necessarily reflect the views of UNSW Australia or the Australian Government Office for Learning and Teaching. We thank those associated with this and previous projects, particularly Lyn Brady, Sue Morris,

Peter Baldwin, Annie Andrews, Annette Olschewski, Leigh Mellish, Jun Mo Jeong, Taylor Innes and Lorayne Botwood.

# Afterword

*Kathryn Coleman*

Five years ago I was working with a team of 'creatives' in a learning and teaching unit in a large Australian research university. To find yourself in a team of artists outside of the art community provides for fantastic opportunities to explore ideas, push boundaries and develop new approaches in education together. Here, I met Adele Flood and Belinda Allen, both creativity researchers and practicing artists. I had found a team where ideas were all worth sharing, exploring and testing. Where creativity was to be applauded and harnessed. Stories, narrative, practice based research and reflection were highlighted as important aspects of our team structure and culture. It was at this time, when Belinda invited me to contribute to the following paper with her for an educational technology conference. It is interesting to go back and begin the conversation again in a collaborative paper, to see that your collective thoughts have not changed all that much and sad at the same time, that we have not seen the uptake of portfolios as much as we would have liked for creativity and personal identity development. I asked Belinda if we could re-visit and re-publish our paper to conclude this collection, because it felt like the afterword, like all of these authors had been in conversation at one of those hilarious conference tables where everyone talks over each other, yet clearly hear what the others are saying, and Belinda and I, excitedly share our ideas on portfolios and creative practice.

This Series, Creativity in Learning and Teaching and more importantly, this collection of chapters in this book, Enabling Reflective Thinking: Reflection and Reflective Practice in Learning and Teaching is like listening in on my colleague's conversations. They are not 'academic' conference papers as such, they are stories that enable your own reflection of practice and prompt experiences and memories or invite new discourse.

To continue the conversation, and follow the narrative and reflective journeys these authors have taken us on, I hope that our revisit of this paper takes the conversation to another space just as we all find ourselves. Sadly, that little team of *creatives*, is no longer working together, but these edited collections and books have tied us loosely together through the new stories we have to tell.

# The Creative Graduate: Cultivating and Assessing Creativity with ePortfolios

*Belinda Allen and Kathryn Coleman*

Changing demands of universities, including technology shifts, the cost of tuition, self-directed digital learning opportunities and graduate employability have all underpinned the growing emphasis on a graduate's capabilities and attributes in recent years. This has led to great reform in Australian universities and seen new forms of teaching, learning and assessment in institutions that place standards, learning and the learner at the center of the lens. Through our work as educators and academic developers we have seen skills, experiences and knowledge gained over a student's learning journey become increasingly personalized, authentic and evidence-based. To evidence this increasingly personalized and blended learning, graduate attributes and capabilities have been reviewed in many universities to enable responsive, creative, adaptable, employable graduates. The 2014, Australian Graduate Outlook Survey (As ranked by employers; ranked by proportion of employers who considered each to be an important selection criterion) tell us that what employers want of graduates is:

- communication skills,
- academic results,
- teamwork skills,
- aptitude,
- interpersonal skills,
- leadership skills,
- work experience,
- cultural fit,
- motivational fit, and
- adaptability.

Where does creativity fit in this list? 'Creativity' is a widely promoted graduate attribute that is more a disposition than a capability or competency. As such it relates to other more defined attributes and capabilities, such as critical reasoning and analytical skills/technical skills, entrepreneurial leadership, independent learning and innovative problem-solving. However, to map and align this attribute to learning opportunities, assessment practices need to become more focused on the evaluation of such generic capabilities, additional to assessment of discipline-specific knowledge. This has implications for the curation of content, learning design and types of assessment across a student's journey. Assessment *as* learning promotes an approach in which the learning assessments occur either formatively or summatively, through assessment design in authentic contexts such as group and team-based learning, reflective practice, experiential learning and problem-based learning using real world learning tasks.

This afterword explores creativity as a graduate capability and attribute, the creative potential of digital learning, and how changing directions in assessment practice could support the assessment of creativity, with a focus on using digital portfolios for assessment and evidence of learning.

## THE CREATIVE GRADUATE

Creativity is increasingly represented in higher education aspiration statements as an attribute that graduates require to successfully engage in contemporary and future professional life. As discussed above, this relates to a range of generic capabilities and skills, but how are these to be embedded into curriculum and assessment practice? This edited collection has investigated a range of strategies, with specific focus on reflection and reflective practice, portfolios and journals.

Portfolios have been widely used in 'creative' disciplines in higher education, and continue to be more prevalent in disciplines where evidence of meeting professional standards across a range of capabilities is critical (Hallam, Harper, McCowan, Hauville, McAllister, & Creagh, 2008; Housego & Parker, 2009; Oliver, Nikoletatos, von Konsky, Wilkinson, Ng, Crowley, Moore, & Townsend, 2009; Oliver & Whelan, 2011). As in traditional portfolio practice, ePortfolio practitioners have traditionally treated the reflective portfolio as solitary and private.

The emergence of digital technologies to support institutional and course wide ePortfolios, allows not only the aggregating and curating of digital artefacts over time, in a wide range of formats, but also peer review and selective sharing via social networks to present and re-present skills, knowledge and experience: "ePortfolios are a space for creating an identity (as a student and as an emerging professional) that links the experiences of the traditional or formal curriculum with the pedagogical and co-curricular experiences that engage and transform learners" (Bass, 2010).

A shift to social pedagogy practices in personalized learning has seen the use of ePortfolios as a site for interaction, exchange, and collaboration in many universities. A course approach has been found to advance student success, make learning visible, support reflection, foster deep learning and can be the catalyst for learning-centered institutional change (Eynon, Gambino & Torok, 2014). Because portfolios are curated collections of artefacts and evidence that the owner designs and presents, they demonstrate applied learning while making learning more meaningful and visible, all the while making new learning connections. EPortfolios have the potential to provide a platform for holistic development and assessment of a range of graduate capabilities related to creativity and creative practice.

## THE IMPORTANCE OF CREATIVITY AS A GRADUATE ATTRIBUTE

Educational and cultural commentators such as Robinson (2000), Florida (2002) and Pink (2005) maintain that apart from any individual humanist benefit, new millennium economic imperatives demand the development of a greater capacity for creativity, among other dispositions such as empathy and collegiality. Robinson (2010) makes a compelling argument for the dismantling of educational paradigms that were developed to suit an industrial age economy, and higher education too has been paying attention to the development of 'creative' graduate attributes such as innovative problem-solving, creative leadership and interdisciplinary practice.

Some transformative learning theorists suggest that new forms and functions of education must urgently engender new visions to deal with complex global problems (Miles, 2002; O'Sullivan, 1999; 2003; O'Sullivan & Morrell, 2002). Barnett proposes that "being-for-uncertainty" is a quality needed by contemporary graduates to manage the 'super complexity' that is characteristic of the contemporary world, characterized by "such dispositions [as] carefulness, thoughtfulness, humility, criticality, receptiveness, resilience, courage and stillness." (Barnett, 2004, p.258).

Industry commentators also assert that university graduates need a range of generic capabilities. A 2010 global study of CEOs by IBM found that creativity was believed to be the most crucial factor for a company's future success (IBM, 2010), while Amabile (1998) has long suggested that industry would benefit by providing opportunities for employees to exercise their creativity, suggesting that businesses require such qualities as expertise, creative thinking skills and motivation.

## What Does it Look Like?

As creativity is increasingly promoted as a desirable learning outcome in different disciplines, and more generically as a graduate attribute in higher education, how can it be characterized in this context?

Conceptions of creativity as differentiated between 'high' (large-C) and 'ordinary' or 'democratic' (small-c" have emerged in recent decades, to support the idea that creativity is not the domain of only the brilliant and eminent, but is achievable by everyone (Csikszentmihalyi, 1996; Craft, 2001). These ideas have more recently been characterized as *second-generation* (McWilliam & Dawson, 2008), emphasizing the social/cultural context and universal and collaborative nature of creativity in contrast to more traditional, individualistic and mysterious. The second-generation focus emphasizes a personal, practical and socially-oriented creativity, and "locates the creative enterprise in the processes and products of collaborative and purposeful activity" (McWilliam & Dawson, 2008, p.633). This second-generation focus on creative capacity building and networking fits the professionally-oriented attributes articulated in higher education aspiration statements and industry skill-set statements.

This characterization of creativity can be seen as behavior in a context, so that it may be more appropriately defined as an enabling disposition (Ivcevic, 2009), rather than as a skill or a capability demonstrated by output or product. 'Creative' behaviors could include taking risks, making connections between disparate fields of knowledge, and being a motivated and independent learner - qualities that could themselves be considered as dispositions, incorporating the affective as well as the cognitive dimension of learning. For instance, some characteristics of creative behavior identified by Tardif and Sternberg (Sternberg, 1988) are: articulate and fluent, good imagination, flexible and skilled decision-maker, copes well with novelty, and finds order in chaos.

## Creativity in Curriculum

### Academic and Student Conceptions

Jackson et al (2006) discovered a range of understandings and definitions by university students and teachers that were complex and frequently contradictory. Some remain attached to romantic and individualist aspects of creativity, and are skeptical that it can be taught. An Australian study of academic teachers also revealed understandings about creativity that combine first- and second-generation conceptions (McWilliam and Dawson, 2009). However, both academics and students believe that creative teaching can enable students to be creative in learning activities and outcomes. Students identified dialogic modes, where students' current understandings or beliefs are addressed, as supportive of creativity, while they felt strongly that prevailing modes of assessment (such as examinations) were generally inhibitive for creativity. Students also expressed frustration at a perceived conflict between being creative and conforming to 'academic' expectations (Oliver et al, 2006).

Academic conceptions across disciplines represented generic features of creativity such as: originality, use of imagination, exploration and risk-taking, making sense of complexity, and story-telling, and many academics believed that development of creativity was important, even though creativity was rarely explicit in learning outcomes or assessment criteria (Jackson & Shaw, 2006).

## Creative Teaching/Creative Learning

To accommodate these features of creativity in curriculum requires the setting of appropriately flexible learning tasks and authentic assessment modes to both promote and support creative responses, and to allow risk-taking and mistake-making in a safe environment. Studies of school teachers have reported that those students who display creative behavioral characteristics (such as playfulness, argumentativeness, independence) tend to be perceived by teachers as non-conformist and disruptive (Craft, 2001; Aljughaiman & Mowrer-Reynolds, 2005). It is not surprising then that students arrive in tertiary education with these behaviors repressed, and creative learning is unlikely to occur without a context in which creative behavior is not only acceptable but supported and rewarded.

Sternberg (1996) has suggested that creativity is best taught through the teacher as a role model for creative practice. This is supported by Jackson et al (2006), who found that both academics and students believe that there is a close correspondence between creative teaching and the opportunity for creative learning. Teachers therefore need opportunities for innovating their own practice in a safe environment to enhance their self perception as creative practitioners.

## Assessing Creativity with Portfolios

Portfolios have the potential to support the development, demonstration and valid assessment of a wide range of personal, professional and academic capabilities, both inside and outside the study program, and develop good professional practice in the documentation, curation and presentation of artefacts. Portfolio assessment can be designed to allow a degree of control over learning pathways and strategies, promoting learner self-direction and motivation, and therefore personalized engagement in learning and related activities.

Portfolios have been widely used in traditionally creative disciplines such as visual art and architecture. However, assessment of creativity, even in creative disciplines, has tended to focus on assessment of product, whereas aspects of creativity such as process, person and place are all deemed to be critical to creative development (De la Harpe et al, 2009). The Studio Teaching Project (ALTC) identified a range of identifiers in these different dimensions for the assessment of creativity, and developed a holistic assessment model to support this. The foci of this model are:

- Outcome dimensions: Product, process and person
- Knowledge and skills: underpinning and core
- Reflective and professional practice – acting like a [creative practitioner]

This model, represented in Figure 1, could be adapted to be more widely applicable across disciplines.

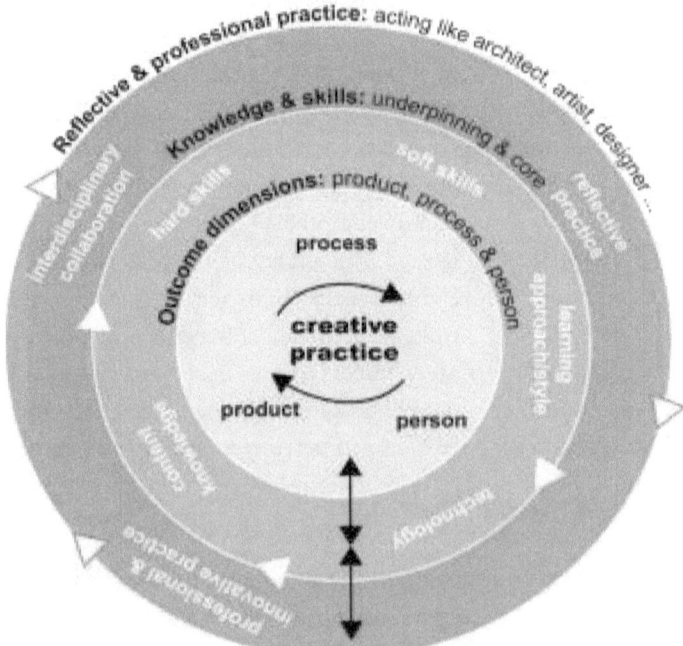

Figure 1: Model for holistic assessment in studio-based disciplines (adapted from De la Harpe et al, 2009, p47)

The reflective aspects of this model are essential to provide the evidence for the 'process' and 'person' outcome dimensions, and the portfolio is an ideal assessment mode for these broader dimensions. Portfolios support the aggregation of selected pieces of evidence to demonstrate learning outcomes and achievements through the curation of artefacts. To leverage the learning benefits of portfolio assessment, this usually includes a reflective dimension, where the learner analyses and evaluates their own learning processes through written reflections, oral presentation and reflective discussion of the portfolio pages or via a reflective statement to lay claim for learning against standards.

As Krause (2006) indicated over ten years ago, "portfolios are a useful vehicle for facilitating critical reflection on one's learning and for compiling and demonstrating evidence of learning and skill development" (p.1) as they catch and preserve the evidence of learning. This critical reflection is imperative for higher education in supporting the development of graduate attributes and offering opportunities for learners to gather and tell their learning journey stories. Provision of evidence of these capabilities often is driven by the student toward the end of the learning cycle in capstone subjects, where students gather evidence for resumes or CVs for accreditation to associations and professional institutions, however, beginning this process early supports a learning-centered pedagogy.

This reflection on learning is important for students as they exit higher education and seek employment in their respective disciplines. Reflective practice and self-assessment of learning is critical for remembering, conceptualizing and analyzing constructed knowledge after time. As Strampel and Oliver (2007) inferred, "reflection is a way of thinking; it is a form of contemplation that determines how one comes to act on new understandings" (p.980). Portfolios are useful tools for this conceptualizing of practice in assessment. They encourage and facilitate student reflection while they compile and develop evidence of learning throughout the learning process and at the completion. Utilizing digital platforms for this reflection can further enhance the learning process, including ongoing thinking and reflection and action on reflection (Schön, 1987).

## CREATIVITY AND DIGITAL MEDIA

### Digital Literacy

Digital literacy is another capability emerging as a critical skill for graduates to function as global professionals in many fields. Prensky's (2001) notion that 'digital native' students are well-versed in technology use in contrast to their 'digital immigrant' teachers have largely been discredited by subsequent research (Kennedy et al, 2008), which found that students are not homogeneous in their use of technology, which tends to be ad hoc and opportunistic. Students need support from their learning environment to not only learn how to use online learning systems, but also to identify, set up and evaluate a range of tools and networks and thereby apply digital production and networking skills to their study and work. While learning management systems (LMS), may have great administrative benefits for teachers, and be useful in providing flexibility to learners, practice for students in using a range of media, publishing and networking tools is likely to be more relevant to their professional lives. Teachers need to be well-versed in digital practice in their discipline to support students to develop the same skills.

Digital literacy inevitably overlaps with information literacy as students have available to them a morass of online information of varying quality and validity, and need to develop the skills to navigate, evaluate, select and contribute to online information. Matthew Allen (2009) refers to 'knowledge networking' as a new paradigm in professional and scholarly practice, and has developed strategies and identified available web applications to support teachers and students in higher education to develop the digital literacies required (Allen, 2011).

**Creative Digital Tools**

Digital media provide a plethora of opportunities for the design, development and presentation of creative portfolios – the tools for creative production have arguably never been so accessible, with almost every student in Australian universities having access to a mobile device incorporating a digital camera, a desktop and/or laptop computer with image, audio and video editing capability, and high-speed internet access to a huge range of productivity software and publication platforms. The social orientation of digital tools is highly supportive of the development of communication and networking skills. These are powerful resources for teachers and learners in the development of the broad range of capabilities intrinsic to creativity. What is required is the scaffolding for learners to produce, critique and publish work relevant to their field of study, in a way that will leverage this potential.

If key characteristics of creative behavior are being able to take risks, step outside of one's comfort zone, and to think both divergently and convergently around different domains of knowledge, this is a meta-capability beyond the scope of any particular communication or publication tool. From this perspective, the design and scaffolding of the learning activity is of primary importance, and is where the creativity of the teacher has the most impact.

## Assessing with ePortfolios

> "[EPortfolios] have the potential for transforming ... curricula through the linking of practice oriented learning and the development of graduate attributes" (Housego & Parker, 2009, p.409).

One of the benefits of a portfolio mode of learning and assessment is that it scaffolds the compilation of evidence and artefacts in a range of media, which is then compiled and curated into a presentation format, or formats, for a variety of purposes. An ePortfolio approach provides additional affordances, in that it not only aggregates artefacts produced in digital form using digital technologies, but that it is integrated into online networking and communication tools to allow a wide range of connectivity and presentation options. The dimensions of practice, learning and research that can be aggregated and organized, and the range of purposes for which an ePortfolio can be used is illustrated in Figure 2.

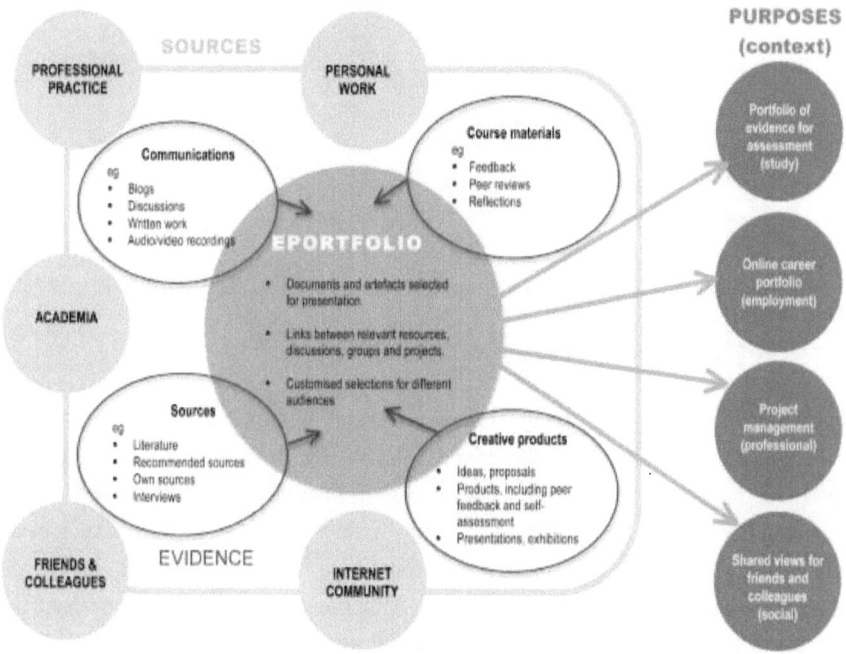

Figure 2: Model for ePortfolio practice

As a pedagogical tool, ePortfolios differ from more traditional folios of practice. As digital tools develop, ePortfolios have the potential to address the lack of integration across existing programs because they can be used across teaching programs and contain all forms of digital artefacts and evidence related to learning from assessment tasks, tests, feedback and student work samples. As ePortfolios are goal-driven, students are self-directed and take ownership of the portfolio collection in a repository, helping students to take responsibility for their own learning artefacts, and for publishing and disseminating their own curated content.

Figure 3 shows the assessment model shown in Figure 1 extrapolated to propose types of evidence that could be presented in an ePortfolio to represent dimensions of creative practice.

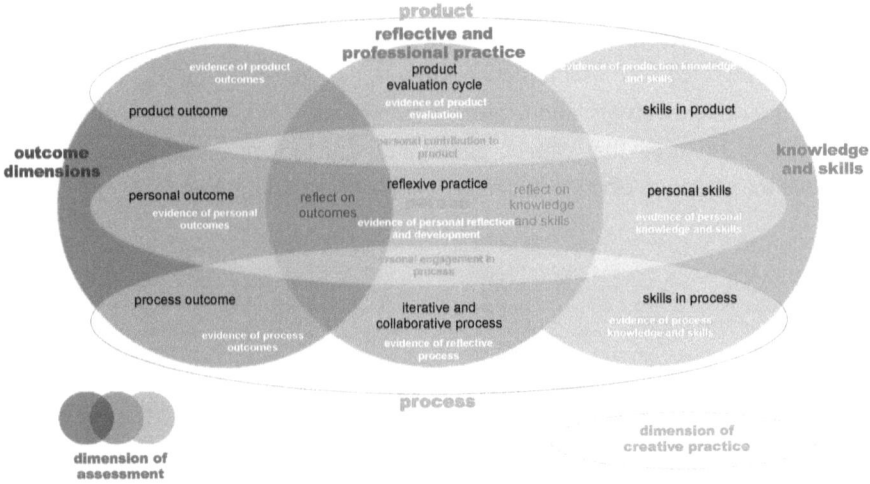

Figure 3: Model for ePortfolio assessment (based on De la Harpe model, Figure 1)

## The Transformative Potential of ePortfolios

Transformation suggests a significant perspective change, which could apply personally to the learner and the teacher, as well as to the curriculum design and the teaching situation. The engagement of teachers in the practices and technologies of ePortfolio use is important if they are to model creative practice, and this may be as confronting and transformative for teachers as it is for learners. Teachers are likely to be already engaged to some degree in development of their own portfolio of work, research and personal activities, and that this could be the basis for the development of their own ePortfolio practice. This academic development process likewise needs to be supported and scaffolded, ideally through a community of practice where they are able to participate in critical reflection and dialogue with peers.

Hughes (2008) has asserted that ePortfolios could be characterized as transformative technology in requiring a change to traditional assessment practices, and to learner and teacher roles in assessment: "Adopting ePortfolios as genre and practice requires us to engage with our learners in meaningful individual and collaborative activities, it requires us to cultivate dialogic cultures which make connections beyond the immediate and it demands that we interrogate notions of authorship and audience" (p.439). Such questions of identity, communication and expression are intrinsic to conceptions of creativity as socially mediated behavior. EPortfolio assessment is able to focus on both cultivating and providing evidence of creative identity and voice, by scaffolding process and supporting evaluation across developmental dimensions (see Figures 2 & 3).

### ePortfolios and Graduate Capabilities

Many characteristics intrinsic to creative behavior are reflected in graduate capabilities that could be evidenced in an ePortfolio. For instance, the University of New South Wales (UNSW) Graduate Capabilities statement aspires to graduates as scholars who are: "capable of independent and collaborative enquiry, rigorous in their analysis, critique and reflection, and able to innovate by applying their knowledge and skills to the solution of novel as well as routine problems" This globally-focused UNSW graduate should be a leader who is "capable of initiating and embracing innovation and change" and be capable of "self- directed practice and independent lifelong learning" (UNSW). These capabilities lend themselves to the objectives of an ePortfolio, where students collect evidence in an authentic context, generating artefacts that demonstrate their problem solving skills and constructed learning through reflection, critique and analysis.

### Further Development in Assessment of Creativity with ePortfolios

This paper has briefly explored how changing directions in assessment practice could support the assessment of creativity, with a focus on using ePortfolios for assessment. Krause (2005) indicated that while ePortfolios had the potential to transform pedagogy; this potential cannot be realized without real curriculum change. Ten years on, we may be witnessing this paradigm shift through open digital badges that warrant the evidence in curated ePortfolios. Endorsing and verifying this curated form of learning with open digital badges is a form of warranting achievement that validates identity as a learner or professional. As Professor Alex Ambrose from University of Notre Dame supports, "the great benefit of the integration (or as he says by the intersection) of ePortfolios and badges is showcasing of relevant co-curricular experience students have at their institution. Digital badges aren't used as certificates and they don't bear credit, however, they along with portfolios provide recognition of student achievement which can have deeper representation than transcripts or more traditional records. Badges integrated with ePortfolios are as seen as supplement to the transcript or resume. Students are usually not obligated to update their ePortfolios every semester, so integrating digital badges with ePortfolios encourage students to do so" (Ambrose, 2015).

## REFERENCES

Aljughaiman, A. & Mowrer-Reynolds, E. (2005). Teachers' conceptions of creativity and creative students. Journal of Creative Behaviour, 39(1), 17-34.

Allen, M. (2011). Learning in Networks of Knowledge (LINK). http://www.knowledgenetworklearning.net/

Allen, M. and Long, J. (2009) Learning as Knowledge Networking: Conceptual Foundations for Revised Uses of the Internet in Higher Education. Proceedings of the World Congress on Engineering and Computer Science 2009 Vol I, October 20-22, 2009, San Francisco, USA. http://netcrit.net/content/wcecslearningasknet2009.pdf

Amabile, T. (1998). How to kill creativity. Harvard business review. Sept-Oct 1998.

Bass, R. (2010). ePortfolios, Presentation to AAEEBL Annual World Conference, July 2010, Boston Mass., USA. Available at: http://assessment.georgetown.edu/program-level-assessment/gathering-evidence-of-student-learning/ePortfolios/

Barnett, R. (2004). Learning for an unknown future. Higher Education Research & Development 23(3): 247-260.

Ambrose, G.A. (2015). ePortfolios and Digital Badges at University of Notre Dame, Europortfolio Life Long Learning Program. Available at: http://www.ePortfolio.eu/resources/contributions/practice/ePortfolios-and-digital-badges-university-notre-dame

Craft, A. (2001). An Analysis of Research and Literature on Creativity in Education: Report prepared for the Qualifications and Curriculum Authority (London, QCA).

Csikszentmihalyi, M. (1997). Creativity: Flow and the psychology of discovery and invention. New York: Harper Collins.

De la Harpe, B., Peterson, F.J., Frankham, N., Zehner, R., Neale, D., Musgrave, E. & McDermott, R. (2009). Assessment focus in studio: What is the most prominent in Architecture, art and design? Journal of Art & Design Education. 28.1.

Eynon, B., Gambino., L. & Torok, J. (2014). What Difference Can ePortfolio Make? *International Journal of ePortfolio,* 4 (1): 95-114.

Florida, R.L. (2002). The rise of the creative class: and how it's transforming work, leisure, community and everyday life. New York: Basic Books.

Hallam, G., Harper, W., McCowan, C. Hauville, K., McAllister, L. & Creagh, T. (2008). Australian ePortfolio Project: ePortfolio use by university students in Australia: Informing excellence in policy and practice. Brisbane: Queensland University of Technology.

Housego, S. & Parker, N. (2009). Positioning ePortfolios in an integrated curriculum. Education & Training, 51(5/6), 408-421.

IBM (2010). Global CEO Study: Creativity Selected as Most Crucial Factor for Future Success.
http://www- 03.ibm.com/press/us/en/pressrelease/31670.wss

Ivcevic, Z. (2009). Creativity Map: Toward the Next Generation of Theories of Creativity. Psychology of Aesthetics, Creativity, and the Arts, Vol. 3, No. 1, 17–21.

Mezirow, J. (1991). Transformative dimensions of adult learning. San Francisco: Jossey-Bass Publishers.

Miles, A. (2002). Feminist perspectives on globalization and integrative transformative learning. In O'Sullivan, E., Morrell, A. & O'Connor, M.A. (2002). Expanding the boundaries of transformative learning: Essays on theory and praxis. Palgrave: NY.

Oliver, B. & Whelan, B. (2011). Designing an e-portfolio for assurance of learning focusing on adoptability and learning analytics, *Australasian journal of educational technology*, 27(6): 1026-1041.

Oliver, B., Nikoletatos, P., von, Konsky B., Wilkinson, H., Ng, J., Crowley, R., Moore, R. & Townsend, R. (2009). Curtin's iPortfolio: An online space for creating, sharing and showcasing evidence of learning, *in ASCILITE 2009 : Same places, different spaces : Proceedings of the 26th ASCILITE conference*, [Australian Society for Computers in Learning in Tertiary Education], [Auckland, N.Z.], pp. 717-719.

Oliver, M., Shah, B., McGoldrick, C. & Edwards, M. (2006). Students' experience of creativity. In Jackson, N., Oliver, M., Shaw, M. & Wisdom, J. eds. (2006). Developing creativity in higher education: an imaginative curriculum. London: Routledge.

O'Sullivan, E. (1999). Transformative learning: Educational vision for the 21st century. Toronto: University of Toronto Press.

O'Sullivan, E. (2003). Bringing a perspective of transformative learning to globalized consumption. International Journal of Consumer Studies. 27 (4) 326–330.

O'Sullivan, E., Morrell, A. & O'Connor, M.A. (2002). Expanding the boundaries of transformative learning: Essays on theory and praxis. New York: Palgrave.

Pink, D. (2005). A whole new mind: Moving from the information age to the conceptual age. New York: Penguin.

Prenksy, M. (2001). Digital Natives, Digital Immigrants. On the Horizon, 9(5). Robinson, K. (2000). Out of our minds: Learning to be creative. Oxford: Capstone.

Robinson, K. (2010). Bring on the learning revolution! TED Talks. http://www.ted.com/talks/sir_ken_robinson_bring_on_the_revolution.html [Retrieved 16.03.11]

Schön, D.A. (1987). Educating the Reflective Practitioner, San Francisco: Jossey-Bass Publishers.

Strampel, K. & Oliver, R. (2007). Using technology to foster reflection in higher education. In ICT: Providing choices for learners and learning. Proceedings ascilite Singapore 2007. http://www.ascilite.org.au/conferences/singapore07/procs/strampel.pdf

UNSW (N.D.). Teaching; Graduate capabilities. http://teaching.unsw.edu.au/graduate-capabilities

## ACKNOWLEDGEMENTS

An earlier version of this chapter was first published as Allen, B. & Coleman, K. (2011). The creative graduate: Cultivating and assessing creativity with ePortfolios. In G. Williams, P. Statham, N. Brown & B. Cleland (Eds.), Changing Demands, Changing Directions. Proceedings ascilite Hobart 2011. (pp.59-69). Available at
http://www.ascilite.org/conferences/hobart11/downloads/papers/Allen-full.pdf

www.ingramcontent.com/pod-product-compliance
Lightning Source LLC
Chambersburg PA
CBHW032145010526
44111CB00035B/1224